Holodomor and Gorta Mór

Advance Reviews

'*Holodomor and Gorta Mór* is the first sustained comparison of two of the most devastating famines in modern European history. By assembling a team of international experts, the editors probe the complex construction of cultural memories of famine in Ireland and the Ukraine. The result is a fascinating collection that will be essential reading for scholars in history, literature and cultural studies.'

—*Dr Enda Delaney, School of History, Classics & Archaeology, University of Edinburgh*

'Writing from broadly diverse vantage points and engaging a variety of competing interpretations of two events that are so different yet so similar, the contributors achieve an amazing effect: historical memory, stripped of its ritualised conventional forms is alive and burning once again, and raises new questions.'

—*Dr Ilya Gerasimov, founder and Executive Editor of 'Ab Imperio'*

'Both the Ukraine and Ireland were devastated by great famines of appalling scale and intensity. These historical traumas, and how they were handled by two very different societies, make for compelling reading. *Holodomor and Gorta Mór* is a pioneering work in parallel histories that opens new vistas on Irish and Ukrainian studies, and indeed on the handling of famine memory more generally. Theoretically sophisticated and resting on deep learning, this multi-authored volume is also characterised by a humane concern for the victims of famine, the survivors and their descendants.'

—*Professor Liam Kennedy, Queen's University Belfast*

'The essays in this pioneering collection provide unexplored comparisons between two wide-scale European famines in contexts of imperialism, politicization and nationalism. They offer transnational, interdisciplinary perspectives on two formative episodes in the colonial past of Europe, thereby contributing significantly to current scholarly debates on trauma, historiography, memory and popular culture.'

—*Marguérite Corporaal, principal investigator of the ERC-project 'Relocated Remembrance: The Great Famine in Irish (Diaspora) Fiction, 1847–1921', Radboud University Nijmegen, the Netherlands*

Holodomor and Gorta Mór

Histories, Memories and Representations of Famine in Ukraine and Ireland

Edited by
Christian Noack, Lindsay Janssen
and Vincent Comerford

ANTHEM PRESS
LONDON · NEW YORK · DELHI

Anthem Press
An imprint of Wimbledon Publishing Company
www.anthempress.com

This edition first published in UK and USA 2014
by ANTHEM PRESS
75–76 Blackfriars Road, London SE1 8HA, UK
or PO Box 9779, London SW19 7ZG, UK
and
244 Madison Ave. #116, New York, NY 10016, USA

First published in hardback by Anthem Press in 2012

© 2014 Christian Noack, Lindsay Janssen and Vincent Comerford
editorial matter and selection; individual chapters © individual contributors

The moral right of the authors has been asserted.

Cover photo: The Kiev Famine Memorial, 2012, courtesy of Olga Papash

All rights reserved. Without limiting the rights under copyright reserved above,
no part of this publication may be reproduced, stored or introduced into
a retrieval system, or transmitted, in any form or by any means
(electronic, mechanical, photocopying, recording or otherwise),
without the prior written permission of both the copyright
owner and the above publisher of this book.

British Library Cataloguing-in-Publication Data
A catalogue record for this book is available from the British Library.

Library of Congress Cataloging-in-Publication Data
The Library of Congress has catalogued the hardcover edition as follows:
Holodomor and Gorta Mór : histories, memories and representations of famine in Ukraine
and Ireland / edited by Christian Noack, Lindsay Janssen and Vincent Comerford.
    pages : illustrations, maps ; cm
    Some articles translated from Russian and Polish.
 Papers of the conference held at Maynooth on November 6–7, 2009.
    Includes bibliographical references and index.
    ISBN 978-0-85728-557-7 (hardcover : alkaline paper)
 1. Ukraine–History–Famine, 1932–1933–Congresses. 2. Ireland–History–
Famine, 1845–1852–Congresses. 3. Famines–Ukraine–20th century–History–Congresses.
4. Famines–Ireland–19th century–History–Congresses. 5. Ukraine–History–Famine, 1932–
    1933–Historiography–Congresses. 6. Ireland–History–Famine, 1845–1852–
    Historiography–Congresses. I. Noack, Christian. II. Janssen, Lindsay. III.
                    Comerford, Vincent.
                  DK508.8374.H654 2012
                    941.5081–dc23
                      2012033890

ISBN-13: 978 1 78308 319 0 (Pbk)
ISBN-10: 1 78308 319 0 (Pbk)

This title is also available as an ebook.

CONTENTS

List of Figures		vii
Acknowledgements		ix
Introduction	Holodomor and Gorta Mór: Histories, Memories and Representations of Famine in Ukraine and Ireland *Christian Noack, Lindsay Janssen and Vincent Comerford*	1
Part I	**Histories, Historiography and Politics**	
Chapter 1	Holodomor in Ukraine 1932–1933: An Interpretation of Facts *Stanislav V. Kulchytskyi (Translated from Russian by Christian Noack)*	19
Chapter 2	Ethnic Issues in the Famine of 1932–1933 in Ukraine *David R. Marples*	35
Chapter 3	Grievance, Scourge or Shame? The Complexity of Attitudes to Ireland's Great Famine *Vincent Comerford*	51
Part II	**Public Commemoration**	
Chapter 4	History and National Identity Construction: The Great Famine in Irish and Ukrainian History Textbooks *Jan Germen Janmaat*	77
Chapter 5	Teaching Hunger: The Great Irish Famine Curriculum in New York State Schools *Maureen O. Murphy*	103
Chapter 6	Remembering Famine Orphans: The Transmission of Famine Memory between Ireland and Quebec *Jason King*	115

Chapter 7	The Irish Famine and Commemorative Culture *Emily Mark-FitzGerald*	145
Part III	**Trauma and Victimisation**	
Chapter 8	Holodomor and the Politics of Memory in Ukraine after Independence *Heorhiy Kasianov (Translated from Russian by Christian Noack)*	167
Chapter 9	The Great Irish Famine in Stories for Children in the Closing Decades of the Twentieth Century *Celia Keenan*	189
Chapter 10	Collective Trauma in a Feature Film: *Golod-33* as One-of-a-Kind *Olga Papash (Translated from Russian by Christian Noack)*	197
Part IV	**New Sources and New Approaches to the Irish and Ukrainian Famines**	
Chapter 11	In Search of New Sources: Polish Diplomatic and Intelligence Reports on the Holodomor *Jan Jacek Bruski (Translated from Polish by Alicja Waligóra-Zblewska and Christian Noack)*	215
Chapter 12	Oral History, Oral Tradition and the Great Famine *Maura Cronin*	231
Chapter 13	Mapping Population Change in Ireland 1841–1851: Quantitative Analysis Using Historical GIS *Mary Kelly, A. Stewart Fotheringham and Martin Charlton*	245
Index		269

LIST OF FIGURES

Figure 6.1	Théophile Hamel, *Le Typhyus* (Notre-Dame-de-Bon-Secours Chapel/Museum Marguerite-Bourgeoys, 1848)	125
Figure 7.1	Elizabeth McLaughlin, *County Famine Memorial Garden* (Roscommon, Co. Roscommon, 1999)	151
Figure 7.2	Maria Pizzuti, *Broken Heart* (Limerick, Co. Limerick, 1997)	152
Figure 7.3	Action from Ireland-sponsored Famine monument (Swinford, Co. Mayo, 1994)	153
Figure 7.4	*The Western New York Irish Famine Memorial* (Buffalo, New York, 1997)	157
Figure 7.5a	*An Gorta Mór Hibernian Memorial* (Irish Hills, Michigan, 1994)	158
Figure 7.5b	*Southern Tier Irish Famine Memorial* (Olean, New York, 2000)	159
Figure 7.6	Eamonn O'Doherty, *Great Hunger Memorial* (Ardsley [Westchester County], New York, 2001)	160
Figure 10.1	Oles Yanchuk, Death of the mother, still from *Golod-33* (1991)	203
Figure 10.2	Oles Yanchuk, Peasants approaching the mill where the sequestered grain is stored, still from *Golod-33* (1991)	206
Figure 13.1	GIS map per cent population change	250
Figure 13.2	GIS map per cent of cropped land in each ED 1851	251
Figure 13.3	GIS map valuation per acre	252

Figure 13.4	GIS map population density on cropped land 1841	253
Figure 13.5	GIS map percentage of crop land under wheat	254
Figure 13.6	GIS map percentage of crop land under oats	255
Figure 13.7	GIS map percentage of crop land under potatoes	256
Figure 13.8	GIS map percentage of crop land under meadow	257
Figure 13.9	GIS map distance to the coast	258
Figure 13.10	GIS map workhouse accessibility	259
Figure 13.11	GWR local parameter estimates for mean elevation	263
Figure 13.12	GWR local parameter estimates for percentage grain on cropped land	264

ACKNOWLEDGEMENTS

This project, like any other, would have been impossible to achieve without the active support of many individuals and institutions. Margaret Kelleher in Ireland, Guido Hausmann in Germany and Andryi Portnov in Ukraine were extremely generous in their advice when we were looking for interested international experts to participate in the conference on which this volume is based.

The Department of History at the National University of Ireland, Maynooth, the Centre for the Study of a Wider Europe, and An Foras Feasa: The Institute for Research in Irish Historical and Cultural Traditions provided the institutional back-up for the conference, entitled 'Holodomor in Ukraine and Great Famine in Ireland: Histories, Representations and Memories'. This brought together scholars from different parts of Europe and North America at Maynooth on 6 and 7 November 2009. The conference was enhanced by the active participation of Professors Kevin B. Nowlan and Cormac Ó Gráda, two celebrated pioneers of famine research.

The editors wish to thank Balazs Apor and his colleagues on the editorial board of the Anthem Series on Russian, East European and Eurasian Studies for their readiness to include our volume. We would also like to thank Laurie Baggen for creating the index. Finally, printing the volume would not have been possible without the generous allocation of a publication grant by the National University of Ireland.

Amsterdam, Nijmegen, Maynooth
Christian Noack, Lindsay Janssen, Vincent Comerford
June 2012

Introduction

HOLODOMOR AND GORTA MÓR: HISTORIES, MEMORIES AND REPRESENTATIONS OF FAMINE IN UKRAINE AND IRELAND

Christian Noack, Lindsay Janssen, Vincent Comerford

Introduction

On 17 April 2012, in the bilingual *Ukrainian Week*, Hennadiy Kazakevych reminded his readers that, 90 years earlier, Ireland had gained its independence from the British Empire, while simultaneously the hopes of militant Ukrainian nationalists were crushed by the Bolsheviks emerging victoriously from the Russian Civil War.[1] Whatever the historical accuracy of this piece, historians of empire have so far paid surprisingly little attention to the many parallels between the histories of Ireland and Ukraine, then provinces of crucial importance for both powers.[2]

An obvious similarity, it would seem, is the centrality of two famines for the development of modern Ireland and modern Ukraine. The traumatic nature of these events has led these peoples, in the words of Kai Erikson, 'to feel estranged from the rest of humanity' and consequently to see their cultural group as somehow distinctive.[3] This combined with the predominance of the national history paradigm leads more often than not to exclusive treatments of both tragedies, usually with an emphasis on the uniqueness of sufferings incurred either by the Irish or by the Ukrainian people. Comparative research on the Great Famine and the Holodomor has so far been attempted mainly in the realm of economic history and principally in the context of global enquiry into the occurrence of famines across time and space.[4]

Some of the parallels between the two famines, separated by 80 years and several thousands of kilometres, are indeed striking. One might point to the occurrence of starvation in key food-producing regions of both empires. Or to the fact that in both cases government policies appeared to hesitate between acceptance of massive population decrease (to put it mildly) and inadequate relief efforts. The list could be continued with reference to the obvious demographic and social consequences.

This is not to deny that any attempt at systematic historical comparison is rendered very difficult by the obvious differences in circumstances and time, and the originating causes of the catastrophes. Beyond this, it seems that the surprising scarcity of comparative studies may perhaps also be attributed to their disjunction in the conventional schemes of periodisation: historians of the 'short' twentieth century, the 'age of extremes' or the 'dark century', customarily refer to the Ukrainian disaster, while earlier famines like the Irish Famine form part of nineteenth-century narratives of colonialism or migration.

More likely, however, the main reason lies in the organisation of the production of our knowledge. Geographically located on the opposite ends of Europe, Irish and Ukrainian history are seldom treated jointly even in syntheses of European history which usually focus on the greater states and societies in Europe and deal with minorities or small independent states at best summarily. Moreover, in the fields of history, historiography and literary studies, researchers with expertise on both Ireland and Ukraine are scarce. And in neither country does the institutional setup of academic research promote intellectual exchange between the two. Among the handful of academic specialists on Eastern Europe currently working in universities in Ireland, none has a primary specialisation on Ukraine; and the reciprocal holds true for expertise on Ireland among the academic specialists on Western Europe in Ukraine.

This volume presents a first attempt at bringing Ukrainian and Irish scholarship into a structured dialogue. Against this backdrop, it can neither provide an exhaustive synthesis in the form of a thorough comparison, nor an in-depth inquiry into possible transnational links. However, given the institutional background described above, a juxtaposition of international scholarship on both cases seemed to provide a possible first step. Such an approach requires a clear focus, and while the historical events in the course of both famines doubtlessly could provide such a lens, the editors chose to concentrate not so much on the history of the famines per se, but rather on their retrospective representation and appropriation in both societies.

The inspiration to review the representations in Ireland and Ukraine was encouraged by recent paradigmatic shifts in history and cultural studies. Against the backdrop of the rapid changes in a time almost interchangeably labelled postmodern, postindustrial or postcolonial, a growing corpus of scholarship in the humanities has focused on the ways cultural knowledge and collective identities are produced. Following the trailblazing studies of scholars like Pierre Nora or Jan and Aleida Assmann, the exploration of national historiography and literary traditions, of public discourses or of collective commemoration of the past has attracted renewed international interest.[5]

For historians, social and cultural scientists, Pierre Nora's seminal studies on the *lieux de mémoire* (sites of memory) in France have proved to be highly influential. Basing himself on Maurice Halbwachs' concept of collective memory as societal practice, Nora argues that with the vanishing of actual *milieux de mémoire* – or places where the past could somehow be experienced – the *lieux de mémoire* have arisen, which are (partially) self-referential sites of memory that can be of a 'material, symbolic and functional' nature. According to Nora, these *lieux* become such an important part of a group's self-identification processes that they should and will not be forgotten.[6] Nora examines the different shapes in which collective memory has been enshrined, and the merits of his project undoubtedly lie in the disclosure of the enormous variety of forms that these *lieux de mémoire* can acquire.[7]

It seems particularly tempting to apply Nora's framework to the evidence in the Ukrainian case, as the collapse of the Soviet Union ended the silence imposed by Stalin precisely when the generation of eyewitnesses was about to disappear. At the same time, the new political regime of independent Ukraine empowered and even conducted collective commemoration. Commemoration by successors and neighbours of the Famine victims on the one hand, and public acts of remembrance organised by the state on the other have not always quite aligned with each other. It would be an oversimplification, therefore, to conflate such political appropriation with collective memory. In Ireland, the Great Famine has never fallen out of popular memory although it struck the island more than one and a half centuries ago.

Following Nora, other scholars have identified the many ways in which power relations come to bear implicitly or explicitly on collective memories, for example in the form of political preferences for specific interpretations of history and their enactment in a form of official commemoration, canonisation in print or educational curricula, and the furbishing of public space with monuments. Such explorations, however, more often than not replicated Nora's straightforward acceptance of the nation (in his case the French) as the main frame of reference, and interrogated the commemorative practice in individual nation-states, Ireland and Ukraine among them.[8] Even when the term 'nation' was applied in cases of (colonial) oppression and 'displacement'[9] with a new and critical awareness, a 'resilient methodological nationalism' prevailed. Methodological nationalism refers to 'the implicit or explicit assumption that the nation-state (still) constitutes the core category of modern social and political order'.[10] The editors of this volume suggest that a comparison of famine representations in two nation-states, Ireland and Ukraine, might not only help to contour the particularities of each of these cases, but also provide a basis for further transnational research. We will return to this question in the concluding part of this introduction.

Besides the suggestion of a comparative approach, this volume aims to integrate interdisciplinary perspectives as well. This is, for one part, the simple recognition of the fact that whether in visual or textual shape, modern print culture (and later film and television) has helped to inscribe such collective memory into everyday life and individual and cultural identities at least as much as educational politics or the erection of public monuments. More importantly, literary and cultural scholars have substantially contributed to the shift in the focus of research from the study of memory to the study of the communication of memory. In other words, the mnemonic medium now receives more emphatic attention. Central to an understanding of the process of mnemonic communication is the notion of mediation: memory is necessarily already mediated as soon as it is performed.[11] Therefore, memory that is passed on – whether it is shared between generations or between different cultural groups and independent of the medium or carrier by which it is transferred – is necessarily mediated in multiple ways. At the same time, these studies have helped to understand the persuasiveness of collective memories by pointing out that multiple mediation does not necessarily imply an increased distance between memory and the remembering subject. As the concepts of 'postmemory' or 'prosthetic memory' demonstrate, 'it becomes possible to have a mediated memory that one nevertheless experiences as real or genuine'.[12] Memories not directly related to one's personal experiences can therefore become part of what an individual perceives as his or her past.

This is an important advance of the concept of collective memory. It implies that memories originally external to the self – whether they originally belonged to predecessors or different cultural groups – can become part of one's self-identification. In this sense, memory behaves in an opaque and 'multidirectional' manner. This term was coined by Michael Rothberg, who argues that 'remembrance both cuts across and binds together diverse spatial, temporal and cultural sites'.[13]

Scholars from a wide array of disciplines – such as cultural memory and cultural trauma studies, psychoanalysis and diaspora studies – also closely examine the mediation and processing of memory between different generations and cultures. Among others, Astrid Erll and Ann Rigney suggest that the formation of cultural memory shares many similarities with the construction of narrative.[14] Both narrative texts and cultural memory are formed by processes of narrativisation. A text is not necessarily a narrative; in fact, a text becomes a narrative through the process of narrativisation. The production of narrative, and here the clear link to the construction of memory becomes visible, concerns 'making-present', selecting what is most important[15] and combining seemingly disparate elements – 'traces of the past'[16] – into meaningful structures.[17]

In such an analysis nationalist ideologues in Ireland can be seen as constructing several distinct, but interrelated, projects of narrativisation. One of these catalogues the misfortunes associated with alien oppression, beginning with the depredations of the Vikings from the eighth century onwards. The Famine was a crowning addition to this list, but only insofar as it could be depicted as the fault of the British. Clearly the failure of the potato was a natural phenomenon, but the government could be accused, fairly or not, of having failed to act appropriately in the face of the disaster. In any case, the emotive potential of the Great Famine was further charged by its association with emigration, which came to be depicted as another agonising infliction. There was much political and cultural rhetoric in the generations after the Famine that was steeped in notions of victimhood and exile.

However its causation might be envisaged, the Great Famine did not fit in with another enduring national narrative, already securely established before 1845. This narrative evoked ancient cultural glory signified by harps, round towers and high crosses, and culminated in the Celtic Revival movement in the decades before and after 1900. By that date the saints and scholars of the golden age had been reinforced in the narrative by a mythic pure-souled peasantry for whom speaking Gaelic and exuding the natural virtues was a quintessential state. Militant republicanism has its own narrative, that of a self-mandating tradition of armed rebellion against foreign rule; the only importance of the famine years in this story is that the Young Irelanders took up arms, however ineffectively, in 1848, thereby forging a new link in the chain. For the less influential militant socialist narrative, associated especially with James Connolly, the Famine was a class crime perpetrated against a peasant proletariat by capitalist exploiters, domestic and foreign.

This melange of interpretative frameworks permitted the Famine to be exploited politically or passed over in silence, depending on the needs of different interests at different times. Quite separate from its presence or absence with respect to political narratives, the Great Famine did figure from the beginning in many works of Irish literature, especially those with a 'diasporic' dimension.[18]

The preconditions for research on collective memories in Ukraine have obviously been much less favourable for most of the period since the historical occurrence of the Holodomor. As a result of the actual denial by the Soviet authorities and the consequent covering up of traces, the ascension of the

1932–33 Famine to its towering position in Ukrainian national history has occurred before our eyes, so to speak. The first cautious references within the Soviet Union did not occur before the 1960s; as yet the commemoration of the Famine and, later, the initiation of academic research were confined to Ukrainians living outside the country. During the 1980s, in a feat that adequately demonstrates the multidirectional nature of cultural memory, the term Holodomor was coined among the diasporic Ukrainians in the United States and Canada, all too obviously alluding to the term Holocaust, just popularised of that time through the American TV series by the same name. Although hampered by the limited access to primary sources, academic research on the history of the Famine began to produce impressive studies like Robert Conquest's famous *The Harvest of Sorrow* (1986). It still being a very sensitive issue at that time, the Soviet authorities felt compelled to produce counterstatements like *Fraud, Famine and Fascism: The Ukrainian Genocide Myth from Hitler to Harvard* (1987).

Simultaneously, the emerging oppositional national movement of Ukraine (Rukh) began to demand official recognition of the fact that Stalin had unleashed a massive famine against Ukrainians in the 1930s. At the same time, historians in Moscow and Kiev re-examined the 1932–33 Famine in the larger contexts of demography or the history of forced collectivisation and industrialisation. First 'revisionist' publications coincided with the collapse of the Soviet Union; and with amazing swiftness the Ukrainian elites, as a rule former communists refashioning themselves as moderate nationalists, incorporated references to the 1932–33 Famine into their rhetorical arsenals.[19] Thus, in the case of the Holodomor, scholars are presented with the perfect case study of the appropriation of memory on different levels; they observe, so to speak, the process of collective commemoration from below (now that the political taboo had been lifted) and its political exploitation from above, under laboratory conditions.[20]

This apparent and very recent politicisation of a historical trauma did not remain an exclusively domestic Ukrainian affair. It was not enough that the Ukrainians, as a nation, united in commemoration and constituted a particular community of those who suffered; 'the identity of a victim always requires affirmation from abroad; otherwise it would remain a sign of weakness and cause of shame'.[21] Particularly during Viktor Yushchenko's presidency (2005–2010), the politicisation of famine commemoration transcended the national context. Yushchenko's administration launched a diplomatic campaign aiming to secure international recognition of the Holodomor as a genocide directed against the Ukrainian people. This was just another reason for the editors of the current volume to embark on a comparative project involving the Irish and Ukrainian famines. With the support of several Irish based scholars of Eastern

Europe, the Centre for the Study of a Wider Europe at the National University of Ireland, Maynooth decided to convene a conference to facilitate an exchange between Irish and Ukrainian scholars. Under the title 'Holodomor in Ukraine and Great Famine in Ireland: Histories, Representations and Memories' this conference, jointly organised by An Foras Feasa: The Institute for Research in Irish Historical and Cultural Traditions, the Centre for the Study of a Wider Europe and the Department of History at the National University of Ireland, Maynooth, finally proceeded on 6 and 7 November 2009.

During the run up to the conference, feedback from scholars working on either country was very encouraging and helpful; nevertheless the composition of a balanced programme remained a challenge. As the number of scholars willing to tackle both countries in a comparative approach turned out to be very limited, the organisers chose to juxtapose papers dealing with comparable issues in either the Irish or Ukrainian case. The panels at the conference aimed at contrasting the politicisation of historiography, the practices of public commemoration and the representations of famine in different types of media, such as literature and film.

A perfect symmetry of papers was neither realistic nor aspired to. The extent of literary representation of the Irish and Ukrainian famines, for example, is very different, as is the corpus of scholarship in each case.[22] The organisers were pleased to discover in the course of the conference that many papers indeed complemented one another significantly, for instance on issues such as politicisation of historiography, or the various aspects of 'victimisation' in Irish and Ukrainian discourses. Hence the current volume assembles substantially revised versions of conference papers, supplemented by some articles published earlier in academic journals.

For publication in this book the contributions have been regrouped in four sections. Part I acquaints the reader with 'Histories, Historiography and Politics' and provides an overview of the historiographies and the key issues in academic and public debates. Chapter 1, written by the widely recognised Ukrainian authority in the field of Holodomor history, Stanislav Kulchytskyi, sets out the main arguments of the proponents of the genocide theory of Holodomor as well as those of their antagonists. Kulchytskyi's main concern is the chronological coincidence of the Famine and other repressive action taken against Ukrainians in 1932–33. Against this backdrop he argues that Stalin's policies were not primarily directed against ethnic Ukrainians, but against the population of the Ukrainian Soviet Republic whose loyalty the Kremlin doubted. 'Holodomor in Ukraine 1932–1933: An Interpretation of Facts' summarises points made in a booklet addressed to a Russian speaking audience which was published by Ukraine's National Academy of Science in 2008.

David Marples' Chapter 2 returns to the academic debate on the Holodomor and the obvious contrast in interpretations put forward by Ukrainian and Western scholars, earlier discussed by Kulchytskyi. Marples, director of the Stasiuk Programme for the Study of Contemporary Ukraine at the Canadian Institute of Ukrainian Studies, University of Alberta in Edmonton, argues that Western works have offered valuable insights into the history of the Famine but tended to neglect the context of nationalities policies. Marples supports Kulchytskyi's argument that national questions remained uppermost in the discussions of party officials about the failure of the 1932 harvest in Ukraine. Like his colleague in Kiev, he remains optimistic that a systematic discussion of the disparate views and the further use of archival evidence will finally enable a clarification of this issue. Previously published in *Europe-Asia Studies* in 2009, 'Ethnic Issues in the Famine of 1932–1933 in Ukraine' is reprinted here as it provides a comprehensive overview of key trends in Western historiography.

In Chapter 3 Vincent Comerford, professor emeritus of modern history at the National University of Ireland, Maynooth, reviews the development of Irish interpretations of the Famine with particular reference to historiography, but also by looking at popular and political attitudes. 'Grievance, Scourge or Shame? The Complexity of Irish Attitudes to the Great Famine' identifies modes of indignation (against the British), ambivalence and amnesia in respect of the calamity. It emerges that since the 1950s study of the Great Famine has been pivotal in the evolution of professional history in Ireland.

Part II is devoted to the logics behind and the practice of different forms of 'Public Commemorations' of the Famines. Two chapters deal with the role of the famines in education. Chapter Four, 'History and National Identity Construction: The Great Famine in Irish and Ukrainian History Textbooks' by Jan Germen Janmaat, senior lecturer in the Comparative Social Sciences at the Institute of Education, London, examines the extent to which textbooks for secondary schools have been influenced by nationalist discourses and traces their changes over time. Janmaat uncovers a trajectory in Irish narratives from very one-sided to gradually more nuanced narratives. The diverse pattern of Ukrainian narratives – surprisingly nuanced narratives from the onset – suggests that states emerging from authoritarian rule need not automatically publicise uniformly nationalist discourses in the period of early independence. Offering the only direct comparison of Irish and Ukrainian material in the volume, Janmaat's study is the reprint of an article first published in the journal *History of Education* (2006).

In Chapter 5 Maureen Murphy from Hofstra University in New York provides a first-hand account of the inclusion of famine history in the New York State school curriculum. 'The Great Irish Famine Curriculum Project' describes Hofstra University's development of a path-breaking programme being taught at state high schools as part of the larger human rights curriculum. This programme illustrates the wide range of areas of learning accessible through an open-minded, evidence-based approach to the study of the Great Famine, not least in a setting such as New York where it can be given meaning for students from a variety of cultural backgrounds as an exploration of comparative experience of hunger, dislocation and lack of entitlement.

In Chapter 6 Jason King, lecturer in the Department of English at the University of Limerick, examines documentary sources related to famine orphans who came to Quebec in 1847–48, to compare contemporary evidence with an enduring legend about the orphans. 'Remembering Famine Orphans: Irish Impressions of Quebec' demonstrates that what remains in popular memory in this case is founded on the myth-making of a generation after the event. King traces this back to a set of pastoral letters, pamphlets and travelogues published in the 1860s, especially John Francis Maguire's *The Irish in America* (1868).

Chapter 7, 'Monuments of the Irish Famine and Commemorative Culture', provides an overview of the memorials and monuments constructed across the globe since 1990 to commemorate the Irish Famine. Emily Mark-FitzGerald from the School of Art History and Cultural Policy at University College Dublin discusses issues of location, funding and the varying formal and aesthetic approaches. Against this backdrop a smaller selection of examples is analysed in detail, drawing out the particulars of their construction and design. On the basis of her findings Mark-FitzGerald reflects on the public visibility of the Famine and the future of this particular form of shaping the Great Famine's past by actors in the present.

Part III of the volume focuses on the issues of trauma and victimisation in representations of the past. Heorhiy Kasianov's contribution (Chapter 8) examines the dynamics within the public debate on the Holodomor in independent Ukraine. Synchronising post-Soviet Ukrainian historiography on the 1932–33 Famine with the recurring political stalemates in Kiev, 'Holodomor and Politics of Memory in Ukraine, 1990–2008' suggests that the political valorisation of the Famine reached its peak under Victor Yushchenko's presidency (2004–2010). However, Kasianov, head of the department of Contemporary History and Politics at the Institute of the History of Ukraine in Kiev, also shows that all preceding presidential regimes, while pursuing controversial political aims, tended to exploit the evocative power of Holodomor recollection to bridge political cleavages within the country.

Celia Keenan, senior lecturer in English and director of the MA in children's literature at St Patrick's College, Dublin, contributes Chapter 9: 'Narrative Challenges: The Great Irish Famine in Recent Stories for Children'. Keenan starts with the observation that children's literature typically tells stories of action, not passivity and concerns itself with black and white ideas of wrong and right. The history of the Great Famine however is not a clear-cut story: heroes and villains are not clearly defined and it is more about passive suffering by the Irish than great deeds. As Keenan shows, this makes the Famine a very difficult and complex topic for typical children's novels. This chapter was first published by Ann Lawson Lucas in the volume *The Presence of the Past in Children's Literature* (2003).

Chapter 10 returns to the Ukrainian case. Olga Papash, doctoral student at the Peter Mohyla Academy in Kiev, reviews the only feature film dedicated to the Holodomor so far. *Golod-33* (The Hunger of '33) was launched in 1991 and narrates the fate of a Ukrainian peasant family during the terrible winter of 1932–33. 'Collective Trauma in a Feature Film: *Golod-33* as One-of-a-Kind' shows how this film, rooted in late Soviet (perestroika) historical critique, foreshadows later developments in Ukrainian historiography and public commemoration: motifs of victimisation and martyrdom are used to render the 'sacrifice' of an earlier generation meaningful for the emerging independent Ukrainian nation.

Part IV of the volume is dedicated to new sources and new approaches in the research on the Irish and Ukrainian famines. In Chapter 11 Jan Jacek Bruski from the Department of History at Jagiellonian University, Krakow, introduces the reader to commonly overlooked sources for the history of the Holodomor: reports of Polish diplomats deployed in Khar'kiv and Kiev during the Famine. 'Polish Diplomatic and Intelligence Reports on the Ukrainian Famine' shows that Polish contemporary sources largely corroborate recent findings in Soviet archives. It also sheds an interesting light on Ukraine's international situation between Poland and the Soviet Union. Indeed, Polish diplomats suggested that what they perceived as Stalin's obvious turn against Ukraine might have been motivated by Soviet doubts about Ukrainian loyalty in case of a future conflict with Poland.

Maura Cronin, senior lecturer in history at Mary Immaculate College, Limerick, reminds us that serious historical research on the Irish Famine conducted during the twentieth century very often depended on oral sources, and not only the testimonies of first-hand witnesses. 'Oral History, Oral Tradition and the Great Famine' discusses the use of oral history and tradition in the reconstruction of the Great Famine. While oral history may tell little about the historical Famine, it speaks volumes about how individuals and communities choose to remember and how values in the present can shape and be shaped by the past. As Cronin argues, oral history informs us how social status, gendered authority roles and significant individuals determine the selection and transmission of memory.

The final chapter of the section and the volume was collectively contributed by Stewart Fotheringham from the School of Geography and Geosciences at the University of St Andrews, and Mary Kelly from the Department of

Geography at the National University of Ireland, Maynooth, and Martin Charlton for the National Centre for Geocomputation at the same university. 'Mapping Population Change in Ireland 1841–1851: Quantitative Analysis Using Historical Geographical Information Systems' demonstrates how new technologies, in this case geographical information systems (GIS), can be used to map, measure and explain the spatially uneven nature of population decline during the Irish Famine. New technology and the application of adequate methods of research enabled the geographers to bridge the gap between two well-documented levels, the national trends and local contexts. An intriguing question resulting from this chapter is whether GIS could also be applied in the Soviet historical and/or geographical context, where similar gaps between the macro and micro levels of famine research have been identified.[23]

The editors suggest that, considered together, the chapters of this volume illustrate the opaque and complex workings of cultural memory by providing comparable insights into two seemingly disparate but on some higher theoretical level linkable cultural traumas which have played constitutive roles for the construction of Irish and Ukrainian cultural memories. The concluding paragraphs of this introduction tentatively outline the directions such comparisons may take.

To begin with the link between historiography and identity politics, the contributions in this volume, while confirming the pre-eminent role the famines play in professional historiography and public commemoration, nuance their respective importance for Irish and Ukrainian nationalism. The fact of having been subordinate polities at the time of their respective famines creates in both Ireland and Ukraine the possibility of finding in those calamities emotionally overpowering evidence and symbol of foreign repression, and an explanation for latter-day national inadequacies. In Ireland, for the most part, this opportunity has tantalised rather than empowered nationalist politics, even if it has been a fairly constant background presence. Pursued beyond the simplifications of the lounge bar ballad or the powerful emotions evoked by images of starvation, the Great Famine quickly raises questions and complications. In post-Soviet Ukraine the Holodomor has provided a much more robust basis for inducing the populace to line up behind leaders. But here also there is clearly ambivalence of attitude and interpretation across the country's political spectrum and its geographical regions. In both countries the government takes an interest in the memorialisation of famines. In Kiev, memory of the Holodomor is something that must be managed vigorously if the government is to keep a grip on legitimacy, a major preoccupation of all presidents since Leonid Kuchma. In Dublin, by contrast, famine commemoration is the relatively minor responsibility of a government minister: the state's concern is merely that the Famine should remain politically inert.

Some measure of equivalence surely subsists between these different levels of resentment on the one hand, and on the other the deductions that can reasonably be made from contemporary empirical evidence. In Ukraine in 1932–33 Stalin initiated and sustained policies that included seizure by force of the entire food supplies of a vast number of people. The issue of culpability can be seen as a question of whether the party secretary thought of himself as directing fatal blows against a distinctive ethnic group, or against the sinews of a potentially secessionist republic, or against a recalcitrant peasantry that failed to meet grain production targets. In the Ireland of the late 1840s the potato crop failed, leaving millions destitute, because of a naturally occurring blight that puzzled officialdom and victims alike. The verdict on culpability then centres on the adequacy of the government's efforts and the humaneness of its intentions in the face of the crisis.

Beyond the level of national identity construction, the contributions to the volume clearly demonstrate a transnational dimension. In both cases, victimisation discourses can be linked to the recent rise of ethical issues in international relations. Ukraine's lobbying for international recognition of the Holodomor as genocide is an obvious case in point and should be further researched in the context of Ukraine's attempts to define its position between Russia, Europe and the United States. In this process Ukraine actively tried to influence political actors and public spheres abroad and simultaneously imported political conjunctures. The drafting of Ukrainian laws against genocide denial is clearly a reflection of larger European trends that regained currency in the wake of the Yugoslav wars.

Clearly the successive Irish governments have stayed aloof from such tendencies, yet the politicised parts of the Irish community in North America displayed a similar leaning in the attempt to achieve the recognition of the Great Famine in the United States. At the end of the day, the inclusion of the Great Famine into the school curriculum in several US states stems from its interpretation as a historical injustice of similar significance to the Holocaust, slavery or Apartheid. Ukrainian communities on the North American continent pursued similar activities prior to USSR's collapse as the Congress hearings of 1984 illustrate. The consultative role many American-Ukrainian and Canadian-Ukrainian activists took in the campaigning for the recognition of the Holodomor in independent Ukraine might have diluted some of the energies in this case. Nonetheless, pro-Irish and pro-Ukrainian activities in this realm certainly constitute another promising topic for future comparative studies on politics of memory in North America.

In this context, Celia Keenan's contribution on children's literature is by no means the odd one out. Significantly Keenan points at the limits of victimisation discourses in terms of identification and, possibly, for mobilisation: narratives built upon victimisation run the risk of denying agency for those who identify with the role of the victim. Worse still, a group constantly stressing its own status as a victim does not only forego alternative development scenarios for the future, but tends to develop immunity towards the suffering of others, as Aleida Assmann reminds us.[24] Olga Papash's analysis of the only Ukrainian feature film produced on the Holodomor echoes this analysis: by its emphatic recurrence to victimisation, the only solution left is some sort of transcendental redemption. At the time of its production (1989–90), this may have been an effective tool in the critique of a decaying secular regime as unethical, but it obviously had a limited appeal in the ensuing period of state and nation building.

Indeed, the contributions focussing on the techniques of public commemoration in Ireland and Ukraine equally demonstrate that collective memory works as a multidirectional construct; it simultaneously influences and is influenced by the memories of different generations and different cultural groups. Mediation, narrativisation and education shape the construction of mnemonic and historiographic narratives. In the context of this volume, the analysis of the Ukrainian case seems somewhat underrepresented. This should be read, however, against the backdrop of the short time that has elapsed since the lifting of Stalin's taboos in the post-Soviet space and the faint resonance of the Famine in the post-war emigration, which was partly stigmatised through factual or alleged collaboration with Nazi Germany. Olga Papash's contribution highlights the rarity of Holodomor novels and films, a paucity that must be related to the surge of recent documental publications fuelling the public debate. The role of historical experts and amateurs as collators and interpreters of such material is discussed by Kulchytskyi and Kasianov. The editors expect, however, that in the wake of the Ukrainian trauma different and possibly conflicting agendas will find literary expression in the (near) future. It is our hope that this book will spark further comparative research, and that it provides insight into the larger workings of cultural recollection (or cultural traumas), not just for the Irish and Ukrainian cases, but also for the overarching theoretical disciplines discussed here.

Finally, the chapters in Part IV of the book dealing with methods and sources suggest that, firstly, not all of the available source material has been thoroughly examined. This goes against conventional wisdom, and is true not just for Ukraine, as Jan Jacek Bruski's presentation of Polish sources shows, but also for Ireland, as Maura Cronin illustrates. In both the Irish and Ukrainian cases new sources are not likely to alter the general line of interpretation; particularly Stanislav Kulchytskyi argues that it is not just impossible, but even unnecessary to produce a written proof of Stalin's intention to starve the Ukrainian countryside. By contrast, new methodological approaches might seriously alter our perceptions. Mary Kelly, Stewart Fotheringham and Martin Charlton demonstrate that the systematic application of new methods and new technologies in the collection, presentation and interpretation of well-known statistical data can significantly advance a more balanced interpretation of historical events. Given the particular significance of the spatial dimension of the 1932–33 Famine in the Ukrainian case, one wonders whether feeding their geographical information systems with Soviet statistical data, as far as it is available, might not help to advance at least the discussion among specialists, which according to David Marples revolves around few recurring issues.

That said, the editors hope that this volume will stimulate further research on the histories, representations and commemorations of the famines, be it either on Ireland or Ukraine or in direct comparison of both countries.

A note on sources and transliteration: Russian and Ukrainian language sources are referenced according to the Library of Congress standards. Where to our knowledge English translations of quoted sources are available, we have referenced those instead of the Russian or Ukrainian originals. In the text of the chapters established English writings of proper names or toponyms are used (i.e. Kiev, Odessa, Moscow, Dnieper, etc. but Khar'kiv), the spelling of Ukrainian proper names in the text was simplified by the omission of apostrophes. The latter were retained in the footnotes, where we reference the place of publication also according to English spelling.

Notes and References

1 Hennadiy Kazakevych, 'Parallel Struggle: 90 Years Ago, When Ireland Gained its Independence from Great Britain, Ukraine Lost its Independence on the Other Side of Europe', *Ukrainian Week*, 17 April 2012, available at http://ukrainianweek.com/History/39376 (accessed 19 April 2012).
2 In his comparative study Dominic Lieven, for example, considers parallels between Scotland and Ukraine instead. See Dominic Lieven, *Empire: The Russian Empire and its Rivals from the Sixteenth Century to the Present* (London: Pimlico, 2003), 419.
3 Kai Erikson, 'Notes on Trauma and Community', in Cathy Caruth (ed.), *Trauma: Explorations in Memory* (Baltimore and London: Johns Hopkins University Press, 1995), 183–99 (194).
4 Cormac Ó Gráda, *Famine. A Short History* (Princeton: Princeton University Press, 2009).
5 Jan Assmann, *Das kulturelle Gedächtnis: Schrift, Erinnerung und politische Identität in frühen Hochkulturen* (Munich: Beck, 1992); English translation: *Cultural Memory and Early Civilization: Writing, Remembrance, and Political Imagination* (Cambridge: Cambridge University Press, 2011); Aleida Assmann, *Erinnerungsräume. Formen und Wandlungen des kulturellen Gedächtnisses* (Munich: Beck, 1999); Aleida Assmann, *Der lange Schatten der Vergangenheit. Erinnerungskultur und Geschichtspolitik* (Munich: Beck, 2006).
6 Pierre Nora 'Between Memory and History: *Les Lieux de Mémoire*', *Representations* 26 (1989): 7–25 (18–19, 23).

7 Pierre Nora, *Les lieux de mémoire*, 3 vols (Paris: Gallimard, 1997–98), English translation: *Rethinking France*, 4 vols (Chicago: University of Chicago Press, 2001–2010).
8 In the case of Ukraine this is more than understandable as independent Ukraine (re-) entered a process of state and nation building in 1991. See: David Marples, *Heroes and Villains: Creating National History in Contemporary Ukraine* (Budapest and New York: Central European University Press, 2007). For Ireland: Ian McBride, *History and Memory in Modern Ireland* (Cambridge: Cambridge University Press, 2001) and Oona Frawley (ed.), *Memory Ireland, volume 1: History and Modernity* (Syracuse: Syracuse University Press, 2011).
9 Angelika Bammer compares the circumstances of an oppressed people at home to the situation of a people in diaspora, pointing out that both are in a position of 'displacement'. See 'Introduction', in Angelika Bammer (ed.), *Displacements* (Bloomington: Indiana University Press, 1994), xi–xx (xi).
10 Daniel Levy, 'Changing Temporalities and the Internationalization of Memory Cultures', in Yifat Gutman, Adam D. Brown and Amy Sodaro (eds), *Memory and the Future, Transnational Politics, Ethics and Society* (Basingstoke: Palgrave Macmillan, 2010), 15–30, (17).
11 Michael Lambek and Paul Antze, 'Introduction: Forecasting Memory', in Paul Antze, Michael Lambek (eds), *Tense Past: Cultural Essays on Trauma and Memory* (New York and London: Routledge, 1996), xi–xxxviii (xii).
12 Alison Landsberg, *Prosthetic Memory: The Transformation of American Remembrance in the Age of Mass Culture* (New York: Columbia University Press, 2004), 17. Marianne Hirsch focuses on the transfer of memory to succeeding generations, and argues accordingly. She informs us that 'the relationship of the second generation to powerful, often traumatic, experiences that preceded their births but that were nevertheless transmitted to them so deeply as to seem to constitute memories in their own right'. Marianne Hirsch, 'The Generation of Postmemory', *Poetics Today* 29 (2008): 103–28 (103).
13 Michael Rothberg, *Multidirectional Memory: Remembering the Holocaust in the Era of Decolonization* (Stanford: Stanford University Press, 2009), 11.
14 See for example Ann Rigney, 'The Point of Stories: On Narrative Communication and Its Cognitive Functions', *Poetics Today* 13 (1992): 263–83; Ann Rigney, 'All This Happened, More or Less: What a Novelist Made of the Bombing of Dresden', *History and Theory* 47 (May 2009): 5–24; Astrid Erll, 'Re-writing as re-visioning, Modes of Representing the "Indian Mutiny" in British Novels, 1857 to 2000', *European Journal of English Studies* 10 (2006): 163–85.
15 Paul Ricœur, 'Narrative Time', *Critical Inquiry* 7 (1980): 169–90 (176).
16 Aleida Assmann, 'Texts, Traces, Trash: The Changing Media of Cultural Memory', *Representations* 56 (Autumn 1996): 123–34, (132).
17 Events are thereby placed in a narratological structure, often providing a narrative with a beginning – middle – end structure, which is not that self-evident in the actual passing of events. See Monika Fludernik, *Towards a 'Natural' Narratology* (London and New York: Routledge, 1996), 45.
18 Marguérite Corporaal, Christopher Cusack and Lindsay Janssen (eds), *Recollecting Hunger: An Anthology. Cultural Memories of the Great Famine in Irish and British Fiction, 1847–1920* (Dublin: Irish Academic Press, 2012).
19 See Jurij Šapoval, 'Lügen und Schweigen. Die unterdrückte Erinnerung an den Holodomor', *Osteuropa* 54, no. 12 (2004): 131–45.
20 Wilfried Jilge, 'Geschichtspolitik in der Ukraine', *Aus Politik und Zeitgeschichte* 8–9 (2007): 24–30.

21 Robert Kindler, 'Opfer ohne Täter. Kasachische und ukrainische Erinnerungen an den Hunger 1932–33', *Osteuropa* 62, no. 3 (2012): 105–20 (quote 114). See also Johan Dietsch: 'Politik des Leids. Der Hunger in der Ukraine 1932/33 und das Paradigma des Vorsatzes', in Matthias Middell, Felix Wemheuer (eds), *Hunger, Ernährung und Rationierungssysteme unter dem Staatssozialismus (1917–2006)* (Frankfurt: Peter Lang, 2011), 327–50.
22 See for example Rolf Göbner, 'Verbrannte Seelen. Der Holodomor in der ukrainischen Belletristik', *Osteuropa* 54, no. 12 (2004): 183–90.
23 Nikolaus Katzer, 'Brot und Herrschaft. Die Hungersnot in der RSFSR', *Osteuropa* 54, no. 12 (2004): 90–110.
24 Assmann, *Der lange Schatten*, 80–81.

Part I

HISTORIES, HISTORIOGRAPHY AND POLITICS

Chapter 1

HOLODOMOR IN UKRAINE 1932–1933: AN INTERPRETATION OF FACTS[1]

Stanislav V. Kulchytskyi
Institute of History at the National Academy of Science of Ukraine

In November 2008 after protracted battles the Verchovna Rada, the Ukrainian parliament, adopted the 'Law on the Holodomor in Ukraine in 1932–1933', characterising the national tragedy of the Holodomor as an 'act of genocide against the Ukrainian people'. In the course of 2008, Ukraine appealed to the United Nations and requested the recognition of this crime committed by Stalin's regime as an act of genocide under the terms of the United Nations Convention. Scholars were called upon to advance the academic discussion on this issue, and the government appealed to a broader public to intensify educational efforts in order to convince the international community as well as the citizens of their own country, Ukraine, that this assessment of the past is valid.

Having gained her independence only recently, Ukraine has to revisit her own past and free it from the norms of historical interpretations that have been prescribed by the *Short course of the History of the Communist Party of the Soviet Union (Bolsheviks)* published in 1938. Ignorance of what happened to Ukrainian citizens in the early 1930s is simply unacceptable. Since Khrushchev's secret speech at the 20th Party Congress we have learned many details about what happened in 1937.[2] Forgetting about the events of 1933 means suppressing the citizens of Ukraine, dividing their historical consciousness and creating obstacles for the nation's consolidation.

The Holodomor as an Act of Genocide

Interpretation of the Holodomor has been politically charged from the very beginning. Striving for clarity in this question, members of the Ukrainian diaspora in North America requested the creation of the special commission in the US Congress for the investigation of the Ukrainian Famine of 1932–33. Due to favourable circumstances and the unanimous support of the Senate and despite the American administration's unwillingness to trouble the already complicated relationship with the Soviet Union any further, a commission was set up in 1986. At the final meeting on 19 April 1988, the commission concluded its work with a report comprising nineteen findings. Among them was the following: Joseph Stalin and his henchmen committed an act of genocide against Ukrainians in 1932–33.[3]

In the same year, 1988, comprehensive research on all aspects of the 1932–33 Famine began in Ukraine. On the occasion of the 70th anniversary of the Holodomor, the Institute of the History of Ukraine at the Ukrainian Academy of Sciences published a survey jointly authored by 30 researchers.[4] The authors presented their book in Moscow in March 2004 on the occasion of a round-table discussion organised by the Institute of Global History at the Russian Academy of Science. It was attended by the best-qualified agrarian historians. In all but one aspect the Russian reviewers agreed with the conclusions of the authors, and summing up the discussion, Viktor Danilov and Ilia Zelenin published an article which concluded: 'If we were to characterise the 1932–33 Holodomor as an "intentional act of genocide against the Ukrainian peasantry", as some historians of Ukraine suggest, this would imply that it was no less a genocide against the Russian peasantry'.[5]

As a matter of fact, the 'Law on the Holodomor' in Ukraine did not achieve any stabilisation in historical interpretation. On the contrary, polemic debates about this tragic period in Ukrainian history intensified within the most heavily politicised parts of society, especially among politicians and political scientists. While accepting the facts (which would have been difficult to deny anyway as millions of Ukrainians undoubtedly died), many discussants rejected the conclusion of genocide.

The 1932–33 Famine in the Light of Historical Research

Discussions on the highly politically charged problem of the Holodomor should avoid emotional interpretations. Furthermore, the task of Ukrainian scholars consists of showing what exactly happened. This is by no means an easy task if we take into consideration that Stalin's most terrible crime was carefully planned and masterfully covered up. All participants should base their historical analysis on a previously agreed terminology. Finally one should make the best possible use of the expertise and experience of Western fellow scholars who approach the problem in a more objective manner.

The author of this chapter published his first scientific study on the Holodomor in 1991.[6] After the meeting with Moscow based scholars in March

2004, it seemed necessary to reinforce the position first taken up in 1991, i.e. the interpretation of the Holodomor as an act of genocide. I have elaborated on my case in two studies published in 2007; the following theses are based on evidence discussed in these books.[7]

It might be helpful to begin at the time when an influential school of interpretation emerged in the West, the school of the so-called 'revisionists'. Their aim was to free the history of the USSR from the critical assessments characteristic of the Cold War era. The revisionists disagreed above all with the prevailing interpretation of the 1932–33 Famine in Ukraine as an act of genocide, an interpretation which was instantly supported in the works of Robert Conquest and James Mace. The revisionists claimed that the grain confiscated from the peasantry was sacrificed for the inviolable cause of industrialisation, and many Russian scholars since have followed this interpretation.

The question remains: was the starvation of hundreds of thousands of people in various regions of the USSR, including Ukraine, triggered by the procurement of grain and its subsequent sale to third countries? And can this policy be considered an act of genocide? We may leave this question to future generations of historians. It is beside the point here. Instead we should concern ourselves with the death of millions of people resulting from the requisition of all edibles under the guise of grain procurement. Up to the last months of 1932 people in Ukraine and in other regions died because their grain was taken away. This led to the death of up to 150,000 peasants in Ukraine during the first half of 1932.[8] From November 1932 onwards, peasants died because they were deprived of other kinds of foodstuffs. At least 3.5 million people died from hunger during the Ukrainian Famine of 1932–33.

Our opponents in the West usually follow certain lines of argumentation to discard the thesis that the Holodomor was an act of genocide. First, they contend that people of different nationalities starved to death in Ukrainian villages. Secondly, they argue that Ukrainians were not persecuted on grounds of their ethnic descent. Thirdly, they ask whether it would be sensible to interpret the Famine as a genocide given the fact that at the same time the Soviet government in 1933 organised large-scale food relief programmes particularly for the populations of Ukraine and the Kuban region.

To differentiate between the victims of different nationalities in Ukrainian villages is not very convincing. It does not provide an answer to the question as to why the number of victims of the Famine was much higher in Soviet Ukraine and in the Kuban region than in other European regions of the USSR in 1933. The answer is fairly simple: this terror was directed against rural regions of Ukraine which were not exclusively inhabited by ethnic Ukrainians.

Whom did Stalin want to annihilate, then? James Mace was among the first to state that Stalin's terror in Ukraine did not target people of a certain nationality or occupation. According to Mace, it was rather directed against the citizens of a Ukrainian state which had emerged from the ruins of the Russian Empire; a state which had only briefly existed during the Civil War and which had been revived in the 1920s under Soviet auspices. As early as 1983, Mace presented a paper at a conference in Montreal dedicated to the Famine in which he put forward his thesis about the destruction through starvation of a Ukrainian civic nation (as opposed to Ukrainians as an ethnic group).[9]

Our opponents argue that the organisation of genocide through famine is incompatible with the provision of massive food relief. Indeed it is indisputable that such help was organised. Robert Davies' and Stephen Wheatcroft's 2004 study on this problem lists 35 governmental decrees dealing with the provision of food to the starving regions of the USSR. The first of these decrees dates from 7 February 1933, the last from 20 July the same year. In total, food relief amounted to 320,000 tons of grain, of which 264,700 tons were dispatched to the Ukrainian Soviet Republic and to the Kuban region. All other regions together received a total of just 55,300 tons.[10]

This data convinced Robert Conquest that the thesis about a genocidal famine must have been wrong. And indeed, a blurb on Davies' and Wheatcroft's books asserted that their conclusions 'differ from earlier ones by many historians, including Robert Conquest'. Conquest himself had reviewed the manuscript at an early stage and his verdict appeared on the same blurb: 'This is really an outstanding contribution to the research on such an important problem'. In their study, Davies and Wheatcroft quote from a letter which they had received from Conquest after the latter had read the draft. In this letter dated September 2003 Conquest asserted that Stalin did not plan the Famine of 1932–3 intentionally, yet he also 'would not have done anything to prevent the tragedy'.[11]

In the light of new evidence about the relief for the starving peasantry of Ukraine which recent research has unearthed, Conquest's dismissal of his own concept of *terror-famine* (in the subtitle of his own seminal study) seems understandable. Yet we should not rush to conclusions.

Peasants, Nationalities, Republics

In my opinion, genocide can occur in two different variants: in the form of ethnic cleansing and as terror through starvation. The genocides against Armenians or Jews are typical examples of the former. What, then, was the Holodomor? Many patriotic Ukrainians tend to describe the Holodomor as the 'Ukrainian Holocaust'. They have no doubts about the validity of the comparison with this universally acknowledged act of genocide; beyond that they are convinced that such comparison will further stimulate the recognition of the Holodomor as a tragedy of similar dimensions.

Such a comparison, however, does little to further their ultimate aim. This becomes even more obvious when we examine the reaction of Jewish public intellectuals in Ukraine on a possible recognition by the state of Israel that the Holodomor has been an act of genocide. The chairman of the Association of Jewish organisations and communities, Joseph Zisels, stated that:

> it would be up to Ukrainian and foreign historians to decide first whether this tragedy can in fact be called ethnic cleansing or not. It seems unacceptable to claim unambiguously that in Ukraine one people exterminated another consciously [...][12]

Obviously Zisels tends to understand the Holodomor as a case of ethnic cleansing, linking it to the corresponding term of Holocaust. Yet this is not the point. We must understand that an act of ethnic cleansing aims to expel a people from a given territory to make space for another. The Nazis used the term *Lebensraum* and based their *Plan Ost* on similar deliberations: its purpose was the elimination of the indigenous populations in a large territory in Eastern Europe up to Crimea for the sake of the creation of *Großdeutschland*.

One could indeed list some evidence that could support the theory of ethnic cleansing in the case of Ukraine, too. Upon arrival in Rostov on the Don on 1 November 1932, Lazar Kaganovich for example addressed the Bureau of the North Caucasian District Committee of the Russian Communist Party[13] and recommended punitive actions against those who did not deliver their quotas during grain procurement. Kaganovich mentioned the possibility of a resettlement of these peasants in the northern territories of the Soviet Union. During a meeting in the Cossack village of Medvedovskaia he openly threatened: 'We will resettle all those to the North who refuse to sow now!' Indeed, during November 1932 more than 60,000 peasants and Cossacks were deported from the Kuban.[14] An All-Union Resettlement Committee was created 15 August 1933. By the end of that year 117,000 collective farmers from Russia and Belorussia were resettled in Ukrainian villages of which the population had vanished during the Famine.[15]

The evidence quoted above does not display one coherent picture. In his study of the different forms of political repression applied by the Kremlin, Ivan Lusiak-Rudnitskyi came to the conclusion that 'Stalin's policy in relation to Ukraine amounted to a massive attempt to break the defiance of the Ukrainian people by the use of physical force. Therefore, it makes obviously no sense to talk about a total extermination of Ukrainians'.[16] This is a position one could agree with. It makes sense to look upon the punitive measure against the

Ukrainian peasantry as a form of terror through hunger rather than as an act of ethnic cleansing. Still, this form of terror corresponds to the norms of the UN Convention on genocide as well. The Convention defines a total or partial annihilation of a human group as genocide. And any form of terror suggests the extermination of a part of a population as a means to terrify the whole entity.

The Kremlin withdrew all foodstuffs from the already starving Ukrainian villages in order to counteract any social unrest. Since an individual deprived of the hope of finding food could hardly be expected to take an active part in protests, the aim was to make starvation as severe as possible. It should be remembered that starvation as a means of terror was first applied in Ukraine as early as 1921, with the aim of crushing the so called 'banditism of kulaks'. At that time such terror occurred in the form of the requisition of foods stocked in the already starving southern provinces. The Famine itself had then been a result of natural circumstances.

Using starvation as a weapon against the Ukrainian peasantry, Stalin at the same time ordered those who were willing and able to participate in agricultural campaigns to be fed through the collective farms. The bulk of food aid sent to Ukraine and the North Caucasus during the first half of 1933 was used first and foremost for this purpose.

Yet another terminological clash complicates an understanding of the core problems of the Holodomor. Basing his interpretation on the evidence of emigrated former Ukrainian citizens, Robert Conquest stated in *Harvest of Sorrow* that this form of terror had been directed against Ukrainians[17]. In a review of this book published in one of the subsequent editions of his *Economic History of the USSR*, Alec Nove insisted that, on the contrary, Stalin's blow had been directed against the peasantry, among which happened to be many Ukrainians, rather than against the Ukrainians, among whom there were many peasants.[18]

Since then scholars have debated whether Stalin annihilated Ukrainians or peasants. But can the question be put as plainly as this? After all it is difficult to imagine that Soviet power persecuted individuals solely on the grounds that they were Ukrainian. Yet it is likewise difficult to imagine that a person could be killed only because he or she belonged to the peasantry. Indeed, the Holodomor of 1932–33 emerged from a specific conjunction of circumstances in place and time. Any attempt at understanding the logic in the Kremlin's activities requires a thorough examination of the intersection between socio-economic and nationalities policies.

A Crisis of Soviet Socio-economic and Nationalities Policies

During the upheavals of 1918–20 the Bolsheviks successfully built up the foundations of a command economy. From 1929 onwards Stalin embarked on a new assault on the peasantry with the aim of executing what Lenin had not achieved earlier: locking up millions of small-scale producers in communes. During the first quarter of 1930 this resulted in massive social unrest. Stalin had to retreat and ordered a temporary halt in the collectivisation campaign.[19] During the next half year the idea of communes was given up and collectivisation was limited to the creation of the less binding *artel*.[20]

It would seem that the history of collectivisation has been fairly well studied. Yet the publication of new documents in five volumes edited by Victor Danilov under the title *Tragediia sovetskoi derevni* (The tragedy of the Soviet village, 1999–2006) substantially altered our understanding. It turned out, for example, that between 1930 and 1932 the Soviet state did not differentiate between state farms (*sovkhozy*) and collective farms (*kolkhozy*): everything produced in the joint economy of collective farms was taken away. While the workers of a state farm (peasants like the *kolkhozniki*) were given a kind of salary, the collective farmers had to content themselves with what they grew on their remaining household plots.

We know that the concept of a workday unit was developed precisely during these three years. The same period witnessed the campaigns against egalitarianism in salaries and discussions on economic and organisational measures to strengthen the collective farms. Still, the law on grain procurement passed in April 1930 had prescribed the amount of grain a collective farmer had to deliver to the state: between a quarter and a third of the total harvest. The larger part of the harvest ought to have been distributed among the farmers according to the amount of workday units they had laboured.[21]

It should have been distributed, but actually it was not. In the wake of the deep global economic crisis between 1929 and 1933 prices for industrial equipment fell worldwide and the Soviet foreign trade organisations bought up what was available at very advantageous prices. Prices for agricultural products, however, declined even more steeply. As nobody was willing to grant long-term loans to the Soviet Union as long as the Tsars' foreign debts were not acknowledged, it became necessary to sell more and more grain to earn foreign currency and to earmark it for the payment of imported machinery. Grain procurement plans grew out of proportion. In the attempt to raise the quantity of grain available for export, the state stripped the collective farms completely of their harvests.

When it became clear that the state would take away all the grain anyway, the peasants displayed little inclination to work seriously for the common good. Nobody bothered to do anything about the weeds that were growing and reducing the amount of grain to be harvested. The peasants started too late to reap the harvest, and the grains were already falling from the stalks. More grain was lost during transportation. On the threshing floor the peasants left a good amount of grain on the stalk, because the only part they could expect to keep was what was left in the straw.

Thus the loss of grain resulted from a lack of material incentives to the collective farmers. But to the Kremlin the catastrophic decline of grain procurement seemed to be explicable only through organised sabotage, or the hiding and pilfering of grain by the peasants themselves. On 7 August 1932 Stalin personally signed a decree of the Central Executive Committee of the RSFSR and the USSR's Council of People's Commissars 'On the protection of the property of state enterprises, *kolkhozes* and cooperatives, and strengthening of the public (socialist) property'. Theft of collective property was threatened with execution, or with imprisonment for no less than ten years in cases with 'mitigating circumstances'.

Despite the measurements taken, the economic crises in the Soviet Union deepened. The Kremlin was forced to cut back sharply on the military budget and on expenses for industrial capacity building. It was the activity of extraordinary procurement commissions, dispatched hastily to the main grain producing regions (Ukraine, North Caucasus and the Volga region) in autumn 1932, which actually caused the Famine. Starvation also occurred in the non-black soil regions; here it was the result of the discontinuation of centralized supply in the wake of the grain shortage.

The state propaganda machine presented these 'food difficulties' as a consequence of the sabotage conducted by kulaks in collective farms. Beyond terror measures, which due to specific reasons were directed primarily against two districts in Ukraine, the Kremlin also resorted to economic measures in its efforts to restore order. The pace of industrialisation was significantly slowed down, and the stocking of food reserves was brought to a halt.

On 19 January 1933 the Council of People's Commissars of the USSR and Central Committee of the Russian Communist Party passed a joint resolution 'On obligatory grain deliveries to the state by collective farms and individual economies'. Can we expect that a single decree could have fundamentally changed the relations between the agricultural producers and the state, holding the 'commanding heights' in the economy? Indeed, we can. The decisions of the tenth Party Congress to replace the system of food confiscation by taxation had been the basis of the New Economic Policies of the 1920s. The 19 January 1933 decree determined that the state could only claim a clearly defined amount of the collective farm's production as natural taxes, and that these amounts would have to be defined at the outset of the agricultural production cycle. The principle of taxation in kind implied that the total amount of grain produced on a collective farm belonged exclusively to the collective farmers, after they settled tax duties with the state in the form of grain deliveries. In that sense the state finally acknowledged collective farmers' ownership over the grain they produced. After this decree, the collectivised agricultural economy acquired the basic outline that characterised it until very recently.

However, it remains to be seen why Stalin, in order to overcome the crisis of 1932, did not content himself with the implementation of this fully rational policy, but supplemented it with terror inflicted on some regions in Ukraine. The problem indeed does not consist solely of the terror through famine directed against the Ukrainian peasantry. The Communist Party of Ukraine, with its membership of half a million, stood in fact at the epicentre of Stalinist repressions. In the years to follow, its strength was diminished by almost 50 per cent, and its leading circles were almost completely wiped out in 1937. By the same token the regime began to prosecute the Ukrainian intelligentsia which had played a leading role in the struggle for national liberation in the years between 1917 and 1920.

The regime directed the most severe forms of repression against the peasantry, but this should not be understood as an attempt to wipe out a social class without national implications. Stalin perfectly understood that the peasantry constituted the backbone of any nation. 'The national question is *in essence* a peasant question', he had stated already in March 1925.[22]

Stalin's letter to Kaganovich dated 11 August 1932 became known to the broader public only in 2000 and has been quoted frequently since. Alarmed by the situation in Ukraine the general secretary deliberated an unusual casting of cadres: he intended to appoint Kaganovich as general secretary of the Central Committee of the Ukrainian party while retaining his position as a secretary of Central Committee of the Russian party. Likewise he thought of attaching the vice-chairman of the Unified State Political Administration (OGPU), the political police, to this mission to Ukraine, also under the provision that Balitskii could keep his former rank. Summing up his view on the situation in Ukraine and on the plan of cadre exchanges, Stalin wrote: 'Without these and similar measures (the economic and political strengthening of Ukraine, above all its border districts, etc.), I repeat, we may lose Ukraine'.[23]

Meanwhile, we also know of the OGPU reports sent back to the Kremlin. The situation was critical everywhere, but to Stalin it seemed to be nowhere as critical as in Ukraine. Here was a national republic with a massive economic and human potential, bordering on Europe. Stalin had not forgotten that between 1917 and 1919 Ukraine had to be conquered three times. He had not forgotten that in early 1920 the fourth All-Ukrainian party conference had refused to vote for a list of candidates recommended by Lenin for the Central Committee. The Ukrainians had elected their own leaders instead. He remembered of course that during the first months of 1930 he had been forced to stop collectivisation because of the social upheavals in Ukrainian territories on the right bank of the Dnieper. But how realistic was the danger of losing Ukraine, in his own words, 'as soon as things start getting worse?'[24]

Our Western colleagues tend to underestimate the national backdrop of the crisis that evolved in the early 1930s. In the starving Ukrainian peasant they frequently see just a peasant, not a citizen of the Ukrainian Soviet state. They treat the Soviet Union as a union of republics created by the so-called 'titular' (ethnic) nations, deprived of any substantial rights. The USSR, however, took on this shape only after the 1932–33 Famine and the terror of 1937 and 1938. Earlier the Soviet Union had been a real confederation of states.

Soviet statehood is a difficult concept both in its primary, i.e. Russian dimension, and in its secondary dimension as a state of many nations. Subject to the dictatorship of the leaders in the Kremlin, the Soviets embodied executive power. Through this power the Party of the Bolsheviks transformed into something like a state structure. Russia remained a state within the Soviet state and the all-Union centre eluded any amalgamation with it: that would have contravened the constitution. At the same time, it prevented the emergence of a competing Russian authority in Moscow.

Regarding the transfer of statehood from the Kremlin to the national republics (among others the RSFSR), which particular risks did the twofold construction of the Soviet state entail? We may distinguish primary and secondary risks: The secondary risk consisted of potential discontent of political functionaries in the republics with the developments in the centre, and their readiness to dissent openly when circumstances would allow for it. For this reason the entire *politburo* of the Ukrainian Communist Party vanished in the repressions, and with them tens of thousands of functionaries and members of the national intelligentsia.

But the primary risk resulted from the particular construction of the vertical authority created by the Kremlin to its own advantage. Soviets, among them also the Soviets in the national republics, held the real executive power in their hands and linked the party with the state apparatus. As long as the Kremlin had full control over these institutions there was no danger of the disintegration of the Soviet Union. If this control were to shift to the regional structures of the party, for example in case of a crisis in the centre, then this threat would become very real indeed. On the grounds of its strong national (non-Soviet) inclination towards traditions of statehood, the Kremlin judged Ukraine to pose the greatest risk.

After the creation of the USSR, the Kremlin embarked on an affirmative nationalities policy (*korenizatsiia*) in the republics, a course of action aimed at a firm anchoring of Soviet power in the non-Russian environment. In Ukraine, *korenizatsiia* quickly transcended the scope of a bureaucratic campaign and turned into an instrument of national revival. At *politburo* meetings on the all-Union level, Ukrainian leaders steadfastly raised the question of incorporation of those RSFSR territories which contained ethnic Ukrainian majorities into the Ukrainian Soviet Republic, pointing at the results of the 1926 all-Union census. Among these territories was the Kuban district. If these petitions were not successful, the Ukrainian leadership managed at least to obtain concessions in the form of the Kremlin's consent to an Ukrainisation of regions outside of the republic where Ukrainians formed a majority. Within a short period of time, Ukrainian became the language of administration, education and mass media in such regions. The Kremlin observed these achievements with growing distrust. A thoroughly 'ukrainised' Kuban would have to be attached to the Ukrainian SSR and would additionally strengthen the human potential of Ukraine within the USSR.

Hence in the second half of 1932 two crises overlapped – the crisis of the Kremlin's socio-economical policies and that of its nationalities policy. As contemporary documents show, Stalin feared above all the outbreak of social unrest in starving Ukraine. The repressions started soon after, and were directed against the Ukrainian peasantry (in the form of terror through famine) as well as against Ukrainian intelligentsia (in the form of individual terror on a massive scale plus the purging of party cells). Supposedly, these repressions were not aimed at members of a particular nationality, but against all citizens of the Ukrainian republic. However, obviously the majority of these citizens were at the same time Ukrainians. Even after having forced it into the strait jacket of the Soviet republic, the Kremlin continued to consider the sheer existence of a Ukrainian citizenry as a menace.

Can Intentionality be Documented?

Every time we state that the government brought the peasantry to complete dependence through the requisition of their food supplies, we are told to produce documentary evidence. No document – no genocide. People who have lived through the Holodomor describe the activities of special brigades that searched peasant households and took away all provisions. Tens, hundreds, thousands of witness reports from different villages add up to a coherent picture. If this is true, there can be just one possible conclusion: these brigades were ordered to confiscate food even if this order was not issued in written form. Nonetheless, we are still asked to produce a written document!

In fact it is possible to present a written document that is relevant to this issue. In November 1932 Stalin sent out extraordinary grain procurement commissions, one headed by Molotov to the Ukrainian SSR and another one under Kaganovich to the Kuban. Following Stalin's instructions, Molotov drafted two decrees, one in the name of the Central Committee of the Ukrainian Communist Party, dated 18 November, and one in the name of the Council of People's Commissars of Ukraine, dated 20 November 1932. Both bore the identical title 'On measures for the improvement of grain procurement'. The final text, approved by Stalin, listed among other points the possibility of punishing peasants through 'fines to be paid in meat or potatoes'.[25]

Taking advantage of the situation emerging in the wake of terrorist action committed by these commissions, the *politburo* of the Russian Communist Party in late 1932 declared the Ukrainisation of the North Caucasus as 'being in the spirit of Petliura'.[26] A joint resolution of the Central Committee of the Russian Communist Party and the Council of Peoples' Commissars of the USSR from 14 December 1932 demanded in the form of an ultimatum that all paperwork of Soviet and cooperative organs, all newspapers and journals in the 'Ukrainianised' regions of the North Caucasus should immediately switch from the Ukrainian to the Russian language, as the latter would be more comprehensible to the population of the Kuban district. Russian should also replace Ukrainian as the language of instruction in schools from the beginning of the next school year.[27]

On 1 January 1933 Stalin sent a telegram to Khar'kiv demanding the delivery of grain. He suggested that the Central Committee of the Ukrainian Communist Party and the Council of Peoples' Commissars should inform, via their village councils, the *kolkhozes*, *kolkhoz* workers and individually operating farmers that:

a. those who voluntarily hand over to the State grain previously stolen and hidden from inventory shall not be repressed;
b. in the case of *kolkhoz* workers, *kolkhozes* and individual farmers who stubbornly persist in keeping grain previously stolen and hidden from inventory, the most severe measures of punishment set out in the Resolution of the Central Executive Committee and Sovnarkom of the USSR from 7 August 1932 'On the protection of property of State enterprises, *kolkhozes* and cooperatives, and the consolidation of socialist property' are to be applied.[28]

This telegram, containing nothing more that the two quoted items, is disconcerting. In the first place, Stalin had never before issued threats against the peasantry of any particular union republic. Moreover, he knew that there was no grain left in Ukraine, since the investigations conducted by the secret police in December had yielded only modest results. The message of the document becomes instantly clear without further explanations if we juxtapose both points: The second point seemingly addressed those who had ignored the first one and who had not delivered grain. But how would you find out who had not delivered hoarded grain? Only by searches! Hence Stalin's telegram was the signal to start those searches.

Those who survived the Holodomor report that during these searches not only potatoes and meat were taken, as laid out in the decree on fines 'to be paid in kind', but all edible products. In this sense, the telegram unmistakably identifies the individual who gave the signal for the requisition of food provisions, as the one who ordered the terror through famine.

Stalin's behaviour has to be analysed in its larger context. At the joint meeting of the *politburo* and *presidium* of the Central Control Commission of the Russian party on 27 November 1932 Stalin had linked the failure of grain procurement not to the methods of forced requisitions[29] but to wrecking and sabotage in collective and state farms. 'Given the fact that collective farms are a socialist form of production', the general secretary declared, 'it would be unwise if communists were not to answer this blow inflicted by some of the collective farmers and collective farms with a devastating counter blow'.[30]

Deflection from the responsibility for the economic collapse which had led to a nationwide famine was the primary reason for the Stalinist leadership's decision to revert to terrorist action. A 'devastating blow' was directed against the largest republic, the one which bordered on Europe, the one which could possibly have used the crisis in the centre ('as soon as things get worse') to put its constitutional right of separation from the USSR into practice.

Stalin, however, was not content with the confiscation of food. On 22 January 1933, he personally drafted a letter (his signature is preserved on the left margin of the document) which opened with the following lines: 'The Central Committee of the Russian Party and the Council of People's Commissars of the USSR have gathered evidence according to which large numbers of peasants left the Kuban and Ukraine for the Central Black Earth and Volga regions, Moscow, Belorussia and the Western provinces in the search of grain'. The Kremlin demanded that heads of the neighbouring territories should close the borders to the Ukrainian Soviet republic and the Kuban district.[31]'

To the survivors of the Holodomor it seemed as if the authorities applied ethnic criteria to determine which parts of the population would fall prey to starvation. The reality was more complex, though. The authorities simultaneously killed and rescued Ukrainian peasants. Pavel Postyshev, who arrived in Ukraine provided with dictatorial authority in January 1933, had been assigned two major tasks: he was to organise the spring sowing and he carried orders 'to liquidate the nationalist inclinations' within the party and Soviet organs in Ukraine. In February he released the food reserves stocked in the Ukrainian SSR in order to feed the starving population. At the same time Postyshev began tightening his grip on the Ukrainian Communist Party and non-party intelligentsia. After the Holodomor and the mass repressions of 1937 and 1938, Ukraine lost its potential for resistance. It goes without saying that this does not apply to the western districts which were incorporated into the USSR in 1939.

The politicians who threw Ukraine into the torment of terrifying repression are no longer alive. Nor does the totalitarian state whose leaders bear responsibility for the Holodomor any longer exist. We should be calm and collected when we revisit the difficult periods of our common past. Yet from the international community we expect the recognition that this crime was indeed an act of genocide. First and foremost we expect this from the Russian Federation, whose population likewise suffered the loss of many millions of lives in the years of Stalin's dictatorial rule.

Notes and References

1 This chapter is a revised and translated version of a brochure originally published in Russian. S. Kul'chitskii, *Ukrainiskii golodomor 1932–1933 gg.: Interpretatsiia faktov* (Kiev: National Academy of Sciences of Ukraine, Institute of Ukrainian History, 2008).
2 The author alludes to the Great Terror of the second half of the 1930s here [translator's note].
3 Cf. the executive summary of the Report to Congress Commission on the Ukrainian Famine. Adopted by the Commission, April 19, 1988, Submitted to Congress, 22 April 1988. United States Government Printing Office: Washington, DC, 1988.
4 *Golod 1932–33 rokiv Ukrainy: prychyny ta naslidky* (Kiev: Naukova dumka, 2003).
5 V. P. Danilov, I. E. Zelenin, 'Organizirovannyi golod. K 70-letiiu obshchekrestianskoi tragedii', *Otechestvennaia istoriia* 5 (2004): 109.
6 S. V. Kul'chyts'kyi, *Tsina 'velikogo perelomu'* (Kiev: Vydavnytstvo Ukraina, 1991).
7 S. V. Kul'chitskii, *Pochemu ON NAS unichtozhal? Stalin i ukrainskii Golodomor* (Kiev: Ukrainiskaia press-gruppa, 2007); S. V. Kul'chyts'kyi, *Holodomor 1932–1933 iak henotsyd: trudnoshchi usvidomlennia* (Kiev: Nash chas, 2008).
8 Kul'chyts'kyi, *Tsina*, 356.
9 'To destroy them as a political factor and a social organism', see James E. Mace, 'The Famine of 1933: A Survey of the Sources', in Roman Serbyn and Bogdan Krawchenko (eds), *The Famine in Ukraine 1932–1933* (Edmonton: CIUS, 1986), 12.
10 Robert W. Davies, Stephen G. Wheatcroft, *The Years of Hunger: Soviet Agriculture, 1931–1933* (New York: Palgrave Macmillan, 2004), 481–4.
11 Ibid., 441.
12 Stanislav Kul'chyts'kyi, 'Treba vidmovliatysia vid poniattia "Ukrains' kyigolokost"' *Forum Natsii*, 11 (2007).
13 Since 1918 the official denomination of the all-Union party was 'Russian Communist Party (Bolsheviks)' [translator's note].
14 S. Kul'chyts'kyi, *Holodomor 1932–1933 rr. iak henotsyd*, 291–2.
15 *Kollektyvizatsiia i holod na Ukraini 1929–1933. Zbirnik dokumentiv i materialiv* (Kiev: Naukova Dumka, 1992), 642.
16 Ivan Lusiak-Rudnits'kyi, *Istorychni ese*, vol. 2 (Kiev: Osnovy, 1994), 297.
17 Robert Conquest, *The Harvest of Sorrow. Soviet Collectivisation and the Terror Famine* (Oxford: Oxford University Press, 1987), 4.
18 Alec Nove, *An Economic History of the U.S.S.R.*, 2nd ed. (Harmondsworth: Penguin, 1989), 170.

19 Cf. Stalin's infamous *Pravda* header: 'Dizzy from Success', 2 March 1930, in Stalin, *Works* (Moscow: Foreign Languages, 1955), 12:197–205 [translator's note].
20 Stalin stated in the same article: 'In the *agricultural artel*, the basic means of production, primarily for grain-farming – labour, use of the land, machines and other implements, draught animals and farm buildings – are socialised. In the *artel*, the household plots (small vegetable gardens, small orchards) the dwelling houses, a part of the dairy cattle, small livestock, poultry, etc., are *not socialised*. They would have been in a commune' [translator's note].
21 Viktor P. Danilov (ed.), *Tragediia sovetskoi derevni: kollektivizatsiia I raskulachivanie; dokumenty i materialy v 5 tomach; 1927–1939, Vol. 2: Noiabr' 1929–dekabr' 1930*. (Moscow: ROSSPEN, 2000), 383–4.
22 Stalin, *Works*, 1925 (Moscow: Foreign Languages, 1954), 7:71. Italics added by author, Stanislav V. Kulchytskyi.
23 *The Stalin-Kaganovich Correspondence 1931–1936* (New Haven: Yale University Press, 2003), 179–81. See also Marples' and Bruski's chapters for extensive quotes from this document.
24 Ibid.
25 Ruslan Pyrih et al. (eds), *Holod 1932–1933 rokiv na Ukraini: Ochyma istorykiv, movoiu dokumentiv* (Kiev: Institut istorii partii, 1990), 254, 257.
26 Symon Petliura (1879–1926) headed one of the independent national Ukrainian governments during the Civil War (1918–1920) [translator's note].
27 Pyrih, *Holod 1932–1933 rokiv*, 293–4.
28 Ibid., 308.
29 A policy which was nonetheless abandoned in January 1933 and replaced with the introduction of natural taxation in kind which was to define the relation between state and collective farms in the future.
30 *Tragediia Sovetskoi derevni*, vol. 3 (Moscow: ROSSPEN, 2001), 559.
31 Ibid., 635–6.

Chapter 2

ETHNIC ISSUES IN THE FAMINE OF 1932–1933 IN UKRAINE[1]

David R. Marples
Director of the Stasiuk Programme for the Study of Contemporary Ukraine,
Canadian Institute of Ukrainian Studies,
University of Alberta, Edmonton

For independent Ukraine, no event has greater significance in the history of the developing nation state than the Famine of 1932–33. It brought about a period of intensive suffering on a hitherto unimagined scale. Although the Famine is becoming integrated into Ukraine's new national history, its progress to that status has been uneven, littered with public disputes and political dissension, and with no consensus among the Ukrainian public as to its scale or, especially, its origins. In part these disputes illustrate the continuing relevance of the Soviet period to life in Ukraine, despite the material and practical steps taken in forging an independent state. The Famine has also generated an emotional academic debate in the West, and no consensus has resulted thus far.[2] Ironically, the social and economic historians who have worked most extensively on this period and published their results are much closer to the former late-Soviet perspective that emerged after the earlier period of silence on the Famine. They conclude that it was namely a result of environmental or climatic conditions rather than part of an official state policy aimed at eliminating Ukrainians as a nation. This chapter explores the debate on the genesis of the Famine and suggests that further emphasis should be given to the national question. This conclusion contrasts with recent discussions in the journal *Europe-Asia Studies*, which, interesting as they are, have often ignored the Ukrainian angle completely and focused on the Famine as an all-Union phenomenon without an ethnic perspective.

A Synopsis of Famine Studies in Ukraine

Ukrainian scholars who write most regularly on the Famine, such as Yurii Shapoval,[3] Stanislav Kulchytskyi,[4] Vasyl Marochko[5] and Petro Panchenko et al.,[6] place emphasis on several factors that appear to elucidate the true causes of the Famine: the rapid introduction of collectivisation in Ukraine compared to other regions; the unreasonable grain quotas placed upon Ukraine; the closure of the borders of Ukraine and the North Caucasus according to Stalin's directive of 22 January 1933 to prevent the migration of starving peasants; the fact that Ukrainian officials informed Moscow of the situation in Ukraine and the imminence of famine as early as 1932 but without any results; Stalin's letter to Kaganovich of 11 August 1932 that outlined his suspicions of the Ukrainian peasantry and his fear of 'losing Ukraine';[7] the fact that the Extraordinary Commission in Ukraine led by Molotov took draconian measures, with its decree of 18 November 1932, confiscating not only grain, but also meat and vegetables, ensuring the inevitability of the peasants starving; the lack of such starvation in other republics, and most specifically Russia and Belorussia; the link between the Famine and the assault on the Ukrainian nation, as manifested by terror and deportations; the purge of cultural and national leaders; and the cessation of the earlier policy of Ukrainisation.[8]

I have simplified these issues but by and large they represent the general tenor of contemporary Ukrainian narratives. Under the leadership of President Viktor Yushchenko, the Famine has taken a central place in the construction of a Ukrainian national history, and the president has taken the personal lead in this campaign.[9] It has also served to designate Russia as the perpetrator and essential 'other' not merely in the 1930s but in the wartime years that followed. The Famine is now represented in school textbooks, and the Ukrainian parliament[10] – albeit by a bare majority – has recognised it as an act of genocide based on the UN definition of that term outlined in 1948, as an attempt to eliminate all or part of a population or nationality group.[11] Ukrainian historians have in part accepted this interpretation based on published works in major historical journals, though there are some serious disagreements. However, the genesis of the Famine issue in Western scholarly works is much more problematic.

The 50th Anniversary and the Famine in Western Scholarship

The year 1983 marked the 50th anniversary of the peak of the Famine and was a watershed for studies of the Famine in the West. Prior to that date very little had appeared in English in scholarly venues on the Ukrainian Famine. A project initiated by the Ukrainian Research Institute at Harvard University resulted in the well known 1986 book on the terror and Famine by Robert Conquest. The book was generally well received though Conquest admitted subsequently that he had lacked sources to confirm his estimates of death tolls. Similarly the Canadian Institute of Ukrainian Studies published a book edited by Roman Serbyn and Bohdan Krawchenko.¹² The subsequent formation of the US Commission on the Ukraine Famine energised research work and in the late 1980s it published three volumes of eyewitness testimony.¹³ In 1990, a negative response to these publications came in the form of an article in *Slavic Review* by Mark B. Tauger, which maintained that the Famine could be explained by the fact that the harvest of 1931 was much lower than initially thought and that grain reserves in the Soviet Union were very low.¹⁴

The reception accorded to Conquest's book provides an indicator of divisions in Western scholarship two decades ago when revelations about the scale of the 1932–33 Famine first came to light. Writing in the *Times Literary Supplement*, Geoffrey A. Hosking concluded that:

> Conquest's research establishes beyond doubt, however, that the Famine was deliberately inflicted there [in Ukraine] for ethnic reasons – it was done in order to undermine the Ukrainian nation, which had been enjoying a unique cultural and linguistic flowering during the 1920s [...] The purge among Ukrainian intellectuals and "bourgeois nationalists" in the Party was carried out much earlier than elsewhere, and more or less coincided with the Famine. Furthermore, GPU guards searched the trains on the border of the Ukraine to prevent food being imported or refugees leaving to seek food elsewhere. There are reports of Russian villages receiving supplies while neighbouring Ukrainian villages across the border were left to starve. All of this indicates that Stalin was pursuing ethnic as well as economic goals.¹⁵

Likewise, the late Peter Wiles of the London School of Economics, commented that Conquest had 'adopted the Ukraine exile view [on the origins of the Famine of 1932–33], and he has persuaded this reviewer'. Wiles also added that Conquest might have placed further emphasis on the North Caucasus, which consisted of at least 'half Ukrainians or Cossacks or – worse – Ukrainian Cossacks'.¹⁶

Craig Whitney, however, disagreed with the theory of genocide:

> The eyewitness testimony may be reliable, but far more debatable is the thesis that the Famine was specifically aimed as an instrument of genocide against the Ukraine. The clear implication of this book is that the author has taken the side of his Ukrainian sources on this issue, even though much of his evidence does not support it well. Mr Conquest's attempts to document the claim that while people were starving in the Ukraine they were being well fed just across the border in Russia fall far short of a rigorous standard – a few citations from 'The Black Deeds of the Kremlin' and other exile sources do not make the case.¹⁷

Similarly the late Alec Nove, in a generally positive review of Conquest's book, advanced one major caveat:

> There is one matter on which one must disagree with Conquest. It is what could be called the Ukrainian aspect. That the majority of those who died in the famine were Ukrainian peasants is not in dispute. But did they die because they were peasants, or because they were Ukrainians? As Conquest himself points out, the largest number of victims proportionately was in fact Kazakhs, and no one has attributed this to Stalin's anti-Kazakh views [...] Yes the Ukrainian countryside suffered terribly. But Conquest seems prone to accept the Ukrainian nationalist myth.[18]

Scholarly divisions on the issue were thus as divided in the mid-1980s as they are today.

As Hiroaki Kuromiya has noted, those who examine the Famine from a general Soviet perspective downplay any specific Ukrainian factor, while specialists on Ukraine generally support the concept of a genocidal famine.[19] The development of the debate on parallel lines has meant that at a time when international governments are recognising the Famine as an act of genocide by Stalin's regime against Ukraine, Western scholars are engaged in a continuing and often heated discussion on whether in fact this was really the case. I would argue also that the debate has taken place in a vacuum: the scholars in question have tended to develop their own theories without communication with 'outsiders'. To be more specific, those who deny that the Famine was genocide do not engage in discussions with scholars who believe that this was the case. This is evident from conferences such as Annual Conference of the American Association for the Advancement of Slavic Studies (AAASS) and from the protracted debate on the pages of *Europe-Asia Studies*. A fundamental divide has developed that has served critically to undermine the issue and at times has taken on a distinctly political hue. Those who have supported the genocide argument have been accused of adopting a political stance, while those who oppose it have been perceived as pro-Soviet or pro-Russian in their political leanings.[20] The most notable work in the school of writing that maintains that the Famine was not genocide is that by Robert W. Davies and Stephen G. Wheatcroft.[21] It is a weighty volume, replete with tables and statistics, and not always easy to comprehend. Nevertheless, it now serves as the main source in English of those who reject any specific Ukrainian factor in the Famine of 1932–33 and, as the title indicates, the authors neither accept the limitations of those two years nor the geographical restrictions of the borders of the Ukrainian SSR.

Davies and Wheatcroft summarise their views in an article in *Europe-Asia Studies*. They comment that the USSR suffered two disastrous harvests in

1931 and 1932, which negated efforts to build up grain stocks. In May 1932, the government reduced targets for the Soviet harvest from 23.5 tons to 19 million tons, and an even lower figure was actually gathered. In Ukraine, they comment, the harvest collection plan was lowered from 5.83 million tons to 3.77 million, with the actual collection being 3.53 million. Once it was aware of the scale of the Famine, the *politburo* issued 35 'top secret decisions' that provided small amounts of food relief to Ukraine and the North Caucasus. These measures were insufficient to prevent mass starvation but they demonstrate the government's efforts to reduce the hardship.[22] They continue by stating that Stalin declined to seek grain relief from abroad because of a crisis in foreign exchange rates and also because of reluctance to expose the real problems in Soviet agriculture. Nevertheless, they state 'we have found no evidence, direct or indirect, that Stalin sought deliberately to starve the peasants'. They also cite a letter from Robert Conquest in which that writer says that he does not believe that Stalin deliberately inflicted the 1933 Famine, but rather put Soviet interests ahead of feeding the starving.[23]

Michael Ellman is more critical of Stalin's regime than Davies and Wheatcroft but nevertheless has reservations about the issue of a deliberate act of genocide. He asks whether one can refer to genocide when most of the alleged victim group survives and comments that when starving peasants fled to the borders of Ukraine, the OGPU[24] could not determine whether or not they were ethnic Ukrainians because they did not carry passports. He cites Davies and Wheatcroft's figure of a 28 per cent reduction of the 1932 procurement quota and points to the state's allocation of seed loans and relief from February to July 1933.[25]

Finally, Kuromiya offers a very careful analysis of the Famine that analyses several factors. He wonders why if Stalin intended to kill Ukrainians he did not announce the fact, as he had declared his earlier objective to eliminate the *kulaks*. He also thinks that such an order would have been comprehended by his subordinates, and that the consequences of imposing a famine would have been impossible to forecast. He concludes that while Stalin was not averse to the occurrence of deaths, 'it is unlikely that he intentionally caused the famine' to eliminate millions. He does acknowledge that Ukraine was seriously afflicted, and that the Soviet leader exhibited suspicion of Ukrainian peasants and Ukrainian nationalists, but he is not convinced that the goal of the Famine was to punish ethnic Ukrainians. He looks also at the perceived foreign threat to the Soviet Union from both the Far East and from Poland, whose agents he believed penetrated Ukraine.[26] Kuromiya's article appeared in June 2008, which indicates the current nature of the academic debate. Unlike some earlier interventions in the debate, he does not dismiss the ethnic factor and his article may represent the start of more all-embracing treatment of the subject matter, difficult as that is to achieve.[27]

The 75th Anniversary of the Famine

On the 75th anniversary of the Famine we have a somewhat paradoxical development: the Ukrainian government has focused on the tragedy as the key event in the history of modern Ukraine, eliminating 54 years of official denial of its existence. Implicitly it is a political issue because it not only differentiates Ukraine from Russian, but also suggests that Russians were the perpetrators, or at the least that the measures were taken by a government centred in the Russian capital, Moscow. However, there is no such consensus in the English-speaking Western countries, whose scholars originally initiated the campaign to reveal the famine, which had been concealed by the Soviet government and sympathetic journalists like Walter Duranty of the *New York Times*.[28] Does it matter? I would argue that it does because ultimately it is the scholarly community that defines and explains events, not governments and public officials or even the United Nations. What should be the next steps in terms of the study of the Famine from the academic perspective?

Davies and Wheatcroft's book focuses on a general Soviet picture rather than a specifically Ukrainian one. Aside from the causal issue, the authors expend many pages discussing the issue of the number of victims, another area in which there is a significant lack of consensus. The ethnic factor and Stalin's nationalities policy are not areas to which the authors pay very close attention. The significance of the ethnic factor in Soviet society perhaps became evident with the collapse of the Soviet Union, when the re-emergence of nations could be construed as the main factor in the failure of the Gorbachev regime.[29] However, it seems fair to suggest that for many decades Western scholars adopted an extensive or all-Union approach – often also a specifically Russian approach – to the study of the Soviet Union.[30] Yet the ethnic factor was pivotal in the 1920s as the adoption of Ukrainisation clearly indicates; it did not just appear in 1932–33. Whether or not Stalin feared the Poles more,[31] within the USSR he was most worried about the Ukrainians, and not least because of the policy introduced in the non-Russian Soviet republics by Lenin, signifying that in makeup they should be national in form, but socialist in content in the 1920s. Thus the importance of the ethnic issue to Stalin's regime needs to be recognised by Western scholars working on the 1932–33 Famine.

Second, what are needed are new scholarly monographs in English to supersede Conquest in particular and to offer an alternative version of events to that offered by Davies and Wheatcroft. This is by no means to suggest that Davies and Wheatcroft's version is in any way wrong or misguided; simply that alternative views exist. Potential volumes are reportedly in the offing at the Ukrainian Research Institute at Harvard University and the Centre for Ukrainian Studies at the University of Ottawa. At the Canadian Institute of Ukrainian Studies, my own project currently has three doctoral students (including one from one of the areas of Ukraine most affected by the Famine) working on the Famine archives, which were copied and purchased from Kiev three years ago.[32] There are over six thousand pages of material so it is not a short-term task. Such works are essential because of the simple fact that more than two decades after the appearance of Conquest's monograph, there is not a single full-length study of the Famine in English. Davies and Wheatcroft's book thus stands alone, though it is not a study of the key issues of the events in Ukraine specifically.

Third, universities in particular need to hold conferences that embrace all aspects of the Famine and from the widest possible academic spectrum, including leading scholars from Ukraine and Russia. The Famine needs also to be integrated into the teaching of history at schools and particularly universities. What tends to happen instead are conferences in which scholars offer like-minded papers under a general title that includes one of the following phrases: Genocidal Famine, Famine-Genocide, Holodomor (death by hunger) or Famine-Holodomor.

Fourth, those scholars working in this area need to publish articles in the most reputable scholarly journals, particularly given the enormity of the event, whatever its causes. Here are some more lamentable facts: the only article on the Ukrainian Famine published in the past two decades in *Slavic Review*, the leading journal in the field in the United States, is that of Mark Tauger, which appeared 18 years ago. *Europe-Asia Studies*, by contrast, has devoted much space to the Famine over the past decade, but not one article has focused on the Ukrainian angle specifically (Kuromiya's comes the closest), and none have supported the notion that the Famine was an act of genocide.[33] Thus at the very least one can state that the spectrum is one-sided. The leading Canadian journal, *Canadian Slavonic Papers*, has not published a single article on the Ukrainian Famine in 17 years.

The Ethnic and National Elements in the Study of the Famine

As an example of the significance of the ethnic or national element in the study of the Ukrainian Famine and, conversely, the folly of ignoring it, let us examine first the proceedings of the Third All-Union Conference of the Communist Party of Ukraine (CPU) in July 1932, available from the Ukrainian Central Archive. The proceedings provide a good indicator of the situation because the conference occurred at a critical time when the failure of the sowing campaign in Ukraine was openly acknowledged, along with the persistence of *kulak* elements in the villages, weak and badly organised collective farms and a general demoralisation in the villages. Starvation was clearly occurring already in several settlements and the CPU forum was convened to discuss the reasons for this disastrous situation. In addition both V. M. Molotov and L. M. Kaganovich arrived from Moscow to witness the discussions and report back to Stalin. Speeches were made by the Ukrainian party secretary, S. V. Kosior,[34] as well as by a host of lesser figures. The discussions were notably frank because Ukrainian party leaders were essentially explaining to their comrades from Moscow why the situation in Ukraine had reached such an impasse. In his introductory remarks, Kosior commented as follows:

> Comrades, many regard the extensive grain procurement plans as a major cause of the current difficulties in Ukraine [...] There have been a fair number of anti-party elements who have obtained party membership in Ukraine. They believe that we plunder Ukraine in favour of Moscow. They reflect kulak theories and sentiments and Petliurite[35] theories.[36]

Kosior returns to this same issue when discussing the failure of the sowing campaign in Uman district (Cherkasy *oblast*):

> It is no accident that in the Uman district the number of mistakes was the highest. Those who are familiar with this area know that one can find the greatest number of Petliurite and kulak elements, their agents, and counter-revolutionaries of various stripes. Our local party organisation is infected in those districts in which we have the most outrageous distortions of plans.[37]

These rather general comments became much more specific when Roman Terekhov, secretary of Khar'kiv *oblast* party committee, took the floor. He reported the prevalence of rumours that Ukraine had been subjected to unfair levels of taxation, that the grain procurement plan was not realistic and the farmers were not in a position to meet the state quotas. What were the sources of such rumours? Terekhov responded as follows:

> The first source is nationalists, who take advantage of our difficult situation to carry out work oriented against Moscow, especially against the Central Committee. It is no secret that people are saying the grain was taken by Moscow. These rumours persist elsewhere: among groups of workers at institutions, among specialists from secondary and higher educational

institutes, etc. They say: when was it the case before that a man from Ukraine had to travel to Leningrad to buy bread? [The answer is] never. Thus the conclusion is that the bread was seized, it was taken away.

Terekhov went on to say that nationalists and petty bourgeoisie both concurred that the Ukrainians had been robbed, that everything had been taken from their villages, and that the grain procurement plans submitted to Ukraine could never have been fulfilled.[38]

The discussions are replete with references to the distinct nature of the Ukrainian villages as compared to other regions of the Soviet Union and the difficulties the communists had in obtaining a secure foothold there. 'Comrade Cherniavskyi'[39] commented that 'the Ukrainian village is the most complex village because of its profound national character and its kulaks'.[40] He was supported later by 'Comrade Zatonskyi'[41] who declared that the rightist elements were attacking the Communist Party of Ukraine for not defending Ukraine enough from the intrusions of the all-Union party authorities in Moscow[42] and by 'Comrade Demchenko',[43] who believed that all political explanations of the errors made in Ukraine could be attributed to Ukrainian chauvinism, the goal of which was to turn Ukraine against Moscow.[44] Finally, the well-known figure of Hryhory I. Petrovskyi, chairman of the All-Ukrainian Central Executive Committee as well as the Ukrainian Central Committee of Poor Peasants (*Komnezam*) and one of Ukraine's most prominent figures,[45] asked himself why Ukraine has so many problems both in spring sowing and grain procurement at this time, answering his own question with the statement that

> Our village is a complicated structure, and everyone in the Soviet Union knows it: we have a strong class of kulaks, nationalism, and chauvinism but nonetheless 70 per cent of Ukrainian households had been collectivised, which is a great accomplishment.[46]

While necessarily taken out of context and amid a plethora of comments about general farming and organisational problems in Ukraine, the minutes of the summer 1932 conference do suggest that the national factor was an element regularly cited by the leaders of the Communist Party of Ukraine. The brief excerpts cited above also encompass many of the elements of the ethnic explanation of the Famine: excessive grain quota targets, requisitions of needed food and the targeting of nationalist elements that continued to predominate in Ukrainian villages, and were turning the local population against Moscow. The references to higher educational institutions in Ukraine indicate perceived links between peasants and the Ukrainian intelligentsia and their collective antipathy toward Moscow. Admittedly, there is nothing in the 1932 party conference to suggest that the Soviet authorities intended to eliminate physically this population but clearly some form of retribution as a counter-measure was implied. The very association, for example of nationalists with *kulaks*, would suggest that there was the possibility that they were similarly singled out as objects for 'liquidation', as well as the fact that 'Ukrainian kulaks' seemed to be offering more resistance to the Soviet authorities than their counterparts elsewhere.

Western scholars generally acknowledge the severe toll of the Stalin purges in Ukraine (and elsewhere) but maintain that the peak of the terror occurred several years after the Famine in Ukraine.[47] Thus, it is asserted, the focus on ethnic nationalism was not notable during the hunger years. However, contemporary reports suggest that the so-called 'struggle with nationalism' in Ukraine occurred earlier than elsewhere in the USSR, partly and paradoxically because of the relative success of the 1920s indigenisation policy initiated by then Ukrainian party boss Lazar Kaganovich, subsequently one of the main figures held responsible for the enormity of the Famine in Ukraine and the North Caucasus and, as noted, a participant in the party conference cited above. One anonymous article, published in late 1933 in a Khar'kiv journal, decried the sort of nationalism espoused by former Commissar of Education, Mykola Skrypnyk.[48] It equated the 'counter-revolution' against the Communist Party in rural Ukraine with the desire of foreign powers to intervene in Ukraine, the coming to power of Hitler in Germany, and the machinations of 'Polish Fascists' and Russian and Ukrainian 'White Guardists' backed by Trotskyists.[49] Shortly afterwards, an article published in the journal of the Council of Nationalities of the Central Executive Committee of the USSR noted that one of the crucial tasks of the party was to respond to the mistakes on the national question that had occurred in Ukraine that were connected with Skrypnyk. The class struggle that had emerged, it continued, pertained not only to the sphere of politics but had had severe consequences in the area of the economy.[50] Given official secrecy about the Famine, one could hardly find a clearer admission of the connection between the ethnic or national issue and the catastrophe that had occurred in the Ukrainian countryside.

A second article published in the summer of 1934 acknowledged that one reason for the removal of the Ukrainian capital from Khar'kiv to Kiev in this same year was to strengthen the agricultural regions of Ukraine. In 1932, the all-Union Communist Party had pointed out the weakening focus of the central organs of Ukraine on agriculture, particularly in the region of the 'Right Bank' (west of the Dniepr River). As a result, *kulak* elements in the villages had tried to undermine the progress of Soviet agriculture and 'to strengthen the counter-revolutionary nationalist position of the class enemies'.[51] The author also noted that *Pravda* had commented that the move of the capital to Kiev in order to bring the central party and Soviet apparatus closer to important agricultural regions had special significance in the further industrialisation and strengthening of Soviet agriculture, 'for the development of national-cultural construction and Bolshevik Ukrainisation'.[52] Admittedly there were other quite logical and historical reasons for transferring the capital to Kiev, but the critical issues of nationalism and its relationship to the problems in agriculture were rarely far from the surface in reports of 1933–34. These writings appeared between three and four years before the peak of the Stalin Purges and indicate that the national issue was identified as the key issue in explaining why the Soviet authorities had encountered so many difficulties in Ukrainian villages during and after the collectivisation campaign. There are good reasons therefore for new analyses at least to take the ethnic or national factor into consideration as it was clearly an issue for the party leadership in Ukraine, and equally for Stalin and the central authorities.

Conclusion

Scholars concur that in terms of the number of victims – between three and ten million[53] – the Famine of 1932–33 constitutes an event of great enormity and significance in the history of the twentieth century and one that devastated Ukraine as well as Ukrainians who lived in the North Caucasus and Kuban regions. However, the study of the genesis of the Famine in the scholarly community has reached an impasse of sorts today, namely the relative neglect of the Ukrainian dimension as manifested in English-language books and articles. Memoirs of survivors have probably been exhausted, particularly given the advanced age of those that remain. Yet, the opportunities have never been more favourable for scholarly studies that are free from any political dimension or preconceived goals, based on solid archival research. Today we have more academic institutions and centres devoted to Ukraine in the West than ever before. Communications with Ukrainian scholars are relatively easy and uninhibited. Many Ukrainian issues have been addressed in scholarly venues in recent years: in order of frequency they are on the Orange Revolution, elections in Ukraine, issues of the Second World War and the complex Ukrainian Revolution of 1917–21. What is needed now is a renewed and determined focus on the Famine of 1932–33 in the English-speaking academic community that includes active engagement between the different schools of thought.

It is naive to believe that the national question can be ignored in such studies; indeed it should be the starting point, along with the question of whether Soviet anxiety about the situation in Ukraine resulted in a drastic solution (the elimination of Ukrainians) or merely ham-handed repression that was indiscriminate rather than targeted, and aimed, as Kosior said, 'to teach the peasants a lesson'. Archival studies to date suggest that there is no 'smoking gun' in the field of the 1932–33 Famine and one should not anticipate finding definitive proof that Stalin had a clearly defined goal to destroy the Ukrainians as a nation. However, it is no longer sufficient to examine the Famine solely from the perspective of Moscow or agricultural statistics either, because the national question was a pre-eminent issue as early as 1933 in Ukraine. There are simply too many references to the role of Ukrainian nationalism and its prevalence in Ukrainian villages, as well as evidence of the removal of prominent cultural and national leaders by the early 1930s to be ignored by Western scholars. On the other hand, the position of the Ukrainian government, and President Yushchenko in particular who seeks to make it a criminal offence to deny that the Famine was genocide, is counterproductive. In embarking on a new series of studies of the Ukrainian Famine, scholars have to start without preconceived notions of what will (and even what 'must') be uncovered. These proposed new works in my view would be a valuable resolution for the 75th anniversary of this tragedy and far more effective than laws issued by various governments (19 at the most recent count) that it was an act of genocide.

Notes and References

1. Originally published in *Europa–Asia Studies* 61, 3 (May 2009): 505–18. Reprinted with kind permission. An earlier version of this article was presented at a weekend forum on the 1932–33 Famine in Ukraine held at the University of Denver, 10–12 October 2008. The author would like to acknowledge the research assistance of his doctoral students Mariya Melentyeva and Eduard Baidaus in the preparation of this article; and Roman Solchanyk for background information and the use of his archives.
2. Many governments have recognised the Famine as an act of genocide, including the United States and Canada. However, it is arguable that such decisions are based more on the efforts of local pressure groups or emotion than on hard evidence. Politicians as a rule do not spend time in archives. Russia unsurprisingly has not accepted this conclusion and neither has the United Kingdom.
3. Yurii Shapoval, 'Proloh trahedii holodomoru. III konferentsiya KP(b)U', *Istoriia Ukrainy* 43 (2002): 1–8.
4. Stanislav V. Kul'chyts'kyi, 'Pam'iat'' pro trydtsiat' tretii', *Istoriia Ukrainy* 24 (1998): 4; Kul'chyts'kyi, 'Skeletons in the Closet in the Light of Perestroika', *Den'*; *The Day Weekly Digest* (4 December), available at: http://www.day.kiev.ua/268404/ (accessed 1 November 2008); Kul'chyts'kyi, *Holod 1932–1933 rr. v Ukraini iak henotsyd* (Kiev: National Academy of Sciences, 2005); Kul'chyts'kyi, 'Holodomor 1932 rr.: mekhanizmy stalins'koho teroru', *Ukrains'kyi istorychnyi zhurnal* 4 (2007): 4–25.
5. Vasyl' Marochko, 'Henotsyd v Ukrains'komu seli 1932–1933 rokiv', in *Holodomor 1932–1933 rokiv iak velychezna trahediia Ukrains'koho narodu. Materialy Vseukrains'koi naukovoi konferentsii. Kiev, 15 listopada 2003* (Kiev: MAUP, 2002); Marochko, 'Kontsepetual'ni

pidvalyny zakhdinoevropeis'koi ta rosiis'koi istoriohrafii holodomoru 1932–1933 rr. v Ukraini', *Ukrains'kyi istorychnyi zhurnal* 3 (2003): 90–103.
6 P. P. Panchenko et al., *Smertiu smert' podolaly: holodomor v Ukraini, 1932–1933* (Kiev: Ukraina, 2003).
7 R. W. Davies, O. V. Khlevniuk, E. A. Rees, L. P. Kosheleva, and L. A. Rogovaya (eds), *The Stalin-Kaganovich Correspondence 1931–36*, translated by Steven Shabad (New Haven: Yale University Press, 2003), 179–81.
8 On the question of famine and terror, see Kul'chyts'kyi, 'Holodomor 1932 rr.: mekhanizmy [...]' and his contribution to this volume.
9 See, for example, http://en.for-ua.com/news/2007/03/19/174029.html (accessed 31 October 2008) and Kasianov's chapter in this volume.
10 The vote was 233 to 1 for an amended version of the resolution introduced initially by President Yushchenko. The other 216 deputies abstained from voting. See the *New York Times*, 29 November 2006.
11 Roman Serbyn, 'The Ukrainian Famine of 1932–1933 as Genocide in the Light of the UN Convention of 1948', *Ukrainian Quarterly* 62 (2006), available at: http://en.for-a.com/news/2007/03/19/174029.html (accessed 8 November 2008).
12 Robert Conquest, *Harvest of Sorrow: Collectivization and the Terror-Famine* (Oxford: Oxford University Press, 1986); Roman Serbyn, Bogdan Krawchenko (eds), *Famine in Ukraine, 1932–1933* (Edmonton, CIUS, 1986).
13 United States Commission on the Ukrainian Famine (1990), in J. E. Mace, L. Heretz (eds), *Oral History Project of the Commission on the Ukraine Famine* (Washington, DC: United States Government Publication Office, 1990).
14 Mark B. Tauger, 'The 1932 Harvest and the Famine of 1933', *Slavic Review* 50 (1990): 70–89. Another response was the book by Douglas Tottle issued by the Soviet publishing agency, Progress Books: *Fraud, Famine, and Fascism: the Ukrainian Genocide Myth from Hitler to Harvard* (Toronto: Progress Books, 1987). Tottle's argument was that the Famine-genocide was fabricated by Ukrainian nationalists in order to conceal their role in the Second World War as collaborators of the Germans.
15 Geoffrey A. Hosking, 'Arranging a Catastrophe', *Times Literary Supplement*, 20 February 1987, 191.
16 Peter Wiles, 'Stalin's Two Famines', *New York Review of Books*, 26 March 1987, 43–5, quote 45.
17 Craig Whitney, 'Starving the Hands that Fed Them', *New York Times Book Review* 26 October 1987, 11–12, quote 12.
18 Alex Nove, 'When the Head is Off', *New Republic*, 3 November 1987, 36–7, quote 37.
19 Hiroaki Kuromiya, 'The Soviet Famine of 1932–33 Reconsidered', *Europe-Asia Studies* 60 (2008): 663–75, here 667.
20 Johan Dietsch, *Making Sense of Suffering: Holocaust and Holodomor in Ukrainian Historical Culture* (Lund: Lund University Press, 2006).
21 R. W. Davies, S. G. Wheatcroft, *The Years of Hunger: Soviet Agriculture, 1931–1933* (Basingstoke: Palgrave Macmillan, 2004).
22 R. W. Davies, S. G. Wheatcroft, 'Stalin and the Soviet Famine of 1932–33: A Reply to Ellman', *Europe-Asia Studies* 58 (2006): 625–33, here 626.
23 Ibid., 628–9.
24 Obedinennoe Gossudarstvennoe Politicheskoe Upravleniye (State Political Administration, the intelligence service and secret police of the Russian Soviet Federative Socialist Republic).

25 Michael Ellman, 'Stalin and the Soviet Famine of 1932–33 Revisited', *Europe-Asia Studies* 59 (2007): 663–93 (684, 686). Ellman, however, is completely dismissive of the Ukrainian version of events in a review of Hiroaki Kuromiya's biography of Stalin in *Europe-Asia Studies*, where he comments in parentheses: 'The notion that Ukraine was uniquely victimised by Soviet famines is just a nationalist fantasy'. M. Ellman, 'Book Review of "Stalin" by Hiroaki Kuromiya', *Europe-Asia Studies* 58 (2006): 985–7.
26 Kuromiya, 'The Soviet Famine [...]', 673.
27 One should note also the book published several years ago by Terry Martin, *The Affirmative Action Empire: Nations and Nationalism in the Soviet Union, 1923–1939* (Ithaca: Cornell University Press, 2001). Martin's position on the 1932–33 Famine seems quite similar to that of Kuromiya. Also, Orlando Figes writes that 'The [Soviet] regime was undoubtedly to blame for the famine. But its policies did not amount to a campaign of "terror-famine", let alone of Genocide, as Conquest and others have implied'. Orlando Figes, *The Whisperers: Private Life in Stalin's Russia* (London: Penguin Books, 2007).
28 On Duranty's role in concealing the Famine from the Western public, see S. J. Taylor, *Stalin's Apologist: Walter Duranty, The New York Times's Man in Moscow* (New York: Oxford University Press, 1990).
29 R. G. Suny, *The Revenge of the Past: Nationalism, Revolution, and the Collapse of the Soviet Union* (Stanford: Stanford University Press, 1993); D. R. Marples, *The Collapse of the Soviet Union, 1985–1991* (Harlow: Longman, 2004).
30 That was at least my impression as an undergraduate in London in the 1970s. Virtually no attention was paid in undergraduate Russian history classes to the nationalities of the Soviet Union.
31 After his noted comment that 'we may lose Ukraine', Stalin went on to write in his letter to Kaganovich: 'Keep in mind that Pilsudski is not daydreaming, and his agents in Ukraine are many times stronger than Redens or Kosior thinks. Keep in mind too that the Ukrainian Communist Party [...] has quite a lot [...] of rotten elements, conscious and unconscious Petliura adherents, and, finally, direct agents of Pilsudski', Davies et al., *Stalin-Kaganovich Correspondence*, 180. See also Bruski's chapter in this volume.
32 Central State Archives of Ukraine, Holodomor: Famine in Ukraine 1932–1933, Central State Archive of Public Organisations, Kiev. 158 microfilm reels.
33 In its earlier form, as *Soviet Studies*, *Europe-Asia Studies* published two of the earliest English-language works about the 1932–33 Famine. Dana Dalrymple: 'The Soviet Famine of 1932–1934', *Soviet Studies* 15 (1964): 250–84; Dana Dalrymple, 'The Soviet Famine of 1932–1934', *Soviet Studies* 16 (1965): 471–4.
34 Stanislav Kosior (1889–1939), a native of Poland, led the Communist Party of Ukraine from 1928 to 1938, and received the Order of Lenin in 1935 for his part in 'successes in collective farm construction in Ukraine'. He was executed toward the end of the Stalinist Purges and rehabilitated in 1956. M. B. Pohrebins'kyi, 'Vydatni diiachi Komunistychnoi partii i Radyans'koi derzhavy: Stanislav Vikentiiovych Kosior', *Ukrains'kyi istorychnoi zhurnal* 11 (1979): 27–35 (33).
35 The reference is to Symon Petliura, 1879–1926, a controversial Ukrainian publicist and statesman, who played a prominent role in Ukraine's quest for statehood after the Russian Revolution and later took part in the invasion of Ukraine in alliance with the Poles. The phrase Petliurite was a derogatory one in Soviet parlance in the same way that 'Banderite' (with reference to nationalist leader Stepan Bandera, 1909–59) was applied in the post-war period. It refers to nationalistic Ukrainians.

36 Central State Archives of Ukraine 2004, Fond 1, Opis 1, Delo N 377, 6 July 1932, 27.
37 Central State Archives of Ukraine 2004, Fond 1, Opis 1, Delo N 377, 6 July 1932, 46.
38 Central State Archives of Ukraine 2004, Fond 1, Opis 1, Delo N 377, 6 July 1932, 273–4.
39 V. I. Cherniavs'kyi (1893–1939), Secretary of the Central Committee (CC) of the Communist Party of Ukraine (CPU) and a candidate member of the CPU Politburo.
40 Central State Archives of Ukraine 2004, Fond 1, Opis 2, Delo N 378, 8 July 1932, 14.
41 V. P. Zatons'kyi was a former Commissar for Education in Ukraine and one of the few ethnic Ukrainian Bolsheviks to take part in the initial Bolshevik takeover in Ukraine in 1918. In the period 1927–33 he was head of the Central Control Commission in the People's Commissariat of Worker-Peasant Inspection. In 1929 he was a plenipotentiary of the CC CPU for grain procurements in Kremenchuk district and evidently objected in the following year to violations of the voluntary nature of collectivisation in Ukraine. M. Rubach, 'Bil'shovyk lenins'koho hartu', *Vitchyzna* 8 (1978): 148–55 (154).
42 Central State Archives of Ukraine 2004, Fond 1, Opis 1, Delo N 377, 6 July 1932, 74.
43 M. N. Demchenko (1896–1937), First Party Secretary of the Kiev Oblast Committee, Communist Party of Ukraine, and a member of the CPU Politburo from 1931.
44 Central State Archives of Ukraine 2004, Fond 1, Opis 1, Delo N 377, 6 July 1932, 81.
45 Dnipropetrovs'k, one of Ukraine's main industrial cities, is named after him. For a brief account of Petrovs'kyi's career, see M. Ponochovnyi, P. Shostak, 'Vseukrains'kyi starosta: do 110-i richnytsi z dnia narodzhennya H.I. Petrovs'koho', *Molod' Ukrainy*, 4 February 1988, 3.
46 Central State Archives of Ukraine 2004, Fond 1, Opis 1, Delo N 377, 6 July 1932, 124.
47 See, for example, Martin, *Affirmative Action Empire*, 309.
48 Mykola O. Skrypnyk (1872–1933) was a leading Ukrainian Bolshevik, who from his position as Commissar for Education, from March 1927 to February 1933, became the chief advocate of the primacy of development of Ukrainian culture in the republic. At the end of his tenure as Education Commissar he was accused of leading a nationalist movement in Ukraine and was purged following the arrival in Ukraine of Stalin's plenipotentiary, Pavel Postyshev. Once again the timing is crucial and his dismissal coincided with the peak of the Famine. He committed suicide on 7 July 1933. See http://www.kmu.gov.ua/control/uk/publish/printable_article?art_id=1261066 (accessed October 2008).
49 'Za proletars'kyi internatsionalizm, proty natsionalizmu', *Za markso-lenins'ku krytyku* 11–12 (November–December 1933): 3–8 (4).
50 'S. D.' 'Bor'ba s natsionalizm i uroki Ukrainy', *Revoliutsiia i natsional'nosti* 1 (January 1934): 15–22 (16).
51 S. Symonenko, 'Da zdravstvuet novaya stolitsa Ukrainy!' *Revoliutsiia i natsional'nosti* 7 (July 1934): 15–22 (17).
52 Ibid., 19.
53 The number of victims of the Famine has elicited as much debate as its causes. See, for example, the following works in English: S. Maksudov, 'The Geography of the Soviet Famine', *Journal of Ukrainian Studies* 8, no. 2 (1983): 52–8; Michael Ellman 'A Note on the Number of 1933 Famine Victims', *Europe-Asia Studies* 43 (1991): 375–9 and Catherine Merridale, 'The 1937 Census and the Limits of Stalinist Rule', *The Historical Journal* 39 (1996): 225–40.

Chapter 3

GRIEVANCE, SCOURGE OR SHAME? THE COMPLEXITY OF ATTITUDES TO IRELAND'S GREAT FAMINE[1]

Vincent Comerford
National University of Ireland, Maynooth

> *Is then our Isle of Heaven accursed and banned,*
> *That all desert her thus? Perish the thought!*
> *Not in such spirit read we Erin's lot;*
> *Full often is adversity's chill breath*
> *More precious than the wealth of India's mine,*
> *High is the comfort of the text divine:*
> *'Whom the Lord loveth, them He chasteneth!'*[2]

The Great Irish Famine occurred in a highly politicised country with a well advanced system of communications, a literacy rate of about 50 per cent, a universally spread local and state bureaucracy and considerable openness to the press, domestic and foreign. Accordingly, it is well documented and extensively remembered. However, both documentation and remembering are incomplete and fragmented in ways that suggest reticence and ambivalence. The Great Famine as national grievance is well posted; but the totality of contemporary response and later remembrance and interpretation is much less clear-cut, incorporating elements of anger, providentialism, embarrassment, guilt and, of course, incomprehension in fluctuating combinations. The present chapter is intended as a tentative exploration of this complexity and of its reflection in history writing. Only limited reference is made to the thriving literary and cultural study of the Great Irish Famine pioneered by Margaret Kelleher, Christopher Morash and others.[3]

Students of the Great Famine have at their disposal a vast array of primary source material ranging from newspapers and travellers' accounts by way of parliamentary papers and debates to estate papers, workhouse records and institutional and private documents of various kinds. Nonetheless, the working out of the fate of individual victims – in disease, dispossession, flight or death – can be traced in only a tiny proportion of cases. And for every townland, village and estate that is well documented there are many more where only basic reconstruction of developments is achievable. The most striking aspect of the surviving evidence for the Famine is the paucity of recorded personal testimony. There is indeed a small set of eye-witness accounts by contemporary visitors. As a prime source of most of the horrific images of starvation, disease, degradation and dispossession that mention of the Great Irish Famine evokes, this is crucial testimony.[4] However, relative to its impact on the contemporary and subsequent life of the country, the record of the period of calamity in late 1840s Ireland is strikingly underendowed with eye witness accounts, reminiscences and recollections of actors or observers. Clearly those living in the 1850s and later decades who had experienced the Great Famine had, with very rare exceptions, little sense of wanting to record what they had witnessed personally in the bad times, or little sense of their contemporaries wishing to share recollections about it.

Canon John O'Rourke (1809–87), who in 1875 published the first monograph history of the Great Famine,[5] would seem at first sight to be an exception to the generalisation about reticence in connection with memory of the subject. However, one of the most remarkable features of this book is the almost total exclusion of the author's own recollections of the period. Throughout the worst years O'Rourke was a student of mature years at Maynooth College, with substantial prior experience of business, associational and devotional life in County Wicklow and Dublin city. While a student he travelled to Dublin to attend meetings of the Repeal Association. He must have possessed vast knowledge of the upheaval of the late 1840s as it affected his relations, business connections, and the Catholic Church. O'Rourke gave his work an air of scientific method by reporting his use of questionnaires, but he seems to have gleaned from these little local information not already available in official and published sources. His findings and the small number of returns that he reports refer mainly to a few notorious famine sites, notably Westport and Skibbereen. A few paragraphs of O'Rourke's own testimony would have been worth much more. His book speaks of the arrival and impact of a nationwide famine, but largely in the abstract. The actual manifestation as described is confined to selected locations. Of course the consequences of the Great Famine were at their most severe on and near the western seaboard, but they were dire almost everywhere.

What seems clear is that O'Rourke (along with his target audience) was in denial about the impact of the Famine on the country at large, but could think and talk about its manifestations in less fortunate parts. The denial in which O'Rourke and his public engaged is compatible with deeply held grievance, but only if that grievance is subordinate to sentiments such as shame and insecurity. To have had the foundations of their society exposed to the world as marked by hunger, disease and reliance on public soup kitchens was a source of deep embarrassment to people who saw themselves as members of an aspiring nationality keenly anxious to be equally respectable with others. Besides, there was for decades a persistent undercurrent of anxiety about a possible recurrence.

The next substantial book on the subject of the Great Famine was published just two decades after O'Rourke's and it is quite explicit about the enduring risk of crop failure leading to calamity on a local basis in the 1890s.[6] W. B. O'Brien was a former government official who had worked as a Poor Law inspector in the late 1840s and was persuaded on his retirement to write an account of the 'phenomenal social calamity' of that period.[7] In fact his principal expression of personal opinion in the book concerns the fear of further distress, related to crop failure and overpopulation on the western seaboard, such as had occurred several times from the late 1870s to the early 1890s. O'Brien also follows O'Rourke in providing scarcely a scintilla of personal recollection of the Great Famine. Instead he summarises and reports upon various official publications and newspapers. His principal account of the horrors of famine suffering comes in the form of a letter dated December 1846 taken from a newspaper, and referring (predictably) to conditions in Skibbereen.[8]

Peter Gray has documented the extent to which the wielders of power and influence at Whitehall and Westminster saw the failure of the potato and the consequent upheaval of society in Ireland as reflecting, or calling for attention to, the designs of providence.[9] Such a viewpoint might dictate policy or merely provide a justificatory pretext for pursuing a line that already appealed on other grounds. The invocation of the will of God could provide succour in coming to terms with calamity for those, inside or outside government, not immediately affected. One of the functions of O'Rourke's work, and probably his clearest purpose in writing it, was to promote a consolatory message. Located significantly at the centre of the book is an encomium for the hundreds of dead lying in the iconic famine pit at Abbeystrewry cemetery outside Skibbereen. He rejoices in the assertion that they died uncomplainingly in acceptance of the will of God. The message is that ultimately the sufferings of this world matter not at all, except insofar as they provide an opportunity to earn greater credit in the next:

> Even in their imperfections and sins, they were like to Him in many ways; they were poor, they were despised, they had not where unto lay their

head; they were long-suffering too; in the deepest pangs which they had suffered from hunger and burning thirst (the last and most terrible effect of hunger), they cursed not, they reviled not, they only yearned for the consolations of their holy religion, and looked hopefully to Him for a better world. It is one of the sweetest consolations taught us by holy faith that the bones now withered and nameless in those famine pits, where they are laid in their shroudless misery, shall one day, touched by His almighty power, be reunited to those happy souls, in a union that can know no end and feel no sorrow.[10]

Religious people of many persuasions reacted to the partial failure of the potatoes in 1845 by invoking the age-old moralising trope about natural disaster as the manifestation of divine displeasure with society in general or with some particular recent offence. Catholic prelates took the opportunity to rail against the legislation of that year which established the non-denominational Queen's Colleges, while Protestants had a choice of targets, the Queen's Colleges or the enhanced funding for Maynooth College also announced in 1845. The irenic Daniel Murray, Catholic archbishop of Dublin, had intimations of the Book of Genesis in August 1846: 'We have heard of old of a seven years famine, and we should not forget that with all our agricultural improvements, we are not yet independent of Providence. Hitherto Sir Robert [Peel, the prime minister] has been our Joseph'.[11] This is an example both of profound unintended irony and of how a religious person can put events in a providential explanatory framework when that suits the rhetorical needs of the occasion, but without any implication of proposing or justifying a policy of fatalism.

In fact, the official response of the Catholic hierarchy to the Great Irish Famine was not by any means along providentialist lines. Indeed, at least one bishop, Maginn of Derry, moved to a quasi-revolutionary critique, and when in 1847 and again in 1850 the bishops spoke with a single voice, they focussed on human rather than divine causation.[12] Bishops and priests on several occasions asserted the priority of life over the rights of property, and in the early summer of 1848 many parochial clergy canvassed the appropriateness of an Irish revolution. But both the prevailing moral theology of their church, and their need to fend off the suspicions of government and of a largely hostile English press, meant that they had little choice but to be seen upholding the rights of property. In the event, almost all the local priests worked energetically to discourage the rebellion that threatened briefly in County Tipperary in the summer of 1848. Earlier that year Archbishop Murray, in an anxious appeal to dissuade priests and people from an uprising, based his case not on theological arguments but on the retributory horrors he had seen inflicted on the country in the wake of the rebellion of 1798.[13]

The current consensus is that around 1 million, or 12 per cent of the Irish population, perished as victims of the Great Famine.[14] Any episode of mass death lends itself to moralising commentary (such as that in the epigraph to this chapter). The best known such response to the Great Famine is that synonymous with the name and writings of John Mitchel – the accusation of malevolent agency by the British government in the name of political economy. From early in the crisis journalists in Dublin associated with the Young Ireland movement promoted a consistently critical interpretation of the government's handling of the issues of food supply and provision of relief. Among them Mitchel had no monopoly of this stance, even if he was to the fore, at least in terms of the vehemence of his language. Convicted of treason felony and transported out of Ireland for Van Diemen's Land in May 1848, he subsequently escaped and made his way to New York, arriving in November 1853. There he founded a newspaper promoting militant Irish nationalism until, following a series of disagreements with other Irish nationalists, he moved to Tennessee in March 1855. At Knoxville he established the *Southern Citizen* in which he published a serialised account of developments in Ireland from 1843 to 1849. In 1860 this appeared in book form in New York under the title *The Last Conquest of Ireland (Perhaps)*.[15]

Mitchel was intent on providing an apologia for radical nationalist politics: the Great Famine was far from being his only concern, but it constituted what he saw as a devastating argument in support of his case. Mitchel was not alone among his contemporaries in advancing a nationalist critique of government policy in response to the failure of the potato crop, but as *The Last Conquest* his telling came to be the most widely circulated. Other nationalist propagandists would reinforce the message and, well before the end of the nineteenth century, the Great Famine was firmly established as one of the grievances available to the propagandists of Irish nationalism.[16] The charge was that, while indeed the failure of the potato had not arisen from human agency, the government had responded either at best ineffectively, and thus failing to save lives, or at worst malevolently, seizing an opportunity to depopulate and reshape Ireland.

However, not all nationalists – not even the most militant ones – utilised the Great Famine in this way or felt comfortable about highlighting it. Released from prison in late 1869, having served four years of incarceration for his role as a leading Fenian conspirator, Charles J. Kickham (subsequently to become president of the supreme council of the Irish Republican Brotherhood) set about writing the fictional account of Irish life that became *Knocknagow, or the Homes of Tipperary*. First published in book form in 1873, it garnered expanded readership following a second edition in 1881, and was reissued more than thirty times over the subsequent seventy years. *Knocknagow* was treasured, and read aloud, and not only in farm families where it might be the only book in the house. It was read to the children of Eamon and Sinéad de Valera in their suburban Dublin home.[17]

While the author of *Knocknagow* is generally careful to avoid references to precise dates or identifiable developments in public life, and the several rambling story lines are weak on chronological structure, the action is clearly set in the 1840s and early 1850s. Having been born in 1828 and having lived for the following three decades and more above his father's drapery shop in Mullinahone, Kickham had a wealth of observation and personal experience on which to draw. And draw on it he did liberally for characters, anecdotes and romantic story lines, but only fleetingly and indirectly with reference to the Great Famine. In fact Kickham does not use the term famine, much less identify explicitly any definite period of crisis to which the term might apply. It was not as if Kickham thought the Famine to be an impossible subject for a novel. There was already a lively school of fiction utilising famine backgrounds and themes, and he had been one of the early practitioners himself.[18]

Knocknagow has no account of the mass failure of the potato crop, and the clearance of the eponymous village of its tenants near the end of the book is not made to relate to economic hardship. The villain of the piece is not crop failure or political economy or malign government, but a self-serving land agent acting behind the back of a well-meaning but ineffective landlord. References to the sufferings of the workhouse poor, and Mitchelite denunciation of the role of the British government, take up little more than the equivalent of a page and come mainly in the dialogue. Meanwhile the authorial voice tells of comic misadventures, fortunes recouped, lost sweethearts found and marriages for love. In this narrative scarcely anyone dies, except for the consumptive girl Norah Lahy, who expires in a miasma of sub-Dickensian bathos. The message of *Knocknagow* is that the homes of rural Ireland have been, and despite vicissitude still remain (if now reduced in number), happy, prosperous and respectable, and that what is required to make this state of affairs secure is the promotion of peasant proprietorship.

The embracing and celebration of *Knocknagow* by the generations of the Land War and Home Rule agitation, of the War of Independence, and of the early decades of self-government, would suggest that a large constituency of nationalists over a considerable period of time felt no need to invoke the Great Famine, and were more than comfortable with an account of their society's antecedents that did not even mention it by name. In and out of fiction, as Christopher Morash has shown, later nineteenth-century Irish Catholics and nationalists can be found regarding the Great Famine as a regrettable but necessary stage in the progress of the country.[19] Justin McCarthy, born in West Cork in 1830 and a long serving Irish Party MP for Longford, wrote in 1879: 'Terrible as the immediate effects of the famine were, it is impossible for any friend of Ireland to say that on the whole it did not bring much good with it'.[20] Generalisations about nationalists and the Famine need to be made with circumspection.

The Gaelic idyll behind the cultural nationalism that came to flourish in the 1890s had little place for the Famine. Patrick Pearse hailed Mitchel as one of the four evangelists of Irish nationality, and delivered a famous graveside oration for O'Donovan Rossa, but he was interested in their intransigent politics rather than their specific views on the Great Famine.[21] When Pearse turned to a policy of military insurrection, the Famine had but little purpose to serve: the proclamation of Easter Week 1916 cited as justification for rebellion the continuity of armed national self-assertion over the centuries and specified only one charge against alien government, that of having fostered division within the nation. Nonetheless, the Famine as grievance or theme had not by any means disappeared completely during the Revival; it had been a particular interest of Maud Gonne, culminating in the attempt to spoil the Dublin visit of Queen Victoria in 1900 by placarding 'the Famine queen'.[22]

The socialist James Connolly in *Labour in Irish History* (1910) provides an uncompromising Marxist interpretation of the Great Famine. He has no interest in personalities or the views of individual actors, holding anyone not embracing a socialist interpretation to be guilty of supporting a system that made mass mortality inevitable. He denies the entitlement of the Young Irelanders, and their bourgeois nationalist successors, to find fault with the conduct of the British government:

> but in this, as in every other measure of the Famine years, they acted consistently upon the lines of capitalist political economy. Within the limits of that social system and its theories their acts are unassailable and unimpeachable; it is only when we reject that system, and the intellectual and social fetters it imposes, that we really acquire the right to denounce the English administration of Ireland during the Famine as a colossal crime against the human race.[23]

There would be few similarly confident interpretations of modern Irish history from that ideological perspective. Indeed, inadequacy of attention to the social and economic dimensions of class is an enduring weakness of Irish historiography, including that on the Great Famine.

A more conventional interpretation of the Famine from the revolutionary period is provided by George O'Brien's *The Economic History of Ireland from the Union to the Famine* (1921). O'Brien would subsequently become professor of National Economics at University College Dublin, at a time when the distinction between 'national' and 'nationalist' was frequently overlooked.

In fact O'Brien devotes surprisingly little space to the Great Famine. He provides a relatively open-minded discussion in terms of economic theory of the question of population levels and food policy in the decades before 1845. His assessment of the government's relief measures subsequently, while critical in tone, is balanced and is related to available statistics. However, his treatment is dry and unappealing to the general reader, and does little to make the subject accessible.[24] O'Brien clearly had no inclination to open a discussion of the Famine. A pioneering article by Patrick Cahalane in 1917 had examined the impact of the late 1840s by reference to the population and agricultural censuses, but it had little impact.[25] Those who wished to hear about the famine at this time were not interested in empirical analysis.

History is about the past, but scholarly history in practice deals only with those parts of the past that can be discussed in a society at any given time. Extensive areas of Irish history have been beyond the bounds of scholarly discourse for stretches of the nineteenth and twentieth centuries, not least the Great Famine. Apart from the works mentioned above, little of scholarly significance about the subject seems to have appeared in print before the late 1940s. It is not that, as in Soviet Ukraine, there was any attempt by the state before or after 1922 to suppress information or discussion. Thanks to a well-established reticence in the wider society combined with the requirement of dogmatic nationalists that it could be discussed only in terms of English malfeasance, the Great Famine had become something of a bugbear for historians. This is not to imply that some ineluctable collective psychological trauma was in play: the explanation was to be found in a somewhat less tragic tactic of cumulative social dissimulation. In any event there was no absolute taboo. In 1937 Liam O'Flaherty published his great novel *Famine*. Insofar as it reflects historiography at all it probably pays more tribute to James Connolly than to anyone else. It certainly lights few lamps for anyone tempted to turn the Famine into a *lieu de memoire* for the 'faith and fatherland' patriotism of the day. The same is true of Gerard Healy's Famine play, *The Dark Stranger*, which had a six week run in Dublin's Gate Theatre in 1945.[26]

The centenary of the Great Famine passed relatively unmarked. However it does appear to have stirred some awareness of the need for research, discussion and enlightenment on the subject. *The Famine, 1845–47: A Survey of its Ravages and Causes* by Timothy O'Herlihy, a Vincentian priest in his late sixties, appeared in 1947. This is a booklet (published at Drogheda) of just over eighty pages and without any critical apparatus. The author has read Mitchel, but clearly does not find his strident harangue to constitute an intellectually satisfying explanation of the Famine. O'Herlihy flits from one famine trope to another, and indeed between different periods of Irish history, formulating some independent observations and questions along the way. Adverting to providentialist interpretations, he ventures a Catholic version of providence at work, and one that he was scarcely the first to imagine: the Great Famine has facilitated the promotion of the faith throughout the world, especially in America and Australia, and saved Catholicism in England and Scotland from possible extinction. In the foreword, echoing O'Rourke, he muses about God's inscrutable designs and the lesson of Job: 'The Lord gave, the Lord took away'.[27] But this is just another take on the subject that fails to satisfy him. He is looking for an explanation that meets the needs of an enquiring mid-twentieth-century mind but can neither formulate it himself nor find out where to search for it. At several points O'Herlihy displays his perspicacity, for example in making comparisons with contemporary food shortages in post-war Europe. His book is effectively a plea for a scholarly historiography of the Famine, and an exemplification of the need for it. He was not alone in his quest.

The same year of 1947 saw the publication of path-breaking scholarly articles on aspects of the Great Famine by T. P. O'Neill[28] and Oliver MacDonagh[29] – clearly the centenary had prompted some stirrings of academic interest. Already in the academic year 1943–44 T. P. O'Neill had been registered at University College Dublin for an MA by research on the administration of Great Famine relief under the supervision of Professor R. Dudley Edwards. Behind the scenes more concerted moves were afoot. Modern historical scholarship had a foothold in Ireland since the nineteenth century and achieved collective identity and national organisation in the later 1930s. Because of the failure of earlier generations to arrive at an agreed national narrative, and because of the contentious political developments of the recent half century, there was much walking on eggshells, and not only around the Great Famine. Remarkably, it was at the behest of the taoiseach, Eamon de Valera (following a suggestion from Dr J. H. Delargy, director of the Irish Folklore Commission) that in 1946 the academic history establishment moved to address that subject. It was as though the permission of the high priest of national pieties was required before the bones could be disturbed. By the mid-1940s even de Valera, the supreme promoter and consumer of dogma, could see the need for study of the Great Famine on the basis of empirical research.

The leaders of the profession in Dublin deemed the subject so large – and possibly so potentially volatile – as to require collaborative treatment, and a project was instituted under the auspices of the Irish Committee for Historical Sciences. The committee prevailed upon the government to provide funding towards expenses and some remuneration of student researchers. Eventually £1,500 was disbursed by the Department of Education. Far from obtaining any influence over the contents of the work, the department scarcely obtained satisfaction about the items of expenditure.[30] Thus, while there was government prompting and funding, the project was far removed from being a state-financed exercise in propagandist history. It came to fruition in 1956 with the publication of *The Great Famine: Studies in Irish History, 1845–52*, edited by R. Dudley Edwards and T. Desmond Williams.[31] The volume consists of seven extensive chapters, each covering a different aspect of the Famine or its context, including agriculture, politics, the working of public relief, famine diseases, and emigration. The foreword is a careful, judicious statement that offers the reader deliverance from dogma, while at the same time displaying deep sensitivity towards received attitudes and assumptions. These key pages in the evolution of Irish historiography are in the names of the editors, and convey their concerns, but are believed to be substantially indebted to one of the contributors, a younger colleague at University College Dublin, Kevin B. Nowlan, holder of a Cambridge PhD on nineteenth-century high politics as they affected Ireland.[32] At this remove *The Great Famine* appears as a rather staid volume, but such was its novelty in 1956, and so keen was the appetite for its subject that the popular *Sunday Independent* newspaper carried advance excerpts, and the book was widely and favourably noticed and sold remarkably well.[33]

The Great Famine was the first work to convey successfully to the wider reading public in independent Ireland an understanding of the function of the modern scholarly study of history: that it was not a closed exercise in national self-justification and confirmation of the prescribed, but rather a venture into exploration of the unknown, and the discovery of intellectually liberating new perspectives from which to make sense of the world, at home and abroad. It was an insight that, conveyed through the schools and a growing output of published works, would over the following half century attract tens of thousands of undergraduates into the country's history departments, and would support an expanding history profession.[34] If *The Great Famine* liberated public attitudes to history, there was a reciprocal effect also: acceptance by the public and the political establishment of the book's empirical approach to the Famine gave the historians a signal that Irish society was ready for critical, evidence-based investigation of the country's past.

What *The Great Famine* may have lacked in reader-friendliness and willingness to engage the emotions was supplied in 1962 with the publication of *The Great Hunger*.[35] The author, Cecil Woodham-Smith, was one of her generation's leading popularisers of nineteenth-century British history. Her books had the great strength not only of being superbly written but also of being based on extensive archival research. To an extent that most professional historians could only envy, she had perfected the art of holding the attention of the reader. *The Great Hunger* covers five years of Irish history in just over four hundred pages of text together with eighty pages of end notes. Its vast readership over half a century has received a factually sound if somewhat sensationalised account of the Great Famine, brilliantly presented. There is no flinching from horror, the suffering of Skibbereen included. An account of the visit of Queen Victoria in 1849 provides a redemptive conclusion, but there is also an alternative, retributive, conclusion with British seamen drowning off the Irish coast in World War II – the neutrality of independent Ireland being represented, rather questionably, as a consequence of the famine. The main conceptual deficiency of *The Great Hunger* is the use of essentialist national stereotypes and other forms of generalisation. Thus, that 'the Irish are fond of children, and family feeling is exceptionally strong'[36] is presented as a timeless given, and the English display 'generosity, tolerance and magnanimity' everywhere they go, except in Ireland, where they never understand.[37]

For all their success as scholarship and communication neither *The Great Famine* nor *The Great Hunger* succeeded in elucidating the explanatory key to their common subject. This was the achievement of Austin Bourke, a professional meteorologist who had developed expertise in predicting the annual onset of potato blight in Ireland before doing scientific work in the 1950s in Chile, where blight then posed a serious problem. In 1967 he completed for the National University of Ireland a PhD thesis on the history of the Great Famine that altered the study of the subject irrevocably, changing, in the words of a biographer, 'the focus of attention from the administrative history of the period to the potato itself, its diseases, and its role in the rural economy'.[38] Appreciation of Bourke's thesis was facilitated by the earlier work of Kenneth Connell on pre-famine population, of S. H. Cousens on Famine mortality, and of Raymond Crotty on Irish agriculture.[39] Bourke's collected articles were assembled for publication in 1993.[40] What the published volume could not hope to convey was a sense of the excitement generated by the lively lectures (illustrated with excellent slides) that he delivered on many occasions and in numerous venues at home and abroad until some years before his death in 1995. The points that he conveyed remain central to a basic grasp of the subject: the rural economy of Ireland was predicated on the ability of perhaps 3 million people to survive almost exclusively on the potato, a nutritious but bulky and unstable food; as it had developed in Ireland the potato had no immunity to the fungus *phytophthora infestans* that came from America by way of seed potatoes brought to Belgium – from where its airborne diffusion affected Ireland partially in 1845 and calamitously in 1846; the blight it caused was a mystery to contemporary science; the partial, once-off failure of 1845 was a disaster, but could be overcome; the 1846 failure signalled (and was seen by contemporaries to signal) the end of the pre-existing rural economy, which had no affordable alternative to the potato for the millions on subsistence; the devastation of the potato was on a scale far in excess of what a parasite normally inflicts on its host, so that even the most pessimistic estimates of the impact of failure underestimated the consequences; managing the transition to a new order was an unprecedented challenge, and facile judgements on the efforts of those in government who faced the challenge should be avoided: the shortfall in the potato crop of 1846 by comparison with a prosperous year may have been in the order of fifteen million tons.[41] All subsequent historical scholarship on the Great Irish Famine stands in the shadow of Austin Bourke.

Bourke's work stands at the beginning of a school which over two generations has taken the scholarly exploration of the Great Famine to an impressively high level of achievement. Its members consist mainly of economic historians and econometricians, including Joel Mokyr.[42] Other major contributors include specialists in intellectual and administrative history, social history, migration history, cartography, geography, epidemiology and medicine, literary and cultural studies and local history.[43] The several available syntheses of this scholarship include, along with other books cited in the footnotes, the following: Liam Kennedy et al, *Mapping the Great Irish Famine*;[44] and Cormac Ó Gráda, *Black '47 and Beyond*.[45] As the culmination of his numerous accomplishments in the field, Ó Gráda has now been able to place the Irish Famine experience in the context of hunger crises across time and around the globe.[46]

More directly in line from the initiative behind *The Great Famine* there emerged a school of Irish agrarian history, based primarily in history departments and reflecting the specialisations of these departments, but with an emphasis on quantitative analysis. The founding figures included W. A. Maguire,[47] W. E. Vaughan and James S. Donnelly, Jr. In terms of source material, the core resource of this genre consists of official publications and the many extant collections of estate papers. While the concentration is mainly on the agricultural economy and socio-political conflict in the post-famine period, this work has a vital connection to the place of the Great Famine in historiography.

One outcome of the famine upheaval was that the class interests of landlords and tenant farmers were set off against one another with a degree of clarity not evident in the more confused circumstances of access to land before 1845. As landlords and tenants were vying with one another in the 1850s, 1860s and 1870s to share the profits of a generally prospering agriculture their conflict was amenable to being identified as one of exploitative tyrannical privilege set against the vulnerable tillers of the soil. It was so identified when the agricultural crisis of the late 1870s led to the conflict over rent, tenure and land ownership generally referred to as the Land War, the first and most incendiary phase of which ran from 1879 to 1882. This was to be followed by smouldering conflict for another three decades or more, as the issue was slowly resolved by the gradual transfer of land ownership through government-facilitated purchase. Throughout this time demonising the landlords was the key strategy of the Land League and other opponents of the existing order. Landlordism became the bête noire of nationalist discourse, excoriated for its roots in the Cromwellian plantation and for centuries of exploitation thereafter, but specifically for an alleged regime of rack-renting and ruthless evictions in the decades before the Land War. For those who accepted it, this critique deprived landlordism of moral legitimacy. As a hegemonic idea promoted by the cadres of the land agitation it was a mechanism for ensuring that their followers remained in line and that any fraternisation with the enemy could be punished by invoking communal wrath and the discipline of the boycott. This demonisation drew on the spirit of antipathy to aristocracy typical of emerging democratic societies – and so struck a chord with non-farming nationalists – while also serving to justify the ambitions of the farmers. While the transfer of ownership of the last 10 per cent or thereabouts of land in the Irish Free State to the occupiers was legislated for by an act of 1923, and the old landlord class quickly lost all status in public life, the term landlord continued to have the most negative connotations for decades to come.[48]

In that context the post-famine rural economy was for historians as challenging as the Great Famine itself. One of the early classics of the social-agrarian genre dealt in depth with the period from 1815 to 1892: James S. Donnelly, Jr, *The Land and People of Nineteenth-Century Cork* (London, 1975). This work, based on a Harvard PhD, is a model of exhaustive research, rigorous analysis and taut writing. It signified the banishment of the dogma and prejudice that had held discourse on the land question in thrall. Far from the outbreak of the Land War having been a response to decades of landlord persecution, the evidence examined by Donnelly showed that over the preceding quarter century on average only about thirty families per year had been evicted without readmission in all of County Cork.[49] The Famine and its horrors are treated in a similarly analytical and measured fashion, for example:

> The awful mortality in the Skibbereen district may have received a disproportionate amount of attention from properly horrified contemporaries, but clearly, the primitive economy of the area, its bottom-heavy social structure, and the almost complete absence of retail facilities doomed its inhabitants to catastrophe.[50]

At last, the trauma of Skibbereen could be discussed in explanatory rather than apocalyptic terms, acknowledging calamity but going beyond it to uncover social structure and measurable cause. Building on the foundations laid by *The Great Famine*, Donnelly, Vaughan[51] and others set new standards for agrarian history in Ireland, in terms both of erudite scholarship and of liberty from the expectation of re-echoing received tropes and lines of interpretation.

Public awareness of political issues was high in the Ireland of 1845. Not only had the constitutional form of the link with Britain been the subject of titanic agitation in preceding years, but the question of poor relief had been a topic of major public debate for more than a decade. Evidence from the localities suggests a widespread assumption at the onset of the crisis that public authority had the capacity to come to the rescue.[52] It is difficult to be certain to what extent the criticism of the government by Mitchel and other Young Ireland journalists reflects the disappointment of this popular expectation. In any event the contemporary, politically-inspired critique of the journalists provided the basis for what would be an enduring condemnation of the government. In this regard the evidence of folklore is of interest. *The Great Famine* has a chapter by Roger McHugh analysing material collected by the Irish Folklore Commission. None of it was collected earlier than the 1940s and so it is quite remote from the Great Famine. Nonetheless there are valuable echoes.

Subsequently, other scholars published their analyses and assessments of the Great Famine material in the general Irish Folklore Commission collection.[53] A number of points stand out from all of these studies. It is very striking that, of the many incidents and actions reported from the Famine, very few concern the immediate family of the informant; a common theme is that things were not bad in the informant's locality: it appears that like the public intellectuals the transmitters of folk memory had a penchant for referring the misery and disgrace of Famine. A quite surprising theme is that of the Famine as retribution for wastefulness in previous times when the potato was abundant. There are many critical references to individual landlords or to the officials on relief works or at soup kitchens, and also to farmers taking advantage of the misfortune of neighbours by outbidding them for tenancy of land. Remarkably, relatively little appears to be recorded by way of condemnation of the government or the British.[54] Those who postulate a continuous tradition of politically-charged resentment arising from unmediated folk memory of the Famine have a case to prove.

A small number of contemporary ballads in English and songs in Irish have been assembled by Christopher Morash[55] and Cormac Ó Gráda[56] respectively. These resemble the folklore material in their authentic illustration of particular local circumstances and individual stances, including various expressions of specific resentments or of general distress. But there is little sense of the intense anti-government animus expressed by contemporary leader writers and political poets in the *Nation* and other newspapers. Pete St John's sentimental patriotic ballad of 1981, *The fields of Athenry*, with its reference to 'the Famine and the crown' (rhymes with 'I rebelled, they ran me down') has become an (unofficial) alternative Irish national anthem in sports stadia, but to attribute its appeal to continuous folk memory of the Famine would be putting the cart before the horse. It almost certainly owes its popularity to the sing-along quality of the ballad rather than the historical echoes in the lyrics.

And the impact of the famine reference owes less to folk memory than to Woodham-Smith. From politicians to popular balladeers to Nobel laureates at home and abroad, most people who know of the Great Famine possess images that have been mediated through the pages of *The Great Hunger*.

The question of government culpability in the handling of the famine crisis highlighted in extreme language by John Mitchel was dealt with in more proportionate terms by O'Rourke. Subsequently the effect of the dogmatising of the famine was to reduce the entire subject to the question of government culpability. (This was rather like confining all discussion of the First World War to the question of who to blame for its outbreak.) The Great Famine came into the realm of academic discourse in the 1940s and 1950s only when scholars felt free to discuss other aspects of the subject. Woodham-Smith moved very far from the positions of John Mitchel and dogmatic nationalists in acknowledging good intent on the part of the government in the first two years of the crisis. She was, however, very critical of the decision to throw all relief on the Poor Law system in late 1847. For this she blamed Sir Charles Wood and Charles Trevelyan at the Treasury, along with Lord John Russell, prime minister from June 1846. This move with its disastrous consequences she attributed to expediency in the face of the British financial crisis of 1847.[57]

Discussion of the culpability of the government has now assumed something like the measured status accorded to it by O'Rourke. While he could blow hot and cold on the subject, the following is O'Rourke's most considered summary of the matter:

> To have met the potato Famine with anything like complete success would have been a Herculean task for any government. The total failure of the food of a nation was [...] a fact new in history; such being the case, no machinery existed extensive enough to neutralize its effects, nor was there extant any plan upon which such machinery could be modelled. Great allowance must be therefore made for the shortcomings of the Government, in a crisis so new and so terrible; but after making the most liberal concessions on this head, it must be admitted that Lord John Russell and his colleagues were painfully unequal to the situation. They either could not or would not use all the appliances within their reach, to save the Irish people.[58]

Most historians or social scientists of recent vintage would probably wish to correct 'the Irish people' to read something such as 'the most vulnerable section of the population of Ireland'. But, subject to some such rewording, O'Rourke's verdict would currently command considerable support from scholars. In particular his framing of the question gets to the nub of the matter.

A search of the bibliographical database Irish History Online[59] under 'famine' produces only a handful of results in total for the 1940s. For the 1980s the figure approaches 200, by the 1990s it is nearly 500, and for the first decade of the new millennium it drops to just over 200. The onset of the one hundred and fiftieth anniversary of the Great Famine in the mid-1990s had given rise to a dramatic upturn of attention to the subject. This was partially fuelled by government initiative, with the establishment in 1994 of an interdepartmental committee, and the subsequent allocation of funding to support research and commemorative events. The relatively modest direct allocation to research was placed under the control of historians who were as unlikely as their predecessors of fifty years earlier to take dictation from the government. The main, but unspoken, concern of the governments of the period 1994–97 as far as the Great Famine anniversary was concerned was to ensure that commemoration nationally or locally did not lead to an unmanageable outbreak of Anglophobia at a tense time in the affairs of Northern Ireland. There militant republican propagandists were recycling John Mitchel's rhetoric, now under the headline 'The Irish Holocaust'.[60]

Manifestations of public interest over the next few years, north and south, included commemorative ceremonies, exhibitions, the unveiling of famine memorials and waves of predominantly unfunded local history research. The most evocative form of commemoration may have been the identification and marking of workhouse cemeteries, typically completely bereft of individual headstones. This phase of communal devising of famine memorial practices contemporaneously with, but separate from, government initiative parallels a similar development in Ukraine in the 1990s, as described in Kasianov's chapter in this volume. This may be the point at which the two famine stories most closely converge.

Just as the neologism Holodomor was adopted almost overnight as recollection of the famine in Ukraine became fashionable, so shortly after, in the mid-1990s, the practice developed of referring to the Great Famine by its Irish language name, An Gorta Mór, even when writing or speaking in English. The usages are not strictly comparable, however, since Holodomor has come to be adopted universally and An Gorta Mór has not. The promotion of each term has a radicalising thrust: in the Irish case the wish to eschew the word famine is based on a questioning of the causality of hunger that owes much more to Amartya Sen's global perspective than it does to Mitchelite nationalism.[61]

In Ireland the contrast with the quiet passing of the centenary fifty years before is striking. Undoubtedly, the opening up of the subject by historians had contributed to the change. In any case, insistent reminders in the media could not but attract public attention, although the emphasis in the media was on a supposed common national memory of the Famine rather than on historical facts or events.[62] However, it was surely the capacity to stand back from the subject that made possible in the 1990s a discourse that would have been unthinkable in the 1940s. The changed economic circumstances of the country mattered very much in this regard. Ireland in 1945 was a country of ration books, looking anxiously at European neighbours menaced by food shortage. It was no time to expend resources on memorialising Famine. By 1995 Ireland was at possibly the most energising stage of an upward economic trajectory, the eventual unhappy downturn of which was more than a decade away. Ironically, this brave new Ireland was founded on the embrace of an economic strategy that was a latter-day mutant of the political economy once excoriated for turning the failure of the potato crop in the 1840s into a famine. There was little advertence to this irony.

A noteworthy feature in the 1990s was the willingness, indeed even eagerness, to entertain explicit comparison between the Great Famine and famines in twentieth-century Africa and Asia. It was a link which two generations earlier would have been too close to the bone. In 1943 the Dáil had voted £200,000 as a contribution to a Red Cross fundraising initiative in support of food relief in liberated parts of Europe and in Bengal. In the course of the debate there appears to have been only rare mention of the Great Famine, and that was very cursory.[63] It was surely not only increased awareness with respect to worldwide hunger, but, more importantly, increased self-confidence and the banishing of a taboo that permitted the link to be made so freely fifty years later. Interestingly, the Famine Museum at Strokestown Park House, opened in 1994, makes a very direct connection between the Irish and other famines. The fact that the former big house of the King-Mahon family, residence of one of the very few landlords murdered during the Great Famine, and now owned and lovingly preserved by local business people Jim and Adeline Callery, could be the site of an even-handed and scholarly display about the Great Famine, was itself a remarkable testament to the maturing of general public attitudes.

For all the temporary public concentration on the Great Famine in 1994–97 there was little enough evidence that either government or people was determined to accord it a central place in the commemorative life of the country on an ongoing basis. The standard style of national commemoration, with a great parade or other display in the centre of the capital, never seemed appropriate. In fact the main commemorative event in 1997 took place in Milltown, a small town in north-west county Cork, admittedly at a well-attended event in a good-sized venue. The National Famine Committee established in 2008 was placed under the auspices of the Department of Community, Rural and Gaeltacht Affairs, which sounds a distinct note of marginalisation. Nonetheless, the focus of the committee appears to be global, continuing the connections with issues of hunger and food security worldwide, and supporting famine commemorative occasions in the USA and elsewhere. It remains to be seen if in Ireland the rituals of an annual day of commemoration will take root. In several localities there are signs of an emerging practice of annual walks to sites associated with the Famine. The walk serves the double purpose of connecting with a famished past that threw so many onto the road and gesturing towards the life-style needs of a present gorged with a surfeit of girth-expanding calories.

Among Irish Americans, ambivalence about the Great Famine has for long appeared to be less pronounced than in Ireland. There was a steady stream of emigration from Ireland to the USA in the years before 1845, and in later decades hundreds of thousands would follow, but the great flood of emigrants during and immediately after the famine years determined the character of the Irish American collectivity defined by Catholicism, Democratic Party politics and militant attitudes to British rule in Ireland.[64] Many of the Great Famine emigrants poured into a collective mentality their personal sense of having been failed by those in power in Ireland, and effectively banished, frequently in distressing circumstances. Those who came more deliberately in calmer times found the communal origin myth so firmly in place that many readily adopted it. In due course to communicate that one's parents or grandparents had come over at 'the potato Famine' became not so much a statement of fact as an assertion of identity. From this perspective the Great Famine fits easily as the work of a nefarious British government and tyrannical Irish landlords. J. J. Lee and Kerby Miller have argued cogently about the psychological mechanisms that led to Irish American Famine survivors transferring to the British government feelings of guilt arising from traumatic intra-familial experience.[65] In response to the adulation of Queen Victoria occasioned by her golden jubilee in 1887 Irish Americans promoted her as a famine ogre.[66] But even in the USA the memory of the Great Famine would scarcely have been carried down over generations on the basis of domestic discourse. It owes its vibrancy to the workings of the ideological support system of a powerful community.

Certain Irish American interests have reacted to official acknowledgement of African American slavery and the Holocaust by seeking parallel recognition of the Great Famine. It is very appropriate that Irish Americans should seek to come to terms with the Great Famine and obtain support in so doing. But the temptation to demand parity by representing what occurred in Ireland in the 1840s as genocide needs to be resisted simply on the basis of honesty. To rebut the allegation of an Irish genocide is relatively easy in an academic setting; to refute it when faced with the emotive rhetoric of identity politics in the public arena is much more difficult. The Great Irish

Famine Curriculum described by Professor Maureen Murphy in Chapter Five provides a striking example of courageous assertion of the claims of evidence-based enquiry as against self-serving shibboleths. The curriculum turns what might have been an exercise in indoctrination into a superlative learning opportunity. Similarly, the contrast in the American context between extremist/opportunist and constructive/open memorialisation is illustrated by Dr Emily Mark-FitzGerald in Chapter Seven.

Even in Irish America no single view of the history of Ireland or of the Great Famine has enjoyed exclusive status. In 1860, as *The Last Conquest* was making its first appearance in book form, the Dublin publisher James Duffy brought out Martin Haverty's *History of Ireland, Ancient and Modern, for the Use of Schools and Colleges, with Questions for Examination at the end of Each Chapter*, in a cramped and skimpy format. While clearly sympathetic to Irish nationality, Haverty (a Mayo-born journalist turned librarian) managed to remain relatively even-handed in a book that closed in tears with the passing of the Act of Union in 1800. A deluxe edition, shorn of the scholastic impedimenta, gilt-edged, sumptuously bound and with dozens of full-page illustrations, was published in New York in 1867 by Thomas Farrell and Son. It was now *A History of Ireland from the Earliest Period to the Present Time* and had several additional chapters bringing the story down to early 1867. While apocalyptic in conjuring up the impact of the Great Famine, Haverty's account, compiled for Irish Americans at the moment when a Fenian insurrection was expected from day to day, has but little echo of Mitchel's view of the respective roles of providence and the government in the Great Famine:

> It was a sad dispensation of divine Providence which came upon Ireland during that year [1845] and 1846 [...] Famine in its most dreadful form, pervaded the whole country; and with famine came its usual attendant, fever of the most malignant kind. Hundreds and thousands were swept to their graves [...] From the government and other sources relief was speedily obtained [...] Lord John Russell now came into power and applied himself diligently to the providing measures [sic] of relief for Ireland [...] The plan was admirably devised and skilfully and energetically carried out, and was for some time very successful in alleviating the prevalent distress [...] From thirty to forty steamers and fourteen or fifteen sailing vessels, were constantly employed in pouring breadstuffs into Ireland, while all the medical aid at the public command was readily rendered for the aid of the sufferers [...] Murmuring, distress, doubt, and death pervaded the land and the spirit of the people seemed to be well-nigh crushed by the load of calamities which had fallen upon them.[67]

This suggests that even in Irish America of the 1860s the Famine as British atrocity was by no means the only marketable interpretation. Nonetheless, the Mitchelite version has enjoyed a higher level of dominance in the USA than in Ireland. Of course Mitchel's views were formed well in advance of his arrival in America. However, the newspaper in which the chapters that became the *The Last Conquest* first appeared was, as we have seen, the pro-slavery *Southern Citizen* conducted by Mitchel himself. This was only one of several journalistic ventures on which he laboured in support of the South and the Confederacy, and – quite specifically, explicitly and repeatedly – black slavery.[68] He was one of the most ardent diehards on the defeated side in the Civil War, losing two sons in the conflict. Nor did he ameliorate his attitude when the war ended. All of this is very material to an evaluation of Mitchel's treatment of Irish history, and is sometimes passed over. Mitchel hated liberalism in all its manifestations. One of those was the government of Lord John Russell. Another was the abolitionist Yankee establishment bent, as Mitchel saw it, on the liberation of the slaves and the destruction of the culture and socio-economic system of the South. When Mitchel was denouncing the British government he was also launching a vicarious assault on the anti-slavery interest in the United States, and providing an object lesson in what could happen to a 'traditional' society falling into the trammels of political economy, free trade and the cash nexus. No doubt his readers in Tennessee and elsewhere in the South got the point.[69] Whatever combination of factors went into Mitchel's exegesis of the Great Famine, concern for the dignity and equality of the individual human being was not one of them. Mitchel was honest in his Carlylean fanaticism and he would scarcely have appreciated latter-day attempts to associate his attitudes with the term 'humanitarian'.

In recorded history most of the inhabited world has been ravaged by war or famine at one time or another, or many times over – including much of continental Europe as late as 1939–45. Accordingly, the theme of traumatic suffering is available to national story tellers of many countries. In this context the Great Famine has particular impact because of the extent of the mortality it involved, without war as cause or complication. The Great Famine will be available as a powerful exemplar for as long as Irish (or Irish American) opinion-formers feel the need to offer communal self-explanation in terms of suffering and victimhood, and a historian has no business estimating for how long this may be. What a historian can venture with some greater confidence is the prediction that for as long as the evidence of the past continues to be explored by people grappling to understand the extremes of human social experience, scholars, and other writers, will revisit time and time again the Ireland of the late 1840s and early 1850s.

Notes and References

1. The author is indebted to Liam Kennedy, W. E. Vaughan and James H. Murphy for their comments on an earlier draft of this chapter; I am solely responsible for any remaining errors.
2. Ellen Fitzsimon, 'Sonnet: 1849', anthologised in Chris Morash (ed.), *The Hungry Voice: the Poetry of the Irish Famine* (Dublin: Irish Academic Press, 1989), 98.
3. Margaret Kelleher, *The Feminization of Famine: Expressions of the Inexpressible?* (Cork: Cork University Press, 1997); Christopher Morash, *Writing the Irish Famine* (Oxford: Clarendon Press, 1995).
4. Kelleher, *Feminization of Famine*, 16–29.
5. John O'Rourke, *The History of the Great Irish Famine of 1847, with Notices of Earlier Irish Famines* (Dublin; London: McGlashan and Gill; James Duffy, Sons and Co., 1875).
6. W. P. O'Brien, *The Great Famine in Ireland and a Retrospect of the Fifty Years 1845–95 with a Sketch of the Present Condition and Future Prospects of the Congested Districts* (London: Downey and Co., 1896).
7. O'Brien, *The Great Famine*, 1.
8. Ibid., 77–81.
9. Peter Gray, *Famine, Land and Politics: British Government and Irish Society, 1843–50* (Dublin: Irish Academic Press, 1999); for another viewpoint see Paul Bew and Robert Haines, *Charles Trevelyan and the Great Irish Famine* (Dublin: Four Courts, 2004).
10. O'Rourke, *Great Irish Famine*, 279.
11. D. A. Kerr, *'A Nation of Beggars'? Priests, People and Politics in Famine Ireland, 1846–52* (Oxford: Clarendon Press, 1994), 33–4.
12. Kerr, *'A Nation of Beggars'?*, 81–3, 228–30.
13. *Tablet*, 12 April 1848, cited in Kerr, *'A Nation of Beggars'?*, 142.
14. See Cormac Ó Gráda, *Famine: A Short History* (Princeton: Princeton University Press, 2009), 23.
15. John Mitchel, *The Last Conquest of Ireland (Perhaps)*, new ed., with introduction by Patrick Maume (Dublin: UCD Press, 2005).
16. J. S. Donnelly, Jr, *The Great Irish Potato Famine* (Stroud: Sutton Publishing, 2001), 245.
17. Information gathered by R. Dudley Edwards from a member of the de Valera family and conveyed to the present author.
18. See M. Corporaal, C. Cusack and L. Janssen (eds), *Recollecting Hunger: An Anthology. Cultural Memories of the Great Hunger in Irish and British Fiction, 1847–1920* (Dublin: Irish Academic Press, 2012).
19. Christopher Morash, *Writing the Irish Famine* (Oxford: Oxford University Press, 1995), 142–51.
20. Justin McCarthy, *A History of Our Own Times* (London, 1879), 424, quoted in Morash, *Writing the Irish Famine*, 149.
21. See Joost Augusteijn, *Patrick Pearse: The Making of a Revolutionary* (London: Palgrave, 2010), 290–3.
22. Kelleher, *Feminization of Famine*, 112–35.
23. James Connolly, *Labour in Irish History* (Dublin: Maunsel and Co., 1910), ch. 13.
24. George O'Brien, *The Economic History of Ireland from the Union to the Famine* (London: Longmans, Green and Co., 1921).
25. Patrick Cahalane, 'An Economic Study of the Great Famine', *Studies* (1917): 95–113.
26. Kelleher, *Feminization of Famine*, 134–44.

27 Timothy O'Herlihy, *The Famine, 1845–47: A Survey of its Ravages and Causes* (Drogheda: Drogheda Independent, 1947), 8. I am grateful to James H. Murphy for biographical information about O'Herlihy.
28 T. P. O'Neill, 'The Famine in Carlow' *Carloviana: Journal of the Old Carlow Society* no. 1 (1947): 16–24.
29 Oliver MacDonagh, 'The Irish Catholic Clergy and Emigration During the Great Famine', *Irish Historical Studies* 5, no. 20 (Sept. 1947): 287–302.
30 Cormac Ó Gráda, 'Making Famine History in Ireland in the 1940s and 1950s', in idem, *Ireland's Great Famine: Interdisciplinary Perspectives* (Dublin: UCD Press, 2006), 234–50.
31 R. D. Edwards and T. D. Williams, *The Great Famine: Studies in Irish History, 1845–52* (Dublin: Browne and Nolan, 1956).
32 Ó Gráda, 'Making Famine History in the 1940s and 1950s'.
33 Ibid. 241.
34 The theoretical issues associated with the historiography of the Famine are explored in Evi Gkotzaridis, *Trials of Irish History: Genesis and Evolution of a Reappraisal, 1938–2000* (London: Routledge, 2006).
35 Cecil Woodham-Smith, *The Great Hunger: Ireland 1845–9* (London: Hamish Hamilton, 1962).
36 Woodham-Smith, *The Great Hunger*, 31.
37 Ibid. 409.
38 Helen Andrews in *Dictionary of Irish Biography* (Cambridge: Cambridge University Press, 2009).
39 K. H. Connell, *The Population of Ireland, 1700–1845* (Oxford: Oxford University Press, 1950); S. H. Cousens, 'Regional Death Rates in Ireland During the Great Famine, from 1846 to 1851', *Population Studies* 24, no.1 (July 1960): 55–74; R. D. Crotty, *Irish Agricultural Production: its Value and Structure* (Cork: Cork University Press, 1966).
40 P. M. A. Bourke, *'The Visitation of God'? The Potato and the Great Irish Famine*, eds. Jacqueline Hill and Cormac Ó Gráda, (Dublin: Lilliput Press, 1993).
41 Ibid., 90.
42 See Joel Mokyr, *Why Ireland Starved: A Quantitative and Analytical History of the Irish Economy, 1800–50* (London: Allen and Unwin, 1983).
43 There is an extensive bibliography in Cormac Ó Gráda, *Ireland's Great Famine: Interdisciplinary Perspectives* (Dublin: UCD Press, 2006).
44 Liam Kennedy, Paul Ell, E. M. Crawford and L. A. Clarkson, *Mapping the Great Irish Famine: A Survey of the Famine Decades* (Dublin: Four Courts Press, 1999).
45 Cormac Ó Gráda, *Black '47 and Beyond: The Great Irish Famine in History, Economy and Memory* (Princeton: Princeton University Press, 1999).
46 Cormac Ó Gráda, *Famine: A Short History* (Princeton: Princeton University Press, 2009).
47 W. A. Maguire, *The Downshire Estates in Ireland, 1801–1845: The Management of Irish Landed Estates in the Early Nineteenth Century* (Oxford: Clarendon Press, 1972).
48 Terence Dooley, *'The Land for the People': The Land Question in Independent Ireland* (Dublin: UCD Press, 2004).
49 James S. Donnelly, Jr, *The Land and the People of Nineteenth-Century Cork: The Rural Economy and the Land Question* (London: Routledge and Kegan Paul, 1975).
50 Ibid., 123.
51 W. E. Vaughan, *Landlords and Tenants in Ireland, 1848–1904* (Dublin: Economic and Social History Society of Ireland, 1984); *Landlords and Tenants in Mid-Victorian Ireland* (Oxford: Clarendon Press, 1994).

52 Kerr, *A Nation of Beggars'?*, 34–42; Christine Kinealy, *This Great Calamity: The Irish Famine, 1845–52* (Dublin: Gill and Macmillan, 1994).
53 Roger McHugh, 'The Famine in Irish Oral Tradition', in Edwards and Williams, *The Great Famine*, 391–436; Cormac Ó Gráda, *An Drochshaol: Béaloideas agus Amhráin* (Dublin: Coiscéim, 1994); Cathal Póirtéir, *Famine Echoes* (Dublin: Gill and Macmillan, 1995); Niall Ó Cíosáin, 'Famine Memory and the Popular Representation of Scarcity', in Ian McBride (ed.), *History and Memory in Modern Ireland* (Cambridge: Cambridge University Press, 2001), 95–117.
54 Ó Gráda, *An Drochshaol*, vi.
55 Morash, *The Hungry Voice*, 268–72.
56 Ó Gráda, *An Drochshaol*, 35–90.
57 Woodham-Smith, *The Great Hunger*, 408.
58 O'Rourke, *Great Irish Famine*, 196–7.
59 Available at http://iho.ie/ (accessed on 27 June 2011).
60 Peter Gray, 'Memory and Commemoration of the Great Irish Famine', in Peter Gray and Kendrick Oliver (eds), *The Memory of Catastrophe* (Manchester: Manchester University Press, 2004), 58.
61 See ibid., 54.
62 For two sceptical commentaries see Cormac Ó Gráda, 'Famine, Trauma and Memory', in idem (ed.), *Ireland's Great Famine: Interdisciplinary Perspectives* (Dublin: UCD Press, 2006) and R. F. Foster, *The Irish Story: Telling Tales and Making it up in Ireland* (London: Allen Lane, 2001).
63 *Dáil Debates 91*, cols. 1987–2015, 11 Nov. 1943.
64 Timothy J. Meagher, *The Columbia Guide to Irish American History* (New York: Columbia University Press, 2005), 60–93, 157–8; T. N. Brown, *Irish–American Nationalism, 1870–1890* (Philadelphia: Lippincott, 1966).
65 J. J. Lee, 'The Famine as History', in Cormac Ó Gráda (ed.), *Famine 150. Commemorative Lecture Series* (Dublin: Teagasc, 1997); Kerby A. Miller, *Emigrants and Exiles: Ireland and the Irish Exodus to North America* (New York: Oxford University Press, 1985), 167–9.
66 James H. Murphy, *Abject Loyalty: Nationalism and Monarchy in Ireland during the Reign of Queen Victoria* (Cork: Cork University Press, 2001), 291.
67 Martin Haverty, *A History of Ireland from the Earliest Period to the Present Time* (New York: Thomas Farrell and Sons, 1867), 791–4.
68 See Maume, introduction to Mitchel, *Last Conquest*, xvii.
69 For the wider context see David T. Gleeson, *The Irish in the South, 1815–77* (Chapel Hill: North Carolina University Press, 2000).

Part II

PUBLIC COMMEMORATION

Chapter 4

HISTORY AND NATIONAL IDENTITY CONSTRUCTION: THE GREAT FAMINE IN IRISH AND UKRAINIAN HISTORY TEXTBOOKS[1]

Jan Germen Janmaat
Institute of Education, London

Ethnocentric views and nationalist biases in textbooks are usually associated with the first half of the twentieth century when national rivalries dominated international affairs and fascist and authoritarian regimes controlled much of the European continent. Marsden, for example, notes that the glorification of war and the vilification of neighbouring states permeated the history and geography textbooks of Great Britain, France, the United States and Germany from the 1880s until the 1940s, despite efforts by the League of Nations to curb rampant chauvinism in textbooks in the interwar period.[2]

After the Second World War politicians and educators concluded that jingoism in textbooks must have contributed to the atrocities committed in the war. Consequently, supported by UNESCO and the Council of Europe, many countries began removing nationalist leanings from their curricula and textbooks.[3] Bilateral agreements were concluded and special commissions set up to identify and eliminate prejudice and stereotypes. Thematically, the emphasis shifted from national to international history and from political and military history, with its tendency to praise national achievements and national heroes, to socio-economic and cultural issues and the daily life of the common person.[4] In their pedagogical objectives, textbooks moved away from the infusion of values, identities and pre-digested, unquestioned knowledge to the promotion of critical thinking, independent analysis and problem solving skills.

Great and unpleasant was the surprise, therefore, when nationalist leanings suddenly reappeared in the textbooks of many states in Central and Eastern

Europe following the collapse of communism. Some would argue that these nationalist colourings are typical of recently or newly independent states, which are generally eager to establish unity within their borders and, therefore, to prioritise nation building over other concerns.[5] Others would link the sudden rise of ethno-national sentiments (and their manifestation in textbooks) to the post-communist transition period, which caused considerable survival stress and left people without a moral compass. In this view nationalism filled the ideological vacuum that communism left behind.[6] Both views seem to imply that nationalist rhetoric is something temporary, characteristic of the early post-independence years: as states grow older and a new social and moral order is established the political and emotional need for identity construction diminishes. This conjecture raises many interesting questions. Are the current historical narratives of new(ly) independent states comparable to those of relatively young West European states in the first few decades after their independence? Have the historical narratives in these West European states evolved from nationalist discourses to more moderate and balanced accounts? If this is the case, can specific factors or circumstances be identified which have triggered this change? Is it likely that the new(ly) independent states follow the same path of development or is it improper to expect history to repeat itself because of changing historical circumstances?

These questions have informed the current study, which compares textbook narratives of Ireland – a young West European state – to those of Ukraine – a new independent post-Soviet state. Specifically it examines representations of the Irish and Ukrainian Famines in the history textbooks of the two countries and explores to what extent these portrayals are coloured by a nationalist discourse. It will track developments in these depictions by analysing successive generations of textbooks that have been in use since state independence. The fact that the two nations experienced the same kind of catastrophe when they were ruled by a foreign power (the United Kingdom in the Irish case, the Soviet Union in the Ukrainian case) is an interesting similarity.[7] Have nationalists in both cases exploited the famines by arguing that the disaster is proof of the ill-willed posture of the foreign power towards their respective nations? Have they, by implication, asserted that the tragedy would not have occurred if their nations had been free from foreign domination?

There are other conspicuous parallels between the two nations. Historically, both the Irish and the Ukrainians were by and large peasant populations tilling lands held predominantly by a landlord class that differed from the peasantry in religion and/or ethnic descent. Their native languages (Irish and Ukrainian) were increasingly surpassed by the imperial languages English and Russian in the nineteenth century.

But there are also differences. Whereas Catholicism gradually came to be seen as synonymous with Irishness in nineteenth-century Ireland, Ukrainians had to fall back on language as the sole marker distinguishing them from Russians. Religion could not be used as a marker of identity as the majority of Ukrainians professed the same belief as their 'elder Slavic brethren' – Eastern Orthodoxy.[8] Second, at the time the famines occurred – 1846 in Ireland and 1933 in Ukraine – the political character of the ruling empires differed completely, with the British Empire exemplifying the classic *laissez faire* state promoting market capitalism and free trade and the Soviet Union constituting the archetypical interventionist state exerting full control over economy and society.

The aims of this chapter are threefold: (1) to assess to what extent the portrayals of the famines in Irish and Ukrainian history textbooks are influenced by a nationalist discourse, (2) to examine changes in the strength of this discourse over time and (3) to use the results of the analysis to explore the validity of several perspectives on the role of historical narratives in national identity construction. The paper starts with a discussion of these perspectives. This is followed by a methodological section that discusses the identification of a nationalist bias and the selection of textbooks. Sections three and four are devoted to the analysis of Irish and Ukrainian textbooks, respectively. The concluding section matches the empirical findings with the aforementioned perspectives.

Perspectives on Historiography and National Identity Construction

The advantage of comparing Ireland and Ukraine is that it allows us to explore the validity of a number of perspectives from political science and history. These perspectives can inform and offer theoretical guidance to textbook studies and can link textbook narratives to wider social processes.

The first perspective sees nationalist historiography as a phenomenon that is characteristic of an ethnic illiberalism. According to Hans Kohn, the founder of this school of thought, ethnic nationalism looked to the past as a source of inspiration, seeing the nation as an eternal, natural and cultural entity defined by common historical experience, culture and descent. He contrasted this with a civic liberal nationalism that 'arose in an effort to build a nation in the political reality and the struggles of the present without too much sentimental regard for the past'.[9] Kohn related the kind of nationalism to class structure: in societies with a strong bourgeoisie (America, Britain, France, the Netherlands and Switzerland) civic nationalism predominated; in traditional agrarian societies (Central and Eastern Europe) ethnic nationalism prevailed.[10]

It must be noted here that Kohn developed his theory in the interwar years, a period when authoritarian intolerant nationalisms triumphed in most parts of Europe. Nonetheless Kohn's theory can hardly be called outdated as it remained an influential theory in the postwar years, inspiring many scholars, journalists and policy-makers and fuelling a heated academic debate that continues to the present day.[11] Although many of his followers interpreted his framework as a crude civic-West/ethnic-East divide,[12] Kohn himself also considered the periphery of Western Europe to be affected by ethnic nationalism, and Ireland in particular.[13] At this point it is relevant to ask how a nation and the image of itself will develop once ethnonationalism has taken root. Are ethnic nations doomed to stay ethnic and illiberal forever? As neither Kohn nor his followers satisfactorily addressed this question, I have no option but to interpret Kohn's framework as a static perspective, as a theory that assumes geographical variations in the understanding of a nationhood to be lasting. In relation to the current study, I infer the following prediction from it: *in both Ireland and Ukraine textbook narratives on the Famine are characterised by a constant nationalist bias since the establishment of state independence.*

Advancing a developmental model, T. Kuzio, a strong critic of Kohn, deals with the question of the static or changing nature of ethnic nations. Drawing on works by A. D. Smith and E. Kaufmann, he argues that both Eastern and Western nations rest on strong ethnic foundations.[14] In Western states civic institutions and practices have been built on and become thoroughly intertwined with these foundations. In his evolutionary model the mix of civic and ethnic elements in a given state is related to the age of that state and to the development of democratic structures – i.e. the younger the state and the more fragile its democracy, the less opportunity it has had to develop civic structures and the more ethnic it still is. In other words, young states may start out by communicating an ethnic conception of the nation – with a concomitant stress on nationalist historiography – but they will gradually adopt more civic features, expressed in a gradual disappearance of the nationalist bias in history textbooks, as the state grows older. Kuzio's model thus echoes those who see nationalist historiography as a temporary phenomenon related to an initial phase of state and nation-building. *His model would predict that Ireland has gradually abandoned a nationalist account of its Famine as it evolved from a traditional agrarian society to a modern democratic postindustrial state and that Ukraine can be expected to follow the same development as it grows older as an independent democratic state.*

A third perspective relates the surge of ethnic nationalism in Eastern Europe and the Soviet successor states to the particular experience with communism. George Schöpflin for instance contends that communism destroyed civil society and the social fabric of communities, leaving people isolated and distrustful of the state. In these circumstances ethnonational identities were the only ones people could fall back on once communism had collapsed. As communism had also wiped out pluralism and views challenging the regime, a vigorous ethnic nationalism excluding oppositional voices had free play.[15] Viktor Stepanenko argues along the same lines. He sees a 'genealogical relatedness' between post-Soviet Ukrainian historiography and its Soviet predecessor in a sense that both accounts of history 'affirm their single vision suppressing the other perspective'.¹⁶ *The perspective linking ethnic nationalism to the communist experience would predict different accounts of the Famine, with Ukraine being likely to adopt a single nationalist narrative and Ireland prone to give neutral and diverse accounts of the Famine from the establishment of the Irish Free State. The nationalist narratives in Ukraine can only be expected to change if democracy and pluralism firmly take root.*

Of course, a two case comparison allows only for a partial testing of the predictions of these models. Many more cases as well as different policy fields would have to be included in the analysis to arrive at a complete evaluation. Yet, the comparison can provide us with some preliminary insights.

Method of Analysis and Selection of Textbooks

For the current study it is crucial to establish what constitutes a nationalist bias and what constitutes a moderate approach in narratives of the famines. This study will use the consensus among historians on a particular topic as a benchmark. Accounts that depart significantly from this consensus in the selection and interpretation of events in favour of the titular group and at the expense of the out-group will be considered nationalist. Accounts that are in line with the consensus will be taken as moderate, neutral or even-handed. A problem that arises here is that the Ukrainian Famine, in contrast to the Irish one, is still a hotly discussed topic among historians. This is not surprising given that Ukrainian historians have only very recently (since 1991) been able to access sources and study the subject seriously. Yet on some crucial issues regarding the Famine a consensus has by and large emerged. Thus historians from various backgrounds (Western, Ukrainian, Ukrainian diaspora) would subscribe to the view that the Famine was not directed specifically at the Ukrainian *nation*, although they would see it as an instrument targeted at the Ukrainian *peasantry* in order to crush the latter's resistance to collectivisation.¹⁷ The consensus on these issues will be used as a yardstick with which to evaluate narratives in Ukrainian textbooks.

Another methodological issue is the qualitative difference between the Irish and the Ukrainian Famine: whereas the former had natural causes, the latter was an artificial disaster, being the result of Stalin's collectivisation campaign, and occurred in other parts of the Soviet Union as well. This means that the narratives of the two famines cannot be judged entirely by the same criteria to determine the degree of nationalist bias. For instance, Irish narratives attributing sole responsibility for the occurrence of the Famine to the British government are *not* in line with the consensus and hence *would* have a nationalist bias. Ukrainian narratives holding the Soviet regime exclusively responsible *do* reflect the consensus and therefore do *not* have a nationalist colouring. Sole responsibility will thus be used as a criterion only in the Irish case. In similar vein, a failure to mention that the Famine also occurred elsewhere *will* be interpreted as a bias in the Ukrainian case but *not* in the Irish case.[18] However, apart from these differences there are a number of common criteria that apply in both cases. For this study I use the following to assess the degree of nationalist bias:

1. the depiction of the Famine as an instrument of genocide (i.e. a policy designed for the physical extermination of the Irish or Ukrainian nation);
2. ethnic boundary-making to create an 'us – them' effect (e.g. labelling the British government and the landlords as 'English' or 'Protestant' in the Irish case; labelling the Soviet government and its agents in Ukraine as 'Russian' or 'Jewish');[19]
3. depicting the in-group (the Irish and the Ukrainians) exclusively as victims and the out-group (the Russians, the English/Protestants) exclusively as perpetrators;
4. failing to mention the motivations the British and Soviet government had for their policies.

The next question that commands attention is the selection of textbooks for the analysis. The current study has tried to be as exhaustive as possible. For the Irish case this has proved difficult, however, as the Irish government from the very inception of the Irish Free State chose to continue the hands-off policy of its British predecessor regarding textbooks (see below). Consequently, no lists have been found of textbooks sanctioned by the Department of Education. Instead, this study relied on the comprehensive selection of textbooks by Brian Mulcahy for his study on the portrayal of English–Irish relations in Irish history textbooks. Mulcahy distinguished two generations of textbooks: the 'purist' ones that were used from independence until the end of the 1960s and which, in his view, stand out for their nationalist tone, anti-Englishness and black-and-white treatment of prominent characters, and the 'moderate' texts, which have been in use from the early 1970s to the present and which 'are generally without such biases and present more neutral accounts of Irish history'.[20] This study follows Mulcahy's periodisation.

I analysed the following textbooks of the first generation:

Hayden, M., and G. A. Moonan. *A Short History of the Irish People from the Earliest Times to the 1920s*. Dublin: Talbot Press, 1921.
Gwynn, S. *The Student's History of Ireland*. London: Longmans, Green, 1925.
Carty, J. *A Junior History of Ireland*. London: Macmillan, 1933.
Casserley, D. *History of Ireland*. Dublin: Talbot Press, 1943.
The Educational History of Ireland: Part I. Dublin: Educational Company of Ireland, 1947.

I analysed the following textbooks of the second generation:

Moody, T. W., and F. X. Martin (eds). *The Course of Irish History*. Cork: Mercier Press, 1967.
Tierney, M., and M. MacCurtain. *The Birth of Modern Ireland*. Dublin: Gill and Macmillan, 1969.
Collins, M. E. *Ireland Three: Union to Present Day*. Dublin: Educational Company, 1972.
Neill, K. *The Age of Steam and Steel*. Dublin: Gill and Macmillan, 1976.
Kirkpatrick, R. *The Nineteenth Century*. Dublin: Folens Publishers, 1980.
Sobolewski, P., and J. McDonald. *Let's Look at History Part 2: Exploring Change*. Dublin: Gill and Macmillan, 1990.
Brockie, G., and R. Walsh. *Focus on the Past: One-Volume Edition*. Dublin: Gill and Macmillan, 1997.

The attentive reader will have noticed that Irish-language textbooks are missing in this selection. It is quite possible that Irish-language history textbooks display a stronger nationalist colouring than their English-language counterparts since many of them have been published by the Christian Brothers, a teaching order feverishly committed to the Irish cause.[21] However, the number of pupils having studied from Irish-language textbooks is not likely to have been large. From the inception of the Irish Free State, Irish fought an uphill battle against English, which continued to be the language of public life and remained the native language of the vast majority of the population. Even in the early postwar years when the state-endorsed Gaelicisation campaign was at its peak, still only about a quarter of all secondary schools taught exclusively in Irish.[22] Under these conditions the impact of Irish-language textbooks is likely to have been minimal, which is the primary reason for not including them in the analysis.

The selection of Ukrainian textbooks was more straightforward as the Ukrainian Ministry of Education to this day closely oversees the textbook writing, production and dissemination process (see below). As lists of officially recommended textbooks could be used, the selection of Ukrainian textbooks (*pidruchnyky*) for the current study is complete. The lists also mention supplementary books (the so-called *posibnyky*), but I decided not to include them in the analysis as schools are not required to use them.

I analysed the following books of the first generation (1993–96):[23]

Kucheruk, O. *Opovidannia z Istorii Ukrainy* (A Tale about the History of Ukraine). Kiev: Osvita, 1993 (fifth grade).
Kul'chitskii, S. V., Y. Kurnosov, and M. V. Koval'. *Istoriia Ukrainy* (History of Ukraine). Kiev: Osvita, 1994 (tenth grade).

Turchenko, F. H. *Noveishaia Istoriia Ukrainy: Chast' Pervaia 1917–1945* (Modern History of Ukraine: Part One 1917–1945). Kiev: Heneza, 1995 (tenth grade).

I analysed the following books of the second generation (1999–2003):[24]

Misan, V. *Opovidannia z Istorii Ukrainy, 5 klas* (A Tale about the History of Ukraine, 5th grade). Kiev: Heneza, 2003 (tenth grade).
Vlasov, V., and O. Danilevs'ka. *Vstup do Istorii Ukrainy, 5 klas* (Introduction to the History of Ukraine). Kiev: Abrys, 1999, 2002 (fifth grade).
Turchenko, F. H. *Novitnia Istoria Ukrainy: Chastyna Persha 1914–1939* (Modern History of Ukraine: Part One 1914–1939). Kiev: Heneza, 1998, 2001 (tenth grade).
Kul'chitskii, S. V., M. V. Koval', and Y. H. Lebedeva. *Istoriia Ukrainy* (History of Ukraine). Kiev: Osvita, 1998 (tenth grade).
Kul'chyts'kyi, S. V., and Y. I. Shapoval. *Novitnia Istoriia Ukrainy (1914–1939)* (Modern History of Ukraine). Kiev: Heneza, 2003 (tenth grade).

The Famine in Irish History Textbooks: The First Generation

The pre-independence education system of Ireland was characterised by strong church involvement, with the Catholic Church managing state-financed denominational schools and appointing teachers from the ranks of priests. After the establishment of the Irish Free State in 1922, Professor Eoin MacNeill, the first minister of education, left this system largely untouched, in exchange for ecclesiastical consent for the Gaelicisation of education, one of MacNeill's key priorities alongside equal opportunities.[25] Championed by the Gaelic League in the decades prior to independence, Gaelicisation was seen as a prerequisite for the conservation and development of a distinct Irish national identity.[26] It had to 'redress the balance and to make compensation' for the neglect of Irish culture under the previous administration.[27] Although the Gaelicisation campaign centred on the issue of the Irish language as a school subject and language of instruction, Irish history did not escape the attention of the educational authorities. History was made a compulsory subject for primary and secondary schools and by 1924 the government had prepared national history curricula that guided pupils to the Intermediate and Leaving Certificate (central exams for secondary education).[28] Central to the history course was Irish national history, which assumed a distinct nationalist flavour.[29] In the words of writer John Broderick:

> The idea of history that we got was that we had been oppressed by our neighbours, the British, for seven hundred years; that the Catholic religion in particular had been suppressed and was persecuted; that there had been a

great revival in the nineteenth century with Catholic Emancipation through Daniel O'Connell, and that Catholicism thrived under that, but that coming into the twentieth century we were being Englified and that was why 1916 came about; this had to be broken, the Irish people had to be shown what their heritage was. In a capsule this was the history of Ireland.[30]

Educational officials instructed teachers to underline the continuity of the Irish separatist idea and highlight the ideals and deeds of national heroes and revolutionaries.[31]

Contrary to what one might expect of a state giving high priority to nationalist history teaching, the Irish state did not intervene in the textbook writing, vetting and adoption process. Initially there was pressure on the Department of Education to establish a list of approved books but the government did not yield to this pressure as it feared the reaction of the commercial publishers.[32] Textbook production was thus left completely to publishers, academics and history teachers. However, the lack of state involvement did not mean that textbooks presented accounts of history that were at odds with official views. To the contrary, according to Roy Foster, the first generation of textbooks dutifully 'memorialised' the institutionalised view of history, a generation moreover that would continue to be used for the next 40 years.[33]

Comparing these books on their representation of the Irish Famine it can be noted first of all that all five are highly critical of the response of the British government to the failure of the 1845 potato crop. The common tenor is that the government acted much too late with measures that were not effective initially. For this reason, the *Educational History* calls the story of the Famine a story of 'hunger, disease and *criminal mismanagement*' (emphasis added).[34] The books are also unanimous in accusing British trade policy, which permitted an unrestrained outflow of grain and meat for export but imposed heavy duties on imported corn, of having seriously aggravated the Famine. Carty is particularly condemning:

> Before the Famine the British Government had been warned that the Irish people lived on the verge of starvation. They gave little heed to these warnings. In the first year of the Famine very little was done to relieve distress. Although the potato failed, there was abundance of food in the country [...] But this food was sent out of Ireland while the people starved. All creeds and parties, Catholics and Protestants, Repealers and Unionists, advised the Government to close the ports, at least for a time. This was not done [...] It was not until the Famine had been raging for nearly two years that effective measures were taken to save the people.[35]

Moreover, both Carty and Gwynn argue that immediate action would have been taken if Ireland had had a government of its own. The latter adds that 'no English Government would have dealt so with Famine in England', implying that the British government simply cared less about Ireland than England. Yet, the book also concedes 'no native government could have prevented famine from following a loss of the potato crop'.[36] Another noteworthy detail is the identification of the British government as 'the other': both Gwynn and Hayden and Moonan refer to it as the 'English' government led by the 'English' prime minister, Lord John Russell.[37]

These accounts, however, are offset by other narratives that dispel the impression that the five books present a one-sided nationalist account of the Famine. Many extracts in the books, for instance, contradict a clear-cut view that sees relations between the English and Irish as purely antagonistic, with a 'hostile other' – 'England', the British government and the landlords – inflicting harm upon an 'innocent us' – the Catholic Irish peasants. First, the books mention the substantial aid funds collected by private organisations in England, America and other countries once news of the disaster had poured in, although these charity efforts, so the books argue, were just a drop in the ocean and could not prevent the catastrophe from occurring. Second, the initial inaction of the British government is interpreted as irresponsible negligence driven by a faulty liberal ideology and insufficient knowledge of the Irish context rather than as a malicious policy of seeing as many Catholic Irish perish or emigrate as possible. Gwynn for instance points out that British politicians were deeply convinced of the correctness of a laissez-faire approach and 'counted it a crime for Government to do anything which could be done by private enterprise and private people'.[38] Or as Casserley puts it: 'The government was sympathetic, but it was not Irish; it knew little about Ireland, and understood nothing about the circum-stances of the case'.[39] Moreover, Hayden and Moonan, Carty and Casserley underline that after the initial unsuccessful measures the British government changed course and finally started implementing effective relief schemes that saved many lives. On the other hand, it is argued that many Irish and certainly those who fled Ireland in search for a better life in the Americas attributed more sinister intentions to the British government. Thus Gwynn states:

> Above all, it was impossible for the Irish not to feel, in spite of all the charity which Englishmen and Englishwomen had shown, that England was glad to see the Catholic Irish leaving their country.[40]

Similarly, in not exactly neutral terms, Hayden and Moonan say:

> The Irish emigrants who, during the Famine years, left their native land for America, carried to their new homes a bitter hatred of England,

to whose prejudices, injustices, and, perhaps, deliberate malice and treachery, they ascribed their sufferings.[41]

Most significantly, however, the books do not depict the landowning class consistently as the hostile Protestant English other. They could have easily done so given the fact that the overwhelming majority of the landlords were descendants of English Protestants who had obtained large tracts of Irish land during the Cromwellian confiscations and the years following William of Orange's victory in the Battle of the Boyne in 1690. Tellingly, the words 'Protestant', 'English' or 'foreign' are never used in combination with the word 'landlord'. In other words, the books do not see the events of the Famine through the prism of an ethnic class struggle between the good Catholic peasant 'us' and the bad Protestant landlord 'them'. Furthermore, most books contend that there were good and bad landlords. Some, they argue, would do everything within their powers to relieve the misery of their tenants, even if this meant losing all their property, while others, mostly absentees, 'subscribed not a penny for their relief, and merely grumbled that their rents were not remitted to them as usual'.[42]

In sum, the books argue that the initial stance of the British government seriously aggravated the Famine, but they refrain from attributing sole responsibility for the occurrence of the Famine to the British government. This government is seen as 'the other' by some authors, indifferent to the plight of the Irish peasant as it refused to take immediate action after the outbreak of the potato disease. British rule in Ireland is seen as a negative phenomenon as a native government – it is argued – would have performed much better. Moreover, none of the books highlight internal differences within the ethnic Irish community, which suggests that all Irish were hit by the Famine equally and that none profited from it. On the other hand, the landlords are not given an explicit ethnic label, nor are they unilaterally dismissed as ruthless exploiters of the tenants. Thus the narrative of the Famine presented by the first generation of textbooks does have a moderate nationalist colouring, but it never develops into a rancorous jingoism, as it neither accuses the 'opponent' of being ill-willed nor exploits all the available historical material to depict social relations in ethnic terms.

Educational Reform and the Second Generation of Textbooks

The end of the 1960s witnessed a major change in history education as a new generation of textbooks appeared that incorporated the tenets of a critical academic historiography. Developing since the 1940s, this 'revisionist' historiography exposed various popular accounts of key historical events as nationalist myths and endorsed the view that Irish history should be seen as 'a complex and ambivalent process rather than a morality tale'.[43] Also the teaching of national history changed as contacts with colleagues and professionals abroad, enabled by the formation of the Irish branch of the European Association of Teachers in 1961, brought Irish history teachers in touch with new views on pedagogical objectives and historical narratives. According to Magee, these international exchanges played a key role in raising the awareness among Irish history teachers that other countries had progressed further in removing from school textbooks 'the distorted judgements and prejudices engendered by recent rivalries'.[44] The changes in history education mirrored wider transformations in education and society. Motivated by a desire to leave the era of economic stagnation and excessive emigration decidedly behind and meet the needs of Ireland's industrialising economy, the Fianna Fail governments of the 1960s introduced sweeping educational reforms geared towards greater provision of education at all levels, more equality of opportunity, more emphasis on vocational, technical and scientific training, and the establishment of a comprehensive curriculum.

Educational reform also had a profound effect on history education and textbooks. A study group set up by the Department of Education on the teaching of history in schools issued a report that marked a turning point in Irish education. The report highlighted the need for new textbooks 'attractively produced and illustrated, and free from the chauvinism and the selective treatment that had disfigured school histories from the establishment of the Irish Free State'.[45] More generally, the reforms heralded a sharp increase of state and parental involvement in education at the expense of the hitherto almighty Catholic Church. The church itself changed as well, moving from a conservative bastion strictly following the orders from the Vatican to an institution primarily concerned with the spiritual and psychological well-being of its adherents.[46] Hence, Ireland was far from immune to the social processes and movements that would so profoundly change the character of Western societies from the end of the 1960s onwards.

The new history textbooks of the late 1960s and early 1970s all echo the changes called for by the report. They differ from the older textbooks in a number of ways. The most notable difference concerns the initial response of the British government. In contrast to their predecessors, the new books state that the British government, headed by Prime Minister Sir Robert Peel in 1845, *did* take immediate action after the outbreak of the disease: 'Peel's relief measures [...] were prompt, skilful, and on the whole successful'.[47] Yet, a new Whig government, the books argue, exchanged the interventionist course for a hands-off policy, in line with the prevailing *laissez-faire* ideology. The state refrained from the purchase and distribution of food, leaving these activities entirely to private enterprise and charity. It would only engage in public works, which were intended to give the poor and hungry an opportunity to work for the state and earn a modest salary. This new policy, the books explain, allowed matters to go from bad to worse so that in the end the government 'admitted defeat' by abandoning public works and extending direct relief.[48] Thus, much more so than their precursors, the books draw attention to the political processes operating in the imperial centre and try to make it understandable why the British government, the main 'other' from an Irish perspective, pursued the policies it did.

The second difference relates to the apportionment of blame for the Famine. Three of the four books explicitly state that it would not do justice to history to assign the sole responsibility for the disaster to the British government and the landlords, or worse to accuse them of deliberately creating the Famine to starve the Irish. Thus Tierney and MacCurtain write:

> Those who sailed from Ireland brought with them a bitter hatred of England and the injustices of Irish landlords. They blamed the English government for the Famine, even suggesting that the Famine had been engineered by the government to reduce the population. They also maintained that there was sufficient food in the country to keep the Irish alive, but that it was exported by the heartless landlord and ruling classes [...] It is true that there was food in Ireland during the Famine, but whether it could have been used to save the situation as a whole is doubtful. Certainly there were very few mills in the country to process the grain, and fewer ovens in which to bake bread. The Famine was caused by the almost total reliance on the potato. The blight was a natural one, and was not introduced into the country by the English.[49]

Pursuing this argument, the new books contend that the Famine was not caused by a single factor but by many. Contrary to the old books, they highlight the role of domestic circumstances. Thus, the habit of early marriage, the creation of large families, the subdivision of holdings into ever smaller patches of land and the lack of opportunities outside agriculture are all seen as having contributed to a growing population pressure on the land and to an excessive reliance on the potato as the primary food crop, thus preparing the way for the devastating impact of the potato blight in 1845 and the years thereafter. Perhaps because of the importance they attach to other than political factors, the books recoil from claiming that the Famine would not have occurred if Ireland had had its own government.

In another and related contrast to their forerunners, the new books devote much more attention to the social, economic and cultural characteristics of

Irish society during the Famine, enabling the student to have a more inside look at the events of the time. Collins, for instance, zooms in on the public works and notes that the pay for labourers was insufficient to feed a family and was often delayed for several weeks. Similarly, Neill provides an extensive narrative on the workhouses. Not only does he inform the reader about the dire conditions in the overcrowded workhouses (no heating, poor food, diseases) but he also writes that the landlords and major farmers paid for their construction and operation, a fact not mentioned by the older textbooks. All seven new books, moreover, support their close examinations of Irish society with illustrations, excerpts from primary sources, tables, graphs and maps. Neill, for instance, uses a map on the intensity of the population decline after the Famine to show how the disaster affected some regions much more than others.[50] In addition, three of the books end their section on the Famine with exercises asking students to reflect on several primary sources and to imagine themselves as mid-nineteenth-century emigrants writing a letter to one's relations back home.

Clearly, therefore, the new books present a more balanced account of the Famine than their predecessors. Their main objectives seem to be to provide a sociological insight into the causes of the Famine and to stimulate student creativity rather than to inculcate a nationalist anti-English outlook and encourage the rote-learning of taken for granted knowledge. This is not to say that the books are not critical of the British government or the landlords. Tierney and MacCurtain for instance note concerning the latter:

> Very few landlords considered it their duty to invest any money in improving the soil or encouraging their tenants to work their holdings in an enlightened way. The Irish landlords took their standards of living from their far richer English brethren and were for the most part living in debt. This led them to exact the last possible penny from their unfortunate tenants.[51]

Yet when dealing with landlord–tenant relations the books are careful not to depict this issue in a one-sided 'Irish/Catholic good – English/Protestant bad' fashion. Thus both Collins and Kirkpatrick remark that it was mostly Irishmen who profited from the bankruptcy of many landlords. By evicting many small farmers and cottiers, these new Irish landowners, they argue, were no less harsh on their tenants than their forerunners:

> Many hundreds of landlords had gone bankrupt during and after the Famine and needed to sell their estates to pay of their debts [...] The new owners were usually businessmen, often wealthy Dublin Catholics, who had little interest beyond making sure of getting the rent on time.[52]

The textbooks appearing in the 1980s and 1990s present historical accounts that are almost an exact copy of those of their immediate precursors. The only feature that distinguishes them from the generation of the 1960s and '70s is the use of even more different visual aids to enliven the narrative. Thus Sobolewski and McDonald rely heavily on comics to tell the story of the Famine.[53] They introduce a narrator in the shape of a comic figure to give critical comments on the events of the time. Similarly, Brockie and Walsh make use of new techniques like bullet points, eyewitness accounts, graphs, and a box with pictures and text showing contrasting conditions in England and Ireland.[54] Thus the youngest generation of textbooks is even more inspired by pupil centred learning.

The Famine in Ukrainian History Textbooks

In Ukraine national renaissance was advocated by Rukh, a popular movement that united the fragmented opposition against the communist party in the late 1980s. As in Ireland, this national revival movement rose to prominence when the country was still part of the larger empire. In Ukraine, however, the period from the inception of the national movement to the establishment of independence was much shorter than in Ireland because Gorbachev's glasnost and perestroika, which had enabled Rukh to flourish, spun out of control so quickly that the Soviet Union broke up before Rukh could have developed into a coherent opposition movement. In fact, while the Baltic nations immediately seized upon the opportunities of glasnost and perestroika by founding popular fronts as early as 1987, the conservative party leadership in Ukraine managed to keep reform at bay and to ignore critical voices until mid-1989. In August of that year, however, the Ukrainian party elite turned its back on Moscow, and transformed itself overnight into 'true Ukrainian patriots' to ensure their political survival.[55] From that moment Rukh quickly gained mass support and became an influential political force, although it never became as popular as the national movements in the Baltics where Soviet rule had left fewer traces (in Ukraine the Russification of the native population had been much more pervasive than in the Baltics).

Nonetheless, undisturbed by the limited appeal of Rukh in the more populous and urbanised Russian-speaking South and East of Ukraine, Leonid Kravchuk, the first president of the new republic, appointed many Rukh members to his government. Once in office these national activists energetically set about establishing and implementing a Ukrainian 'affirmative action' programme designed to undo Russification and make Ukrainian the sole language used in public domains. Although, as in Ireland, the emphasis was on language, national history followed closely in the hierarchy of priorities. In contrast to its Irish counterpart, the Ukrainian Ministry of Education assumed control not only over history curricula and examinations but also over the textbook production and adoption process and has continued to do so until the present. In cooperation with the National Academy of Sciences, the Academy of Pedagogical Sciences and private publishers and foundations, it organises annual competitions for new textbooks. A jury composed of scholars and experts evaluates the books on readability, overall quality and correspondence to the curriculum plan. The books passing the competition are subsequently tried and tested in several school districts. Only after a successful probation period in schools do the books receive the approval of the Ministry of Education and will they be included on the list of officially recommended textbooks.[56] Schools are obliged to use the standard recommended textbooks but are free to use any kind of additional materials.

The Ministry split history education in schools into two subjects – History of Ukraine and World History. The institution of a separate course on national history is indicative of the importance assigned to the subject in promoting national identity. This is also underlined by statements in the curriculum plans for national history. The 1996 plan, for instance, asserts that one of the course's objectives is to 'educate pupils in a patriotic spirit so that they cultivate a love for their nation'.[57]

The curriculum for History of Ukraine acquaints pupils with the Famine on two occasions in their school career, in the fifth grade when a bird's-eye view of national history is presented and in the tenth grade when the history of the first half of the twentieth century is discussed. Given the direct political causes of the Ukrainian Famine one would expect the first post-independence textbook for the fifth grade to display a particularly one-sided and condemning account, but that is not quite the case. Thus it states:

> The harvest of 1932 was not any less successful than those of the previous years. Hence there was no reason for the Famine. Stalin, however, wanted to accelerate industrialisation – to build more factories and build them quicker. He needed a lot of money for that. Therefore it was decided to increase the sale of corn abroad and to get the corn from Ukrainian peasants at any price. At the same time Stalin expected that he could put the Ukrainian peasants, who had shown more resistance to collectivisation than for instance the Russian peasantry, under heavy pressure with this measure. However, as the peasants made up a substantial part of the Ukrainian population, the Famine basically meant the starvation of the Ukrainian nation.[58]

True, on the one hand the book contends that Stalin specifically attacked the Ukrainian peasantry with the Famine. One could argue that this constitutes a nationalist distortion as the Famine also claimed many victims in areas outside Ukraine, notably in the lower Volga and Kuban regions.[59] On the other hand the book does not argue that the Ukrainian nation was deliberately attacked by the Soviet regime. In fact, the book gives a meaningful explanation for the exceptional vigour of the collectivisation campaign in Ukraine: the Ukrainian peasantry resisted collectivisation more than the Russian peasantry. In addition it states that the policy of food confiscations was primarily motivated by Stalin's desire to industrialise the country. These remarks attenuate the impression that the Soviet regime was particularly hostile to the Ukrainians.

In 1994 two parallel textbooks for the tenth grade appeared, followed a year later by Russian translations for the (steadily decreasing number of) Russian schools in Ukraine. The first of these books, *Istoria Ukrainy* by Stanislav Kul'chitskii et al., was still a trial version, the Ukrainian edition of which numbered 500,000 copies and the Russian one 300,000 copies.[60] The second book, *Noveishaia Istoriia Ukrainy* by Fedir Turchenko, was a genuine textbook of which more than one million copies were printed.[61] This book, which closely followed the curriculum, came to be the standard textbook used in schools.[62] A comparison of the two books reveals that, despite presenting the same facts about the famine period, the latter presents a more radical interpretation of events than the former. This is first of all reflected in the terminology. Turchenko's text is littered with words carrying strong negative value judgements, all of which are used to characterise Stalin's regime. We read, for example, about the 'cruel crimes' of Stalinism, about 'cruel aggressors', the 'monstrous' scale of the Famine in Ukraine, victims of the 'genocide' of 1932–33, and about a totalitarian regime 'terrorising' the countryside.[63] Kul'chitskii et al. are equally condemning of Stalin's regime but refrain from using emotionally charged terms.

A second difference concerns the identification of the victims. Whereas Kul'chitskii et al. argue that the collectivisation campaign and the confiscations of food were aimed solely at the peasants – 'In reality however these activities were consciously geared towards the slow physical annihilation of peasant families'[64] – Turchenko tends to extend victimhood to the whole Ukrainian nation. Thus he opens his account of the Famine with the following statement: 'One of the most cruel crimes committed by Stalinism against the Ukrainian nation was the Famine of 1932–1933'.[65] In the concluding paragraph he writes:

> The Tragedy of 1932–1933 decisively crushed the resistance against the Kolchoz-feudal system and essentially blew up the forces that stood up for the vexed national rights. This is precisely what the totalitarian regime aimed for, what its representatives in Ukraine cynically discussed.[66]

These extracts leave the impression that the rest of the Ukrainian nation was as much assailed by the Soviet authorities as the peasants resisting collectivisation. Although Turchenko acknowledges that regions with an intensive agriculture outside Ukraine, such as the North Caucasus, the Kuban, the lower Volga and North Kazakhstan, also suffered greatly from the Famine, he claims that it assumed 'the most monstrous proportions' in Ukraine.[67] In fact, the radical tone of Turchenko's book extends to other topics. Thus its account of the Second World War offended many left-wing deputies in the Ukrainian parliament, who felt that the book's portrayal of Ukraine as a neutral victim of both warring parties in the Second World War, as suffering from both Nazi terror and the re-institution of the 'Stalinist totalitarian regime', was a serious misrepresentation of reality.[68]

Another conspicuous contrast between Kul'chitskii et al. and Turchenko concerns the achievements of collectivised agriculture in the years following the Famine. Whereas the former presents a predominantly upbeat account of the initial results of the Kolkhozes and Sovkhozes, the latter mentions only negative consequences of the collectivisation. Thus, Kul'chitskii et al. argue that because of improvements in the organisational structure and in the technological and mechanical support the collective farms managed quickly to overcome the food crisis (they substantiate this claim by showing how the harvest of corn rose from 317 million pood[69] in 1933 to 496 million pood in 1937). In addition they state that the collective farms started diversifying their agricultural activities and that the *kolkhozniki* (workers on Kolkhozes) were granted interest-free credits for the purchase of cattle.[70] For Turchenko collectivisation brought nothing but misery. He contends that 'the forced labour' [in collective farms] was not very effective, that the Kolkhozniki were paid 'appallingly low' prices for their produce and that due to the collectivisation drive the peasantry lost its 'entrepreneurial spirit, individualism and work ethos', held to be its most valuable character traits.[71]

This brief review of the first generation of textbooks tells us that despite the unanimous strong condemnation of the role of the Soviet regime in the unfolding of the Famine, there are considerable differences between the textbooks in tone and, to a lesser extent, selection of events. The books further do not claim that Stalin specifically targeted the Ukrainian nation with the Famine, although Turchenko, the most influential textbook of the three, is more ambiguous on this issue. Moreover, none of them engages in ethnic stereotyping as the Soviet government and the officials responsible for the collectivisation programme in Ukraine are not marked as Russians or Jews. Thus, the conclusion seems warranted that the books have not exploited the available historical material for nationalist purposes to the fullest extent. Yet, the downside of not addressing ethnic differences is that the books do not provide anecdotes that would present Ukrainians in an unfavourable light. Thus the participation of many ethnic Ukrainians in the grain-requisition bands that pillaged the countryside[72] is an unpleasant fact not mentioned by any of the textbooks. This leaves the impression that ethnic Ukrainians were only victims of the collectivisation campaign.

In 1994 President Kravchuk had to make way for Leonid Kuchma, a Russian speaking Ukrainian from Dnipropetrovs'k, who advocated closer ties with Russia and favoured granting Russian official status. However, once in power, Kuchma failed to keep his promise to lift the status of Russian. The officials appointed by him, such as the education ministers Mykhailo Zgurovskyi and Vasyl Kremen, consolidated the cultural policies established by the previous administration. This change of form but not of content is by and large reflected in the textbooks. Thus, the newest book for the fifth grade written by Misan presents an account of the Famine which is almost similar to that of Kucheruk.[73] It also mentions the reluctance of the Ukrainian peasantry to enter the collective farms and the reasons Stalin had for pursuing the collectivisation of agriculture ('the construction of new factories, power plants and dwellings').[74] Remarkably, another book for the fifth grade (Vlasov and Danilevs'ka 1999), published some years earlier, is more radical in tone. It makes extensive use of the strong normative terminology so often found in nationalist narratives and does not address the main reason for the regime to undertake collectivisation.[75] It also fails to mention that the famine occurred in other areas of the Soviet Union as well. Moreover, it seems dangerously close to supporting the view that the Famine was as much directed at the Ukrainian nation as at the peasantry. The book for instance states:

> The second half of the 1920s saw the beginning of the violent establishment of collective enterprises – Kolkhozes. The land, horses, cattle and working tools were taken from the farmers by means of force [...] Having been [independent, JGJ] corn-growers for generations, they became tenants without rights – *kolkhoznik* [...] To resolutely break the resistance of the Ukrainian corn-growers the Bolshevist leaders in Moscow decided to organise a deliberate famine [...] Simultaneously with the extermination of the Ukrainian peasantry, the Bolshevik government started waging a war against Ukrainian education, academia and art.[76]

The textbooks for the tenth grade did not change much in content either. The later editions of Turchenko, for instance, contain only marginal alterations.[77] They lost some of the most controversial terms – we do not see the word 'genocide' anymore – and include an acknowledgement that the government offered some help to the peasantry in the late spring of 1933, but in all other respects their accounts of the Famine are an exact copy of that of its predecessor. The new editions of Kul'chitskii do contain some noteworthy changes compared with their forerunner.[78] Although the content mostly stayed the same, the form of the narrative is different with less text and the inclusion of several pieces of documentary evidence and a map showing the regional variations in intensity of the Famine. Students, moreover, are asked to draw their own conclusions from the presented documents. These modifications in form could be an indication that pedagogical motivations (readability, developing interpretation and presentation skills) are becoming more important than nation-building objectives.

Change might indeed be in the air as the Ministry of Education recently approved a supplementary book for the tenth grade that was prepared by the all-Ukrainian association of history teachers Nova Doba in cooperation with the European Standing Conference of History Teachers' Associations (Euroclio), and many Ukrainian and Western experts.[79] This book closely resembles Western textbooks in approach and teaching method as it presents a variety of historical sources and encourages pupils to work independently and make their own inferences from the material presented.

Discussion

The analysis of textbooks has shown that Ireland started out with moderately nationalist accounts of the Famine and has exchanged these for balanced narratives since the end of the 1960s. Educational reform, contacts with history teachers abroad, the loss of influence of the Catholic Church, and the appearance of a generation of critically minded historians have all contributed to this change. The textbooks appearing from the 1960s not only have more balanced accounts of the Famine but also highlight socio-economic themes and micro-histories and present the material in a more diverse manner, inviting pupils to work independently with the textbooks. They thus reflect a shift away from rote learning and the cultivation of an Irish national consciousness as pedagogical objectives to fostering broad sociological understanding, critical thinking skills and an attitude of independent enquiry. The Irish pattern of textbook narratives clearly lends support to Kuzio's developmental perspective. As noted above, this perspective expected neutral historiography to gradually replace nationalistically inspired narratives as part of a change from ethnic to civic nations in young states growing to maturity and consolidating democratic structures.

Unsurprisingly, the Ukrainian textbooks are highly disapproving of the policy of the Soviet government during the years of the Famine. They all highlight the many deaths from starvation in the countryside and argue that the government consciously used a policy of famine to crush the resistance of the peasantry to the collectivisation of agriculture. Ukrainians are only portrayed as victims of the Famine: the participation of ethnic Ukrainians in the food confiscation brigades is omitted. Nonetheless, the variation among textbooks in tone and content is conspicuous. Whereas some follow the (emerging) international historical consensus closely, others are much more radical in the selection and interpretation of materials, and hence can be said to display several nationalist distortions. The most influential textbook (written by Turchenko for the tenth grade) falls into the last category. It contrasts sharply with its main competitor (the tenth-grade textbook written by Kul'chitskii et al.) in the account of the Famine and of the first results of the collectivised system.

This variation in Ukrainian textbook narratives is difficult for the three perspectives on nationalist historiography to explain. It certainly does not support the postcommunist perspective, which expected to see a uniform nationalist account of the Famine replacing an equally uniform but ideologically different Soviet account. Paradoxically, while the Ukrainian state exerts more control over the textbook production and dissemination process than the early Irish state did, the Ukrainian textbooks are at least as varied in tone and content as their Irish counterparts in the 1920s and 1930s. State supervision thus need not stand in the way of a variety of opinions. Possibly, state control of textbooks is more token than real given that the textbook review and selection process is mostly undertaken by peers (academics and teachers) and not by civil servants from the Department of Education.

The finding that the Ukrainian textbook narratives are in fact quite varied is of great significance. It indicates that a monolithic politicised historiography is not automatically replaced by an equally intolerant nationalist discourse in young states emerging from a period of authoritarian rule, contrary to the expectation of leading theories. This conclusion is still tentative, however, as many other topics and other countries need to be drawn into the comparison to arrive at a more finite judgement. In this regard it is interesting to briefly review textbook issues in other post-Soviet states to assess whether Ukraine is the exception confirming the rule or whether other post-Soviet states also show a diversity of textbook narratives.

To begin with Kazakhstan, Carolyn Kissane has described how the post-Soviet government has seized on history education to promote a de-Sovietised Kazakh ethno-national identity. After independence it instituted a separate national history course for which it ordered new textbooks to be written. These textbooks paint Russian–Kazakh relations in antagonistic terms: Russia is depicted as a hostile neighbour that violently incorporated Kazakhstan in the nineteenth century to exploit it as a colony. However, the new programme for the course of World History, issued in 2000, counterbalances the ethno-nationalism of these textbooks by adopting a multi-ethnic approach that sees

Russian–Kazakh relations in a more positive light. Nonetheless, as of 1999, schools were no longer permitted to use textbooks for World History published outside Kazakhstan, which sharply reduced options for teachers to acquaint themselves and their pupils with different perspectives.[80]

In Russia history education is no longer as monolithic as it used to be either. Robert Maier recounts how a fierce battle erupted in the mid-1990s between reform-minded historians who sought to challenge nationalist myths in Russia's history and practitioners and politicians who held more traditional views. Interestingly, he mentions the example of a modern textbook endorsed by the Federal Ministry of Education that was blacklisted by the *Duma* of the Voronezh region. The deputies of this local parliament believed that the book, which was partly financed by the Soros Foundation, 'undermined the dignity of the "fatherland's" history and culture' and was a conscious attempt by foreign agents to poison the minds of innocent Russian children.[81]

Moldova presents another case of a post-Soviet state where different interpretations and approaches to the past coexist in an uneasy manner. The controversy in this country concerns the recent attempt by the communist government to replace the two courses of History of the Romanians and World History by the single course Integrated History, which combines national and international history. This initiative was welcomed by the Council of Europe, Euroclio and Western scholars who had criticised the History of Romanians course and its textbooks for having a pro-Romanian bias that excludes the country's minorities. However, at the grassroots level ethnic Romanian teachers and parents rejected the new course, which they saw as a shrewd and covert manoeuvre by the government to re-Sovietise and de-nationalise the Romanian Moldovans.[82]

These examples show that a diversity of historical interpretations is not just confined to Ukraine among the post-Soviet states. However, it is doubtful whether this diversity also reflects a conviction that diverging historical views are part of a democratic society and therefore deserve respect. Judging from the eruptions of anger following textbook reform and from the attempts at both central and local levels to censor unwanted interpretations, the emerging pluralism of historical thought may well be fledgling and temporary. It remains to be seen, for instance, whether the current Russian government, which has declared patriotic education a key priority,[83] is as committed to a diversity of opinions as the government of the mid-1990s was when Maier carried out his study. Moreover, Ukraine and the other three countries examined are relatively open post-Soviet societies. It is unlikely that the authoritarian regimes of Belarus and Turkmenistan are permitting a diversity of historical views.

This brings us back to textbook developments in Ukraine. As noted before, a supplementary book has recently appeared that echoed Western books in pedagogical approach. Tellingly, this book resulted from a cooperation project between the Ukrainian Association of History Teachers and Euroclio. A clear parallel can be drawn here with the Irish context where contacts with history teachers abroad have also marked the beginning of new approaches in teaching aids and materials. International contacts are thus important for the incorporation of new views and approaches. Indeed, it is difficult to imagine pluralist even-handed histories, which by necessity are the product of discussions with peers abroad, being written in an isolated society ruled by an (authoritarian) regime fearful of foreign influences that might undermine its hold on power. In this regard, it can be expected that history textbook writing in Ukraine will increasingly open up to the outside world after a pro-Western reform minded government came to power following the turbulent presidential elections in December 2004, provided this government remains committed to democracy, freedom of speech and the rule of law.

Notes and References

1 First published in *History of Education* 35, no. 3 (2006): 345–68. The author is grateful to Andy Green and to the two anonymous *History of Education* reviewers for their useful comments on earlier drafts of this article. The British Academy is thanked for providing the financial support that made the research for this article possible.
2 William E. Marsden, '"Poisoned History": A Comparative Study of Nationalism, Propaganda and the Treatment of War and Peace in the Late Nineteenth- and Early Twentieth-Century School Curriculum', *History of Education* 29 (2000): 29–47.
3 In 1949 for example UNESCO published a programme for peace education that was intended as a model for school books to follow. See UNESCO (ed.), *A Handbook for the Improvement of Textbooks and Teaching Materials as Aids to International Understanding* (Paris: UNESCO, 1949).
4 Volker R. Berghahn and H. Schissler, 'Introduction: History Textbooks and Perceptions of the Past', in V. R. Berghahn and H. Schissler (eds), *Perceptions of History: International Textbook Research on Britain, Germany and the United States* (Oxford: Berg, 1987), 3.
5 David Coulby, 'Educational Responses to Diversity within the State', in D. Coulby, J. Gundara and C. Jones (eds), *World Yearbook of Education: Intercultural Education* (London: Kogan Page, 1997); Costa Carras, 'Preface', in C. Koulouri (ed.), *Teaching the History of South-Eastern Europe* (Thessaloniki: Center for Democracy and Reconciliation in Southeast Europe, 2001).
6 Michael Ignatieff, *Blood and Belonging: A Journey into the New Nationalism* (London: Vintage, 1994); Jack Snyder, 'Nationalism and the Crisis of the Post-Soviet State', *Survival* 35 (1993): 5–26.
7 From the Act of Union in 1800, which abolished the parliament in Dublin, to the proclamation of the Irish Free State, Ireland was an integral part of the United Kingdom of Great Britain and Ireland. The Soviet Union was formally a federal state with autonomous Union Republics, one of which was Ukraine. Formally these republics also had the right to leave the Union. In practice, however, the Soviet Union was a highly centralised state.

8 This argument has to be qualified somewhat as Ukraine now has several Orthodox churches all claiming to represent the community of Orthodox believers in Ukraine. A sizeable minority, concentrated in the western part of Ukraine, professes the Greek Catholic or Uniate religion.
9 Hans Kohn, 'Western and Eastern Nationalism', in J. Hutchinson and A. D. Smith (eds), *Nationalism* (Oxford: Oxford University Press, 1994), 164.
10 Hans Kohn, *The Idea of Nationalism: A Study in its Origins and Background* (New York: Macmillan, 1944).
11 Well-known journalists and scholars influenced by Kohn's writings, for example, are Michael Ignatieff (see note 6), and Liah Greenfeld, *Nationalism: Five Roads to Modernity* (Cambridge, MA: Harvard University Press, 1992). For scholars critical of the Kohn framework see Will Kymlicka, 'Misunderstanding nationalism', in R. Beiner (ed.), *Theorizing Nationalism* (Albany: State University of New York Press, 1999) and Stephen Shulman, 'Challenging the Civic/Ethnic and West/East Dichotomies in the Study of Nationalism', *Comparative Political Studies* 55 (2002): 554–85.
12 John Plamenatz, 'Two Types of Nationalism', in E. Kamenka (ed.) *Nationalism: The Nature and Evolution of an Idea* (London: Edward Arnold, 1976); Stephen Velychenko, *Shaping Identity in Eastern Europe and Russia: Soviet-Russian and Polish Accounts of Ukrainian History, 1914–1991* (New York: St Martin's Press, 1993). Velychenko for instance contends that nationalist sentiments are much stronger in the 'poorer, authoritarian' societies 'east of the Elbe' than in the 'wealthier, pluralist and constitutional societies' of the West, and that national historiography has emotive and even explosive potential in the former if it is deemed essential for group survival (ibid., 18).
13 Kohn is not alone in seeing Irish nationalism developing in an ethno-cultural direction from the 1870s. See, for instance, Bill Kissane, 'Nineteenth-Century Nationalism in Finland and Ireland: A Comparative Analysis', *Nationalism and Ethnic Politics* 6 (2000), 25–42.
14 Taras Kuzio, 'The Myth of the Civic State: A Critical Survey of Hans Kohn's Framework for Understanding Nationalism', *Ethnic and Racial Studies* 25 (2002): 20–39; Anthony D. Smith, *National Identity* (London: Penguin, 1991); Eric Kaufmann, 'Ethnic or Civic Nation? Theorizing the American Case', *Canadian Review of Studies in Nationalism* 27 (2000):133–55.
15 George Schöpflin, *Nations, Identity, Power* (London: Hurst & Company, 2000).
16 Viktor Stepanenko, *The Construction of Identity and School Policy in Ukraine* (New York: Nova Science Publishers, 1999), 113.
17 Bogdan Krawchenko, *Social Change and National Consciousness in Twentieth-Century Ukraine* (London: Macmillan, 1985); Orest Subtelny, *Ukraine: A History* (Toronto: University of Toronto Press, 1994); Andrew Wilson, *The Ukrainians: Unexpected Nation* (New Haven: Yale University Press, 2002). Wilson for instance labels the Ukrainian Famine as 'deliberate and brutal, but part of an ideological rather than a national war' (ibid., 145).
18 The potato blight also struck other parts of the British Isles and caused great hardship there (notably in Scotland), but mass starvation was narrowly avoided.
19 In addition to a rapidly growing Russian minority prewar Ukraine had a sizeable Jewish population of primarily urban dwellers.
20 Brian J. Mulcahy, *A Study of the Relationship between Ireland and England as Portrayed in Irish Post-Primary School History Text Books, Published Since 1922, and Dealing with the Period 1800 to the Present* (PhD diss., University of Hull, 1988), 2. The two textbooks from the 1990s selected for the analysis (see below) were not part of Mulcahy's study.
21 Thomas O'Donoghue, *The Catholic Church and the Secondary School Curriculum in Ireland, 1922–1962* (New York: Peter Lang, 1999).

22 Ibid., 79.
23 These books can be found on the list of approved textbooks for the 1996–97 school year. This list was published in *Informatsiinyi Zbirnyk Ministerstva Osvity Ukrainy* (Collection of Information of the Ministry of Education of Ukraine) no. 12 (1996): 4–6.
24 These books can be found on the list of approved textbooks for the 2004–2005 school year. This list was published in *Osvita Ukrainy* (Education of Ukraine) nos. 60–61 (2004): 15–18.
25 Sean Farren, *The Politics of Irish Education 1920–65* (Belfast: Queen's University of Belfast, Institute of Irish Studies, 1995); Thomas A. O'Donoghue, 'Catholic Influence and the Secondary School Curriculum in Ireland, 1922–1962', *History of Education Review* 28 (1999): 16–29.
26 John M. Coolahan, *A Study of Curricular Policy for the Primary and Secondary Schools of Ireland, 1900–1935, with Special Reference to the Irish Language and Irish History* (PhD diss., Trinity College Dublin, 1973).
27 Quoted in Farren, *The Politics of Irish Education*, 107.
28 Mulcahy, *A Study of the Relationship*.
29 John Magee, 'The Teaching of Irish History in Irish Schools', *The Northern Teacher* 10 (1970): 15–21.
30 O'Donoghue, *The Catholic Church*, 69.
31 R. F. Foster, 'History and the Irish Question', in C. Brady (ed.), *Interpreting Irish History: The Debate on Historical Revisionism* (Dublin: Irish Academic Press, 1994).
32 Gabriel Doherty, 'The Irish History Textbook, 1900–1960. Problems and Development', *Oideas* 42 (1994): 5–25.
33 Foster, 'History and the Irish Question', 139.
34. *The Educational History of Ireland*, 97.
35 Carty, *A Junior History of Ireland*, 72, 73.
36 Gwynn, *The Student's History of Ireland*, 261.
37 Ibid., 260, 261; Hayden and Moonan, *A Short History*, 496, 497.
38 Gwynn, *The Student's History of Ireland*, 261
39 Casserley, *History of Ireland*, 108.
40 Ibid., 268.
41 Hayden and Moonan, *A Short History*, 499.
42 Ibid., 498.
43 Foster, 'History and the Irish Question', 140.
44 Magee, 'The Teaching of Irish History in Irish Schools', 17.
45 Ibid., 16.
46 O'Donoghue, 'Catholic Influence'.
47 R. Green, 'The Great Famine (1845–50)', in T. W. Moody and F. X. Martin (eds), *The Course of Irish History* (Cork: Mercier Press, 1967), 268.
48 Ibid., 270.
49 Tierney and MacCurtain, *The Birth of Modern Ireland*, 59.
50 Neill, *The Age of Steam and Steal*, 57.
51 Tierney and MacCurtain, *The Birth of Modern Ireland*, 54.
52 Kirkpatrick, *The Nineteenth Century*, 156.
53 Sobolewski and McDonald, *Let's Look at History Part 2*.
54 Brockie and Walsh, *Focus on the Past*.
55 E. Krylach and S. Kul'chytskyi. 'Die Diskussionen in der Ukraine über die Schulbücher zur Vaterländischen Geschichte', in I. de Keghel and R. Maier (eds), *Auf den Kehrichthaufen der Geschichte? Der Umgang mit der sozialistischen Vergangenheit* (Hannover: Hahnsche Buchhandlung, 1999).

56 Nancy Popson, 'The Ukrainian History Textbook: Introducing Children to the Ukrainian Nation', *Nationalities Papers* 29 (2001): 325–50; see also Jan Germen Janmaat, 'Identity Construction and Education: The History of Ukraine in Soviet and Post-Soviet Schoolbooks', in T. Kuzio and P. D'Anieri (eds), *Dilemmas of State-Led Nation Building in Ukraine* (London: Praeger, 2002), 171–89.
57 *Prohramy dlia Serednoi Zahal'noosvitn'oi Shkoly: Istoriia Ukrainy 5–11 Klasy; Vsesvitnia Istoriia 6–11 Klasy* (Programmes for Secondary Comprehensive Schools: History of Ukraine, grades 5–11; World History, grades 6–11) (Kiev: Perun, 1996): 9.
58 Kucheruk, *Opovidannia z Istorii Ukrainy*, 186.
59 Wilson, *The Ukrainians: Unexpected Nation*.
60 Kul'chitskii, Kurnosov and Koval', *Istoriia Ukrainy*.
61 Turchenko, *Noveishaia Istoriia Ukrainy*. The title is given in a transcription from Russian as I read the Russian translation of the Ukrainian original. The same applies for Kul'chitskii, Kurnosov and Koval', *Istoriia Ukrainy*.
62 Krylach and Kul'chytskyi, 'Die Diskussionen in der Ukraine'.
63 Turchenko, *Noveishaia Istoria Ukrainy*, 225–8.
64 Kul'chitskii, Kurnosov and Koval', *Istoriia Ukrainy*, 194.
65 Turchenko, *Noveishaia Istoria Ukrainy*, 225.
66 Ibid., 227.
67 Ibid.
68 Krylach and Kul'chytskyi, 'Die Diskussionen in der Ukraine'. For the quotation see Turchenko, *Noveishaia Istoriia Ukrainy*, 310.
69 One pood is 16.38 kg.
70 Kul'chitskii, Kurnosov and Koval', *Istoriia Ukrainy*, 255.
71 Turchenko, *Noveishaia Istoriia Ukrainy*, 230.
72 Wilson, *The Ukrainians: Unexpected Nation*.
73 Misan, *Opovidannia z Istoriia Ukrainy*.
74 Ibid., 170.
75 Vlasov and Danilevs'ka, *Vstup do Istorii Ukrainy*.
76 Ibid., 234–5.
77 Turchenko, *Novitnia Istoria Ukrainy*.
78 Kul'chitskii, Koval' and Lebedeva, *Istoriia Ukrainy*; Kul'chyts'kyi and Shapoval, *Novitnia Istoriia Ukrainy*.
79 Y. Komarov, V. Mysan, A. Osmolovs'kyi, S. Bilonozhko and O. Zaitsev. *Istoriia Epokhy Ochyma Liudyny: Ukraina ta Evropa y 1900–1939 Rokakh, 10 Klas* (Kiev: Heneza, 2004). This book is included in the list of textbooks and supplementary books for the 2004–2005 school year. See *Osvita Ukrainy* (note 25).
80 Carolyn Kissane, 'History Education in Transit: Where to for Kazakhstan?' *Comparative Education* 41 (2005): 45–69.
81 Robert Maier, 'Learning about Europe and the World: Schools, Teachers, and Textbooks in Russia after 1991', in H. Schissler and Y. N. Soysal (eds), *The Nation, Europe, and the World: Textbooks and Curricula in Transition* (Oxford: Berghahn Books 2005), 144.
82 Elizabeth A. Anderson, 'Backwards, Forwards, or Both? Moldovan Teachers' Relationships to the State and the Nation', *European Education* 37, no. 3 (2005): 53–67.
83 Nelli Piattoeva, 'Citizenship education as an expression of democratisation and nation-building processes in Russia', *European Education* 37, no. 3 (2005): 38–52.

Chapter 5

TEACHING HUNGER: THE GREAT IRISH FAMINE CURRICULUM IN NEW YORK STATE SCHOOLS

Maureen O. Murphy
Hofstra University, New York

The impetus for the Great Irish Famine Curriculum originated from initiatives that came from both sides of the narrow street in Albany, New York, that separates the chambers of the New York State Legislature from the headquarters of the New York State Education Department. In 1996, the State Education Department began to distribute copies of its new Learning Standards, the performance-based learning criteria designed to improve the quality of education in the State's public schools. A new set of assessments would be designed to ensure that all pupils in grades four, eight and eleven had reached the appropriate standards of competence in each of the middle and secondary school subjects. Because the assessments would be performance-based, no curricula were provided for the new standards.

The following year, on the 150th anniversary of the worst year of the Great Irish Famine, Ann Garvey, president of the American Irish Teachers Association, approached Assemblyman Joseph Crowley, a member of the New York State Legislature, to urge that the a study of the Great Irish Famine be a required strand in the State Education Department's Human Rights Curriculum which, at that time, included the Atlantic Slave Trade and the European Holocaust. Crowley introduced the bill and steered it though the legislative process where it had enthusiastic bi-partisan support and was passed after a short debate. The Legislature and the Office of the Governor provided a budget of $200,000 to develop the curriculum and issued a call for submissions.[1]

The Hofstra University team of Maureen Murphy, Alan Singer and Maureen Miletta, subject specialists who are teacher educators, responded with an application that described a curriculum framed by the new Learning Standards in all of the disciplines: career development, civics, dance, economics, family and consumer science, fine arts, geography, history, language arts, math, music, science, technology and the performing arts, that would teach the Great Irish Famine as a model of a way to teach about hunger and homelessness. The Hofstra team's proposal included a narrative that described its pedagogy and a budget that explained how the State grant would support the development and field testing phases as well as the publication of the curriculum in paper and in electronic form for each of New York State's public and private elementary, middle and secondary schools. On 22 October 1998, the Hofstra team was notified that its application was the winning proposal. It succeeded, in part, because it included a Board of Advisors composed of Irish and American Great Irish Famine historians to supervise the academic quality of the project. It proposed to integrate its Great Irish Famine Curriculum with the Learning Standards, and it promised to deliver an effective interactive, interdisciplinary pedagogy with a more inclusive vision than the exceptionalism that characterised other applicants' submissions.

James V. Mullin, chair of the New Jersey Irish Famine Curriculum Committee that became part of New Jersey's Holocaust Education Curriculum, an unsuccessful applicant for the New York State grant, was the Hofstra grant's most persistent critic.[2] He challenged the team at professional meetings and criticised the Great Irish Famine Curriculum in *The Irish People* for being too easy on the British government. While Mullin answered that he wanted students to make up their own minds whether the Great Irish Famine was genocide, his curriculum is a narrative to be mastered. The Hofstra Great Irish Famine Curriculum asks students to think like historians: to examine a variety of primary source documents and to draw their own conclusions. As educators, we trust the integrity of the sources and the ability of students to read with understanding, to draw conclusions based on evidence and to speak and write with clarity. Faced with a variety of historical evidence and given a variety of ways to approach the material and to make meaning of it, students studying the curriculum learn what the lessons of the Great Irish Famine have to teach us today about hunger and homelessness. We endeavour to engage students in actively responding to these issues. In addition, the curriculum seeks to enhance students' awareness and appreciation of the experiences and identities of diverse peoples who have suffered from hunger and homelessness in the past and in the world today.

One of our goals in designing the Great Irish Famine Curriculum was to write Ireland into the teaching of world history, a required subject in secondary schools in New York State. We provide content-rich lessons in the other disciplines that facilitate students' demonstration of mastery of the Learning

Standards. We promised in our proposal to produce 24 lessons; in fact, we produced 150 interdisciplinary, project-based lessons for students in grades 4–12. The Great Irish Famine Curriculum, as one of the strands of the state's Human Rights Curriculum, asks students to look at the common themes: human suffering and the development of policies and strategies to remedy or ameliorate conditions responsible for slavery, genocide and famine. Our lessons that focus on the Great Irish Famine in the context of other famines are designed to develop students' understanding of the factors that contribute to hunger and to encourage them to develop an awareness of hunger in their own communities and to become active volunteers in programs and organisations that offer food and other support and services to the poor.

Our Great Irish Famine Curriculum asks students to consider four major questions. The first asked students to consider the forces that shaped Ireland and the world before the Great Irish Famine. Did the 'Columbian Encounter', British and European colonialism and the Industrial Revolution contribute to the conditions that created the Great Irish Famine and the Irish diaspora? These topics prompt students and teachers to read, think, speak and write about some of the big questions in world history. How can a thing or event transform history? What role does religion play in human history? How does technology change the way people live and work? Are famines more often acts of nature or are they the result of decisions made by people and governments? What are the consequences of ethnic prejudice? What is the responsibility of a government in the time of disaster? What is the responsibility of the media when it reports the news? What are the responsibilities of individuals when they are faced with injustice or calamity? What are the origins and consequences of imperialism? What constitutes human rights and how are they protected? What is genocide? Can individuals and groups shape the future?

Our first question involved looking at the historical forces, social conditions and political concepts like colonialism and family and developing an understanding of family and community life in Ireland before the Great Irish Famine. Concerned that students realise that while the rural Irish lived in conditions of economic poverty, they had a rich cultural life, we included lessons about oral tradition, music, dance and sport in pre-famine Ireland. Our attention to the community aspects of wake traditions prepared students for the significance of the bleak, often clandestine, burials of those who died during the Great Irish Famine. (Many local 1997 famine commemorations were sited in the famine graveyards to mark posthumously the hastily buried dead.)

We introduced the conditions in rural Ireland that would have made the country vulnerable in the event of a natural or economic disaster: endemic poverty, chronic unemployment, substandard housing on land occupied by tenants who lived with the threat of eviction. One of the most frequently taught lessons is the one that asks students to be part of a team of experts charged with predicting the areas of Ireland most likely to suffer in the event of a crisis. Using housing information and mapping the population density and the percentage of arable land of Irish counties, students are able to judge accurately which counties would be most vulnerable. What is most interesting about the lesson is the way that students apply their Great Irish Famine predictions to contemporary events. Students in Brooklyn as well as students in Gorey, Co. Wexford who were testing a New York State Great Irish Famine Curriculum module saw immediately the correspondences between an ability to predict the impact of the Famine on particular locations and the knowledge prior to Hurricane Katrina of what particular areas of the city of New Orleans would be exposed in the event of an extraordinary sea surge; later groups of students have learned how to make similar predictions about areas in danger of heavy flooding or earthquakes.

The second question asks whether the Great Irish Famine was an act of nature. This question with its subtext that asks whether the Great Irish Famine constitutes a case of genocide is the most sensitive lesson in the Curriculum because it had informed the politics of the discussion of the requirement that the Famine be part of the State's Human Rights Curriculum. Students examine print and non-print sources about genocide and analyse data: graphs, charts, photographs, illustrations and political cartoons. They study three events, chosen from a list of five, that resulted in the death of massive numbers of particular people: in Armenia, in Europe during the Holocaust, in Bosnia, in Rwanda and in East Timor, to determine whether the events meet the United Nations' definition of an act of genocide. They discover that the term *genocide* is a recent one, a term coined by Raphael Lemkin in his book *Axis Rule in Occupied Europe* (1944) and that the United Nation's Convention on Prevention and Punishment of the Crime of Genocide, 1951 stipulated that genocide consists of:

> any of the following acts committed with intent to destroy in whole or in part, a national, ethnic, racial or religious group, such as: a) killing members of the group; b) causing serious bodily or mental harm to members of the group; c) deliberately inflicting on the group conditions of life calculated to bring about its physical destruction in whole or in part; d) imposing measures intended to prevent births within the group; e) forcibly transferring children of the group to another group.[3]

Then students examine primary sources and the conflicting interpretations about British policy during the Great Irish Famine to determine whether that event meets the definition of the term genocide. Students bring their findings to a 'democratic dialogue', a learning activity that promotes a thorough examination of complex issues. Unlike a debate, there are no winners and losers. Instead, the format allows for students to formulate a strong case for their interpretations, to present opinions backed by supportive documentation, to question other opinions and to engage in a dialogue about complicated issues. This lesson was extensively field tested; it is one of the learning experiences most frequently used in the classroom. Experience with the 'democratic dialogue', particularly with the student presentations, suggests that their analysis of the Great Irish Famine recognises that the question of genocide and the Great Irish Famine is a complex one because the United Nations definition requires the demonstration of intentionality; there is no sanction for those groups who fail to take action. Students tend not to find evidence of British intentionality during the Great Irish Famine, but they are typically highly critical of the British policy that failed to provide timely and appropriate relief to the Irish. It is an important insight for students. They see that we are responsible not only for what we do, but also for what we fail to do. As a result, after their 'democratic dialogue', students frequently spend a lot of time discussing how to frame language to charge people responsible with the failure to act or to act appropriately. Students' conclusions about the question whether British policy constituted genocide generally align with current expert opinion. While genocide continues to inform some versions of the nationalist narrative, it is not the interpretation of the Great Irish Famine accepted by most historians today.

The curriculum does not, on the other hand, undermine the contemporary British government's culpability. The students look at Tony Blair's message to the Irish people on 31 May 1997, which contained the following statement:

> The Famine was a defining event in the history of Ireland and Britain. It has left deep scars. That one million people should have died in what was then part of the richest and most powerful nation in the world is something that still causes pain as we reflect on it today. Those who governed in London at the time failed their people through standing by while a crop failure turned into a massive human tragedy.

Students generally conclude that while Blair's message was not an apology, his expression of remorse constituted an implicit apology. Blair took responsibility on behalf of the British government and expressed regret.[4] We revisit the Blair message later when we talk about reconciliation and forgiveness as the last step in any permanent peace process.

Having identified government leaders who failed to take appropriate action, we were equally concerned with providing models of compassionate and responsible behaviour to students. Students re-create the relief organisations that New Yorkers founded in 1847 to aid the Irish during the Great Irish Famine and decide how best to plan and execute such relief campaigns. They also design appropriate public relations materials to make the plight of the Irish poor known to their fellow New Yorkers. They read simulated grant applications and debate how best to allocate their 'funds' to realise the greatest possible good. Another series of lessons ask students to read Seamus Heaney's 1966 poem 'For the Commander of the *Eliza*', a poem that alludes to an episode in Cecil Woodham Smith's *The Great Hunger* (1962). It describes the Whitehall reprimand given to Sir James Dombrain, inspector general of the Coast Guards, for disregarding orders to transport grain to Westport depot and instead giving it to the hungry people of the Westport sector for free. Students were asked to distinguish between the moral and civil law in that instance and to identify and discuss other examples of civil disobedience (Sophocles' *Antigone*, Henry Thoreau's 'Civil Disobedience' and Rosa Parks's refusal to give up her seat to a white man after being ordered to do so by bus driver James F. Blake in Montgomery, Alabama in 1955).

The third question asks students to examine ways that the Great Irish Famine changed Ireland and the world. Since the Irish have played a significant role in New York State history and in American history, many of these lessons have been adopted by colleagues teaching immigration units or immigration electives. As we considered the experience of the Irish in the United States, our advisers strongly recommended that our lessons about the Irish in America not be simply an Irish success story. We created lessons about the New York City Draft Riots of 1863 to demonstrate the complexity of the Irish experience. Other lesson about prejudice and stereotyping provide historical models to consider when students confront discrimination against immigrants today. A very popular lesson is our 'Emigrant's Trunk' which asks students to pack their trunks for America. The lessons have encouraged immigrant students to share their own experiences and to talk with their families about the decisions they made about leaving home and their experience as immigrants. In one of our test sites, English as a Second Language (ESL) students organised their artefacts and wrote captions and narratives in their home languages and in their newly-acquired English for a classroom museum exhibition for their school and community.

Our fourth and final question asks students to think about the legacy of the Great Irish Famine: folk legends of hospitality rewarded, proverbs like '*Ar scáth a chéile, a mhaireann na daoine*' (people live in each other's shadow/protection) that remind students of our obligations to each other. Other lessons focus on art, music and literature produced by contemporary artists, musicians and writers that reflect the losses experienced during the famine decade, losses that survive in the Irish landscape and in oral and written tradition. The persistence of memory in art offers students opportunities to consider the way that our view of the present is shaped by the past, the moral choices encoded in those events and the strategies for reconciling past and present. The local and national monuments, created to mark the 150th anniversary of the Great Irish Famine offer students opportunities to study and to evaluate the way that such commemorations help mourners live with loss. They also have opportunities to think about cultures of commemoration and to design their own famine or diaspora memorials.

The closing lessons in the curriculum remind students that there is still hunger in the world today. We designed lessons to raise awareness of hunger in students' own communities some of which are among the most affluent in the country. We identify particular groups (children, the elderly, returned service personnel), the causes of local hunger, and create plans of action to recruit volunteers for local hunger-related service projects. During the current economic crisis, students have observed the increased numbers of people seeking aid from soup kitchens and food pantries. We work with the schools that required or encouraged service projects to consider how their students can respond to this most basic need. We also suggest these activities to students who are members of scout troops or faith-based groups.

Our three lessons about famine in the world today focus on hunger in sub-Saharan Africa. This was the one part of the curriculum that used lessons that we did not create ourselves. They were provided courtesy of Trócaire (from the Gaelic for mercy/compassion), the Irish NGO aid organisation that works with local partners in more than a hundred developing countries around the world. The Great Irish Famine Curriculum ends with a meditation about hunger in memory and how people experience, remember and reconcile the traumatic events in their past. This lesson provides a way to examine the trauma of the Great Irish Famine with other narratives of loss and suffering. Students examine the different narratives of national trauma particularly the new methodologies and models that interrogate a variety of primary source documents. We leave students with the words of Hannah Arendt in *The Human Condition* (1998) who speaks about being liberated from the past by forgiving and being bound to the future by promising

> The possible redemption from the predicament of irreversibility – of being unable to undo what one has done though one did not, could not, have known what he was doing – is the faculty of forgiving. The remedy for unpredictability, for the chaotic uncertainty of the future, is contained in the faculty to make and keep promises. The two faculties belong together in so far as one of them, forgiving, serves to undo the

deeds of the past, whose 'sins' hang like Damocles' sword over every new generation; and the other, binding oneself through promises, serves to set up in the ocean of uncertainty, which the future is by definition, islands of security without which not even continuity, let alone durability of any kind, would be possible in the relationships between men.[5]

In the spirit of Arendt, the curriculum concludes with students planning an annual school famine remembrance day with a proclamation and a promise to work with others to do something to eliminate the poverty that causes hunger and homelessness.

Before we published the Great Irish Famine Curriculum, we field-tested our lessons in diverse settings: in inner-city schools, in rural areas of New York State and in suburban settings. We worked with students who brought a variety of backgrounds, experiences, interests and abilities to the classroom, and we learned to make the material accessible to those students so that they could grasp the concepts of the lesson, discuss and write about the material and participate in the project-based learning experiences that are an essential part of the curriculum. In some cases we created two and three versions of texts to provide content rich texts for students of different reading levels. These texts allow students to participate fully in class discussions and to be active participants in learning activities. We also planned lessons for special education classes and for students in English as a Second Language classes. Teachers report that students' interest level has increased significantly and their attendance has improved. The degree of engagement that students had with the text never failed to impress those who came to observe the curriculum in the classroom.

The first copies of the Great Irish Famine Curriculum were ready on 20 July 2001. Copies were mailed to every school, public and private, in New York State on Friday, 7 September 2001. A high-profile, state-level roll out was planned for later in September, but the 11 September tragedy postponed the launch indefinitely. Instead, Murphy and Singer worked on a smaller, local and regional scale with teachers, schools, district professional development programs and professional organisations to introduce the curriculum and to model lessons.

Since we teach our students to differentiate between fact and opinion, we asked those interested in evaluating the efficacy of the curriculum to examine the accounts of those like Harry Browne of the *Irish Times* who have actually seen students working with the curriculum[6]. The national Ancient Order of Hibernians historian Mike McCormick monitored the curriculum closely and visited school sites. He concluded that while our curriculum differed from the one he and some of his colleagues had envisaged, and while he would have preferred coverage of topics like the penal laws, having seen the curriculum in the classroom, he endorsed it. He was present on 23 November 2002, at the 82nd annual conference of the National Council for the Social Studies in Phoenix, Arizona when the Great Irish Famine Curriculum was awarded the Council's Programs of Excellence Award.

The curriculum has had an influence beyond the individual classroom. The students' Great Irish Famine Museum brought more than a hundred students from schools in Brooklyn, Queens and Nassau County to Hofstra in December 2001 to exhibit and to interpret their projects for one another and for visitors. At the same time, the Irish Arts Center in New York City developed 'The Big Potato', a ninety-minute workshop and performance based on the Great Irish Famine Curriculum. The centre presented the programme to some 5,000 children at 25 city schools and community centres. During President Mary McAleese's visit to New York for the 2010 Great Irish Famine commemoration, she visited fifth graders at PS 197 in Brooklyn who presented her with copies of their 'big books' about the Great Irish Famine to share with Dublin schoolchildren.

The Great Irish Famine Curriculum has a permanent place in the New York City landscape. In 1999, when Governor Pataki charged the Battery Park City Authority with creating a memorial to the Great Irish Famine on a half-acre site within the shadow of the World Trade Center, Murphy was invited to serve as the memorial's historian. As plans for the memorial progressed, its purpose changed from a Great Irish Famine memorial to the Irish Hunger Memorial. The curriculum is represented in some of the quotations in the mile of texts on the memorial's frosted glass panels and in the audio loops with passages translated into Amharic, English, German, Irish, Russian and Spanish that speak to the Great Irish Famine and to examples of famine in other parts of the world. The addition of the World Hunger Information Center across from the Irish Hunger Memorial site provides visitors with information about current world hunger sites and international relief programs.

Since publishing the Great Irish Famine Curriculum, we have taught workshops for teachers and curriculum specialists all over the state, in New Jersey and in Massachusetts.[7] We have taught master classes in the Great Irish Famine in teacher education programs at the National University of Ireland, Maynooth and St Patrick's, Drumcondra, at the University of São Paulo, at the University of Kyoto and at international gatherings of the American Conference for Irish Studies and the International Association for the Study of Irish Literature. Murphy has team-taught lessons in a Great Irish Famine module with Liz Russell at the Gorey International School in Co. Wexford. The National Council for the Social Studies' *Middle Level Learning* offered a special supplement on the Great Irish Famine Curriculum

(September–October 2000), and Murphy and Singer served as consulting editors and writers to a special famine issue of *Calliope* (April 2006).

While it may appear that our lessons asking students to look at the Great Irish Famine comparatively with famines in India and sub-Saharan Africa is a departure from our original brief from the New York State Education Department to create a curriculum to teach about Great Irish Famine, we were impressed with Margaret Kelleher's pioneering study of the visual and verbal imagery of famine in *The Feminization of Famine. Expression of the Inexpressible?* (1997) that demonstrated the effectiveness of studying the Great Irish Famine comparatively. Our decision to study the Great Irish Famine comparatively anticipated Cormac Ó Gráda's integrative approach to his analytical history of world famines in *Famine: A History* (2009).

The National University Ireland, Maynooth Centre for the Study of Wider Europe's '*Holodomor* in Ukraine and The Great Famine in Ireland: Histories, Theories and Memories' conference offered yet another opportunity to discuss the famines in Ireland and in Ukraine comparatively in the context of current famine scholarship, a scholarship informed by historiographical methods and sources. Conference papers and discussions focused on the common theme of hunger and human rights. These opportunities to meet and consider famines comparatively, especially in terms of local conditions, demonstrate the complexity of famine causes for scholars and the challenges of redress for policymakers. For those of us who teach, questions about curriculum and pedagogy complement concerns about content. The New York State Great Irish Famine Curriculum suggests some ways to study hunger and homelessness with students in order to prepare the next generation to develop the strategies to understand and solve the more fundamental problems of human rights to food and shelter.

Notes and References

1 Thomas J. Archdeacon, 'The Irish Famine in American School Curricula', *Éire-Ireland* 37, nos. 1–2 (Spring/Summer 2002): 130–52, analyses the New York State Legislature's adoption of the Great Irish Famine Curriculum in the context of the politics of the interpretation of the Famine. It includes the exchange between then Governor George Pataki and the British Ambassador John Kerr when Pataki charged, in a press release of 9 October 1996, that the British denied the Irish access to food during the Great Irish Famine.
2 Mullin's curriculum is available on the Nebraska Department of Education website; it was distributed to schools in New Jersey in 1996. James V. Mullin, 'The New Jersey Famine Curriculum: a Report', *Éire-Ireland* 36, nos. 1–2 (Spring/Summer 2002): 119–29.
3 UN General Assembly, *Convention on prevention and punishment of the crime of genocide*, A/RES/260, 9 December 1948.

4 During her historic visit to Ireland in May 2011 Queen Elizabeth II expressed her own regrets about historic relations between Britain and Ireland. She did not mention the Great Irish Famine specifically.
5 Hannah Arendt, *The Human Condition* (Chicago: University of Chicago Press, 1998), 237.
6 Harry Browne, 'U.S. using the Irish past to shape its future', The Education and Living Supplement, *Irish Times*, 24 April 2001.
7 *The Great Irish Famine Curriculum* (Albany: New York State Education Department, 2011) is available for $15.00 post-paid from the Publication Office, New York State Education Department, Washington Avenue, Albany 12234. *The Great Irish Famine Curriculum* is also available on the New York State Education Department website.

Chapter 6

REMEMBERING FAMINE ORPHANS: THE TRANSMISSION OF FAMINE MEMORY BETWEEN IRELAND AND QUEBEC

Jason King
University of Limerick

The adoption of Irish Famine orphans by French-Canadian families has long been remembered in Quebec as a traumatic historical experience that nevertheless brought the French and Irish closer together. It is commonplace to note that many of these famine orphans kept their Irish surnames but became fully integrated into French-Canadian society. In the 'Orphans' Heritage Minute – a genre of sixty-second capsule history broadcast frequently by the Canadian Broadcasting Corporation in the 1990s – French-Canadian 'sympathy for the victims' and endeavours to 'preserve the Irish identity of the children' are specifically emphasised.[1] This chapter examines the documentary sources on which the popular memory of the famine orphans is based. In particular, it suggests that their memory can be traced not to contemporary records and correspondences between the French-Canadian and Irish clerics, religious and lay benefactors and government officials who first ministered to the famine migrants on Grosse Isle and in Montreal in 1847,[2] but rather to a set of pastoral letters, pamphlets, didactic novels and travelogues published a generation after the Famine in the 1860s, especially John Francis Maguire's *The Irish in America* (1868).

Broadly speaking, I want to argue that in the period between their adoptions in 1847–1848 and the recollection of these events two decades later, the famine orphans became inscribed as 'figures of memory'[3] in Irish and Canadian popular consciousness. More specifically, it is my contention that John Francis Maguire's *The Irish in America* provided the conduit through which the memory of the famine orphans was popularised. Implicit in this memory is the generosity of French-Canadian families who allowed them to keep their Irish names and cultural identity. In the 'Orphans' Heritage Minute, Montreal Bishop Ignace Bourget's magnanimous gesture of permitting the orphan Molly Johnson to keep her Irish name 'in memory of her homeland' is emphasised as being a significant part of Canadian heritage. Thus, whereas Bishop Bourget initially confers 'the proud new name' of Bélanger on Molly Johnson and proclaims her a 'Canadian now', he then relents at the behest of her new French-Canadian family to honour her dying mother's wish 'to keep her Irish name'. As we will see, the emphasis on the posthumous fulfilment of a maternal pledge is a recurring motif in the transmission of famine memory between Ireland and Quebec. In the 'Orphans' Heritage Minute, however, its meaning is changed from a pledge to preserve the orphans' sense of Catholic piety and religious fidelity into a different injunction to cultivate and respect their distinctive Irish identity. The implication is that there is no contradiction between becoming Canadian and the retention of an Irish cultural heritage. The memory of the famine orphans is perceived as an integral part of Canadian heritage because it exemplifies that accommodation rather than assimilation defines the process by which immigrants and cultural minorities become integrated into Canadian society.

Hence, the adoption of the famine orphans is recollected in Canada as epitomising a tradition of tolerance of cultural diversity, whereas in Ireland it is remembered in speeches by Mary Robinson and others as evidence of the historical obligation of the Irish to receive immigrants in the same spirit of hospitality. As the recipients of French-Canadian generosity, the orphans created a legacy for the Irish nation to constructively engage with its own diaspora as well as displaced migrants in the developing world. Indeed, President Mary Robinson's celebrated 'Cherishing the Irish Diaspora' address (1995) drew on their memory and echoed Maguire's claim that 'the orphan children were gathered to the homes and hearts of the generous Canadians' in her commemoration of those 'French-Canadian families who braved fever and shared their food, who took the Irish into their homes and into their heritage'.[4] Her remarks were intended to signal a new era of Irish openness to the developing world and the host societies into which members of the Irish diaspora had settled over generations as defining themes of her presidency.

Like most forms of collective memory, this impression of the famine orphans as models of integration appears somewhat anachronistic. There is no evidence during the Famine itself that Irish children were idealised in this fashion. On the contrary, the popular memory of the famine orphans was actually shaped and moulded two decades later during a moment of ethnic friction and heightened tension between Quebec's Irish and

French-Canadians in the autumn of 1866. More specifically, it was the convergence of two distinct events in November 1866 that crystallised their memory in Canadian and Irish popular consciousness. The first was Montreal Bishop Ignace Bourget's plan to subdivide Notre-Dame-de-Montreal parish into a number of smaller ones, which was perceived by the city's Irish clergy and members of the laity to threaten their control over St Patrick's Church, the autonomy of Irish Catholic religious and social institutions and to fragment the city's Irish community at large. The controversy mobilised Montreal's Irish clerical and lay leadership, such as Father Patrick Dowd and Thomas D'Arcy McGee, to struggle to preserve their religious and social institutions from French-Canadian ecclesiastical encroachment.[5] At the same time, the nationalist MP and founder of the *Cork Examiner*, John Francis Maguire, had travelled to Quebec City and Montreal, where he met Father Dowd and D'Arcy McGee, between 4 and 10 November 1866, in order to gather material for *The Irish in America*, which was published on both sides of the Atlantic in 1868.[6] In spite of the fact, however, that he visited Montreal at a time of heightened tension between the city's Irish-Catholic and French-Canadian co-religionists, Maguire portrays their relations in a conciliatory fashion, because he sought evidence of successful Irish integration abroad to contrast with the maladministration of British rule in Ireland.

It is my contention that Maguire's narrative contains the first detailed evocation of the myth of the famine orphans; that is, the popular belief that their adoptions into French-Canadian families epitomised an enduring ideal of cultural conciliation. As such, it is a myth that originated and took shape at the very moment that popular recollections of the famine orphans were passing from lived experience into the 'post-memory' of their arrival in Quebec. The most common beliefs about the orphans were based not on eye-witness reminiscences but rather Maguire's 'imaginative investment, projection' and second-hand recollection of their adoptions, his 'traumatic recall' of the event 'at a generational remove'.[7] Although he was obviously not descended from Quebec's famine Irish, Maguire's record of their reminiscences in *The Irish in America* came to define their sense of cultural inheritance. His book provided the vehicle for the mediation of their memory not only in its transmission to a wider public and subsequent generations: but also, perhaps more importantly, in its perception of the orphans as symbols of reconciliation between rival French-Canadian and Irish Catholic versions of the past. In essence, Maguire created the myth of the famine orphans by recasting them in memory during a moment of ethnic and religious tension as models of integration, exemplary immigrants who brought together the French and Irish communities in their symbolic embodiment of cultural and spiritual kinship. Their myth took shape not in spite of but rather because of the deteriorating relations between Irish

Catholics and French-Canadians that gave reminiscences of past benevolence a heightened significance. More than anyone else, Maguire defined the meaning of famine orphan adoptions as a parable of cultural conciliation. His narrative was the first published text to encapsulate the three core motifs that define their popular memory: namely i) the posthumous fulfilment of the maternal pledge to preserve their Catholic religious identity, ii) the processions of orphans led by priests from the fever sheds into surrounding communities and iii) the retention of their Irish surnames after their adoption into French-Canadian families.

Famine Orphans in Ireland and Quebec

The first of these motifs, the posthumous fulfilment of the maternal pledge, is derived from a broader discourse of the feminisation of Famine which has been comprehensively examined by Margaret Kelleher. In her groundbreaking study, Kelleher claims that both eye-witness and literary accounts of the Irish Famine repeatedly emphasise the spectacle of maternal suffering. 'One of the most frequent figures in Famine texts', she notes, 'is that of a hunger stricken mother, holding a child to her breast [...] The spectacle of mother and child becomes iconic', she suggests, especially 'the woman's inability to feed her child, the absence of nourishment from the mother's breast [...] In some depictions, the mother has died with the child still attempting to suckle.'[8] In each of these iconic representations, the absence of maternal nourishment becomes a synecdoche for the infertility of the land.

However, the specific image of the dying Irish mother relinquishing her children to the care of the Catholic Church, is unique to Quebec. There was, in fact, a fundamental difference in perception of the famine orphans in Ireland and North America. In North America, they appeared much more conspicuous in the Atlantic ports in which they congregated than in Ireland, where the famine orphans tended to be more widely dispersed and rapidly absorbed into the workhouse network beyond the purview of most observers. By 1850, Irish children were so noticeable on the streets of Boston, Montreal and New York that they had created the impetus for a new genre of fiction 'adapted to the condition of the poor orphan boys' in Mary Anne Sadlier's *Willy Burke; or the Irish Orphan in America* (1850) and Father John T. Roddan's *John O'Brien, or the Orphan of Boston: a Tale of Real Life* (1850).[9] Sadlier and Roddan sought to transform the predominant, Dickensian image of the orphan from an object of charity and compassion into an exemplary figure of Catholic piety. In contrast with English Victorian novelists, they eschewed character traits of psychological complexity and realist depictions of poverty to emphasise the sense of resilience and resistance to proselytism that their orphan protagonists embodied. The anxiety their works expressed about the proselytisation of Irish orphans was not without foundation: recent research indicates that Catholic children housed in the Emigrant Orphan Asylum in St John, New Brunswick, were invariably adopted into Protestant families.[10] Maguire charges that a similar fate befell many famine orphans in Kingston, where adoptive parents 'of a different faith secured a certain proportion of the children, who are now perhaps bitter opponents of the creed of their fathers'.[11]

In New York City, it was not until a generation after the Famine, in 1863, that the Catholic Protectory was established to safeguard delinquent and destitute Irish children from being institutionalised in Protestant reformatories, as documented in Sadlier's novel *Aunt Honor's Keepsake* (1863).[12] More to the point, her earlier novel *Willy Burke* was her first to feature a dying Irish mother entrusting her children to the custody of a priest to prevent her 'poor orphans' from 'losin' their faith'.[13] 'I just wanted to see your reverence an' the children here', declares Willy Burke's mother on her deathbed, 'so that I might give them up to your care before I leave this world.' The achievement of narrative closure through 'the bald contrivance of the deathbed legacy' was a commonplace in Catholic fiction, as Charles Fanning notes:[14] but Sadlier's depiction of the maternal pledge was also corroborated by the personal reminiscences of the famine emigrants themselves. John Francis Maguire was intimately familiar with Mary Anne Sadlier, not only because she was the publisher of the North American edition of his text, but she was also one of his correspondents.[15] In *The Irish in America*, his portrayal of famine orphan adoptions appears to combine the conventions of Catholic fiction with eyewitness recollections of Irish emigrants and those who ministered to them on their deathbeds and in the fever sheds in Montreal.

By contrast, the figure of the famine orphan was much less conspicuous in Ireland than in the famine ports of North America. Under the Irish Poor Law (1838), it was not only orphaned but also destitute or pauper children who were institutionalised in workhouses and segregated from their families as a precondition for relief.[16] The containment of vulnerable children in these institutions rendered them largely invisible to casual observers and travellers in mid nineteenth century Ireland; the stigma and 'enduring shame' of workhouse incarceration further restricted reminiscences of them in subsequent Irish folkloric impressions and popular memory.[17] In consequence, children were generally perceived as appendages of their stricken mothers in travellers' accounts, while orphans were glimpsed only in passing or as already housed in institutional settings. One of the most poignant glimpses in Asenath Nicholson's *Annals of the Famine in Ireland* (1851), for example, is

> of a little orphan girl, who had crept into a hole in the bank and died one night, with no one to spread her death-bed, or to close her eyes, or wash

and fit her for the grave. She died unheeded, the dogs lacerated her body, gnawed her bones, and strewed them about the bog.[18]

The brevity and starkness of her description attests to the utterly marginal position of orphaned children who fell outside of either familial or institutional networks of care.

The prior existence of the Irish Poor Law also meant that even compassionate observers could abdicate themselves from any sense of personal responsibility in caring for desperate children. In the *Recollections of Aubrey De Vere* (1897), De Vere recalls 'roaming over the famine stricken moors and bogs' near Kilkee, Co. Clare, with the Poor Law stewards William Monsell and Lord Arundel, where they paid a visit:

> to a deserted cabin among the morasses. Its only inmate was a little infant, whose mother was most likely seeking milk for it. On slightly moving the tattered coverlet of the cradle, a shiver ran over the whole body of the infant, and the next moment the dark emaciated little face relapsed again into stillness. Probably the mother returned to find her child dead.[19]

Their response to the plight of this shivering infant is revealing. Although William Monsell 'burst into a flood of tears' and subsequently donated 200 pounds to the local relief fund, none of them care for or comfort the distressed child as it hovers between life and death. Their compassion is exercised through the provision of institutional rather than individual aid. The shuddering child is caught between an absent mother and the prospect of institutional relief, yet is abandoned to his or her fate. For all of the pathos of the spectacle of maternal suffering, the Famine-stricken mother still offered a modicum of care and nourishment. Even more desperate was the plight of abandoned children who appear marginal in eyewitness and literary accounts of the famine. Scattered, isolated and neglected, they left little imprint on famine memory.

The image of the orphan in the workhouse was no less grim. In the *Gleanings in the West of Ireland* (1850), the Reverend Sydney Godolphin Osborne recounts his experiences of visiting and inspecting a number of workhouses between Limerick and Mayo in 1850, much of which he also published in the *Times*. Like many travellers in famine Ireland, he glimpsed in passing orphans struggling to survive whom he felt powerless to assist.[20] Unlike most famine accounts though, Osborne's narrative appears exceptional in its emphasis on the immiseration of children in workhouse settings. Indeed, many of his gleanings are focalised around the spectacle of the institutionalised, suffering child: 'I know well what the appearance of a really famine-stricken child is', he remarks at the beginning of his tour in the Limerick workhouse. The children there, he claims, provide 'a spectacle to fill any humane heart with indignation': 'very many were mere skeletons.' Recent research indicates that conditions had rapidly deteriorated in the Limerick workhouse shortly before Osborne's visit,[21] but he found similarly neglected children in most of the Poor Law unions through which he travelled. After observing a particularly emaciated child in the Galway workhouse, Osborne remarks of:

> this little blanched piece of skeletoned humanity [...] one felt very thankful that [he] must soon die; he neither spoke nor moved – such children never do: I have sometimes liked to think, that at a certain stage of workhouse misery, the child's spirit has so far escaped from the decaying frame, that nothing remains, which can appreciate neglect, or be sensible of real pain.[22]

The seeming insensitivity of such children to the extent of their deprivation might well alleviate their pain, but also inhibited communication and any sense of identification with others.

Conversely, the widespread lack of compassion and empathy for destitute and dying children struck Osborne as a 'libel on humanity'.[23] He was particularly appalled by what he perceived as the stifling of maternal instincts in the workhouse setting. 'What I would pray to see would be, *mothers*', he avows, 'women who have learned at their own breasts, on their own knees, the language, the character of childhood; making these poor suffering things, objects for practical works of love'. The absence of such maternal affection Osborne regarded as a symptom of their institutional degradation. Ultimately, in his view, the Poor Law simply protracted the suffering of the children it was supposed to provide for by confining them in workhouses which were but way stations to the grave.

By contrast, the sheer proliferation of famine orphans in the fever sheds of Grosse Isle and Montreal during the summer of 1847 immediately overwhelmed the scant institutional supports that existed, and created a new context in which their adoptions into French-Canadian families became iconic as a site of memory. Recent studies of the archival records of the religious orders who ministered to the famine Irish in Montreal – many of which have never been examined by professional scholars[24] – indicate both the impact and scale of maternal loss and parental mortality that left hundreds of orphans in the city. Marianna O'Gallagher provides an overview of these accounts of mainly French-Canadian female religious congregations, such as the Sisters of Providence and Sisters of Charity or Grey Nuns, which contain 'graphic reports [...] [of] children lifted from the arms of dying mothers, a baby trying to suckle a dead mother'.[25] 'We held one poor woman in the throes of death, her suckling infant still latched to her breast',[26] reads one such Grey Nun testimonial. According to Doyle Driedger, by June of 1847, there were over five hundred orphans in the fever sheds in Montreal, at least eighty of whom 'were newborns, suckling infants lifted from the stone-cold breast of a dead mother. Unable to feed them, the nuns laid the hungry, wailing babies four to six to a berth [...] [where] many died of starvation.'[27] These images of famished infants plucked from the maternal breast recur in the archival records of the nuns who first tended to them. As surrogate parents, they appear no more capable of providing succour for malnourished children than their emaciated and apathetic mothers were in the cabins, fields and workhouses of Ireland.

Yet from the beginning, the spectacle of children suffering in Quebec created the impression that their welfare was a public responsibility, whereas in Ireland the workhouse regime was increasingly funded only through levies on Irish property. Margaret Kelleher and Melissa Fegan both explore the ways in which encounters with famine victims were often envisioned as a form of spectacle in Irish literary and travel narratives that precluded communication or interaction between observer and observed. The frequent glimpses of emaciated, skeletal and spectral figures from across the threshold of cabin entrances, carriage windows, distant fields and behind workhouse walls not only demarcated their class differences but also rendered the former 'in effect the voyeur of Irish distress'.[28] Invariably, these sightings of famine victims occurred in a context for which the term 'spectacle' was something of a misnomer, as they tended not to seek attention but rather to 'evade inspection'.[29]

Motifs of Famine Memory I – Orphan Processions

By contrast, the famine orphans in Quebec quickly became a public spectacle because they were gathered in processions which were intended to display them before potential benefactors. O'Gallagher and Doyle Driedger each call attention to the same event on 11 July 1847, when Bishop Bourget personally escorted a procession of Irish orphans from the fever sheds in Montreal into a temporary asylum run by the Sisters of Providence in the heart of the city. 'In the midst of these desolate scenes, there was nothing more touching', notes the congregation's annalist,

> than the spectacle of a multitude of little children, hardly knowing what it meant to be alive, and already so miserable, rolling around pell-mell helplessly on the paving, without even the failing hand of a mother to help them.
>
> The dreadful misery of these innocents was painful to the eyes of Monseigneur Bourget [...]

On July 11 our sisters collected all the children from the sheds [...]

We hastened to get six carriages, in each of which rode two Sisters who held the smallest ones on their knees and in their arms. Some were only days or even hours old.

Monseigneur Bourget preceded us in his carriage. Everyone hastened to see the touching cortege, which even the Protestants stopped to admire.[30]

Bishop Bourget himself recalled the same event in a pastoral letter in March 1848. According to Bourget:

it was one of the most touching moments of my life [...] At the head of this numerous family of orphans, we travelled through the streets of the city to take them to the hospices that had been prepared for them. The spectacle of these hundreds of children, emaciated by hunger, covered in rags and succumbing to attacks of this terrible malady [typhus] that had deprived them of their parents was too poignant to ever forget.[31]

Both accounts suggest that there is a performative dimension to the orphans' procession. Whereas in Ireland priests were often called upon to assuage and disperse hungry, importunate crowds before they became unruly, Bishop Bourget personally assembled and placed himself at the 'head of this numerous family of orphans' to symbolise their acceptance into the wider community. The carefully orchestrated spectacle was clearly intended to impress upon all who beheld it, Catholic as well as Protestant, that the famine orphans belonged in their midst. In fact, it could be argued that they took their place within a rich processional culture of events like Corpus Christi or *Fête-Dieu* parades which habituated French-Canadian parishioners to regard the orphans as already within the fold. Shortly before Bourget escorted them from the sheds, 'a large number of school children formed part of [a] procession', notable for 'the scrupulous neatness of their attire', to mark the festival of St Jean Baptiste.[32] More to the point, Bourget's emphasis on his role as the orphans' paterfamilias underscored his injunction that they be accepted not only into the community but the very families of his diocese.

Not everyone who beheld the orphans though was inclined to admire them. Either by accident or design, the orphans' procession became a politically charged event. By 11 July, medical and political opinion in Montreal had become divided over whether to move the fever sheds from their central location by the Lachine Canal to Windmill Point, where they were ultimately relocated on the outskirts of the city, or further down river to the more remote Boucherville Islands, which pitted the mayor John Easton Mills against the city's Board of Health, whose fusillades were published in the *Pilot*. It is important to emphasise that the *Pilot* was in every respect an Irish-Canadian newspaper, established by the Irish Protestant Francis Hincks in 1844 to mobilise Irish Catholic support for the reformist Baldwin-Lafontaine coalition and Responsible Government, which was achieved in 1848.[33] The anxieties it expressed about inadequately quarantined fever victims were in no way unreasonable: by 11 July, typhus had spread to the populace at large and fatalities in the city exceeded those in the sheds.[34] Indeed, on Saturday 10 July, three thousand people had demonstrated in Montreal's Bonsecours Market against 'the proximity of the city to the Sheds' which 'rendered them altogether unfit for […] purpose',[35] according to the *Pilot*. On the basis of second-hand information from 'a respectable practicing physician', the paper also took exception to the orphans' procession itself: 'several carts filled with young children were removed from the Sheds and brought into St Catherine Street', it noted. 'We are not informed as to the persons or the authority who dictated this movement, by which the pestilential disease of the Sheds is at once introduced into the city.' The *Pilot*'s information was clearly second hand, because not one person who actually saw the orphans' procession could have had the slightest doubt about who authorised it: the man, of course, who led it, Montreal's Bishop Ignace Bourget. Above all else, the orphans' procession was a display of unfettered ecclesiastical power. Had the Bishop not placed himself at its head, the children might never have left the sheds. On both a political and spatial level, their procession was a carefully cultivated spectacle of integration that brought them into, and not out of, the city.

One month after leading the orphan procession, Bourget also sought to memorialise their suffering and pay tribute to the nuns who cared for them by commissioning a votive painting, Théophile Hamel's *Le Typhus* (c. 1849), which became both a commemorative artefact and a medium of intercession. As Bourget declared in a pastoral letter (13 August 1847), the painting would depict 'the typhus seeking an entrance into this city, but checked at its gates by the [Virgin Mary's] powerful protection'.[36] Théophile Hamel's *Le Typhus* was subsequently installed in Montreal's Notre-Dame-de-Bonsecours church, where it portrays the experiences recorded in the annals of the Sisters of Providence and Charity: in the foreground and middle ground of the painting, the nuns provide comfort and remove infants from the breasts of dying mothers, under the Virgin Mary's watchful eye and against the backdrop of a fever shed and panoramic view of the city. Beneath the celestial figure of the Virgin on billowing clouds, behind the spectacle of salvation depicted in the fever sheds, church spires appear silhouetted in the background against the horizon which represent the orphans' pathway from

Figure 6.1. Théophile Hamel, *Le Typhyus* (Notre-Dame-de-Bon-Secours Chapel/Museum Marguerite-Bourgeoys, 1848)

quarantine, under clerical protection, into the heart of the city. *Le Typhus* is thus both a votive offering and a history painting that visually recalls each of the three orders of nuns who ministered to the famine Irish in turn. As John Francis Maguire recounts:

> First came the Grey Nuns, strong in love and faith [...] [then] the Sisters of Providence came to their assistance, and took their place by the side of the dying strangers. But when even their aid did not suffice to meet the emergency, the [Hotel Dieu] Sisters of St Joseph, though cloistered nuns, received the permission of the Bishop to share with their sister religious the hardships and dangers of labour by day and night.[37]

In creating commemorative artefacts like Hamel's painting and instigating the orphans' procession, Bishop Bourget helped transform the children into figures of memory 'too poignant to ever forget'.

The mass adoption of famine orphans thus quickly became ritualised as a spectacle in its own right. As was the case with Bishop Bourget in Montreal, French-Canadian and Irish priests serving at the quarantine station on Grosse Isle also escorted processions of orphans from the island to be adopted into French-Canadian families. Like Bourget, they positioned themselves at the head of these processions in the symbolic role of paterfamilias to deliver the children en masse into the waiting arms of French-Canadian mothers who were assembled in groups to receive them. The movements of famine orphans were thus of necessity improvised yet also highly ritualised occasions that marked their transition from Irish Catholic into French-Canadian families. In taking custody of the children, the priest led them on a rite of passage from their place of loss and presided over their adoption.

The sense of communal responsibility engendered by these processions can be discerned in the reminiscences of the Reverend Bernard O'Reilly, who served on Grosse Isle from 6 to 14 July 1847 and then helped escort a party of orphans to the town of Trois Rivières, on 18 July.[38] Fathers 'Harper and O'Reilly went through here this morning, in great spirits. Charitable people everywhere are arguing over who is to have the orphans whom they have brought from Quebec', observed Father Thomas Cook in Trois Rivières.[39] Their procession was also reported in the *Gazette* and the *Pilot*, both of which noted that 'in less than an hour [they] found worthy *habitants* with either small families, or who had no children, to adopt these poor little destitute orphans and to secure for them the comforts of a home and the care of parents, under [their] immediate eye'. According to the *Pilot*, such adoptions attest to 'the humane and Christian dispositions of our [French-] Canadian brethren' in spite 'of the calumny which imputes to them hostility to the Irish race'.[40] Five years later in a lecture in New York, O'Reilly recalled this moment and paid tribute to the 'Bishops, Priests, Nuns, and people of Canada, in 1847', but most especially

> the French Canadian people: for, [...] as each Parish Priest returned from Quarantine, or from Montreal, the parishioners came forward to meet them at the landing places with long trains of carriages, to escort the Priest and his numerous orphans home. And touching was the meeting of those French mothers with the little children misfortune gave them.[41]

As a parish priest himself who was born in Ireland, O'Reilly provides one of the first documented Irish expressions of gratitude for French-Canadian generosity in 1847. His reminiscences of 'the meeting of those French mothers with the little children misfortune gave them' – the scenario depicted in the 'Orphans' Heritage Minute – became increasingly elaborate in later years. Indeed, O'Reilly expounds upon his experiences in *The Mirror of True Womanhood; A Book of Instruction for Women in the World* that was first published in 1877 and then reprinted in 16 editions by 1883. In *The Mirror of True Womanhood*, he claims to 'remember returning from quarantine, in the second week of July, with the Rev. John Harper', after having:

> spent a fortnight among the fever-sheds, and [having] had, at the urgent request of their parishioners, brought home with them a large number of orphans [...] We had been delayed [...], and on our arrival about midnight at Three Rivers, we found a crowd of eager and excited women, mothers of families all of them, waiting and watching for us [...] It was a spectacle worthy of the admiration of angels, which was beheld that sultry midnight in July, these farmers' wives, weeping every one of them with that holy emotion which the sweetest charity creates, pressing around their pastor and choosing, when they could, in the uncertain light, the child that pleased them best, or accepting joyously and folding in a motherly embrace the little orphan allotted to them.[42]

Such reminiscences are no doubt embellished, but unquestionably attest to the religious connotations of the orphans' procession that delivered Irish children into the arms of French-Canadian mothers who waited so steadfastly to receive them. In both O'Reilly's and popular memory, their adoptions were recollected as a form of religious devotion.

Motif of Famine Memory II – Posthumous Fulfilment of Maternal Pledge

Thus, a distinct iconography developed around famine orphan adoptions during the summer of 1847, but it was not until a generation later that it became popularised in texts like O'Reilly's *Mirror of True Womanhood* (1877) and especially John Francis Maguire's *The Irish in America* (1868). There has been relatively little research on the construction and transmission of famine memory in North America in the decades after 1847, although both Mark McGowan and James Donnelly have examined its dissemination in the writing of Irish nationalists such as John Mitchel, Thomas D'Arcy McGee and Maguire in the 1860s in particular.[43] Unlike Mitchel or McGee, however, Maguire's interpretation of famine memory was based on the interviews he conducted with people who actually lived through the experience in Canada and the United States. His tour of North America in 1866 was motivated by his desire to find evidence that the Irish fared better abroad than under British rule at home. The importance of *The Irish in America* lies both in the fact he came to Quebec City and Montreal to converse with famine emigrants and those who ministered to them and that the book found a mass readership on both sides of the Atlantic. Because he was editor of the *Cork Examiner*, the paper reported in detail on Maguire's travels and reprinted the numerous reviews his book received. The extensive publicity generated by these reviews and sales provided the conduit through which the memory of the famine orphans was popularised, both in an Irish and international context.

More importantly, Maguire's evocation of the famine orphans is the first to combine all three core motifs that recur in popular memory: i) the posthumous fulfilment of the maternal pledge to maintain their Catholic identity, ii) the children's procession from the fever sheds into nearby communities and iii) the retention of their Irish surnames after their adoption into French-Canadian families. He repeatedly emphasises the spectacle of the dying Irish mother bequeathing her children to the care of Catholic clergy who preside over their adoption into French-Canadian households. In his own words:

> This deplorable havoc of human life left hundreds of orphans dependent upon the compassion of the public; and nobly was the unconscious appeal of this multitude of destitute little ones responded to by the French Canadians. Half naked, squalid, covered with vermin generated by hunger, fever, and the foulness of the ship's hold, perhaps with the germs of plague lurking in their vitiated blood, these helpless innocents of every age – from the infant taken from the bosom of its dead mother to the child that could barely tell the name of its parents – were gathered under the fostering protection of the church.[44]

Under the fostering protection of the church, the famine orphans became the objects of French-Canadian compassion and devotion. The infant taken from the bosom of its dead mother was regarded with particular adoration. But it was the maternal injunction to preserve the infant's Catholic faith that Maguire adverts to as the formative experience that bound together the figures of the Irish and French-Canadian mother as icons of familial and religious fidelity. The adoption of famine orphans thus represented the posthumous fulfilment of a maternal pledge that enjoined the French-Canadian mother to take the place of her Irish predecessor, at the behest of the church, as her sacred responsibility: 'before she died, the pious mother – the Irish Catholic mother – left them to the good God, and the good God now gives them to you', Maguire recounts as a common priestly injunction. He also imputes a nationalist perspective to the Catholic clergy who entreated French-Canadian mothers to adopt the famine orphans: because 'they were starved out of their own country by bad laws, and their fathers and their poor mothers now lie in the great grave at Grosse Isle. Poor mothers!' Maguire recollects a priest exhorting his female congregation. 'They could not remain with their little ones. You will be mothers to them', he implored. In fulfilment of their maternal pledge, French-Canadian mothers epitomised an ideal of cultural and spiritual kinship with their Irish predecessors that the orphans came to embody.

The spectacles of the orphan procession and self-sacrifice of the priests and nuns who ministered to the famine Irish also feature prominently in *The Irish in America*. Maguire describes a 'long procession of waggons' transporting the children from the temporary care of the priest 'to a Canadian home'. He also quotes accurately from the annals of the Sisters of Charity, although it is unclear how he gained access to these unpublished, French language archival records that remain all but unknown even to specialists in the field.[45] Whether it be the fever-stricken Bishop Bourget 'hovering between life and death' or the priests and nuns, 'a few Irish, the majority French Canadians, [who] caught the infection', images of clerical self-sacrifice recur in the annals that Maguire draws on in his account. 'Among the priests who fell a sacrifice to their duty in the fever-sheds of Montreal was Father Richards', he writes, the founder of the city's Irish Catholic community. Before his own demise, Father Richards sought to 'provide for the safety of the hundreds of orphan children, whom the death of their parents had left to the mercy of the charitable', Maguire notes. In his solicitude for the orphans, Father Richards is reported to have requested straw from the Mayor, which elicited the reply: 'I wish it was gold, for his sake.' Shortly thereafter, when each of them died, 'both Protestant mayor and Catholic priest "had gone where straw and gold are of equal value", wrote the Sister already mentioned', Maguire recounts almost verbatim from the annals of the Sisters of Charity. The Sister in question would appear to be

Martine Reid, who in the annals recalls that after Father Richards requested straw from the Mayor: 'quelques jours plus tard, tous deux étaient allés là où l'or et la paille sont de même valeur.'[46] Aside from citing their archival records, Maguire also describes the cultural artefacts that commemorate the Grey Nuns such as Théophile Hamel's 'memorial painting' *Le Typhus*. In Maguire's view, it provides an iconic representation of 'the horrors and the glories of the fever-shed – the dying Irish, strong in their faith – the ministering Sisters, shedding peace on the pillow of suffering – the holy Bishop, affording the last consolations of religion to those to whom the world was then as nothing'.[47]

Yet for all of Maguire's emphasis on French-Canadian compassion for the famine Irish, his visit took place at a time of heightened ethnic friction and social tension between them. In fact, Maguire travelled to Montreal during a particularly tumultuous period in November 1866, when the Fenian scare was at its height after the battle of Ridgeway in June and Montreal's Irish community was in open conflict with Bishop Bourget over his plan to reorganise the city's parishes. For example, on 8 November, the very day that Maguire was 'meeting the very *élite* of [his] countrymen of all denominations' in Montreal, touring the city's 'magnificent' colleges, convents, hospitals, asylums and schools including 'the grand church of St Patrick, of which the Irish are justly proud',[48] and dining with D'Arcy McGee at the St James Club,[49] that same afternoon both McGee and Father Dowd had submitted a petition in Saint Patrick's Sacristy on behalf of their congregation to protest against Bourget's redistricting plan.[50] In the war of words that ensued between Bishop Bourget and the clerical and lay leaders of Montreal's Irish community, the memory of the famine orphans served both to accentuate and reconcile their differences.

Their differences became especially pronounced in an exchange of pastoral letters and pamphlets published in the immediate aftermath of Maguire's visit. For example, in a pastoral letter read in St Patrick's Church on 23 November, Bishop Bourget all but accused the Irish of ingratitude, questioning if they had forgotten 'when the ravages of the typhus left the children of your countrymen by hundreds, orphans on our shores, did we did not make an appeal to all our Diocese, to obtain for them other fathers and mothers, who as you know, reared them and cherished them as their own?'[51] His insinuation that the Irish were forgetful and ungrateful for the sacrifice made by French-Canadians in caring for the famine orphans two decades beforehand incensed Father Dowd and D'Arcy McGee, who took the unusual step of publishing a pamphlet entitled *The Case of St Patrick's Congregation* that warned of the likelihood of 'bloodshed' and 'a domestic war between Irish and Canadian Catholics throughout the city' if the Bishop's plan was brought to fruition.[52] These were extraordinary admonitions in the aftermath of the battle of Ridgeway when the Irish were under intense scrutiny for any incitement to violence. As stated in the pamphlet:

> Your Lordship, referring to the sad events of 1847, is pleased to call us an 'unfortunate' people. In 1866 we are still 'unfortunate' – for your Lordship will not allow us to forget our sad destinies. The memory of all past afflictions must be kept fresh: and all the charities of which we have been the sad recipients, must be turned into an argument to force us to surrender, in silence, all the advantages of our present condition, which we owe to our own efforts, [...] and the generous sympathy of our immediate Pastors.[53]

Thus, the Irish community sought to emphasise its resilience and self-reliance in overcoming its 'sad destiny' rather than its dependence on Bourget and French-Canadian co-religionists a generation beforehand. As the first public document to be issued by an Irish community in Quebec, *The Case of St Patrick's Congregation* represents a highly significant foundational narrative that was determined to define the Irish in terms of their advantageous 'present condition' of prosperity and self-sufficiency instead of past afflictions. The pamphlet's emphasis on 'our own efforts' and 'our immediate Pastors' refutes Bourget's insinuation that the Irish community survived only under his tutelage.

And yet, in this highly fraught environment, the one area of common ground that *The Case of St Patrick's Congregation* conceded to Bishop Bourget was that he and his fellow French-Canadian clergy did indeed undertake 'good work' and 'noble charity' for the 'Irish alone' in ministering and caring for the famine orphans twenty years beforehand. It acknowledged that 'the Appeal made by your Lordship to the Diocese and to various institutions of charity, and Education, in favour of the Typhus Orphans' was 'a noble deed of charity for your Lordship – a noble deed for the individuals and Communities who became the kind parents of the fatherless little ones'.[54] The memory of this generosity stands out as the only undisputed event in otherwise vigorously contested Irish-Catholic and French-Canadian versions of the past.

In a second pamphlet, however, published by Father Dowd, the image of the famine orphan itself is transformed from a symbol of French-Canadian benevolence into one of Irish resilience and communal self-reliance. In his *Objections and Remonstrances against the Dismemberment of the Ancient Parish of Montreal* (1867), Dowd makes public the petition that he had submitted to Bishop Bourget on 8 November 1866, the very day that John Francis Maguire arrived in the city. According to Father Dowd, Bourget's plan to reorganise the parish threatens the cohesion of the city's Irish community and especially the institution of St Patrick's Orphan Asylum that it had supported since 1850. He also intimates that Bourget is evicting the famine Irish from the very institutions they created less for reasons of ecclesiastical necessity than his own aggrandisement. 'I cannot look upon the labour of years about to be destroyed', Dowd protests,

> the monuments of charity raised and sustained by union of our whole people, [...] so long happily collected together under the shadow of their beloved St Patrick's, about to be driven from his sanctuary, as not belonging to them; – thus bringing back to their memory that they were once before driven from their native land, as if it were not their home.[55]

Far from being beholden to Bishop Bourget, the Famine Irish now perceive him as complicit in their persecution. Father Dowd also appeals to Bourget's self-image as a paterfamilias 'to whom the faithful children of St Patrick always looked as a second father [...] not to inflict upon them the cruel blow of a second dispersion'. It is their fate, in particular, Dowd suggests, that is most imperilled by Bourget's decision. In his own words:

> The St Patrick's Orphan Asylum contains about two hundred and fifty (250) inmates. They are mostly the children of Ireland's exiles. They are the favorite charge of St Patrick's congregation which contributes on an average eight thousand dollars ($8,000) a year for their support [...] This creditable state of things is owing to the present condition of St Patrick's Congregation. All have a common spirit, under a common direction. They work together as one man, animated by this unity of spirit, guided by this unity of direction. Thus, though comparatively poor, they have been enabled to give to charity sums of money which have earned for them the reputation they justly possess. Divide St Patrick's Congregation, and you destroy all this [...] In this state of things, where will our poor orphans find eight thousand dollars a year for their support? The decree of erection, that will scatter the St Patrick's Congregation, will be the death warrant of the St Patrick's Orphan Asylum. Yes, its first victims will be the little ones, whom God left fatherless, but whom that decree will leave houseless and friendless in a strange land.[56]

In Father Dowd's view, the adoption of famine orphans into French-Canadian families was but a prelude to the Irish community taking responsibility for their welfare through the establishment of St Patrick's Asylum. Their salvation, he insists, was the creation of a specifically Irish 'institution which we, strangers here, have built out of the sweat of our brow to save the orphan children of our own race from vice and heresy'. In Father Dowd's recollection, their arrival provided an impetus for Irish institution building and communal self-realisation that owed little to Bishop Bourget's ministrations. He even puts a price on the loss of communal autonomy that 'the little ones' would suffer from if not defended against French-Canadian ecclesiastical encroachment. The former paterfamilias of the famine orphans is accused of disinheriting his spiritual progeny from the very asylum their community created for their care.

Immediately before Bishop Bourget issued his pastoral letter and *The Case of St Patrick's Congregation* and *Objections and Remonstrances* pamphlets were published, John Francis Maguire had met with Montreal's Irish community leaders, such as Father Dowd and D'Arcy McGee, and his narrative provides an invaluable record of how they perceived themselves and their relations with French-Canadians. In *The Irish in America*, Maguire repeats their pamphlets' claims that it was through their own self-sufficiency and the salutary influence of 'the good fathers of St Patrick's'[57] that Quebec's Irish community persevered against the adversity of the Famine. Of these 'good priests', Maguire specifically praises the work of Father Dowd, whom he credits with reuniting a disconsolate Irish orphan adopted into a French-Canadian family with her living father back in Ireland.[58] More significantly, Maguire reproduces not Bishop Bourget's but the Irish Catholic version of events concerning the founding of their community in Montreal. In *The Case of St Patrick's Congregation* pamphlet, it is claimed that 'in 1815, the Irish were first assembled by themselves, as a people, in the little church of Bonsecours, by the lamented Father Richards',[59] whereas Bishop Bourget insisted in his pastoral letter that it was his French-Canadian predecessor, Bishop Lartigue, who first ministered to Montreal's Irish community in 1825. This was no petty discrepancy between rival French and Irish Catholic versions of parochial history. For Irish Catholics in Montreal, their assembly as a people under Father Richards was the founding event in their communal myth of origin. In *The Irish in America*, Maguire corroborates this origin myth and notes that it was Father Richards who 'took compassion upon the handful of exiles who were then friendless and unknown, [...] to speak to them in a language which they understood'.[60] Thus, where Bishop Bourget's pastoral letter gave his fellow French-Canadian Bishop Lartigue credit for first assembling the Irish in Montreal 'as a people' in the eyes of the church, Maguire recounts the Irish community's own version of events to help set the record straight. At the same time though, Maguire also pays homage to the courage and generosity displayed by Bishop Bourget, his fellow French-Canadian clergy and the French community in general, in caring for the famine orphans and allowing Irish Catholicism to flourish in Quebec.

Motif of Famine Memory III – Retention of Irish Surnames

More specifically, Maguire's narrative seems to mediate between Montreal's Irish and French-Canadian versions of the past, and to conciliate both groups in its detailed evocation of the myth of the famine orphans. As noted, he recounts at length how French-Canadians responded to their plight, often after specific injunctions from their clergy were made on behalf of dying Irish mothers: the scenario of posthumous fulfilment of the maternal pledge depicted in the 'Orphans' Heritage Minute. It is the very malleability of their identity that makes the famine orphans ideal emissaries between Quebec's French and Irish communities, Maguire suggests. For example, he recalls how 'the prayers of a dying [Irish] mother were indeed heard' when her 'affrighted children'[61] were taken in by a French-Canadian family that raised her son to become a Catholic priest who served both communities in turn. Soon after the boy's adoption, 'his generous protectors' suspected that he might be

> a little mute, or that he had momentarily lost the power of speech through fright or starvation. But at the end of a fortnight he relieved them of their fears by uttering some words of, to them, an unknown language; and from that moment the spell, wrought as it were, by the cold hand of his dying mother, passed from the spirit of the boy, and he thenceforth clung with the fondness of youth to his second parents. The Irish orphan soon spoke the language of his new home, though he never lost the memory of the fever shed and the awful death-bed, or of his weeping sisters, and the last words spoken by the faithful Christian woman who commended him to the protection of God and His Blessed Mother.[62]

As he matures, the boy discovers his vocation and enters the priesthood to minister to both French and Irish Catholic congregations. 'Of his Irish name, which he was able to retain, he is very proud', Maguire recounts; 'and though his tongue is more that of a French Canadian, his feelings and sympathies are with the people of his country and his birth'.

Equally at home in English and in French, the famine orphan's ordination represents not just the posthumous fulfilment of a maternal pledge, but also the resolution of tension between French and Irish forms of Catholicism. Language and memory are compounded into a singular, hybrid French and Irish identity that is shaped in the image of the Irish orphan: 'the spirit of the boy' epitomises an ideal of adaptability and linguistic facility that binds the French and Irish communities together. The formative experience 'of the fever sheds and the awful death-beds' takes on the qualities of a fable in Maguire's prose, in which the famine orphans symbolise the consolidation of a fluid Franco-Irish identity.

Maguire thus imagines the adoption of the famine orphans to be a synecdoche for the integration of the Irish into French-Canadian society as a whole. 'Absorbed thus into the families of the French-speaking population' – he recounts:

> even the older Irish orphans soon lost almost every memory of their former home and of their parents, and grew up French Canadians in every respect save the more vigorous constitution for which they were indebted to nature. It is not, therefore, a rare thing to behold a tall strapping, fair-skinned young fellow, with an unmistakable Irish face, who speaks and thinks as a French Canadian. Thus genuine Irish names – as Cassidy or Lonergan, or Sullivan, or Quinn, or Murphy – are to be heard of at this day in many of the homes of the kindly *habitans* of Lower Canada.'[63]

Maguire's portrayal of Irish orphans who kept their Irish names but 'grew up French Canadians in every respect' popularised their image as symbols of integration long before the 'Orphans' Heritage Minute was made. The retention of their cultural heritage and preservation of their 'genuine Irish names' were never emphasised before the publication of *The Irish in America*. Furthermore, the widespread acclaim Maguire's book received transmitted his impressions of the famine orphans to both an international and Irish readership. For example, the *Freeman's Journal* declared that 'the anecdotes told by Mr Maguire about those little children are full of interest'. 'Thousands of orphans survived this havoc of human life in which the ministering priests had their share, and the greater portion of those destitute children were [sic] adopted by the French Canadians.'[64] Similarly, *Blackwoods* was struck by 'the self devotion of the Catholic clergy and religious Sisterhoods; and last, but not least remarkable, of the Canadian *habitans* who adopted the surviving orphans into their own families'.[65] According to *The Dublin Review*, 'the ship-fever; the horrors of Grosse Isle; the noble devotion of the priests and the sisters, who had to shelter and protect [Irish] orphans [...] make up a story *not* to be read without deep emotion'.[66] It is clear from the tone of each of these accounts that the story of the famine orphans is being disseminated from Quebec to Ireland for the first time.

Conclusion

Ultimately, the figure of the famine orphan served to symbolically bridge but not substantially breach Quebec's cultural divide, providing subsequent generations of Irish Quebecers with a sense of affinity with their French-Canadian co-religionists even while both groups struggled for control of the

Catholic Church through which their collective identities were increasingly defined. Because they had been concentrated in the fever sheds of Grosse Isle and Montreal and made visible in public processions rather than scattered and immiserated in the vast network of Irish workhouses, the famine orphans loom much larger in Irish cultural memory in Quebec than in Ireland itself. The endeavours of French-Canadian and Irish clerics such as Bishop Bourget and Bernard O'Reilly to make the children conspicuous to facilitate their adoptions heightened their profile before would-be benefactors and in popular recollection. Religious archival records and cultural artefacts like Hamel's painting *Le Typhus* attest to the formative experience of the fever sheds in which Irish children were orphaned and removed from the breast of dying mothers who pledged their care to the church. The fulfilment of their pledge through the adoption of Famine orphans into French-Canadian families became the focal point of commemoration in the transmission of famine memory between Ireland and Quebec.

It was only a generation after the Famine, however, that these memories crystallised and were popularised in texts like Maguire's and O'Reilly's when relations between Quebec's Irish and French-Canadian communities had become particularly fraught. As the Irish beneficiaries of French-Canadian compassion, the orphans appeared to be, in a cultural sense, immaculately conceived, effortlessly integrated into French-Canadian society without the anxieties of assimilation or apprehension of cultural and linguistic decline that epitomised Bourget's redistricting controversy. They were summoned to memory as reminders of the instinctive good will that the French and Irish should have felt toward one another now that they appeared to be in open conflict. Although usually invoked in a spirit of conciliation, their memories definitively took shape during moments of social discord. Communal tensions and ethnic rivalries with French-Canadians were set aside by the symbol of the famine orphans. Thus, there was little difference between the ways in which Bishop Bourget, Bernard O'Reilly, Mary Anne Sadlier, Thomas D'Arcy McGee and Father Patrick Dowd, or John Francis Maguire imagined their reception into French-Canadian society, as the posthumous fulfilment of a maternal pledge. But they perceived differently the interrelation between the French and Irish communities in Quebec that the famine orphans were held to symbolise. Whereas Bishop Bourget recalled his ministrations to them as proof of his good intentions towards the Irish in Montreal, Maguire celebrated their integration as evidence of emigrant success. By contrast, Quebec's Irish communities tended to idealise the famine orphans as intermediaries with the French-Canadian majority with whom they were having increasingly little contact. They were recalled not only as the beneficiaries of French-Canadian compassion, but also as symbols of Irish resilience and self-reliance in overcoming their 'sad destiny'. Their memories appear compensatory for the varying degrees of tension that existed between Quebec's Irish Catholics and French-Canadians in the latter nineteenth century.

The legacy of the famine orphans thus was based on the elision of ethnic and religious conflict as much as Maguire's recollections. His perceptions of the orphans were not fully internalised by the Irish in Quebec until the semi-centennial commemoration of the Famine at the end of the nineteenth century, when their relations with French-Canadians had become less strained. Before then Irish visitors to Quebec like Maguire were more likely to acknowledge the 'kindly *habitans* of Lower Canada'[67] than were members of its Irish communities, who sought to emphasise their present prosperity rather than past affliction. Two years after the publication of *The Irish in America*, another traveller from Cork, the Reverend M. B. Buckley, followed largely in Maguire's footsteps in 1870–1871 to raise funds for Cork's Cathedral of St Mary and St Anne, as recounted in his *Diary of a Tour in America* (1889). Like Maguire, Buckley was a guest of Father Dowd and struck by the fractious relations between his congregation and their French co-religionists. 'A great antipathy seems to exist between them and the Irish, clearly not on religious grounds, inasmuch as both are Catholics', he observed, yet both were 'embittered as much, if not more, by political and national prejudices as by differences of religious faith. In many places efforts have been made by ecclesiastical authorities to blend the two nationalities', he added, 'but oil and water are not more dissociable'.[68] Labour conflict and the 'difference of language must [...] create a barrier against international fusion, or thorough sympathy between races', remarked Maguire in a similar fashion in *The Irish in America*.[69]

The myth of the famine orphans as figures of 'blended nationality' was thus cultivated by Irish travelers who were highly cognizant of French and Irish antipathy. Like Maguire, Buckley regarded the memory of French-Canadian generosity in 1847 as being more significant than the 'political and national prejudices' he bore witness to. 'Let the Irish at home ever remember [...] with gratitude', he declared, that 'a holy rivalry sprung up amongst the inhabitants of Quebec, Canadian as well as Irish, for possession of the children [...] [who were] rescued by charity from a terrible fate': 'the starving, dying thousands found sympathy with the French-Canadians of Montreal', he avowed. His injunction to remember a 'holy rivalry' rather than ethnic animosity between the French and Irish cast the orphans as emblems of 'blended nationality' against a backdrop of more recent hostility. Also like Maguire, Buckley emphasised the adaptability of the orphans who 'were brought up by the Canadians [and now] cannot speak one word of English. The French language, as well as French parents, had been adopted as their own'.[70] By contrast, the later commemorative publications of Quebec's Irish communities tended to stress their struggle for self-sufficiency rather than acknowledge acts of French-Canadian generosity in the past,[71] much in the same spirit as the *Case of St Patrick's Congregation* and *Objections and Remonstrances* pamphlets discussed above. In the case of J. J. Curran's *Golden Jubilee of St Patrick's Orphan Asylum* (1902), the adoption of famine orphans was recalled as a temporary expedient 'that was tried and did not work well',[72] necessitating the creation of an Irish orphanage in the first place. In their remembrance of famine orphans, travellers like Maguire and Buckley more readily acknowledged an Irish debt of gratitude to French Canadians than their long settled compatriots in Quebec, whose perceptions of their co-religionists were more fraught.

The impression of the orphans as the progeny of 'blended nationality' did not become widespread amongst the Irish in Quebec until the famine semi-centennial commemoration at the end of the nineteenth century. Elsewhere I have argued that the semi-centennial both coincided with and reflected a new spirit of rapprochement between the province's Irish Catholics and French Canadians whose relations were becoming redefined in a less antagonistic fashion.[73] What concerns us here is the extent to which Maguire's perception of famine orphans was internalised as a defining feature of a less insular Irish communal self-image in Quebec. On 29 August 1897, the Ancient Order of Hibernians organised a mass pilgrimage to Grosse Isle that inspired Charles Fitzpatrick, the Irish-Canadian solicitor general, to propose a campaign for a permanent monument; commemorative emphasis was placed on the 'devotion of the French clergy of Canada, not a few of whom had sacrificed themselves [...] [in] their sympathy for a plague-stricken and afflicted race'.[74] His proposal came to fruition with the erection of a Celtic Cross on Grosse Isle, with its trilingual English, French and Gaelic inscriptions, as well as the publication of J. A. Jordan's *The Grosse Isle Tragedy* in 1909. Every dignitary at the unveiling of the Celtic Cross paid tribute to the spirit of 'brotherly love' and 'kindness' exemplified by 'French Canadians, who soothed the dying hours of [...] Irish exiles, and later assumed the duties of parents towards their orphan children'.[75] The creation of monuments and public observances on Grosse Isle, especially under the recent stewardship of Parks Canada, has generated much critical interest;[76] what is less well known is that their commemorative emphasis on the orphans was first cultivated and mediated in Maguire's account. The most extensive eye-witness testimonial reproduced in J. A. Jordan's *The Grosse Isle Tragedy* is erroneously attributed to Bernard O'Reilly, but actually seamlessly and skillfully amalgamates his reminiscences with Maguire's recollections of how 'the greater portion of the orphans of the Grosse Isle tragedy were adopted' into French-Canadian families.[77]

Their legacy is now preserved unevenly at the national and international level while more localised impressions of the orphans have begun to fade. In a recent documentary about the return of the Ancient Order of Hibernians to Grosse Isle in 2009, the only French-Canadian present at the event, Société St Jean-Baptiste president Gilles Dubord, appears completely incongruous in his proud recollection 'of what the Québécois did during the time of 1847 when they took in and adopted the Irish orphans into their homes'.[78] Even more precipitous has been the decline of communal memory of the orphans in Montreal. The closure of St Patrick's Asylum in the early 1970s was commemorated with 'no memorial or other reminder of the Orphanage's existence in the city';[79] but proceeds from the sale of its property were used to establish a registered charity now worth over $13 million, the Montreal St Patrick's Foundation, which has recently become embroiled in controversy for its attempt to evict elderly tenants from a low-rent residential property it owns in a manner that was subsequently 'ruled invalid'.[80] The controversy generated considerable media exposure,[81] but the Irish origins of the institution and its close association with the Irish community evoked little comment. Whereas once Father Dowd fought tenaciously to protect Irish orphans from suffering 'the cruel blow of a second dispersion', their descendants now issue eviction letters to society's most vulnerable in the name of the institution he created. His conception of the asylum as a 'monument of charity raised and sustained by union of our whole people' has faded from Irish communal consciousness in Montreal.[82] As figureheads of a strictly financial legacy, the orphans in memory now preside over the eviction of the elderly.

These localised instances of faded remembrance stand in stark contrast with the national and international memory of the orphans in the Heritage Minute and President Robinson's address which attest to Maguire's influence. The uneven spread of their legacy in no way diminishes his significance in having cultivated the myth of the famine orphans in the first place. Paradoxically, it is a parable of conciliation created against a backdrop of ethno-religious tension that is indicative of Irish integration in Quebec. If John Francis Maguire provided the conduit through which the myth of the famine orphans was popularised, then he drew heavily from the wellsprings of Irish communal memory in Quebec City and Montreal. By 1866, these Irish communities were well established and had acquired the characteristics that would continue to define them. My final point is that integration is not only a geo-political and socio-economic phenomenon, but a cultural one as well. The integration of immigrant and minority communities occurs when they develop the capacity to tell stories about themselves, to create founding narratives and myths of origin that help define their place, *on their own terms*, within the host society. The memory of the famine orphans provided Quebec's Irish with one such founding myth: a story of self-reliance and social acceptance by their French-speaking brethren that acknowledged religious affinity without compromising their ethnic and linguistic identity. The famine orphans feature more prominently in Irish cultural memory in Quebec than earlier arrivals because they embody an ideal of integration that reconciles ethnic and linguistic difference with a sense of shared religious belief as the basis for acceptance and belonging in French Canada. As Montreal's French and Irish communities were increasingly estranged from one another during the 1860s, the famine orphans became perceived as symbols of reconciliation. The catalyst that had transformed them into enduring figures of memory was Maguire's visit at a time of heightened ethnic friction between the French and Irish that accentuated recollections of their former amity. More than anyone else, he provided the conduit through which the famine orphans' myth was transmitted and popularised.

Notes and References

1 'Orphans' Heritage Minute', Historica Dominion Institute, http://www.histori.ca/minutes/minute.do?id=10165 (accessed 25 June 2011).
2 These records have been meticulously compiled and interpreted in Mariana O'Gallagher and Rose Masson Dompierre, *Eyewitness Grosse Isle 1847* (Ste Foy, Quebec: Carraig Books, 1995). Also see, Marianna O'Gallagher, *Grosse Île: Gateway to Canada, 1832–1937* (Ste Foy, Quebec: Carraig Books, 1984); Marianna O'Gallagher, 'The Orphans of Grosse Île: Canada and the Adoption of Irish Famine Orphans, 1847–48', in Patrick O'Sullivan (ed.), *The Irish World Wide: The Meaning of the Famine*, 6 vols (London and Washington: Leicester University Press, 1997), 6: ch. 4; Andre Charbonneau and Andre Sevigny, *1847, Grosse Île: A Record of Daily Events* (Ottawa: Canadian Government Publishing, 1997).
3 Jan Assmann, 'Collective Memory and Cultural Identity', *New German Critique* 65 (1995): 129.
4 John Francis Maguire, *The Irish in America* (Montreal and New York: D. and J. Sadlier, 1868), 148; Mary Robinson, 'Cherishing the Irish Diaspora' (Address to the Houses of the Oireachtas, on a matter of public importance), 2 February 1995, http://www.gov.ie/oireachtas/Addresses/02Feb1995.htm (accessed 25 June 2011).
5 I have examined the causes of the controversy in detail in Jason King, 'L'Historiographie Irlando-Québécoise: Conflits et Conciliations entre Canadiens Français et Irlandais', *Bulletin d'Histoire Politique du Québec* 18, no. 3 (2010): 24–31; also see Rosalyn Trigger, 'The Geopolitics of the Irish-Catholic Parish in Nineteenth Century Montreal', *Journal of Historical Geography* 27, no. 4 (2001): 553–72.
6 Maguire, *Irish in America*.
7 Marianne Hirsch, 'The Generation of Postmemory', *Poetics Today* 29, no. 1 (2008): 106–7.
8 Margaret Kelleher, *The Feminization of Famine: Expressions of the Inexpressible* (Durham, NC: Duke University Press, 1997), 22–3.
9 Orestes Brownson, *Brownson's Quarterly Review* 4 (January 1850): 131.
10 Peter D. Murphy, *Poor Ignorant Children: Irish Famine Orphans in Saint John, New Brunswick* (Halifax: Saint Mary's University, 1999), 26.
11 Maguire, *Irish in America*, 150.

12 Mary Ann Sadlier, *Aunt Honor's Keepsake* (Montreal and New York: D. and J. Sadlier, 1863). Also see Maureen Fitzgerald, *Habits of Compassion: Irish Catholic Nuns and the Origins of New York's Welfare System, 1830–1920* (Urbana and Chicago: University of Illinois Press, 2006), chs 3–4.
13 Mary Anne Sadlier, *Willy Burke; or the Irish Orphan in America* (Boston: Thomas P. Noonan, 1850), 99, 101.
14 Charles Fanning, *The Irish Voice in America: 250 Years of Irish-American Fiction*, 2nd edn (Lexington: University of Kentucky Press, 2000), 119.
15 In his *Diary of a Tour in America*, based on a journey that followed largely in Maguire's footsteps four years after he first travelled to North America, the Reverend Michael Buckley notes that in New York he had called upon 'Mrs Sadlier [...] [who] has obtained fame as a writer of fiction' after presenting her with a personalised letter of introduction 'from John Francis Maguire, M.P.' M. B. Buckley, *Diary of a Tour in America. By M. B. Buckley, of Cork, Ireland. A Special Missionary in North America and Canada in 1870 and 1871* (Dublin: Sealy, Bryers and Walker, 1889), 23.
16 Michelle O'Mahony, *Famine in Cork City: Famine Life at Cork Union Workhouse* (Cork: Mercier Press, 2005), ch. 4.
17 Cormac Ó Gráda, 'Famine, Trauma, Memory', *Béaloideas* 69 (2001): 135.
18 Asenath Nicholson, *Annals of the Famine in Ireland* (1851), Maureen Murphy (ed.) (Dublin: Lilliput Press, 1998), 87.
19 Aubrey De Vere, *Recollections of Aubrey De Vere* (New York: E. Arnold, 1897), 250.
20 While en route from Kilrush to Ennis, he 'overtook two children', he recalls, 'from 10 to 12 years of age; one, himself very far from strong, [...] supporting the staggering steps of the other, evidently sinking in the last stage of famine. I know not how far he had to go, before he found a shelter on earth', Osborne adds, but 'I feel comforted in my assurance that his hours were numbered there.' Lord Sydney Godolphin Osborne, *Gleanings in the West of Ireland* (London: T. and W. Boone, 1850), 33.
21 Michael D'Arcy Ryan, 'Commissioners, Guardians and Paupers: Life and Death in the Limerick Poor Law Union, 1838–1850' (unpublished PhD thesis, Concordia University, 2005), 204–33.
22 Osborne, *Gleanings*, 53.
23 Osborne, *Gleanings*, 74, 131.
24 The archival records for the female religious orders who ministered to Famine emigrants in Montreal in 1847, such as the Sisters of Charity or Grey Nuns, the Sisters of Providence and the Sisters of St Joseph or 'Hotel Dieu' congregation, are internally classified as follows. Archival Services and Collections, Maison de Mère d'Youville, Sisters of Charity of Montreal, 'Grey Nuns'. Annals of the Sisters of Charity, 'Ancien Journal' I (1847): 491–515; 'Ancien Journal' II (1847): 319–510; 'La terrible epidemie de 1847': 1–150; Providence Archives Montreal, *Mother House of Montreal Chronicles, 1828–1864* (May 1847–March 1848): 72–85; *Notes Historiques des Souers de la Providence 1799–1893*: 46–62; Positio *of Mother Emilie Tavernier-Gamelin*: 168–72, 201; *The Institute of Providence* tome II: 111–63, 170–71; *Institute of Providence* tome IV: 145–61, 165–76; 'Typhus Orphans Register', 'St-Jérôme-Émilien/Saint Patrick Hospital Chronicles (M6)'; *Activités Hospitalières des Soeurs de Charité de la Providence (au Canada et en Pays des Missions)*: 18–23 (D2259.H2.2 (775) – AG-Cb1.1); St Joseph Province Archives. Soeur Césarine Raymond, *Annales des Hospitalières de Saint-Joseph de l'Hôtel-Dieu de Montréal, 1756–1861*, chs 12–13.
25 Marianna O'Gallagher, 'The Orphans of Grosse Île', 102.

26　Quoted in Sharon Doyle Driedger, *An Irish Heart: How A Small Community Changed Canada* (Toronto: HarperCollins, 2010), 43.
27　Doyle Driedger, *Irish Heart*, 43–4.
28　Kelleher, *Feminization*, 21, 65; Melissa Fegan, *Literature and the Irish Famine, 1845–1919* (Oxford: Clarendon Press, 2002), 98.
29　Kelleher, *Feminization*, 25.
30　O'Gallagher, 'Orphans', 101–2.
31　Quoted in Doyle Driedger, *Irish Heart*, 44.
32　*The Gazette*, June 25, 1847.
33　See Jason King, 'L'Historiographie Irlando-Québécoise', 16–19.
34　Doyle Driedger, 48.
35　*The Pilot*, 13 July 1847.
36　Bishop Bourget, pastoral letter, 13 August 1847, cited in *The Extracts of Providence* tome II, 135. Providence Archive. Also see Jacques Des Rochers, '*Le Typhus*, History of a Painting', in Patricia Simpson and Louise Pothier (eds), *Notre-Dame-de-Bon-Secours: A Chapel and its Neighbourhood*, (Montreal: Fides, 2001), 92.
37　Maguire, *Irish in America*, 145.
38　For a detailed study of Bernard O'Reilly's response to the Famine Irish in Quebec, see Jason King, 'The Genealogy of *Famine Diary* in Ireland and Quebec: Ireland's Famine Migration in Historical Fiction, Historiography and Memory', *Éire-Ireland* 47 (2012): 45–69.
39　Mariana O'Gallagher and Rose Masson Dompierre, *Eyewitness Grosse Isle 1847*, 106.
40　*The Gazette*, 20 July 1847; *Pilot*, 22 July 1847.
41　Bernard O'Reilly, 'The Irish Emigration of 1847', *True Witness and Catholic Chronicle*, 17 December 1852.
42　Bernard O'Reilly, *The Mirror of True Womanhood; A Book of Instruction for Women in the World* (New York: Excelsior Publishing House, 1877), 98.
43　Mark McGowan, *Creating Canadian Historical Memory: The Case of the Famine Migration of 1847* (Ottawa: Canadian Historical Association, Canada's Ethnic Group Series, no. 30, 2006), 6; James S. Donnelly, Jr, 'The Construction of the Memory of the Famine in Ireland and the Irish Diaspora, 1850–1900', *Éire-Ireland* 31 (1996): 1–2, 42–3, 48.
44　Maguire, *Irish in America*, 138, 139.
45　Because of overcrowding in the fever sheds, he observes, 'patients lay, sometimes two together, looking, as a Sister of Charity since wrote, 'as if they were in their coffins', from the box-like appearance of their wretched beds' (145). Maguire's description is derived almost verbatim from the annals of the Sisters of Charity entitled 'Ancien Journal', vol. I, 1847, in which it is written: 'L'expression manque pour dire l'état affreux où étaient ces malades, couchés jusqu'à trois dans des espèces de lits ou plutôt de grabats qu'on avait fabriqués à la hâte, et qui offraient l'aspect de cercueils' (497).
46　Annals of the Sisters of Charity, 'Ancien Journal' I (1847), 512.
47　Maguire, *Irish in America*, 48.
48　Maguire, *Irish in America*, 96, 99, 101.
49　*Morning Chronicle and Commercial and Shipping Gazette* (Quebec), 9 November 1866.
50　The event was later described in the *Montreal Herald and Daily Commercial Gazette*, 4 December 1866. It was also reported in the *Morning Chronicle* that a large demonstration was held and 'six thousand English speaking Catholics have petitioned against the dismemberment of the Old Parish of Montreal, as it would deprive them of St Patrick's Church […] [and] the Pope had not commanded dismemberment' (10 November 1866).

51 Pastoral Letter of 21 November 1866. Reprinted in Anon. *The Case of St Patrick's Congregation as to the Erection of a New Canonical Parish of St Patrick's, Montreal, Published by Order of the Committee of the Congregation*, (Montreal, 11 December 1866), 12.
52 Anon. *Case of St Patrick's Congregation*, 25.
53 Ibid., 19.
54 Ibid., 22.
55 Father Patrick Dowd, *Objections and Remonstrances against the Dismemberment of the Ancient Parish of Montreal, and the Proposed Erections of the Parishes of St James and St Patricks, made at Meetings held in September and November, 1866* (Montreal: John Lovell, 1867), 14.
56 Dowd, *Objections*, 15.
57 Maguire, *Irish in America*, 101.
58 Maguire, *Irish in America*, 145.
59 Anon. *Case of St Patrick's Congregation*, 19.
60 Maguire, *Irish in America*, 97.
61 Maguire, *Irish in America*, 142.
62 Maguire, *Irish in America*, 143.
63 Maguire, *Irish in America*, 143–4.
64 *Freeman's Journal*, 23 December 1867.
65 Reprinted in the *Cork Examiner*, 3 February 1868.
66 Reprinted in the *Cork Examiner*, 17 April 1868.
67 Maguire, *Irish in America*, 144.
68 Buckley, *Diary of a Tour in America*, 53–4.
69 Maguire, *The Irish in America*, 99.
70 Buckley, *Diary of a Tour in America*, 64, 81, 81.
71 See James O'Leary, *History of the Irish Catholics of Quebec: Saint Patrick's Church to the Death of Rev. P. McMahon* (Quebec: Daily Telegraph Print, 1895); J. J. Curran (ed.), *Golden Jubilee of the Reverend Fathers Dowd and Toupin, with Historical Sketches of the Irish Community* (Montreal: John Lovell & Son, 1887); J. J. Curran (ed.), *Golden Jubilee of St Patrick's Orphan Asylum. The Works of Father Dowd, O'Brien and Quinlivan with Biographies and Illustrations* (Montreal: Catholic Institute for Deaf Mutes, 1902).
72 J. J. Curran (ed.), *Golden Jubilee of St Patrick's Orphan Asylum*, 43.
73 Jason King, 'L'Historiographie Irlando-Québécoise', 27–9.
74 '1847–1897. The Excursion to Grosse Isle on the Steamer Canada. Hundreds of Quebecers Honor the Memory of the Dead – An Imposing Spectacle', *Quebec Daily Telegraph*, 30 August 1897. Also see 'Ireland's Dead at Grosse Isle. Hon. Mr Fitzpatrick Makes a Timely Suggestion', *Quebec Daily Telegraph*, 1 September 1897; 'Irish Dead at Grosse Isle', *Quebec Daily Telegraph*, 2 September 1897.
75 J. A. Jordan, *The Grosse Isle Tragedy and the Monument to the Irish Fever Victims, 1847* (Quebec: Telegraph Printing Company, 1909), 95.
76 Marianna O'Gallagher, *Grosse Île: Gateway to Canada*, 85–108; Colin McMahon, 'Quarantining the Past: Commemorating the Great Irish Famine on Grosse Île', (unpublished master's thesis, Concordia University 2001); Kathleen O'Brien, 'Language, Monuments, and the Politics of Memory in Quebec and Ireland', *Éire-Ireland* 38, nos. 1 and 2 (2003): 141–60; Rhona Richman-Kenneally, 'Now you don't see it, now you do: Situating the Irish in the material culture at Grosse Île', *Éire-Ireland* 38, nos. 3 and 4 (2003): 33–53; David Valone and Christine Kinealy (eds), *Ireland's Great Hunger: Silence, Memory, and Commemoration* (Lanham: University Press of America, 2002), 271–333. For a broad overview, see Jason King, 'Remembering and Forgetting

the Famine Irish in Quebec: Genuine and False Memoirs, Communal Memory, and Migration', *Irish Review* 44 (2012): 20–41.
77 J. A. Jordan, *The Grosse Isle Tragedy*, 68. The transition from Bernard O'Reilly to John Francis Maguire's reminiscences occurs in the second paragraph on page 68.
78 Ronald Rudin and Robert McMahon, *Remembering a Memory: A Film about the Celtic Cross on Grosse-Île* (Montreal: Concordia University, 2011). Gilles Dubord appears at minute 22. http://rememberingamemory.concordia.ca/index.html (accessed 25 June 2011).
79 Ned Eustace, 'May 30, 2005, the 150th Anniversary of the St Patrick's Orphanage Act of Incorporation', *Nuacht: Community Newsletter of St Patrick's Society* 8, no. 2 (2005): 1.
80 Sarah Leavitt, 'Marian Hall Termination Notice Deemed Invalid', *West Island Chronicle* (May 31 2011); also see Alycia Ambroziak, 'Tenants Avoid Eviction – For Now', the *Gazette*, 16 June 2011.
81 Sarah Leavitt, 'West Island Seniors Evicted', *West Island Chronicle*, 28 February 2011; Karen Seidman, 'Beaconsfield Seniors ordered out of Building', *Gazette*, 10 March 2011; 'West Island Seniors Face Eviction', CTV Montreal, 2 March 2011. http://montreal.ctv.ca/servlet/an/local/CTVNews/20110302/mtl_evict_110302/20110302/?hub=MontrealHome (accessed 25 June 2011).
82 Dowd, *Objections*, 14, 15.

Chapter 7

THE IRISH FAMINE AND COMMEMORATIVE CULTURE

Emily Mark-FitzGerald
University College Dublin

In Ireland [...] the dislocations produced by rapid economic growth may help explain the recent surge of interest in the traumatic experience of the 1840s Famine [...] there remains a demand for some historical continuity, a collective identity rooted in a distinctive 'Irish' past and the Famine appeared to many to offer a focus that was at once catastrophic, local, diasporic and relevant to the modern world.[1]

Unlike so many events of Ireland's history, the Irish Famine of the 1840s is a relative newcomer to the commemorative stage. The 150th anniversary of the Famine in the mid-1990s occasioned a remarkable outpouring of events and activities, new research and the construction of new memorials and monuments. Yet the rapid multiplication of these forms of public engagement with famine memory is particularly striking due to the relative absence of commemorative activity before the 1990s, save for a few isolated events. In contrast, the centenary of the Famine in the 1940s was a muted affair, producing a commissioned volume of historical essays (not published until 1956)[2] and the Irish Folklore Commission Famine survey undertaken in 1944–45, and little in the way of public or popular events. Set against the massive celebrations and attention (both official and popular) which greeted the 50th anniversary of the 1916 Easter Rising in 1966,[3] this famine 'silence' formed a common backdrop to many 1990s commentators' own commemorative musings, frequently interpreted as an unwillingness or inability of previous generations to confront the 'traumatic' experience of the Famine. Certainly the proximity of famine memories for those alive in the 1940s (who might only be separated by a generation or two from direct experience of the Famine) rendered commemoration an unlikely prospect, its cataclysmic effects still not wholly understood nor studied.[4]

However the 1990s characterisation of the 1940s anniversary as a psychological 'repression' of famine memory (a view which of course privileged more contemporary, psychoanalytically 'correct' means of confronting the historical past) often failed to account for the very pragmatic reasons why the Famine failed to register on the commemorative front. Unlike the mythologising of 1916, promoted by de Valera's government to affirm a teleologic ascendancy of the new Irish State (and their central position within it), there is little doubt the Famine sat awkwardly with existing traditions of national and popular commemoration, with its lack of central characters, linear narrative, heroic episodes or key dates. The geographic and social imbalance of the Famine's devastation and the complexities of its legacy (still very potent in the 1940s and the source of much bitterness, particularly with respect to land ownership) further rendered any form of communal agreement over its memory unlikely. Indeed the experience of Famine hardly seemed a threat consigned to the distant past, as severe food shortages experienced in Ireland in 1946 and 1947 sparked a series of debates in the Dáil over exportation of goods from Ireland to a war-torn Europe,[5] and Ireland's heavy economic reliance on the United Kingdom in the postwar period also likely discouraged calls for national commemorations.

Indeed if the St Patrick's Day edition of the American magazine *Collier's* in 1951 is any indication – its cover optimistically emblazoned 'Ireland Today: From Great Famine to Great Future' – there existed considerable feeling that improvements to Ireland's economic and political condition could only be achieved through a forward-looking confidence: a future where the Famine past held little relevance.

Why then the astounding reversal of attention and activity in the 1990s directed towards commemorating the Irish Famine, and what forms did it take? Prompted in the first instance by the activities of local historical societies and the NGO sector in the 1980s (who championed Ireland's Famine commemorations as a means of drawing awareness to contemporary African famine), by the mid-1990s a widespread commemorative 'Famine Fever'[6] in Ireland and its diaspora was clearly evident. Cathal Póirtéir's 16-part RTÉ radio series *Famine Echoes* (broadcast in 1995) did much to keep famine history alive in the popular consciousness, along with numerous television documentaries and dramas broadcast on famine subjects during the commemorative period, and the plethora of one-off theatrical events, lectures, poetry readings, musical performances, exhibitions and other activities carried out locally and nationally.[7] An unprecedented number of famine interpretative centres and museums also launched in Ireland around the period of the anniversary, most notably the Famine Museum in Strokestown, Co. Roscommon in 1994, the unveiling of the major 'Emigrants' exhibition in 1994 at the Ulster American Folk Park and the opening of St Mary's Famine Church in Thurles, Co. Tipperary in 1995. The desire to engage, interpret and consume famine history and memory was matched by offerings of all kinds, from the serious to silly: alongside a surge of newly published academic histories one could also purchase children's books (Kerby Miller's *Journey of Hope*[8] and Laura Wilson's *How I Survived the Irish Famine*[9] are but two examples), kitsch mementoes (such as the *Irish Independent*'s offer of limited edition emigrant collector dolls for £795 per pair[10]) and pay for it all using a limited edition Ancient Order of Hibernians Famine commemorative credit card.

Preconditions for commemoration invariably include historical distance, economic stability and available models/modes of commemorative expression, and the Ireland charging into its Celtic Tiger renaissance certainly possessed all three. Growing prosperity, intensified connection with its diaspora and the rise of global 'memory cultures' in the 1990s (remarked upon by Pierre Nora, Andreas Huyssen and many others) had an indelible impact on the scale of the Famine's commemoration. Undoubtedly one of the most significant outcomes of the anniversary period has been the construction of more than one hundred public memorials over a period of approximately fifteen years in Ireland, Northern Ireland, England, Scotland, Wales, Canada, the United States and Australia, a phenomenon that continues into the present. These monuments ranged from grassroots, community-led projects to complex public artworks with multi-million budgets, and they continue to multiply: in 2002 Brian Tolle's $5 million *Irish Hunger Memorial* was unveiled in Lower Manhattan, just blocks from the World Trade Center Site; in 2003 Glenna Goodacre's $3 million *Irish Memorial* was unveiled in Philadelphia in a prime location along the city's historic waterfront; and in July 2007 the $3.5 million Ireland Park was opened to great fanfare in Toronto.

The geographical scope and number of commemorations to an event separated from participants by three or four generations is remarkable, but of course this development should be seen in the context of a widespread enthusiasm in the 1990s for the construction of high-profile museums and memory sites dedicated to the subject of nineteenth-century immigration: Ellis Island in New York, the transformation of the quarantine island Grosse Île in Quebec into a national heritage site, the Immigration Museum in Melbourne and the launch of France's first major museum to immigration (Cité Nationale de l'Histoire de l'Immigration) in Paris in 2008.

As the most visible legacy of the anniversary, these public famine monuments reflect a plurality of famine memory discourses – witnesses to the clash of history and memory articulated through the visual language of commemoration, and signposts along the search for an adequate representational approach to famine. As Christopher Morash has observed:

> In the case of the Famine, it is the event itself which eludes definition. There is no single clear consensus as to what constituted the Famine [...] there are no framing texts; there is no ceremonial beginning, no ceremonial ending [...] Like all past events the Famine is primarily a retrospective textual creation. The starvation, the emigration, and the disease epidemics of the late 1840s have become 'the Famine' because it was possible to inscribe those disparate, but interrelated events in a relatively cohesive narrative. For those of us born after the event, the representation has become the reality.[11]

Certainly public commemoration, as a highly symbolic and complex form of social activity, has increasingly been subject to analyses that link its performance to the sustenance of collective or social memory. Whilst the fashion to describe such practices as 'memory' work remains current, we may also simply define commemorative practice as a core form of cultural behaviour, a means by which groups organise their knowledge and understanding of the past into narrative and representational forms for an external audience with the ambition to transmit this knowledge (or 'memory') across generations.

The remainder of this essay will address these representations of the Famine as constructed through the form of the community memorial and monument, offering an overview of the phenomenon of famine community commemoration in Ireland and the United States (focused on issues of siting, formal/aesthetic approaches, funding and political context) and some observations on the intersection of famine visuality, ideology and social memory.[12] These community monuments range enormously in scale, ambition, cost and consequence: from small gravesite markers dotted across the Irish countryside to more elaborate diasporic monuments often taking many years to realise. In using the term 'community commemoration' a distinction is made here between modest, locally-orientated commissions (all under the €1 million mark) managed by grassroots community groups (some of which, but certainly not all, involved the participation of professional visual artists); as opposed to the smaller in number (but higher-profile) complex and expensive public famine memorial artworks guided by centralised civic committees, such as the projects in New York City (2002), Sydney (1999), Murrisk, Co. Mayo (1997), Toronto (2007) or Quebec (1998). Although it is these prominent monuments which have most frequently attracted response and analysis (in the case of the famine, Brian Tolle's *Irish Hunger Memorial* in New York and Rowan Gillespie's *Famine* in Dublin have garnered the bulk of public attention),[13] community-level commemorative activity offers a unique insight into the prosaic business of commemoration and its outcomes: the functioning of commemorative committees, range of fundraising activities, commissioning of artists, physical construction of the works and their ongoing maintenance reveal much about the significance of the famine past for agents in the present. These local monuments rarely featured in any kind of national press and their level of artistic achievement is often too low to warrant any particular praise on aesthetic grounds. However, community monuments retain a particular value in the study of monumental visual practices as they present an alternative and more frequently direct view of the social experience and memory of the Famine marked by the scars of protracted civic negotiation and politicised appropriation, of artistic vision and compromise and of struggles between competing versions of Irish history and identity.

Ireland

In Ireland, unlike so many previous epochs of historical commemorations where local efforts piggy-backed onto or modified narratives enshrined at the national level (as with the 1798 rebellion, Easter Rising, or the First World War), the Famine was an intensely local experience, not one which occurred at a remove from daily life.[14] It was an enormously complex event experienced variably according to location, replete with local anecdote and evocative textual descriptions available in newspapers and archival records, and open to a wide range of compelling human and emotional narratives.

What general observations might be made at the outset about the phenomenon of famine memorialisation in the Republic? The geographic distribution of memorials was relatively broad, spanning 19 of the 26 counties, with a slightly larger proportion located in the western counties.[15] Certainly the west of Ireland endured some of the worst suffering of the famine period and the devastating impact of mass emigration, its landscape marked with many visual reminders of dramatic shifts in nineteenth-century agriculture and land ownership – empty cottage ruins and endlessly subdivided smallholdings – making the higher incidence of famine memorialisation in this region unsurprising. Yet the reclamation of famine landscapes (particularly graveyards and workhouses) proved to be an important dimension of commemorative activity across Ireland even in those counties that proportionately suffered less during the famine period.[16] As attested by the list of grants awarded by the National Famine Commemoration Committee (the main provider of government funds for commemorative efforts), much of the funding for local commemorative projects was driven towards the preservation and restoration of these famine sites, whether or not they eventually received an additional commemoration in the form of a contemporary famine monument/memorial.[17]

Unusually for most widespread commemorative movements, the memorialisation of the Famine in Ireland has been a largely rural phenomenon. To date no sculptural/three-dimensional famine memorials have been erected in Cork, Kilkenny nor Waterford city; only Dublin and Limerick witnessed the addition of monuments during the mid-1990s (and Galway in 2012). Most famine monuments to be found in Ireland are located in small towns and villages, often in outlying locations and only very rarely placed in prominent public space. Although a few were designed with a tourist or external audience in mind (Skibbereen is one notable example, as its multiple monument sites now form the centre of a well-developed heritage trail), many are devoid of prominent signage and/or permanent interpretative fixtures. The siting of memorials at remote places of local significance, even at the expense of wider appreciation and footfall, suggests a very different relationship with famine memory than is frequently found in the diaspora. As a consequence of siting choices, many community monuments in Ireland are unknown to a wider audience, and some just over a decade old are currently in a state of disrepair or returning to formerly derelict conditions. The social performance of memory seems to be central in sustaining the relevance and prominence of local famine monuments, whether through annual famine walks, layering of famine monuments into pre-existing sites of contemplation or prayer or ongoing commemorative activities sited at the monument.

Considered together, the formal range of Irish Famine memorials is impressive, if occasionally bizarre: examples include bronze figurative groups (as in Roscommon, Co. Roscommon, 1999, Figure 7.1), high crosses (as in Longford, Co. Longford, 1995), commemorative stones (Carraroe, Co. Galway, 1997), recycled famine-era artefacts (Carrick-on-Shannon, Co. Leitrim, 1998), reconstructed peasant dwellings (Newmarket, Co. Kilkenny, 1999) and even a fountain in the shape of a giant, anatomically correct heart (Limerick, Co. Limerick, 1997, Figure 7.2)[18] However the function of many local monuments as memorials to the famine dead has encouraged a significant conservatism of form and symbol, with crosses, religiously-inflected grave monuments and simple, durable stone markers often (though not exclusively) preferred over works of public art or complex symbolic memorials. Occasionally visual artists were commissioned to create monument designs, but often the modest scale, budget and intent of the markers meant that local monument makers were employed to design and produce the finished memorials. With many monuments standing as proxy or sign for the now-vanished famine bodies which lie beneath the ground where they stand, figurative monuments in Ireland are few in number.

Stone and bronze predominate as materials, and the emotional tenor of most memorials is keyed at a much more sombre and darker pitch than will

Figure 7.1. Elizabeth McLaughlin, *County Famine Memorial Garden* (Roscommon, Co. Roscommon, 1999)

Figure 7.2. Maria Pizzuti, *Broken Heart* (Limerick, Co. Limerick, 1997)

be found elsewhere in the diaspora. Excessive textual interpretation or lists of sponsors/donors are usually eschewed, and in several cases there is no explanatory text whatsoever – suggesting that these committees considered textual explication of their monuments either unnecessary, inappropriate or at odds with the intended function of the memorial. Those memorials which do include interpretative text overwhelmingly refer to the impact of the Famine in local terms, laced with occasional reference to general historical facts of the Famine, but focused on specifics of place and the suffering which occurred in the locality. Accordingly most memorials focus not on themes of emigration, renewal or triumph over adversity (as in many diasporic examples), but rather death, absence and unknowable loss. Major narrative themes wrought by Irish memorials include an acknowledgment of past neglect of the famine poor, expressions of sorrow and solemn remembrance (often conveyed through religious symbology and Biblical references) and the direction of viewer attention to the sacred state of famine spaces. Many also make reference to historical texts from the locality (letters, workhouse reports, etc.) and include text in Irish, often utilising local dialects.

The government attention paid to commemorative activities in the mid-1990s sparked occasional laments in the Irish media of an emergent 'Famine

THE IRISH FAMINE AND COMMEMORATIVE CULTURE 153

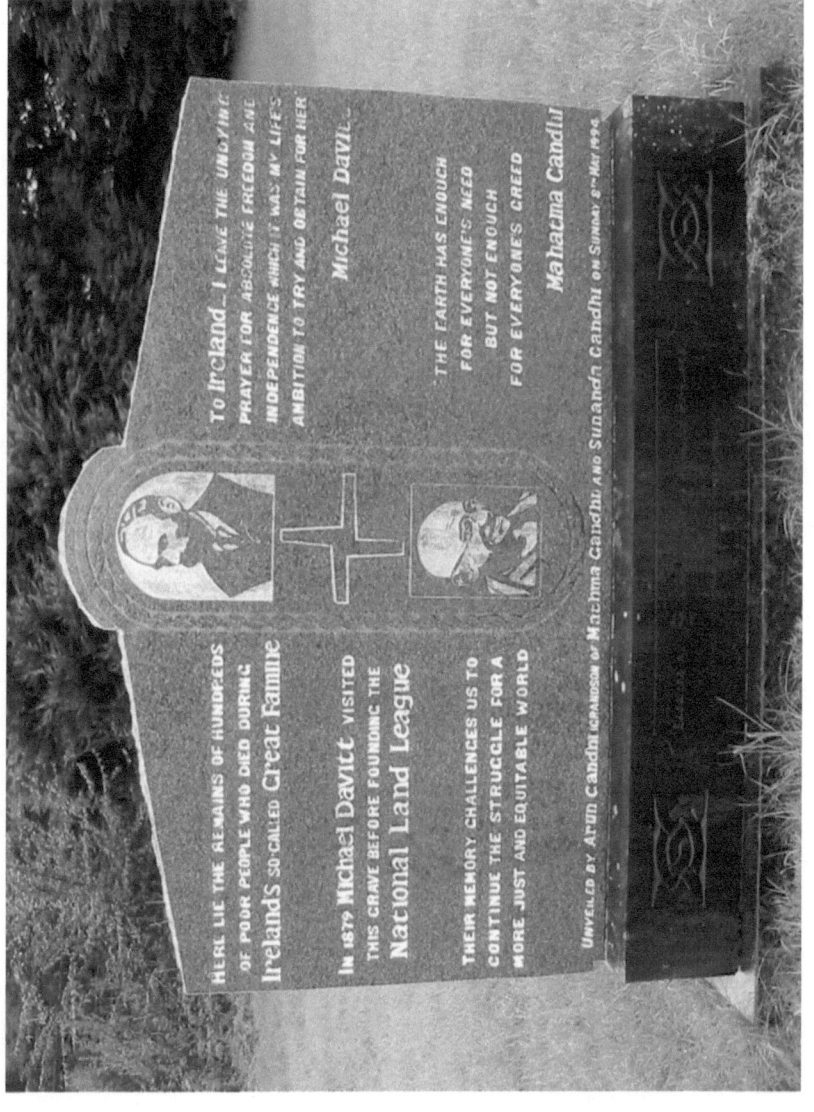

Figure 7.3. Action from Ireland-sponsored Famine monument (Swinford, Co. Mayo, 1994)

industry', an instrumentalist charge similarly levelled by historian Roy Foster.[19] Yet the term 'industry' connotes more centrality, structure and figures of dominance than the range of commemorative activity would actually indicate. Rather, the process of memorialisation in Ireland bore a fluid and largely grassroots character, highly individualised in particular communities and in proportion to levels of local interest in the anniversary. Whilst the Famine Commemoration Committee and its budget provided a national touchpoint, some funding and the official stamp of approbation, far more local projects were conceived and achieved independently of any real assistance at governmental level, either from a thematic, managerial or financial point of view. The majority of memorial projects were seeded and developed by small groups of committed local individuals, usually with little or no experience with public art or commemorative activities, often as outgrowths of local historical or heritage societies, and funding was nearly entirely privately raised.

The 150th anniversary of the Famine in Ireland revolved around several key preoccupations: the alignment of the anniversary with Third World relief issues and humanitarian aid, the centrality of the diaspora in shaping famine memory and the moral and emotional responsibility of remembrance as exhorted by many commemorationists, most particularly President Mary Robinson. These emphases were manifested through the budget allocations of the National Famine Commemoration Committee; the key role played by NGOs, particularly Action from Ireland and Concern[20] (see the monument in Swinford, Co. Mayo, 1994, Figure 7.3); and diasporic groups during the commemorative period; and the emergence of both popular and academic writing which has positioned the Famine within discursive frameworks of historical trauma.[21] With such calls for apologies, for 'healing' or for activism, famine memory has been endlessly instrumentalised and refracted, denying the emphatic wholeness and inviolability pronounced by those with competing agendas of remembrance.

The construction of community famine memorials in Ireland over the last decade thus centred on the connection of the anniversary in the Republic with the reawakening of local memories of the famine and the marking out of neglected sites for a primarily local audience. Their engagements with famine places and spaces of suffering have emphasised the act of mourning, the reconstitution of the absent body and a connection to the Irish landscape, past and present. What then of the production of community monuments in the diaspora – particularly in the United States?

The United States

Whether historicised, eulogised or celebrated, Irish America has always dominated the story of emigration from Ireland. The extensive historiography of Irish America bears witness to its enduring popularity as a subject and the inexhaustible demand for re-tellings of how the Irish came to America, and what they did once they got there.[22] Indeed the high profile of some sectors of the Irish community in the United States and the diasporic statistics frequently cited can obscure a sober reality: Irish America is actually getting smaller. Between 1990 and 2000 the number of people reporting Irish ancestry actually decreased by 21.2 per cent, a drop of some 8 million people.[23] At the same time interest in asserting Irish cultural identity and heritage within the United States is as strong as ever; moreover there is a growing awareness that the traditional association of Irish America with east coast big-city enclaves distorts the true demographic picture: Portland, Oregon and Phoenix, Arizona (both home to recently constructed famine monuments in 2008/1999 respectively) boast Irish populations that are proportionally twice as large as New York City's.

Such is the paradox of Irish America: if absolute numbers are shrinking, what can explain its amplified presence? What is it about the contemporary moment that has influenced such passionate expression, despite the demographic reality of ever-weakening links to immigrant ancestors? The sociologist Reginald Byron's 1999 study of the contemporary Irish-American community in Albany, New York offers some possible answers to why it is that fifth- and sixth-generation Irish Americans may frequently identify themselves as more 'Irish' than those previous generations who actually *were* more Irish. According to Byron's findings the faltering of actual, felt individual links to Irish ancestry and the ensuing commodification of Irish heritage has reinforced the representation of the Famine as a mythic explanatory event:

> the anthropomorphic interpretation of the Famine, as the event that is popularly believed to have caused the Irish diaspora, has assumed mythic status and now informs most people's understandings of the 'immigrant experience'.[24]

American community famine monuments offer visual evidence confirming Byron's description of mythic narratives colliding with personal interpretations, particularly in the observation that global notions of Irishness have been grafted onto local sites in increasingly paradigmatic ways. In terms of siting, nearly all US community monuments represented new commissions in cities or towns with very few physical traces of famine history still evident. As opposed to most Irish monuments, many do not occupy innately resonant or meaningful locations, although a site with some limited historical significance was often acquired, though more frequently they were sited in local parks or peripheral public locations. Furthermore, while in the Republic of Ireland Famine memory remains to some extent a widespread, *living* memory, these local monuments often constitute the sole civic gesture towards famine history and/or Irish identity within a crowded multicultural public space.

Formally speaking, the representational choices and themes adopted for US diasporic community famine memorials have focused overwhelmingly on emigration, genealogical links and reification of the imagined Irish ancestor or artefactual 'pieces' of Ireland. Commemorative committees' relationship to the Famine was frequently expressed through textual or symbolic declarations of genealogical ties, often directly inscribed by committee participants onto the physical memorials. The extensive recording of family names, insertion of symbolic stone elements from places like Cobh, the Cliffs of Moher or Connemara, and frequent reference in inscriptions to 'our ancestors' and the duty of remembrance borne by descendants are common elements across US famine memorials. Funding for many such small projects derived from the sale of physical space enabling participants to commemorate their own personal genealogy, and the literal representation of genealogy in the shape of bronze figural family groups predominates many memorial sites, presenting a simulated Irish ancestor(s) usually based on nineteenth-century engraved prototypes, which seek to inspire an emotional connection between viewer and subject.[25]

Slippage is common between the categories of 'Irish immigrant' and 'Famine immigrant'; claims of descent from famine immigrants form a powerful (though diffuse) emotional image which strikes close to the core of an oft-expressed form of Irish-American identity, although such identifications need not have a factual basis to be persuasive.[26] These memorials set out to make material a resounding claim: '*We* (the viewers, the constructors) are Famine immigrants'. By focusing almost exclusively on the theme of emigration and its connection to the existence of the latter-day commemorating group, these monuments foreground an Irish-American teleology which uses the Famine's anniversary as an occasion for reasserting an ethnic selfhood, not simply the translation of historical experience for a contemporary audience.

The prevalence of genealogical themes and the recourse to traditional Irish symbology and antiquated heroic aesthetics is perhaps unsurprising given the funding and sponsorship of most US Irish memorials, most frequently local divisions of the Ancient Order of Hibernians (AOH), the conservative Catholic fraternal organisation active in protecting a traditional vision of Irish-American heritage since the nineteenth century. Unlike in Ireland where community commemorations varied widely according to particulars of place and local experience, the pre-existing social networks that connect various AOH divisions with organisations like the Friendly Sons of St Patrick and the Emerald Society helped to ensure a close connection between many memorials in disparate locations. For example, the project in Buffalo, New York (1997)

THE IRISH FAMINE AND COMMEMORATIVE CULTURE   157

Figure 7.4. *The Western New York Irish Famine Memorial* (Buffalo, New York, 1997)

(Figure 7.4) utilised a replica standing stone as its main feature, surrounding the stone with smaller quaystones rescued by the commemorative committee during the renovation of Penrose Quay in Cork (a point of emigrant departure in the nineteenth century). Quaystones surplus to the Buffalo project's requirements were subsequently given to other projects: one in Irish Hills,

Figure 7.5a. *An Gorta Mór Hibernian Memorial* (Irish Hills, Michigan, 1994)

Michigan (1994) and the other in Olean, New York (2000) (Figures 7.5a and 7.5b), both of which transformed the humble quaystone into an elevated relic at the centre of their commemorative landscapes.

These threads linking US community monuments – including the recycling of construction materials and inscriptions, tapping of the same artists to

Figure 7.5b. *Southern Tier Irish Famine Memorial* (Olean, New York, 2000)

complete multiple commissions, attending each others' unveiling ceremonies and referencing each others' projects on websites – has created a remarkable series of connections between them, unlike most Irish projects which tended to be commissioned and managed independently. The need for extensive private fundraising and multi-year project timelines has meant that many groups remain

Figure 7.6. Eamonn O'Doherty, *Great Hunger Memorial* (Ardsley [Westchester County], New York, 2001)

deeply attached to their memorial projects, as opposed to Irish examples where links often dissipated quickly after the realisation of a project.

In terms of the political framing of famine, it is here we may observe some of the most profound differences between the United States and Ireland. Declarations of genocide and British culpability for the Famine have a significant presence within American memorials (an articulation almost entirely absent in the Irish context). A strongly nationalist sensibility pervades far more American memorials than any other variety, probably due to the influence of the AOH in commemorative activities and the persistence of nationalist framings of Irish-American experience with the Famine as originating point. Almost no mention has been made at any American famine memorial site of contemporary immigration policy or experience – a more politically divisive subject in the US than famine aid, which no doubt would have met with little consensus among commemorative committees. In the few instances where controversy has dogged a community memorial project, it did not concern commemorative symbolism or formal decisions, but rather money, political influence and the assignation of credit for the memorial gesture – as in the case of the monument in Ardsley, New York (2001) (Figure 7.6), where the commemorative committee split into two rival groups who wound up suing each other over control of the raised funds and final credit for the finished monument.[27]

In a related vein, the reiteration and defence of traditional notions of Irish ethnic identity found expression in most US monuments; in almost every diasporic example the 'Irish community' is cited as if a monolithic and tangible entity, though the notion of such cohesion is of course inevitably an illusion. The anxieties underlying some of these efforts – fears over a declining solidarity in the Irish community, or the competition with other ethnic groups for public space and recognition – are palpable. The emphatic characterisation of the Irish as an oppressed group in the US (however contrary to their present social status), while couched in an 'educational' narrative explicating the Irish Famine experience, seems rooted in the hope that with increased awareness of the Famine in America, in the words of one Irish-American famine commentator 'Now, for the first time since they were obliged to blend in, the Irish will stand out again, just as blacks, Jews, Hispanics and Chinese do'.[28]

In conclusion, what observations can be made about the intersection of the visual and the political at the site of local famine commemoration? The majority of community famine monuments in both Ireland and the US display an intensely conservative visual approach: in the case of the US, the deployment of famine clichés and Irish ethnic stereotypes still abounds – there is no shortage of shamrocks, coffin ships nor Bridgets on plinths.[29] In the case of Ireland, the issue of form has not always exercised the imagination of committees, who have often employed monumental sculptors to churn out variations of grave monuments with famine-related inscriptions.

All too often the visual 'vocabulary' of famine remembrance is taken to be self-evident, as if thatched cottages, emigrant ships and emaciated figures are 'natural' images of famine with unquestionable emotional power. Yet this assumption is no more true than the belief that minimalism or abstraction are 'natural' commemorative forms of the Holocaust: such choices have everything to do with the history of the event's visuality, current political concerns and aesthetic preferences, and relationships across commemorative communities that reinforce circularity. Post-traumatic frames of reference, Third World politics, the urgency to sustain Irish diasporic identity or the very fact of such a commemorative explosion itself – all are symptoms of the *Kunstwollen* of our own time.

In the aggregate, what unfolds from the simple command 'remember the Famine' is a motley crew of sculptural memorials confirming the suspicion that we cannot possibly locate a singular 'authentic' famine experience in a visual form. In an age of globalisation and the reduction of complex historical realities into a consumable 'heritage', the Famine remains a dislocation whose contradictions outnumber its certainties. We have moved no small distance from the solemn and sparse commemorations of the 1945 Fianna Fáil government to Michael Flatley's 2005 dance extravaganza *Celtic Tiger*, featuring an extensive famine sequence complete with scantily rag-clad dancers, projections of burning cottages and mock evictions. Whether the future of famine representation will remain locked in an obsession with self-affirmation, political instrumentalisation and conservative visual practices remains open; what is indelible is the stamp our present preoccupations have made on the construction of the famine past.

Notes and References

1 Peter Gray and Kendrick Oliver, 'The Memory of Catastrophe', *History Today* 51, no. 2 (February 2001): 13.
2 R. Dudley Edwards and T. Desmond Williams (eds), *The Great Famine: Studies in Irish History, 1845–52* (Dublin: Irish Committee of Historical Sciences by Browne and Nolan, 1956). For an account of the gestation of this volume see Cormac Ó Gráda, 'Making History in Ireland in the 1940s and 1950s: The Saga of the Great Famine', *Irish Review* Spring/Summer, no. 12 (1992).
3 Mary Daly and Margaret O'Callaghan (eds), *1916 in 1966: Commemorating the Easter Rising* (Dublin: Royal Irish Academy, 2007).
4 Writing on the perception of 1940s historians' 'silence' on the Famine, UCC historian Joe Lee has noted the very small number of university historians actually working on Irish subjects at the time. J. J. Lee, '150 Years: The Famine', *Irish Independent*, 19 August 1995.
5 See Dáil Éireann Debates, 'Committee on Finance, Vote 72 – Alleviation of Distress' (1947).
6 Cormac Ó Gráda, 'After the Famine Fever', *Irish Times*, 19 May 2001.

7 For details of the commemorative activities see National Famine Commemoration Committee, *Ireland's Famine: Commemoration and Awareness* (Dublin: Famine Commemoration Committee, 1995); National Famine Commemoration Committee, 'Directory of Commemorative Events' (Department of the Taoiseach, 1995); Don Mullan (ed.), *A Glimmer of Light: An Overview of Great Hunger Commemorative Events in Ireland and Throughout the World* (Dublin: Concern Worldwide, 1995). See also Peter Gray, 'Memory and Commemoration of the Great Irish Famine', in Peter Gray and Kendrick Oliver (eds), *The Memory of Catastrophe* (Manchester: Manchester University Press, 2004).
8 Kerby Miller and Patricia Mulholland Miller, *Journey of Hope: The Story of Irish Immigration to America* (San Francisco: Chronicle Books, 2001).
9 Laura Wilson, *How I Survived the Irish Famine* (Dublin: Gill and Macmillan, 2000).
10 The makers of the dolls, the Crolly Doll Factory of Donegal, currently offers 'Kathleen, the Tattie Hoker' Famine doll for a more reasonable €100.
11 Christopher Morash, *Writing the Irish Famine* (Oxford: Clarendon Press, 1995), 2–3.
12 Information on the monuments discussed in this essay is derived from extensive site visits, interviews and archival research conducted between 2003–2007: Emily Mark, 'Memorials and Monuments to the Irish Famine: Commemorative Art and History' (PhD dissertation, University College Dublin, 2008).
13 On Tolle's work see David Frankel, 'Hunger Artist: David Frankel on Brian Tolle', *ArtForum* (Summer 2002); Richard Kearney, 'Exchanging Memories: New York Famine Memorial', in *Navigations: Collected Irish Essays, 1976–2006* (Syracuse: Syracuse University Press, 2006); Niamh Ann Kelly, 'Remembering Homelessness in the Great Irish Famine', in David Valone (ed.), *Ireland's Great Hunger: Relief, Representation, and Remembrance* (Lanham: University Press of America, 2010). Gillespie's monument is probably the most visited and photographed Famine monument in Ireland: Tom Burke, 'Sculpting Life: The Work of Rowan Gillespie', (Moondance Productions in association with RTÉ, 2007).
14 In this context Guy Beiner's review of the 1898 commemorations of 1798 is particularly insightful, taking into account the manner in which official forms of commemoration were modified locally in line with specific interests and individual concerns: Guy Beiner, 'Negotiations of Memory: Rethinking 1798 Commemoration', *Irish Review* 26 (2000): 60–70.
15 Very few Famine memorials were erected in the North in the 1990s, with the largest concentration (four) in Co. Fermanagh. Two of the monuments (in Irvinestown, 1997 and Ardess, 2006) are similar in form and siting to their cousins in the Republic, as simple stone markers noting the position of mass graves. The third in Enniskillen was a more elaborate cross-border project (designed by sculptor Eamonn O'Doherty, 1996) that received funding from both governments, and served as the launch site for the Irish government's official start of commemorations.
16 Joel Mokyr's statistical survey lists Mayo, Sligo, Roscommon, Galway and Leitrim as suffering the highest degree of excess Famine mortality between 1846–1851; and Dublin, Wexford, Carlow, Kildare and Derry suffering least: Joel Mokyr, *Why Ireland Starved: A Quantitative and Analytical History of the Irish Economy, 1800–1850* (London: Allen and Unwin, 1983). It is unwise to draw too many conclusions about the geographic distribution of Famine monuments due to the small sample involved; however, the information to hand would suggest that the extent of historical suffering per region does not have a particularly strong correlation with rates of contemporary physical memorialisation. For example, Co. Limerick is home to four Famine memorials, while Cavan (which suffered nearly five times the excess mortality) has none recorded to date.

17 *National Famine Commemoration Committee Expenditures, 1995–97*, Commemoration Office, Department of the Taoiseach, 1 July 1998.
18 Maria Pizzuti's *Broken Heart* fountain in Limerick is one of the most unusual monuments to the Famine, won through a competition held for Dublin Institute of Technology (DIT) final year students in sculpture in 1997 and partially funded by the Per Cent for Art scheme. The bronze heart was sculpted using architectural bronze and welded; in line with the project brief the sculpture incorporates a water feature that flows water through the valves of the upstanding heart form.
19 Roy Foster, *The Irish Story: Telling Tales and Making It up in Ireland* (London: Allen Lane and the Penguin Press, 2001), 28.
20 Monuments produced directly by or in collaboration with NGOs include examples in Swinford, Co. Mayo; Doolough, Co. Mayo; and Callan, Co. Kilkenny (all erected in 1994). Indeed, calls for the Famine's commemoration from overseas aid agencies predated by at least a decade the government's establishment of an 'official' commemorative period (1995–97); the National Famine Commemoration Committee was formally launched at Action from Ireland's seventh annual 'Famine Walk' in Louisburgh, Co. Mayo in 1994.
21 Engagement with the discourse of historical trauma features prominently in several essays published in Tom Hayden (ed.), *Irish Hunger: Personal Reflections on the Legacy of the Famine* (Boulder and Dublin: Roberts Rinehart Publishers and Wolfhound Press, 1997).
22 The very notion that an 'Irish America' exists (or has ever existed) as a unified collective entity is undoubtedly questionable; histories which have traditionally reinforced the idea of an Irish ethnic 'sub-nation' are gradually being supplemented (if not supplanted) by those which question the basis of assuming ethnic collectives.
23 United States Census, 1990 and 2000. http://www.census.gov/.
24 Reginald Byron, *Irish America* (Oxford and New York: Oxford University Press, 1999), 294–5.
25 Engravings published in the *Illustrated London News* (particularly the image of 'Bridget O'Donnell and Children', 22 December 1849) form the most common source material used by recent projects: examples include monuments in Providence, Rhode Island (2007); Cleveland, Ohio (2000); and Keansburg, New Jersey (1997). See also Emily Mark-FitzGerald, 'Towards a Famine Art History: Invention, Reception, and Repetition from the Nineteenth Century to the Twentieth', in David Valone (ed.), *Ireland's Great Hunger*.
26 Byron makes this point forcefully in his analysis: 'Despite the common perception that today's generations of people of Irish ancestry are "the children of the Famine", there has been so much generational mixing over the last 150 years that it is questionable how many people having some fifth-generation ancestry are even preponderantly the descendants of Famine immigrants', Byron, *Irish America*, 145.
27 Thomas Staudter, 'Dispute Overshadows Hunger Sculpture', *New York Times*, 2 September 2001; Thomas Staudter, 'Dispute on Hunger Sculpture Lingers', *New York Times*, 3 February 2002.
28 Sean Kenny, 'A Nightmare Revisited', in Tom Hayden (ed.), *Irish Hunger: Reflections on the Legacy of the Famine* (Boulder and Dublin: Roberts Rinehart Publishers and Wolfhound Press, 1997), 190.
29 The extraordinary monument in Oak Forest, Illinois (1999) is perhaps the most extreme example, squashing every conceivable Irish symbolic cliché (emigrant ship, thatched cottage, Celtic cross, potato furrows, spectral 'death head' figure and an emaciated family) into its high-relief bronze surface.

Part III

TRAUMA AND VICTIMISATION

Chapter 8

HOLODOMOR AND THE POLITICS OF MEMORY IN UKRAINE AFTER INDEPENDENCE[1]

Heorhiy Kasianov
Institute of the History of Ukraine, Kiev

The 1932–33 Famine emerged as a topic in Ukrainian public and political discourse during the mid-1980s and formed part of an overall critique of the Soviet past. The usual set of stereotypical clichés about the Holodomor and their discursive representations read just about as follows:

During 1932 and 1933 the Ukrainian nation was subject to genocide. Under Stalin's leadership a famine was planned and executed by the ruling elite in Moscow with the aim of breaking the Ukrainian nation's possible resistance to the building of communism. The main target of this organised famine[2] was the individualistic and freedom-loving Ukrainian peasantry, and with it the 'backbone of the nation' was broken. At the same time, the national intelligentsia likewise faced repression and the nation was effectively beheaded. Between 7 and 10 million people died from starvation (this is at least the number that ex-president Yushchenko and politicians used to quote; scholars are more cautious and prefer to speak about three and a half to four million victims of the Famine). The Famine struck the Ukrainian nation and its genetic potential beyond remedy, and the consequences of this blow are felt to the present day. Many of the problems Ukraine currently encounters in its state- and nation-building efforts are consequences of the totalitarian rule to which Ukrainian nation has been subdued; the Holodomor being one of its main symptoms. The Holodomor was the greatest tragedy the Ukrainian nation experienced during the twentieth century. This was a tragedy of global dimensions, no less tragic than the Holocaust.

In the field of politics, the ideological and mobilising potential of the topic was instantly realised. Already during the term of President Leonid Kravchuk

(1991–94) the 'totalitarian past' in general and the Famine of 1932–33 in particular played an active role in the political rhetoric of the president and his followers. Kravchuk condemned past actions as 'illicit totalitarianism' to successfully distance himself and his image from this past and the crimes mentioned. In this he sided with parts of the 'national-democratic' establishment that used similar topics for political legitimisation and strove to leave behind their recent and not always unsullied past as members of the nomenclatura. Among the advocates of a 'Nuremberg trial on communism' were quite a few representatives of the literary establishment who owed their careers to the old regime. They now sided with dissidents in the quest for a comfortable position in the new situation. Hence the condemnation of 'totalitarianism' played an important ideological role and 'totalitarianism' was now represented as the Ukrainian nation's main foe. The past could easily be held responsible for all the embarrassing obstacles in the processes of the 'national rebirth' and state building. The 1932–33 Famine fitted ideally into this construction which explained, blamed and legitimised: all present difficulties could be traced back to unfavourable historical conditions or the evil intentions of 'the other'.

As far as Leonid Kuchma's presidency (1994–2004) is concerned, the problem of how to deal with the Soviet past and its 'original sins' initially lacked substantial meaning. Kuchma began to attach importance to these questions only when the political conflict with his opponents came to a head. Kuchma's directives on the commemoration of the 1932–33 Famine by no means coincide accidentally with the peak of political confrontation: such was the case during the 1998 parliamentary elections and the run up to the presidential elections one year later, and again in 2002 during the next parliamentary elections. At that time Kuchma faced the movement Arise, Ukraine! aiming at his resignation. On the eve of the upcoming presidential elections in 2003, Kuchma made another manoeuvre since a faction of the presidential majority in the parliament had joined the initiative of the opposition and recognised the 1932–33 Famine as an act of genocide. In order to prevent the opposition from gaining credibility in this field the president launched his own initiative.

A combination of ideological and pragmatic political motives, based on personal convictions, can be observed for Victor Yushchenko's term (2005–2010). For Yushchenko the politics of history constituted one of the main pillars of nation building, and the Famine of 1932–33 was at the very core of his understanding of the past. To be sure, even in his case the turn towards history was clearly motivated by political calculations. It is certainly not accidental that the active promotion of the historical subject of the 1932–33 Famine by the Ukrainian president coincided with the escalation of the power struggle between 2006 and 2008. Beyond that, one may assume that Yushchenko's politics of history were to a significant degree motivated by the fact that the president and his supporters (the remaining right wing and the national democrats, as well as some representatives of the diaspora) genuinely believed in a nationally orientated humanistic policy serving as a source of moral recovery for Ukrainian society and the facilitation of political unity. The use of history would be just one component of this policy.

The 'Uncovering' of the Holodomor under President Kravchuk, 1992–1994

A decree on the financing of a memorial complex called *Kolokola mira* (Bell of peace) in the town of Lubny in the Poltava district, issued on 26 August 1992 by Prime Minister V. Fokin, was the first official reaction to the Famine issued by the government of the newly created independent Ukrainian state. The decree was never fully implemented, particularly in its financial dimension, yet in Lubny a memorial was erected in form of a mound crowned by an enormous bell and cross.

In 1993, on the occasion of the 60th anniversary of the 1932–33 tragedy, the political leadership set out to discuss commemorative measures. President Kravchuk actively supported the idea of holding various acts of remembrance at state level. He was pushed by cultural officials from the ranks of the national democrats in the president's entourage[3] and by high ranking returnees from the diaspora. By that time the latter had established themselves as vocal participants and moral persuaders in debates on Ukrainian cultural policies.[4] Hence Kravchuk was caught between two stools: he had to abstain from overtly radical exploits and declarations, while simultaneously balancing between nation building and the condemnation of the 'criminal totalitarian regime', of which he himself of course was a product.

On 19 February 1993 Leonid Kravchuk issued a decree which became the first of a whole series of official statements by the presidential administration on the topic of the 1932–33 Famine. It was the point of departure for the active pursuit of the politics of history in the new Ukrainian state. Although pretty technical in character – the document basically contained instructions for various state organs on how to organise official events, essentially for the so-called 'Days of Sorrow' in September 1993 – this decree was a benchmark in the ideological exploration of the topic of the 1932–33 Famine. Already the title of the decree, 'On measures connected to the 60th anniversary of the Holodomor in Ukraine'[5], contained the ideologically significant term Holodomor, which would, in the years to come, transform from a literary metaphor into an academic, political and even juridicial notion. The title of the decree did not merely sanction the use of the term, but also a certain opinion on, and an understanding and interpretation of the 1932–33 Famine which now became official. To a degree, the term Holodomor already encoded information on the reasons and the consequences of the tragedy, and defined the limits of possible interpretation.

Beyond that, the decree was a first attempt to internationalise the question of the 1932–33 Famine: The Ministry of Foreign Affairs was instructed to contact UNESCO with a request to enter a reference to the tragedy into its calendar. Likewise, it deserves mentioning that 13 representatives of the Ukrainian diaspora in the West and other CIS countries were invited to join the organisation committee for the Days of Sorrow. These invitees headed the biggest Ukrainian associations outside the state, and there were even two non-Ukrainians among them: the American scholar James Mace and his British colleague Robert Conquest. With the support of the diaspora, they had helped create the canonical academic interpretation of the 1932–33 Famine.

Evidently, the decree did not include any detailed instructions of a political or ideological kind as Kravchuk tried to steer clear of extremes. Nonetheless, some of the national democrats among his followers tried to exacerbate the situation. In May 1993 the organisational committee for the Days of Sorrow operating under government tutorship suggested a programme of official commemoration which contained the proposal of a tribunal on those deemed responsible for the Holodomor.[6] Moreover, it was suggested that the whole string of events, now titled 'Days of Sorrow and Commemoration for the Victims of the Holodomor', should be realised as a large-scale public enterprise. Some of the best film directors in the country, Yuri Il'enko, Mykola Mashchenko and Leonid Osyka were invited to contribute.

In June 1993, the Association of Holodomor Investigators in Ukraine, founded one year earlier, suggested that the Ukrainian parliament should appoint a provisional commission to examine the 1932–33 Famine. This association united several dozens of people from different regions of Ukraine interested in the topic; among them were professional historians. According to their suggestion, the commission

> could, on the basis of sources brought to light by academic research, qualify the Holodomor as a crime against the Ukrainian people, as an imminent act of genocide that seriously endangered its [the Ukrainian people's] genetic reproduction and its cultural potential.[7]

The association, led by the former dissident and founder of the Ukrainian Republican Party, Levko Luk'ianenko, also suggested transferring the 'case' to the International Court of Justice in The Hague.

In the month of July of 1993, Mikola Zhulinskii, deputy prime minister of the government and chairman of the organisational committee, came to the *Verkhovna*

Rada with the suggestion to organise a hearing on the 1932–33 Famine during parliamentary sessions. The parliament's reply was an attempt to prevaricate, wrapped in bureaucratic propositions: it contained the proposal to commission a historical report, the name of a keynote speaker, and a draft for a statement by the parliament. Further consultations made it clear that, as elections drew closer, there was little chance to have the famine issue debated while the parliament was in session. Beyond that, the background of the deputies, elected (prior to Ukrainian independence) in 1990 when the majority vote still went for communist candidates, excluded any public event exposing the 'crimes of the communist regime'.

As a result, the first significant and government-supported public commemoration of the 1932–33 Famine carried every sign of a compromise between radical and moderate scripts. No national tribunal or theatrical staging came about. This would, however, not prevent the costs for such a tribunal from amounting to half of the budget for the Days of Sorrow.[8] Nor did any of the parliamentary hearings planned for the anniversary take place. Instead, President Leonid Kravchuk participated in an international conference titled 'Holodomor in the Ukraine 1932–1933: Causes and Consequences'. His participation sent an important signal to the partisans of the radical scenario and was taken as a symbolic token for the highest authorities' interest in a 're-establishment of historical truth'. In his opening speech, Leonid Kravchuk declared:

> I do basically agree that this [the Famine] was a planned incident, that this was a genocide committed against our own people. But I would not stop here. Yes, it was against our own people, but it was not committed on orders from another centre.[9]

This was a risky remark as ten years earlier, on the occasion of the 50th anniversary of the 1932–33 Famine then functioning as Head of the Ukrainian Communist Party's Department for Agitation and Propaganda, the same Leonid Kravchuk had actively participated in counterpropaganda against the 'anti-Soviet campaigns organised in the West in connection with the so-called "50th anniversary of the artificial famine in Ukraine"'.[10] Incidentally this was passed over in silence both by the former dissidents supporting the president and the representatives of the diaspora, whose 'nationalist imaginations' of the Famine had been the target of Kravchuk's ideological zeal not so long ago. For these groups it was politically important what he said and did at present, and not what he had said and done in the past. Against this backdrop, insistence on 'historical truth' seemed to be dispensable.

The conference mentioned above may also serve as an example of the extreme polarisation which surrounded the topic of the 1932–33 Famine. Among the speakers scholars were easily outnumbered by public figures and politicians, and the latter surpassed the former also in terms of the force and the emotions with which they dealt with the subject. The 1932–33 Famine was mentioned in the context of topics like Ukraine's future as a nuclear power, the division of assets formerly belonging to the Soviet Union; and the status of Sevastopol and the Crimea.

The year 1993 was the point of departure after which the Ukrainian state, or at least the presidential administration and the executive branch (boundaries between the branches were hardly distinguishable), began to pursue the politics of history more actively. Their policy aimed at a conversion of the 1932–33 Famine into the main and fundamental symbol of a national historic myth. Following directives from the highest state authorities, the same year saw events and procedures put in place which were intended to become recurring commemorative routines performed across the whole country. In a sense, this politics of history blended state and public practices. Processions, requiems and the erection of crosses on the graves of the famine victims, for example, had been organised locally earlier and independently of the state by organisations that initially stood in opposition to the government. The difference was overcome and now these initiatives received the blessing of the state. More often than not, however, support remained at a rhetorical level, as the 1990s would turn out to be the decade of the deepest socio-economic crises, and of unprecedented private appropriation of public property. Under these circumstances the funding of any policy concerned with history became a prerogative of the Ukrainian diaspora; and this is particularly true for the history of the 1932–33 Famine.[11]

It should be mentioned, however, that in the same year 1993 a first all-Ukrainian commemorational event was organised after Kravchuk's government had issued a corresponding decree. On 10 September 1993 the national flags on all government buildings across the country were dropped to half-mast for four hours.[12] At the same time the idea of undertaking a second Nuremberg trial on communism emerged among some of the public organisations. Behind it was the same Association of Holodomor Investigators in Ukraine, founded in 1992. Although the Associations of Prisoners and Victims of Repression and Memorial supported the idea, the tribunal was held as late as 2000, and in Lithuania.[13]

Amnesia or Pragmatism? History and Memory under Leonid Kuchma, 1994–2005

As mentioned earlier, the role of ideological factors in state policy diminished during Kuchma's presidency. Kuchma, a technocrat, was preoccupied with economic problems, with the establishment of personal control beyond limits of property and with the introduction of a system of checks and balances within the administration. The struggle for power and its redistribution, however, required to take ideological problems into account. Therefore it would be incorrect to assume that politics of history under Leonid Kuchma could be summarised as an attempt to realise a 'project of amnesia'.[14] It would be more precise to talk about 'pragmatism' in the politics of history, and the 1932–33 Famine as an object of such policies proves the point again.

A governmental decree dedicated to the 65th anniversary of the 1932–33 Famine in October 1998[15] contained the already customary list of commemorative events. In November of the same year Kuchma proclaimed an official Day of Commemoration in another specifically dedicated decree: the last Saturday in November was from now on declared Day of Remembrance for the Victims of the Holodomors.[16] The use of the word Holodomor in its plural form clearly reflected the idea that the famines of 1921–23, 1932–33 and 1946–47 were directly linked and proof of a policy towards the Ukrainian people that Moscow pursued uniformly and continuously. In October 2000 Leonid Kuchma altered the denomination of the commemoration day again: it was now called the Day of Remembrance for the Victims of Holodomor and Political Repressions. Thus the symbolic territory of remembrance was enlarged. In July 2004, at the height of the campaign for his succession in which Kuchma pulled the strings, he changed the denomination back into Day of Remembrance for the Victims of Holodomors and Political Repressions, thus returning the initial plural.[17]

In February 2002, during the year of parliamentary elections which contestants and commentators alike regarded as a showdown of strength preceding the presidential elections, Kuchma issued another commemorative decree titled 'Measures in Connection with the 70th Anniversary of the Holodomor in Ukraine'.[18] This is an interesting document as it lists as recommendations for the executive bodies practically all the commemorative practices in relation to the 1932–33 Famine as they developed during the 1990s. Most likely, it was an attempt to regain the initiative, as the appeal to the tragic historical past was a convenient means of displaying one's own humanitarian attitudes. At the same time it prevented any appropriation of the past in contexts less opportune for the president. Towards the end of that year, on 6 December 2002, Kuchma ordered the construction of a memorial complex for the victims of the Holodomor and repressions in Kiev. This project, however, was only realised in November 2008 after his presidency had ended. It should be added that other 'ideological' decrees by Kuchma, including those on historical memory, were implemented without enthusiasm, superficially or not at all by the presidential administration in the regions and municipalities. Reports on commemorative events linked to the 1932–33 Famine sent back 'from below' read as very formal bureaucratic carbon prints of the initial orders.[19]

2003 – A Quantum Leap in the Handling of the Holodomor?

During 2003, politicians and authorities displayed a growing interest in the problem of the 1932–33 Famine. The 70th anniversary coincided with renewed political tensions within Ukraine, which in their turn were caused by the approaching presidential elections and Kuchma's attempts to impose political changes shifting the balance between presidency and parliament in favour of the former. It should be added that 2003 also saw the anniversary of other problematic historical events like the Polish-Ukrainian conflicts over Volhynia (1943–44), also known as the 'Vohlynian massacre'.[20] And finally, 2003 had been declared the Year of Russia in Ukraine, which added a particular dimension to the political debates about the 1932–33 Famine, in particular among those factions of the political spectrum that customarily regarded Russia as the eternal suppressor of Ukraine.

Against this backdrop, the anniversary of the 1932–33 Famine could not but play an important role in the political debates of the day. The extremely heterogeneous opposition was unified only by the desire to prevent Kuchma from concentrating overwhelming power in his hands. The opposition instantly disintegrated after the centre-right parties teamed up in the block Our Ukraine under the leadership of Victor Yushchenko, publicly insisted on a parliamentary hearing on the 1932–33 Famine. Occasional allies of Our Ukraine, the Communists categorically rejected this idea. In return, and with the blessing of Kuchma, parties run by the oligarchs supported the initiative, although they were not genuinely interested in the politics of history.

The parliamentary hearing in the *Verkhovna Rada* took finally place on 12 February 2003. The parliamentary speeches of that day constituted a distinctive compendium of ideological clichés on the subject of totalitarian crimes. The national democrats and their allies from the right would routinely direct their diatribes against the 'criminal totalitarian regime', including the present regime which they considered to be no less criminal. The invectives against the government were readily supported by the communists, who, in their turn, rejected any responsibility for the crimes of their predecessors, as suggested by the national democrats and the political right. Of course, all orators interspersed their remarks on the Holodomor with references to the present situation in Ukraine.

The representatives of power themselves related the contemporary problems to the grave traumas of the past. Deputy Prime Minister Dmytro Tabachnyk deemed the

> excesses of the hungry year of 1933 not a by-gone historical experience, but one of the deepest socio-demographic catastrophes of the twentieth

century. It is a moral and psychological wound that does not heal, one that torments the memory of survivors with unbearable pain. The socio-physiological feeling of fear caused by mass repressions and famines lives on in the consciousness of many generations. It has been engraved into the genetic type of the nation and it significantly retards the democratisation of our society.[21]

The authorities thus duplicated interpretations brought forward by the national democrats and rightists: according to them, the Holodomor extinguished the Ukrainian elite, dealt a devastating blow to the whole nation and destroyed its genetic stock. The former writer and deputy of the Our Ukraine faction, Pavlo Movchan, declared that 'the energy, intellectual, and creative force of our nation had been discontinued for many years. Any form of resistance against these acts of suppression in all spheres of national and public life has been crushed'.[22]

The left reinvigorated the years of Famine 1932 and 1933 in a different manner. Communist leader Petro Simonenko declared that a genocide was actually happening at present, and that is was futile to look for it in the past: 'From this tribune I propose to and demand from the gentlemen in power not to indulge in slander of the Soviet past, but to answer for their current criminal deeds which amount to politics of genocide'.[23]

On 14 May 2003, upon recommendation of the parliamentary hearings, the *Verkhovna Rada* held a special session dedicated to the 1932–33 Famine, which, according to information distributed by the public organisation Laboratory for Legislative Initiatives, lasted only a few minutes. In the absence of the communist deputies, the legally necessary majority of 226 deputies passed the wording of a 'Declaration to the Ukrainian people', in which the 1932–33 Famine was described as a genocide against the Ukrainian people:

> We consider that in independent Ukraine the terrible truth about these years must be released by the state, in so far as the Holodomor of 1932–33 was consciously organised by the Stalinist regime and must be publicly condemned by Ukrainian society and the international community as one of the manifestations of genocide in world history, and as one with the highest number of victims.[24]

From this time onwards the term 'genocide' was irrevocably established as a denominator for the 1932–33 Famine in the vocabulary of the authorities. This is true for the presidential administration as well as for the executive and the legislative powers. The same year 2003 also witnessed the first endeavour to see the 1932–33 Famine recognised by the largest of the international organisations, the United Nations.

Haunted by History? Viktor Yushchenko's Presidency, 2005–2010

The ideological reinvigoration of the Famine and political allusions to the topic reached a new level in the wake of the 2004 'Orange Revolution'. References to the traumatic historical experience became an unavoidable element of important public appearances of President Viktor Yushchenko, and mentioning the 1932–33 Famine formed an almost imperative subject of his speeches. The Famine already figured in the president's inaugural speech in January 2005. The first international addresses of Viktor Yushchenko in the European Parliament and on the occasion of a joint session of the chambers of the US Congress also referred to the problem of the 1932–33 Famine.[25]

Yushchenko issued the first of a series of presidential decrees concerning the politics of history in June 2005. It was titled 'On additional measures serving the perpetual commemoration of victims of political repressions and the Holodomors in Ukraine'. The first decree mentioned contained a section suggesting the draft of a law on 'the political and judicial assessment of Holodomors in Ukraine'.[26] The use of the expression 'political and judicial assessment' may have signalled some legal incompetence on the part of the president and his advisors, or it indeed reflected his conviction that a correlation of law with politics was permissible and even necessary. Again, the use of the word Holodomor in its plural form borrowed the idea that the famines of 1921–23, 1932–33 and 1946–47 were directly linked and proof of a uniform and continuous policy of the Kremlin directed against Ukraine. The same decree represented a landmark in other respects as well: it suggested that the government should 'solve the question' of the creation of a 'National Memory Institute' by November that year.

The president issued another decree on 4 November 2005 in which the government was primarily obliged to draft a law on the 'political and judicial assessment'. In doing so, the president did not await the government's assessment and described the Holodomor as a 'genocide against the Ukrainian people' and called for additional measures in order to achieve international recognition that the 1932–33 Famine had indeed been a genocide. The decree contained a repeated call for the creation of a National Memory Institute, now with a two week deadline.[27] With this decree the state also embarked on a commemorative campaign dedicated to the 75th anniversary of the 1932–33 Famine. The government created an organisational committee[28] which never became active due to the renewed stand-off between government and parliament in the wake of the 2006 parliamentary elections.

In September 2006 the president received an open letter from a group claiming to represent the 'scholarly community', in fact a gathering of peoples' deputies, politicians and representatives of the diaspora with rather remote links to academia. The authors asked the president to set up two different days of remembrance, one for the commemoration of the victims of the Holodomors, and one for commemoration for the victims of political repressions. The request was motivated by the desire to distinguish between wolves and sheep: finally some of the perpetrators, the authors of the letter pointed out, had then ended up as victims of the repressions themselves.[29] The content of this letter was symptomatic in the sense that these 'scholars in society' were ready to support the president in the unfolding campaign for the transformation of the Holodomor into a historical symbol shared by the entire nation, for its transformation into a symbolic marker of the nation.

Victor Yushchenko himself tried to create another organisation committee for the preparation and realisation of the Day of Remembrance for Victims of the Holodomors and Political Repressions in October 2006. This time he commissioned representatives of two antagonistic groups within the state bureaucracy as co-chairs, one from the presidential secretariat, and one from the government's secretariat which was controlled by Viktor Yushchenko's political opponents. At the same time he ordered Ukraine's foreign ministry to step up activities with the aim of a 'recognition by the international community that the 1932–33 Holodomor had been a genocide against the Ukrainian people and one of the greatest tragedies in the history of mankind'.[30]

Together with the National Memory Institute the presidential secretariat organised a round table discussion titled 'Holodomor 1932–1933 – genocide in Ukraine' which was held on 16 October 2006. The organisers hoped that an open letter by the participants to the president would demonstrate public support for the state's initiative to achieve a 'political and judicial assessment of the Holodomor'.[31] They called the tragedy of 1932–33 'the apogee of the long struggle of the USSR's totalitarian regime against the Ukrainian people's fight for liberation, and in particular against the Ukrainian peasantry'. Its recognition as genocide was understood as 'the indubitable task of the contemporary generation of Ukrainian politicians, and in particular of the body of parliamentary deputies'. Politicians from the 'regions where the Great Hunger struck with particular violence during the years 1932–1933, i.e. the East, South and the Centre' were called upon to display particular zeal in the realisation of the 'indubitable task'.[32] The political geography behind that statement is fairly easy to decipher: This appeal was addressed to deputies from regions opposing the president's party, and their allies, the communists and socialists.

Holodomor – Genocide and its Denial

On 2 November 2006 President Viktor Yushchenko used his constitutional prerogative to introduce a priority law 'On the 1932–33 Holodomor' in the *Verkhovna Rada*. Three out of six articles of the draft opened up a new stage in the politics of history in Ukraine. The first article defined the 'Holodomor of 1932–1933 as a genocide against the Ukrainian nation', the second prohibited any 'denial of the fact of the Holodomor', while the sixth article suggested making the 'public denial of the 1932–1933 Holodomor in Ukraine an accountable offence'.[33] It deserves mentioning that until this point even the most narrow-minded leftists had not denied the fact of the 1932–3 Famine. Accounts of the events had become parts of the history curricula in schools and colleges in Ukraine, and national Days of Commemoration and other nation-wide rituals had been established. The presidential initiative was clearly designed to provoke rejection on the part of the opposition, which would have made it subject to reprimand and moral discredit. Indeed, the autumn of 2006 saw the intensification of the tiresome struggle between the president and the oppositional parliamentary majority that had elected Viktor Yanukovich's government.

Predictably, the draft of the law triggered protest from the president's opponents. The Party of the Regions proposed a competing draft, without the items on the genocide and the accountability before the law. The passionate parliamentary debate on the presidential draft in the *Verkhovna Rada* on 28 November 2006 turned into a mutual apportionment of blame. Both legislative proposals, the presidential and the alternative one, were rejected. Still, a compromise was found and on this basis a law was passed with the votes of Our Ukraine, the Block Yulia Timoshenko and the socialists. The categorisation of the Holodomor as a genocide was retained; it was supplemented with a reference to 'other nationalities of the USSR as victims of the famine', and the item threatening the denial of the Holodomor with administrative penalties was dropped. It was replaced by a different phrasing, according to which 'the pubic denial of the 1932–1933 Holodomor is regarded as an insult to the five million victims of the Holodomor, as a vilification of the dignity of the Ukrainian people and is declared unlawful'.[34]

The adoption of the law in this form was just a prelude to more radical measures. On 21 December 2006 two deputies from the Our Ukraine's faction introduced a bill requiring changes in Ukraine's criminal code which was titled 'On responsibility for the public denial of the 1932–33 Holodomor as a genocide against the Ukrainian people'.[35] The president took upon himself the next legislative initiative on 28 March 2007, introducing the draft of a bill titled 'On the introduction of changes in the criminal and criminal-procedural codes of Ukraine (on responsibility for the denial of Holodomor)'. It suggested the introduction of legal persecution for 'the denial of the 1932–33 Holodomor as a genocide against the Ukrainian people and of the Holocaust as a genocide against the Jewish people'.[36] The draft suggested sanctioning these denials if performed publicly, and also the dissemination of material containing them, with fines of between one and three hundred times the minimum wage,[37] or sentences of up to four years of imprisonment.[38]

It is difficult to come up with a rational explanation for Viktor Yushchenko's pressure to criminalise not merely alleged denials of the fact but also of differing interpretations of the tragic events of the past. The draft contained direct references to laws existing in European countries, and included references to the issue of the Holocaust, which was conceived to add weight to the president's initiative through analogies with European practice, the draft contained direct references to laws existing in European countries.[39]

Explanatory notes on the draft included a number of very interesting expressions. It was emphasised, for example, that the

> passing of the law will facilitate the consolidation of the Ukrainian people and the citizens of all other nationalities around the rejection of all forms of aggression, it will further the respect for the lives, rights and freedoms of the citizens, strengthen mutual understanding between the nationalities and reinforce the concord of the citizens of Ukraine.[40]

The document contains little in the way of explanation on how precisely the criminal persecution for the 'incorrect' interpretation of the Holodomor or the Holocaust would assist the attainment of the noble aims listed above. Furthermore, the presidential argumentation in favour of the law is even more interesting in the light of sociological data published on the president's own website. 'The Holodomor', it read,

> reached its biggest extent in those regions where the electoral base of the Anti-Crisis-Coalition[41] is concentrated. As a result of insufficient information, Soviet propaganda and an indifferent position of the leaders of the coalition, the population of these territories does not understand the present consequences of the tragedy. According to sociological polls, only 40 per cent (of those who gave a definite answer) agree that the Verkhovna Rada should pass a law which would recognise the 1932–33 Holodomor as an act of genocide against the Ukrainian people. The figure for the South is 64 per cent, which is still lower than the average figure for Ukraine in total (71.4 per cent).[42]

The presidential initiative precipitated angry protests by political opponents, and disapproval or incomprehension from parts of the intelligentsia. The main academic advisory board of the *Verkhovna Rada* pointed out that the suggestion aimed at criminalising acts which had to be considered as 'a form of expression of particular opinions and convictions', while the constitution would allow such restrictions only in clearly defined circumstances, under which the presidential project would not fall.[43]

The draft of the law provoked a storm of predominantly negative comments and had no chances of passing in the *Verkhovna Rada*. Using his prerogatives as the Speaker, Oleksandr Moroz put it on the parliamentary agenda only for the end of May 2007, although it had been introduced as 'urgent' by the presidential administration. Incidentally, the president accused the Anti-Crisis Coalition of trying to usurp power and dissolved the *Verkhovna Rada* already on 1 April 2007. He would repeat this practice another three times during the following year and a half. Interestingly, though, this draft law became the object of active political negotiations with the Anti-Crisis Coalition during the spring of 2007. It was included in a package for a political compromise which contained, among other things, draft laws on constitutional changes and on the opposition.[44] It is also interesting that at the height of the political crisis between representatives of authority, the president found the time to sign two decrees which split up a commemorative date: the third Sunday in May was now dedicated to the Commemoration of the Victims of Political Repressions, while the last Saturday in November continued to be celebrated as the Day of Remembrance for the Victims of the Holodomors.[45]

In October 2007, when parliamentary re-elections before the end of term seemed to offer chances of a parliamentary majority, Viktor Yushchenko affirmed his intention to push his law project through the renewed parliament. He delivered on his promise in December, when he included the draft in a package of 13 'urgent' bills. It deserves attention that the argumentation on the need to introduce criminal persecution for the 'denial' of the *Holodomor* and the Holocaust as genocides was built on the 'requirement to prevent corresponding behaviour, and thus the prevention of any threat to the public or any damage to physical or juridical bodies, to society or to the state'.[46] One month later the presidential draft was revived through the legislative initiative of two deputies from the presidential faction Our Ukraine – Popular Self-Defence. The deputies modestly demanded sanctions for the denial of the *Holodomor* only; perpetrators would be punished with imprisonment from six month up to three years.[47] At the same time it remained unclear for which offence such draconian punishment was proposed: in one passage of the explanatory note to the draft the denial of the *Holodomor* was mentioned, in another the denial that the *Holodomor* had been a genocide, and a third section threatened to sanction the 'denial of the fact of a genocide against the Ukrainian people'.[48]

'Ukraine Remembers, the World Acknowledges'

Simultaneously, an unprecedented ideological and political campaign was launched under Viktor Yushchenko's direct involvement. He personally headed an organisational committee created for the purpose of transforming the 1932–33 Famine into the central mobilising symbol of Ukraine's national history; into a symbol for the greatest humanitarian catastrophe of the twentieth century, which had exceeded the Holocaust and other examples of genocide in its effects. This campaign under the catch-phrase 'Ukraine remembers, the world acknowledges' began in spring 2007 and reached its climax in November 2008 on the occasion of the 75th anniversary of the 1932–33 Famine.

The campaign targeted basically two audiences – a domestic and an international one. A string of commemorative, propagandistic and cultural events in Ukraine was organised with the help of, on the one hand, state bureaucracy; in particular the regional and municipal administration directly subordinated to the president plus the security services. On the other hand it drew on the support of thousands of volunteers who sincerely wished to honour the victims of the Famine. Outside the state the diplomatic service undertook unprecedented efforts to obtain international recognition for the thesis that the 1932–33 Famine had been a genocide against the Ukrainian people.

One of the core concerns of the campaign was the compilation of a national Book of Memory which the names of all victims of the 1932–33 Famine should be registered. The compilation of the book became a grandiose commemorative project employing tens of thousands of citizens across Ukraine, including those regions that had not been exposed to the Famine but had become the home of eyewitnesses later on. Coordination groups emerged under the tutelage of district and regional state organs to organise the collection of information on those who suffered or died from the Famine in 1932–33. These coordination groups managed the activities of hundreds of local groups which collected evidence on the spot, predominantly in villages. The local groups consisted of teachers, students, pupils of local schools, librarians, museum staff and local historians, club directors and so on. They tracked down eyewitnesses, interviewed them and worked with the archives of the registry offices. By November 2008 the compilation of 18 regional volumes plus one all-Ukrainian volume of the book of memory was concluded. These volumes registered information about more than 800,000 victims of the Famine.

Simultaneously, Ukraine saw commemorative mass events like Light a Candle, Inextinguishable Candle or 33 Minutes.[49] Meetings and concerts were arranged and literary and arts competitions organised. Pupils competed for the best essays on the subject, commemorative talks were held in schools. Wreaths and bouquets were placed at memorial sites; museums, schools and libraries hosted exhibitions, crosses and other memorials were erected in sites of remembrance; rose gardens were planted and new memorial sites created.[50]

These measures were supplemented by the above mentioned passing of laws and the subsequent juridical validation of the Holodomor as a genocide; and the preparation of further laws that would sanction any other public interpretation of the tragedy. The state also financed the publication of academic research on the 1932–33 Famine through competitive grants for publishers and authors. Still, the expected stream of publications did not materialise. It seems that not many historians were ready to answer the call for 'the correct version of the tragedy of the past'.[51]

Finally, the most characteristic feature of the 2007–2008 campaign was the unprecedented active involvement of the president and his diplomatic services with the aim of international recognition for the interpretation of the 1932–33 Famine as an act of genocide against the Ukrainian people. Viktor Yushchenko personally presided over the international committee for the ceremonies dedicated to the 75th anniversary of the 1932–33 Famine. This committee comprised representatives of the largest associations of the Ukrainian diaspora; yet such committees would usually be chaired by the Deputy Prime Minister for Humanitarian Affairs. During meetings with leaders of important international organisations in years 2005 to 2008, Viktor Yushchenko asked for support for the dissemination of knowledge about the 1932–33 Famine across the borders and its recognition as an act of genocide. A standing committee was installed in Ukraine's Ministry of Foreign Affairs in order to provide 'position papers' and to coordinate the diplomatic missions' efforts to popularise knowledge about the Holodomor. This group and the heads of the diplomatic missions in the respective countries closely collaborated with the local diaspora organisations. Thanks to their lobbying of the latter, the 1932–33 Famine was recognised as a genocide by the legislative organs of the United States, Canada and Australia. Between 1993 and 2008 the parliaments of 13 countries recognised the 1932–33 Famine as a genocide against the Ukrainian people. The diplomatic efforts to achieve the same decisions on the level of international organisation proved to be futile, though. In 2007 and 2008 the OSCE Parliamentary Assembly, the European Parliament and the UNESCO passed resolutions on the 1932–33 Famine, but the term 'genocide', all efforts of the Ukrainian diplomatic services notwithstanding, found no mention.

In these endeavours the Ukrainian authorities faced the stiffest resistance from the Russian leadership. The latter regarded these efforts as damaging Russia's international prestige as the legal successor of the USSR. 'A genocide against Ukrainians organised by Bolshevist Moscow' was, according to the Russian authorities' reading, the more or less subtly gilded subtext of the whole 2007–2008 campaign. As a reaction, Ukrainian efforts to achieve recognition of the 1932–33 Famine as a genocide were blocked. Since the spring of 2007 a silent but ferocious war was fought in the representation of the United Nations, in the UNESCO and the OSCE, which only occasionally surfaced through notes issued by the foreign ministries of both countries. Formally, the more aggressive and more flexible Russian diplomacy gained a victory, although both sides suffered equal amounts of moral damage. It should not be overlooked that with Israel there was a third player involved in the struggle. The rare comments made by Israeli diplomats clearly make a simple statement: the Holocaust is the main example of a genocide in the twentieth century. Therefore, according to their opinion, many terms would be appropriate to characterise the Holodomor, an enormous tragedy or a crime against humanity, as the European parliament had stated, but certainly not the term 'genocide'.

As a preliminary conclusion it seems fair to say that the politics of history in independent Ukraine basically followed the set of standard practices and tendencies typical for the post-communist transitions. That is, according to the voluntary aberrance, a development from 'authoritarianism' towards 'democracy'. Similar processes can be observed in all countries of the former Soviet Union and also of the former 'socialist camp'. Almost ubiquitously, the formation of a communal identity of the new citizens of the new states is based, as in Ukraine, upon the principle of ethno-cultural exclusivity of the titular nation, the singularity of its historical development and its future aspirations, and the quest for finding explanations in the past and outside one's own nation for current difficulties. Everywhere history is used as an argument in political debates to define the relations to neighbouring states, and this is particularly true for the relations with Russia as the successor state of the USSR (or the Russian empire). Everywhere this policy is devised and realised by a state bureaucracy that declares the attainment of unity and civic identity as ultimate goals; and everywhere this policy leads to internal conflicts and to disagreement in international relations. And everywhere professional historians become involved in this policy which always leads to conflicts between the state bureaucracy, habitually dictating the 'correct' interpretation of history to historians, and the scholarly community.

Notes and References

1 This chapter develops some thoughts published earlier in Georgy Kasyanov, 'Ukraine: The Holodomor and nation-building', in Samuel A. Greene (ed.), *Engaging History: The Problems & Politics of Memory in Russia and the Post-Socialist Space* (Carnegie Moscow Centre Working Papers 2/2010), 37–50; available online at http://www.carnegieendowment.org/files/WP_2_2010_engaging.pdf (accessed 9 May 2011).

2 It goes without saying that there are several versions. In a more radical variant, the planned character of the Famine is emphasised. In another it emerges as the consequence of the attempted collectivisation of the individual peasant households, and the Famine is represented as a way to neutralise the peasantry. Excessive procurement and requisition of grain, the seizure of peasant provisions and the blockade of starving territories are cited as the main instruments used to bring about the Famine. Stanislav Kulchytsky's works present the most scholarly-oriented version of this standard narrative of the Holodomor. See S. V. Kul'chitskii, *Pochemu on nas unichtozhal?* (Kiev: Ukrainskaia press-gruppa, 2007).

3 Some of those deserve mentioning, like Mykola Zhulinskii, Ukraine's vice president for humanitarian questions in 1993, Ivan Dziuba, minister of culture, Dmytro Pavl'chko, head of the Verkhovna Rada's (the Ukrainian parliament's) Committee on International Affairs, Ivan Drach, head of the Council of the 'Association for Relations with Ukrainians Living Abroad'. Cf. the decree of the president of the Ukraine 'Pro zakhody u zv'iazki z 60-mi rokovynamy Holodomoru v Ukraini', *Golos Ukrainy*, 25 March 1993.

4 The list of organisations represented in the organisational committee for the preparation of ceremonies dedicated to the 60th anniversary of the Holodomor indicates their influences on the course of events: the Ukrainian Congress Committee of America, the Ukrainian National Aid (USA), the Congress of Canadian Ukrainians, the World Congress of Free Ukrainians (Canada), the Ukrainian National Council (USA), the Union of Ukrainian Organisations in Australia.

5 Ukaz prezidenta Ukrainy vid 19.20.1993 'Pro zakhody u zv'iazku z 60-mi rokovynamy Holodomoru v Ukraini', www.zakon.rada.gov.ua (accessed 20 July 2003).

6 The group for the preparation of the tribunal included well-known public figures and writers from the ranks of the national democrats, for example Ivan Drach, Pavel Movchan or Volodymyr Javorskii. They all begun their career under Soviet rule and communism; now they had no problems to enter the ranks of a new *nomenklatura* consisting mainly of representatives of the old one.

7 'Propozitsii shchodo vshanuvannia 60-kh rokovin golodomoru v Ukrainy', from the author's archive.

8 This would, however, not prevent the costs for such a tribunal from amounting to half of the budget for the Days of Sorrow. According to accounts, a sum of 288.5 million *Kupokarbovancy* was spent in total. The costs for the national tribunal, a requiem and procession under the cross were declared to have amounted 148.6 million. 'Koshtoris vitrat, pov'iazannykh z provedenniam Dniv Skorboti i Pam'iati zhertv golodomoru v Ukraini 1932–3rr'. From the author's archive.

9 Leonid Kravchuk, 'My ne maemo prava znekhtuvati urokamy mynuloho', in *Holodomor 1932–33 rr. v Ukraini: prychyny i naslidky. Mizhnarodna naukova konferentsiia. Kiev, 9–10 veresnia 1993 r. Materialy* (Kiev: Instytut istoriii Ukrainy NAN Ukrainy, 1995), 10.

10 For details see Volodymyr Lytvyn, *Ukraina: Politika, politiki, vlast'. Na fone politicheskogo portreta L. Kravchuka* (Kiev: Al'ternativy, 1997), 98–101.

HOLODOMOR AND THE POLITICS OF MEMORY IN UKRAINE   185

11 To quote two very graphic examples: More than ten books compiled by the Association of Holodomor Investigators in Ukraine have been published with grants by one US businessman of Ukrainian descent, Marian Kots. Oleg Yanchuk's film *Golod-33*, discussed in Olga Papash's chapter in this volume and first shown on the day of the referendum on Ukraine's independence on 1 December 1991 was also realised with financial support from the Ukrainian diaspora.
12 Kabinet ministriv Ukrainy Postanova vid 10 veresnia 1993 r. No. 718 'Pro vshanuvannia pam'iati zhertv golodomoru v Ukraini u 1932–1933 rokakh', at http://zakon.rada.gov.ua/cgi-bin/laws/main.cgi?nreg=718-93-%EF (accessed 10 November 2011).
13 Rokas M. Tracevskis, 'Tribunal on communism announces its verdict', *Baltic Times*, 5 October 2000. See: http://www.baltictimes.com/news/articles/2714/ (accessed 10 November 2011).
14 This interpretation has been suggested by some scholars and publicists. See G. Grabovich, 'Ukraina: pidsumki stolittia', *Kritika* (1999), 11; M. Riabchuk, 'Pot'omkins'kyi iuvilei, abo shche raz pro amnistiiu, amneziiu ta "sladkoemnist"' postkomunistychnoi vlady v Ukraini', *Suchasnist'* 2004, 3; S. Kul'chyts'kyi, 'Demografichni naslidki golodu-genotsidu 1933 r. v Ukrainii,' in *Henotsyd ukrains'kogo narodu: istorychna pam'iat' ta polityko-pravova otsinka. Mizhnarodna naukovo-teoretychna konferentsiia. Materialy* (Kiev: Kots, 2003), 8.
15 Kabinet ministriv Ukrainy Postanova vid 26 zhovtnia [Oktober] 1998 r. No. 1696 'Pro 65-ti rokovyni Holodomoru v Ukraini', at http://zakon.nau.ua/doc/?uid=1059.1375.0 (accessed 10 November 2011).
16 Ukaz prezydenta Ukrainy 'Pro vstanovlennia dnia pam'iati zhertv golodomoriv' vid 26.11.1998, No. 1310/98, at http://zakon1.rada.gov.ua/cgi-bin/laws/main.cgi?nreg=1310%2F98 (accessed 10 November 2011).
17 Ibid.
18 'Pro zakhody u zv'iazku z 70-mi rokovynami golodomoru v Ukraini. Ukaz Prezydenta Ukrainy', at http://zakon.rada.gov.ua/cgi-bin/laws/main.cgi?nreg=275%2F2002 in *Uriadovyi kur'er*, (accessed 10 November 2011).
19 In the Khar'kiv region, for example, the local executive power conducted a 'Day of Public Information'. It was reported back that 'the heads and deputy heads of the regional administration, the heads and deputy heads of the district administrations and the municipal authorities, and also directors of enterprises, organs and other associations of the region' took part in this enterprise. Document no longer available online.
20 It was discussed in both Poland and Ukraine in very sharp tones, and the debate was characterised by mutual accusations of a lack of interest in the historical truth. On both sides radical right and nationalist forces spurred the discussion; Together with Poland's president Alexander Kwasniewski, Leonid Kuchma positioned himself as an arbitrator, while libertarian intellectuals called for mutual excuses and reconciliation.
21 Parlaments'ki slukhannia 'Shchodo vshanuvannia pam'iati Holodomoru 1932–3 rokiv', 12 liutogo [February] 2003 roku. (Kiev: Verkhovnaia Rada, Kabinet Ministrov, 2003).
22 Ibid.
23 Ibid.
24 'Zverennia do Ukrains'kogo narodu uchastnikiv spetsial'nogo zasidannia Verkhovnoi Rady Ukrainy shchodo vshanuvannia pam'iati zhertv Holodomoru 1932–33 rokiv', at http://zakon.rada.gov.ua/cgi-bin/laws/main.cgi?nreg789%2D15 (accessed 20 October 2007).
25 The truly unprecedented efforts of the 'orange' president in the field of the politics of history and commemoration provoked equally unprecedented critique from his

political opponents and even some of his allies. Observers have tried to explain this particular propensity for ideological components. On the one hand, they conceded that personal motives of moral and ethic nature may have played a role; on the other they assumed that practical reasons, like the use of the topic in order to raise the personal prestige of the president and to negatively mark his political opponents, have been important motives. The Ukrainian writer Mykola Riabchuk is a representative of the first trend, the Canadian political scientist Dominique Arel of the second. Cf. M. Riabchuk, 'Holodomor: The Politics of Memory and Political Infighting in Contemporary Ukraine', *The Harriman Review* 16, no. 2 (2008): 3–9; S. Bilen'kyi, 'Konferentsiia pro Golodomor v Toronto', at www.utoronto.ca/jacyk/Holod%20ukr.doc (accessed 25 February 2009). A review of many interviews and speeches on the 1932-33 Famine by Viktor Yushchenko would suggest that moral and ethical motives actually play an important role and that Viktor Yushchenko has been and continues to be deeply impressed by evidence on the tragedy. Nonetheless it is difficult not to take notice of the coincidence of an increased interest in the exploitation of the famine topic with the intensification of political conflicts within Ukraine during the years 2006 to 2008. At the same time, the politics of history that were designed to overcome the 'Soviet heritage' bore deep imprints of Soviet administrative methods. This is pertinently illustrated by the ways in which the 2006–2008 commemorative campaign was organised with massive utilisation of administrative resources; the ways in which alternative interpretations of the 1932 33 Famine were, sometimes quite aggressively, rejected; the ways in which scholarly estimates on the numbers of victims were ignored, finally also by the efforts to punish the 'denial of the Holodomor and the Holocaust' with administrative or criminal persecution and the selection of the memorial site referring to the 1932–33 tragedy in complete ignorance of Kiev's historical landscape.

26 Ukaz Prezidenta Ukrainy 'Pro dodatkovi zakhodi shodo uvichnennia pam'iati zhertv politichnykh repressij ta Holodomoriv v Ukraini', at http://www.president.gov.ua/documents/2982.html (accessed 10 November 2011).

27 The creation of the institute was quite a painful process, in the absence of a clear cut conception or an understanding of its future function. Poland's parliament had created its Institute of National Remembrance – Commission for the Prosecution of Crimes against the Polish Nation (IPN) in 1998 with a special bill. There was little chance to repeat the Polish example successfully in Ukraine, partly due to the incompetence of the initiators, partly due to disagreements between the initiators and those potentially commissioned with the realisation of the initiative. Besides representatives of the government and scholars, representatives of public organisations interested in the matter, yet with clearly diverging ideas like Memorial, the Association of the Politically Repressed and Political Prisoners or the Association of Holodomor Investigators, took part in preparatory discussions. The institute was finally founded in May 2006 and became an active promoter of president Yushchenko's ideas. Cf. the internet site of the institute at www.memory.gov.ua (accessed 10 November 2011).

28 Ukaz Prezydenta Ukrainy 'Pro vshanuvannia zhertv ta postradalykh vid golodomoriv v Ukraini', at http://www.president.gov.ua/documents/3456.html (accessed 10 November 2011).

29 Zvernennia naukovoi hromads'kosti do Prezydenta Ukrainy Viktora Yushchenka pro zaprovadzhennia postinoi kalendarnoi dati vshanuvannia pam'iati zhertv Holodomoru 1932–33 rr. V Ukraini, at http://www.podilr.gov.ua/?page=63&cat_id=0&a_id=273&parent_id=&l=&page=63&lang_id=1 (accessed 10 November 2011).

30 Ukaz Prezydenta Ukrainy vid 12 zhovtnia [October] 2006 'Pro vidznachennia y 2006 rotsi Dnia pam'iati zhertv Holodomoriv ta politichykh repressii', at http://www.president.gov.ua/documents/5087.html (accessed 10 November 2011).
31 The term 'political and juridical assessment' might seem like an oxymoron to foreign observers only. In fact it reflects quite adequately a concept of law in Ukraine and across the post-Soviet space which equates law and politics, and which sees the former determined by the latter.
32 'Zvernenia uchastnykiv kruhlogo stolu 'Golodomor 1932–3 rokiv – henotsid v Ukraini'. The document is no longer available at the presidential website. A copy is accessible at http://www.rv.gov.ua/sitenew/main/en/publication/content/218.htm (accessed 10 November 2011). I contacted some of the 'signatories' or presumed authors of this document and asked them to comment. As it turned out, not only had they not signed it, they had not even seen the text.
33 'Prezydent Ukrainy vnis na rozghliad parlamentu Zakon Ukrainy "Pro Holodomor 1932–3 rokiv v Ukrainy"'. The document is no longer available at the presidential website. A copy is accessible at http://www.mfa.gov.ua/belarus/ua/news/detail/2953.htm (accessed 10 November 2011).
34 Zakon Ukrainy 'Pro Golodomor 1932–3 rokiv v Ukrainy', at http://zakon.rada.gov.ua/cgi-bin/laws/main.cgi?nreg=376-16 (accessed 10 November 2011).
35 http://gska2.rada.gov.ua/pls/zweb_n?webproc4_1?id=&pf3511=29140. Link no longer available (10 November 2007).
36 'Poiasniuval'na zapyska do proektu Zakonu Ukrainy "Pro vnesennia zmin do Kryminal'nogo ta Kryminal'no-protsesual'nogo kodeksiv Ukrainy"', 2. From the author's personal archive. The document was copied from the official site of the Vekhovna Rada Ukrainy at http://gska2.rada.gov.ua/pls/zweb_n?webproc4_1?id=&pf3511=29881 (in October 2007 but has been removed since). A copy is available at http://www.esstaff.com.ua/index.php/laws-dogs/90-law-crime-about (accessed 10 November 2011).
37 Which would have been the equivalent of 1,700 to 5,100 *Hrivna*; or between $340 and $1,020 USD.
38 'Poiasniuval'na zapyska do proektu Zakonu Ukrainy "Pro vnesennia zmin do Kryminal'nogo ta Kryminal'no-protsesual'nogo kodeksiv Ukrainy"', 2 (see note 36).
39 In the context of legislation the use of the term 'denial of the Holocaust' is not entirely correct. The legislation of states belonging to the European Union and of the European Union itself targets the prevention of a public justification of Nazism, the trivialisation of its crimes, the public denial or justification of specific acts of genocide or crimes against humanity, the instigation of radial hate and the crimes of communism. The 'denial of the Holocaust' figures in this legislation as a specific case and it is not pursued everywhere. Beyond that, this kind of legislation has recently become the target of increasingly active criticism by liberal forces in society that consider it limiting to the freedom of expression. For an interesting scholarly critique of the sensitivity of such legislation and the complications of corresponding terminology see Robert M. Hayden, '"Genocide denial" – Laws as Secular Heresy: A Critical Analysis with Reference to Bosnia', *Slavic Review* 67, no. 2 (2008): 384–407.
40 Poiasniuval'na zapyska do proektu Zakonu Ukrainy 'Pro vnesennia zmin do Kryminal'nogo ta Kryminal'no-protsesual'nogo kodeksiv Ukrainy', (see note 36).
41 The Party of the Regions, the Communist and the Socialist called themselves 'Anti-Crisis Coalition' when they joined forces in June 2006 and formed a parliamentary

majority and a government. The conflict between this coalition and the presidents became the central issue in the political life of the country.

42 'Viznannia golodomory 1932–3 rokiv aktom genotsidu Ukrain'kogo narodu, at the official internet site of the president of Ukraine', at http://www.prezident.gov.ua./content/p_150_18.html (accessed 31 October 2007, no longer accessible).

43 'Visnovok na proekt Zakonu Ukrainy "Pro vnesennia zmin do Kryminal'nogo ta Kryminal'no-protsesual'nogo kodeksiv Ukrainy"', 1–2. From the author's archive.

44 'Yushchenko perezavatazhiv matritsiu', *Ukrains'ka Pravda*, 25 April 2007.

45 Ukaz Prezidenta Ukrainy 'Pro zakhody u zv'iazku z 70-mi rokovynami Velikogo terroru – masovykh politychnykh prepresii 1937–1938 rokiv vid 21.05.2007', http://www.president.gov.ua/documents/6153.html (accessed 10 November 2011).

46 'Poiasniuval'na zapyska do proektu Zakonu Ukrainy "Pro vnesnnia zmin do Kryminal'nogo ta Kryminal'no-protsesual'nogo kodeksiv Ukrainy"', http://gska2.rada.gov.ua/pls/zweb_n/webproc4_1?id=&pf3511=30933 (accessed 10 November 2011).

47 'Proekt Zakonu pro vnesennia zmin do Kriminal'nogo kodeksu Ukrainy (shchodo vidpodvidal'nosti za publichne zaperechennia faktu Golodomory 1932–1933 rokiv, iak genotsid narodu)' http://gska2.rada.gov.ua/pls/zweb_n/webproc4_1?id=&pf3511=31473 (accessed 10 November 2011).

48 Ibid.

49 'Light a Candle' is a yearly event and conceived to be all-Ukrainian. It was organised for the first time in 2003. On the day of remembrance for the victims of the 1932–33 Famine (the last Saturday in November) all participants are invited to set up a burning candle in their window. The 'Inextinguishable Candle' is fabricated from ca. two hundred kilograms of the best bee wax collected across Ukraine and moulded into the form of wheat-shape sheaves. In the course of the year 2008 it was passed from country to country (33 in total according to the year of the tragedy) and everywhere the arrival was celebrated with requiems and commemorative meetings. In the autumn of the same year, the candle was exhibited in all regions of Ukraine. The 'Inextinguishable Candle' accomplished its journey in the Memorial Complex which was opened in November 2008 in Kiev, where it became one of the permanent exhibits. '33 Minutes' was a public event performed from June to November 2008 in public places that had been dedicated to or close to memorials for the 'representatives of the totalitarian regime'. In those places the names and surnames of victims of the 1932–33 Famine were read out aloud for 33 minutes during each public holiday.

50 The 'Snowball Tree Boscage' consisting of more than two hundred snowball trees was planted by deputies of the parliament under Viktor Yushchenko's guidance on the steep bank of the Dnieper; close to the Kiev Caves monastery. This is the location of the Memorial Complex opened in November 2008, with a 26m high candle shaped monument as the central element.

51 Stanislav Kulchytskyi, who began his research already in the mid-1980s, became the most important scholar in the development of Holodomor historiography. Researchers in the field tend to read his numerous publications in Ukraine and abroad as translations of the state's official position on the Holodomor. Yet this is only partially fair, as Stanislav Kulchytskyi, even if he advances the interpretation of the Holodomor as an act of genocide, does not share the extreme positions of President Yushchenko and of parts of the Ukrainian diaspora. In his latest interpretation, the genocide was not directed against ethnic Ukrainians, but against the 'citizens of the Ukrainian state'. In his estimates the numbers of victims also significantly differ from what was proclaimed by Viktor Yushchenko. See Kulchytskyi's chapter in this volume.

Chapter 9

THE GREAT IRISH FAMINE IN STORIES FOR CHILDREN IN THE CLOSING DECADES OF THE TWENTIETH CENTURY[1]

Celia Keenan
St Patrick's College, Dublin

This essay examines representations of the Great Irish Famine in stories for children written by British and Irish authors towards the end of the twentieth century. The texts, selected from among a large number of publications, represent the best of their kind in this writer's view.

The story of the Great Irish Famine of the 1840s is one of the most problematic episodes in Irish history. It is such an emotive story that efforts to commemorate the 150th anniversary of 'Black '47' aroused passionate debate in Ireland. The *Irish Times* printed an angry series of letters arguing that a concert of popular music was not a suitable way to remember the deaths of a million people.

A letter from the British prime minister Tony Blair on the subject was deeply appreciated in Ireland for observations such as these: 'that one million people should have died in what was then part of one of the richest and most powerful nations in the world is something that causes pain as we reflect on it today' and 'those who governed in London at the time failed their people through standing by while a crop failure turned into a massive human tragedy'. However, his comments were not universally welcomed in Britain, where *The Times* accused him of pandering to the Irish tendency to engage in self-pity.[2]

Given the level of unease with the memory of the Famine and that its history has been written only relatively recently (frequently by women historians), it is not surprising that efforts to tell the story to children should prove difficult for British and Irish writers alike.[3] The subject is intrinsically difficult to shape into narratives for children. It lacks some of the ingredients of a good children's tale, and the most important of these is the potential for action. The Great Famine is a story of mass suffering. The children's writer must do justice to that without the relief that adventures or conflict provide, and without over-indulging in suffering and despair in the manner of a horror story. The second and related missing ingredient is that of an agreed villain. Only in the most extreme nationalist history can it be suggested that the Famine was simple genocide by the British. Only in the most extreme Unionist version of the story can the lazy Irish peasants or the greedy Irish landlords be solely blamed.[4] People writing for children like to use strong plots, clear characterisation and simple explanations for events. Even characterisation becomes difficult in famine narratives. There is a tendency for the hungry to become indistinguishable from each other, mere objects of pity and horror.

Three writers – Walter Macken, David Rees and Michael Mullen – who were interested in the Famine and who wrote historical novels for children chose not to write about the famine for children, but did so for adults. The fact that these three writers avoided telling their famine story to children may be indicative of an awareness of problems inherent in the notion of famine as a subject for children's books.

However children's writers towards the end of the twentieth century began to set their stories in the famine period. An opportunistic element may have had some part to play in the fact that in 1997, the year of the 150th anniversary, no fewer than four children's novels about the Famine were published in Ireland, one of which seemed to me to be an exploitative, poorly written novel that insults Irish Famine victims and the Choctaw people of America, who contributed $470 for Irish Famine relief in a time of great tribulation for themselves.[5]

Writers resort to a variety of expedients to make the Famine in some way tellable to children. One device used by several novelists is to abandon the Famine quite early in the novel, so that the narrative becomes an emigration story, usually to North America. This transforms a tale of suffering into one of adventure, travel to exciting places, chance encounters and the opportunity to make fortunes. This is the pattern in Michael Morpurgo's *Twist of Gold* (1983), Arthur McKeown's *Famine* (1997), Michael Smith's *Boston! Boston!* (1997) and Colette McCormack's *Mary Anne's Famine* (1995). In a number of novels with this pattern a family survives intact, or is re-united in North America. This is the structure most likely to offer a happy ending, which often includes love, marriage and prosperity. The most explicit expression of this comes at the end of McKeown's story *Famine* where the elderly father (in West Virginia) says, "'It's a long way from Ballymore, Maggie. I'm glad we made the decision to come here all those years ago." "Yes, I'm glad we came too", Maggie replied. "It was a hard journey but we have a good life here"'.[6]

One novel, Soinbhe Lally's *The Hungry Wind* (1997), uses the emigration plot in an unusual way. The destination is Australia, not North America, and the long journey comes quite late in the novel. The bulk of the novel is an account of the experiences of two sisters in the workhouse, an institution avoided as a location for action in all the other novels. Issues of pubertal sexuality and sexual exploitation by the master of the workhouse are confronted. There is a note of hope in the end, but not a happy ending.

A significant absence in Irish Famine novels in this period is that not a single one of them gives an account of emigration to Britain, yet during the period of the Great Famine Britain was the destination of the vast majority of refugees. Between 1841 and 1851 the number of people born in Ireland and taking up residence in Britain doubled. These people provided a sizeable proportion of the workforce in the industrial areas of Yorkshire and Lancashire and had a profound effect on the culture of the towns they found refuge in.[7] My suspicion is that these English stories of migration are not being told because they do not conform to the national myth of freedom. Freedom can be found in America or in Australia, but not in the bosom of the ancient oppressor. The Irish relationship with England has been too problematic to tell this story yet. Until very recently there was a particular sense of failure or shame about Irish emigration to England.

If there are omissions in the stories that Irish writers tell about the Famine, there are difficulties for British writers too. A particular difficulty seems to be created by the role of British soldiers in Ireland during the Famine. Soldiers would have been the most obvious manifestation of English power in Ireland. They were Englishmen, not Irish. In Irish accounts they figure in two ways: assisting at evictions and protecting stocks of food from hordes of starving people. In two novels by British writers, Michael Morpurgo's *Twist of Gold* (1983) and Elizabeth Lutzeier's *The Coldest Winter* (1991) an individual soldier behaves in a way that would be frankly unthinkable in a novel by an Irish writer. In both novels a kind soldier is appalled at the role he is forced to play in Ireland and gives food, money in the form of a gold coin and physical protection to starving children. In both cases his intervention is pivotal to the narrative. Morpurgo's soldier even includes fishing lessons in his benevolence:

> "One day I'll not be here to feed you, and you must learn to live from the land. There's people dying in this country because they don't know where to look for their food. They've dug the potatoes for so long they've forgotten. Eels are there in plenty if you can only catch them, and I shall teach you."[8]

An unconscious colonial condescension here assumes that the natives need to be taught how to exploit their own land by a representative of the colonial power. The assumption that country boys would not know how to fish is absurd and the historical fact that fishing rights belonged to landlords is ignored. Elizabeth Lutzeier's novel is much more nuanced, but her soldier gives a gold coin to the hero Eamonn saying, 'Here buy yourself something to eat'.[9] The soldier does not seem to know the value of the coin. We later discover it is enough to pay rent for almost a year. Lutzeier recognises that the device of the soldier giving the boy so much money is an unusual one; later in the novel another character is surprised at the soldier's altruistic gesture: 'the baker's wife had never heard of any soldier giving away money before'.[10]

Lutzeier's novel is very fine; her initial focus is on the peasant boy Eamonn's family – poor, hungry and evicted from their home. She succeeds where many other famine novelists fail, giving an intelligent consciousness to her characters, so that we can identify with them. They are not mere victims and objects. Hence it was a real disappointment that although she avoided using emigration as a way of escaping from the implications of famine, she resorted to a related device. In chapter five, she shifts the centre of interest from hungry, Catholic, peasant Eamonn, to the middle-class, Protestant and altruistic Kate, and her and her family's efforts to alleviate famine misery. In a sense Lutzeier retreats from her central story to tell a different story of how the Irish were saved by charity, and Eamonn Kennedy and his family, who were so well drawn in the earlier part of the novel, become victims and objects of charity. Of course what is really happening is that the political implications of the Famine are avoided.

One novel that is more explicitly political in its intentions is Northern Irish writer, Eve Bunting's famine adventure novel, *The Haunting of Kildoran Abbey* (1978), originally published in the USA. The perspective is clearly northern Unionist. In the beginning the hungry children blame England for their misery and threaten revenge. However, they are proved wrong. England turns out to be Ireland's saviour, symbolised by the presence of an English boy, Christopher, and the all-benevolent Lord Lieutenant of Ireland, Lord Bessborough, who says, 'I have always found the Irish to be a simple people but not stupid. It's difficult to believe that if you have been a good landlord all these years they would turn against you for no reason'.[11] In this novel the villains are unscrupulous Irish landlords, whom England would no doubt punish, if only she knew: 'It's hard for him [the Lord Lieutenant] to know when something needs remedying when it looks alright on the surface', one of the characters says and Colum, the reformed rebel, says, 'It's hard for us to understand that there can be justice if we look for it'.[12] The problem is that the simple Enid-Blyton-like adventure story sits a little uneasily alongside the colonial polemics.

There are a number of points to be made about the treatment of religion in almost all of these novels. The most striking point is that they all avoid the most common motif of traditional famine lore, the proselytising dimension of the soup kitchens, or 'soupers' as they were known. If people converted from Catholicism to Protestantism the phrase used was 'they took the soup'[13] (the charity of the Quakers was the one strong exception in this myth for their charity was seen as being disinterested). There is no hint of this sectarian tension to be found in any of the selected modern novels for children. Another point about the depiction of religion in modern novels for children is the unflattering way that Catholic priests are frequently depicted: plump with smooth hands, eating cheese, eating fried bacon, taking money from desperate people, giving clichéd sermons about sin and self-indulgence to the starving. This may be a reflection of modern Irish anti-clericalism, for there is no evidence of it in famine folklore, where the priest is often as poor as the people and is often their only comfort. Yeats' poem, 'The Ballad of Father Gilligan', comes closer to the traditional image of the famine priest as one who exhausts himself through devoted care for the sick.[14]

It is only in books published towards the end of the twentieth century that the depiction of Protestant victims of the Famine occurs. In McKeown's 1997 book *Famine*, Joe and his daughter are Protestant, Co. Antrim farmers who live in comfort on the fruits of their farming and linen-weaving until the Famine strikes. They leave their farm and sell their loom and emigrate to America with their savings and their Bible and are able to buy a farm in West Virginia. They hear stories about the Famine from other less fortunate people on their journey to America, an example of a very obvious distancing device. In a sense they conform to stereotypes of Protestant prosperity and the Unionist myth that the Famine spared Ulster, a myth exposed by Christine Kinealy.[15] Only in Lally's *The Hungry Wind* do we find Protestant victims of destitution and exploitation – Hannah and Rachel in the workhouse – who can speak Irish and who find comfort in their Bible, particularly in the story of Jonah in the belly of the whale.

Perhaps the greatest cultural effect of the Great Famine was the near destruction of the Irish language; many of the writers are aware of this and it occasionally causes problems in their narratives. Sometimes we are told that families speak only Irish and then find that they have learned very good English in a matter of months. Sometimes they tell each other to speak quietly so that soldiers will not hear what they are saying. Lally is the only writer who integrates the language issue into her plot and characterisation in a creative way; thus, when her Irish-speaking heroine wants to explain about the sexual abuse of another girl by the workhouse master, she is overwhelmed by the fluency of her interrogator's English, loses her confidence in her own ability to speak English, and so justice fails.

One of the strangest references to the Irish language occurs in Ann Pilling's novel *Black Harvest* (1983) in which three modern English children holidaying in Ireland are possessed by the ghosts of a family which died in the Famine. When the English children hear an old man talking, 'the voice was shrill and harsh. They couldn't tell whether he was speaking Irish or just making horrible noises [...] he was letting out a stream of foul Irish [...] spitting the words out, slavering'.[16] The English family suffers all the pangs of hunger. The baby almost dies and the dog pines away, until the famine grave is found and the original victims are given a proper burial. It is a ghost story, indeed a horror story that is redolent of a post-colonial sense of guilt and a desire to atone for past wrongs. The suffering is internalised and in a sense becomes 'ours' rather than 'theirs'. It finds an interesting solution to a narrative problem by setting its story in the contemporary world.

Marita Conlon-McKenna's *Under the Hawthorn Tree* (1990) is one of the best-known Irish Famine stories for children, and it too finds ways around some of the problems of this kind of narrative. Her narrative is simple, third person and stays with the Famine from beginning to end. It has no unbelievable adventures, no great gifts, no magic, no soldiers with money. Three children set out in search of their great-aunts after they are evicted from their home. In order to make their suffering tolerable Conlon-McKenna emphasises the beauty of nature, the changes of the seasons and the colours of the sky, gorse, hawthorn and bluebells. Famine narratives usually assume that all nature, not just the potato, has failed. Here, like the vision of nature, women's story-telling is a device used to relieve suffering. The mother tells tales of her grandmother and aunts, and her daughter Eily repeats these tales. Women's domestic skills function as emblems of hope. The tragedy of the baby's death is framed by the fact that she is buried in a little white robe which had been made by her grandmother for her mother's christening and that she is buried under a hawthorn tree which protected the living children at play and will now protect the dead child. The hawthorn is where people traditionally buried infants who died before they were christened, a fairy burial place, a sacred place where memories are kept. Myth, legend, storytelling and religious tradition are all used to humanise a nightmare world. Conlon-McKenna's characters are always allowed to speak for themselves; loyalty and resourcefulness are what save them. This is a deceptively simple narrative in which the courage of ordinary people triumphs.

A strikingly beautiful and stark picture book extends the parameters of famine literature for children. Starkly beautiful black and white illustrations and a simple elegiac text bring the suffering of the Choctaw and Irish nations together in *The Long March* (1998) by Marie-Louise Fitzpatrick. The effect is to universalise pain without diminishing it. The fact that both nations are called 'Potato People' highlights their common humanity.[17]

Famine stories for children in Ireland reverse a tendency that is prevalent in other forms of Irish fiction for children which typically reject urban life and its values in favour of a romantic rural ideal. Famine narratives end with rural children finding refuge in the comfort of large towns and cities whether in Ireland or in America. The horrors of the Irish Famine are an antidote to the fashionable notion that most human problems are caused by urban living.

In summary, the challenge of writing stories about the Famine for children has created some difficulties common to all writers who have chosen to write about it; related to the nature of the material, these derive from the lack of conflict or of action and the passivity of the victims. As a subject it also poses problems specific to writers from particular cultures or traditions. In the present very largely post-colonial culture of Ireland and the post-imperial culture of Britain, it is not surprising that a process of revision should continue. Post-colonial angst is not experienced solely by the colonised nation. British writers also feel the need to re-examine their colonial history in the light of dramatically changed relationships with the larger world. Children's writers are conscious of the burden of the past in a particularly acute way because they believe that their books may influence the values and even the actions of young people. It is therefore not surprising that the truth is sometimes somewhat approximate. For a British writer of children's fiction it is difficult to depict a world in which a British soldier is merely an oppressor. For an Irish writer it is difficult to depict Britain as a refuge from the Famine. In both cases cherished national narratives are challenged.

Notes and References

1. An earlier version of this chapter was published in Ann Lawson Lucas (ed.), *The Presence of the Past in Children's Literature* (Westport: Praeger Publishers, 2003).
    The author wishes to acknowledge with gratitude the assistance of Valerie Coghlan, librarian at the Church of Ireland College of Education, Dublin; Robert Dunbar, Dublin; Rosemary Hetherington, librarian Dublin Public Libraries; Professor Margaret Kelleher, NUI Maynooth; and Dr Martin Maguire, Dundalk Institute of Technology.
2. *Irish Times*, 5 June 1997.
3. Cecil Woodham-Smith, *The Great Hunger: Ireland 1845–1849* (London: Hamish Hamilton, 1962); Mary Daly, *The Famine in Ireland* (Dundalk: Dundalgan Press, 1986); Christine Kinealy, *This Great Calamity: The Irish Famine 1845–52* (Dublin: Gill and Macmillan, 1994); Margaret Kelleher, *The Feminization of Famine: Expressions of the Inexpressible?* (Cork: Cork University Press, 1997).
4. *Unionist* is the term used to denote that political view which supports the union of Great Britain and Northern Ireland.
5. The Choctaw, mentioned in Colin Vard, *Trail of Tears* (Dublin: Mentor Books, 1997), were forced to march to distant territories on the confiscation of their homelands at this time, many dying on the journey.

6 Arthur McKeown, *Famine* (Dublin: Poolbeg Press, 1997), 42.
7 Frank Neal, *Sectarian Violence: The Liverpool Experience 1819–1914, An Aspect of Anglo-Irish History* (Manchester: Manchester University Press, 1988), 80–104.
8 Michael Morpurgo, *Twist of Gold* (Kingswood : Kaye and Ward, 1983), 23.
9 Elizabeth Lutzeier, *The Coldest Winter* (Dublin: Wolfhound Press, 1996), 19 (first published 1991).
10 Ibid., 36.
11 Eve Bunting, *The Haunting of Kildoran Abbey* (New York and London: F. Warne, 1978), 139.
12 Ibid., 153.
13 Desmond Bowen, *Souperism: Myth or Reality: A Study in Souperism* (Cork: Mercier Press, 1970).
14 Cathal Póirtéir, *Famine Echoes* (Dublin: Mercier Press, 1995).
15 Christine Kinealy and Trevor Parkhill, *The Famine in Ulster* (Belfast: Ulster Historical Foundation, 1997).
16 Ann Cheetham (Pilling), *Black Harvest* (London: Armada, 1983), 22.
17 Marie-Louise Fitzpatrick, *The Long March* (Dublin: Wolfhound Press, 1998).

Chapter 10

COLLECTIVE TRAUMA IN A FEATURE FILM: *GOLOD-33* AS ONE-OF-A-KIND

Olga Papash
Kyiv-Mohyla Academy

The subject of the Ukrainian Famine is so intensely distressing that any critique of its representation in the arts runs the risk of being mistaken as an attempted denial of the fact of the Famine itself. The term 'Holodomor', coined during the 1980s by the Ukrainian diaspora in North America to describe the intentional extermination of people on a massive scale through hunger, has since become a cornerstone in the process of state building in independent Ukraine and in the formation of a national identity.

It goes without saying that events during the Famine in the early 1930s have been traumatic. In current discussions on the 1932–33 Famine, figures of up to 10 million victims are quoted.[1] While the latter figure is certainly excessive, it is almost unconditionally taken for granted in the current Ukrainian historiographical mainstream, as Heorhiy Kasianov has shown.[2] Still, any significant reduction of the number of victims would not alter the situation much, as we would still be dealing with millions of premature deaths. Unlike the victims of the Holocaust, those of the Ukrainian Famine still await an adequate visual representation of their sufferings. The only attempt undertaken so far in the realm of fictional films has been Oleg Yanchuk's 1991 picture *Golod-33*. Surprisingly, this film has not been subjected to a thorough analysis as a contribution to collective commemoration either. In other words, while the Famine itself has left a considerable mark on contemporary public discourse in Ukraine, its only cinematographic representation seems to have rapidly fallen into oblivion.

A Visual Contribution to an Emerging Debate

Golod-33 (Hunger-33), written by Sergei D'iachenko and Les' Taniuk and directed by Oleg Yanchuk, was produced by the Dovzhenko National Studios for Feature Films in Kiev in 1991. It is based on a novel by the writer Vasilii Barka titled *The Yellow Prince*, in which the author, already in American exile in the 1950s, reprocessed his own impression of the 1932–33 Famine. Barka was born in 1908 and had himself repeatedly faced accusation of being a 'bourgeois nationalist' after he had published first poems in Ukraine during the 1930s. Under the occupational regime in the Second World War he was deported to forced labour in Germany where he remained for some time after the war before moving to the United States in 1950. *The Yellow Prince* was first published in book form in New York in 1963. Commenting on his novel Barka stressed that it did not merely narrate events during the 1932–33 Famine, but more generally discussed the communist regime's efforts to annihilate Christianity and the Ukrainian nation.[3]

Against this backdrop the adaptation of the *Yellow Prince* for the screen was first of all a political statement. The film called for the further national consolidation of the Ukraine and strove to support the mobilisation of Ukrainians in the struggle for political independence. Hence, for all its intents and purposes, it can hardly be expected to have engaged in a historically adequate representation of events as they had unfolded during the 1930s. Rather, the film must be read as a manifesto, and the form of this manifesto remains exclusively artistic and cinematographic. Therefore it should be analysed by aesthetic criteria rather than being judged in its political or even moral dimensions.

The question why *Golod-33* has remained the only fictional film produced on the subject remains to be answered even twenty years after its launch. A number of factors may have played a role here, not least the changing political situation. Yet in my opinion the main reason has been the complete demise of the Soviet-Ukrainian film industry in the wake of the economic crises. Indeed, Yanchuk's film, completely independent in terms of the topic and context, was still produced during the late perestroika period by Soviet studios. In this sense its creation in the Dovzhenko studios may be attributed to the inertia of the Soviet production system. By the time the Famine had acquired its towering role in the historical narrative under President Yushchenko, Ukraine simply lacked the facilities to engage in a cinematographic project of a similar scope. While several documentary films on the Famine were produced, no further feature film complemented *Golod-33*.

During the early 1990s, when Ukraine had just achieved independence, the quest to expose and fill the lacunae of Soviet historiography characterised the intellectual climate. Of course the Famine that was rampant in the country in 1932 and 1933 turned out to be one of the most intensely debated issues in Ukrainian–Soviet history. It had been eliminated from the USSR's official historical narrative for obvious reasons. As a matter of fact, already on

7 February 1990 the Central Committee of the Ukrainian Communist Party had issued a decree 'On the 1932–33 Famine in Ukraine and the Publication of Related Archival Materials'. As even the fact of a famine had been denied for decades and any public reference to it banned, the publication of this decree was a significant step: 'It meant more than just a concession on the part of the Communist Party; it was rather the latter's total capitulation on one of the most important battlefields in the struggle to rewrite history'.[4] It was symptomatic that this quest to fill the blank pages of history, in particular with respect to the 1932–33 Famine, coincided with the spasmodic tremors of Soviet statehood which led to its final deconstruction. By no means accidentally the first public screening was organised on the eve of the all-Ukrainian referendum on independence scheduled for the 1 December 1991. Yanchuk, then a young graduate from Kiev's National University for Theatre, Cinema and Television working at the Dovzhenko Film-Studios, launched his film at the first peak of public interest.

Yanchuk's filmed manifesto was intended to serve as an eye-opener for his compatriots and to expose them to 'historical truth'. At the same time, it was hoped that film might fulfil the same mission on the international arena. While books like Robert Conquest's *Harvest of Sorrow* (1986) had stirred up a degree of discussion during the 1980s, Ukrainian intellectuals felt that public opinion in the West had remained grossly ignorant about the occurrence of a famine in Ukraine during the 1930s. Against this backdrop the film represented a distinctive 'political action against communist tyranny'.[5] Hence during and after the collapse of the Soviet Union, *Golod-33* performed several functions in that it provided political orientation on the one hand, and furthered dissociation from the Soviet past on the other. It inspired a sense of belonging to the Ukrainian nation and, in this, it pointed at ways to overcome the appalling past. The importance of the film's political and cultural mission was acknowledged through the award of the main prize at the Ivan Mikolaichuk All-Ukrainian Film Festival in November 1991.

Adapting the Novel for the Film

How did the director approach his project? At the outset, Yanchuk had to address a number of challenging tasks. Not only would he have to decide from which angle he would approach this tragic chapter in Ukrainian history: against the backdrop of the long term suppression of information about the events, how could he break this silence and cover events that were almost incomprehensible to any viewer, or at any rate difficult to interpret adequately? How could he represent distressing experiences which went beyond the scope of rational understanding? After all, he was dealing with historical events which would continue to be denied by some parts of Ukraine's political spectrum some twenty years after the declaration of Ukrainian independence.

It goes without saying that any interpretation of the film has to take into account that *Golod-33* was in the first place an individual director's attempt to answer these questions, and as such his answers deserve detailed analysis. At the same time Yanchuk was responding to an ideological challenge broadly disseminated during the late 1980s and early 1990s. In other words, he took an active stance in the quest for the consolidation and for the further development of a Ukrainian national identity.

By necessity, the focus on the Famine is narrowed in both Yanchuk's film and in Barka's novel: as readers and viewers we observe the members of a single Ukrainian peasant family starving to death, one after the other. The chronological frame of the film is limited to the period between the autumn of 1932, when communist henchmen took away the last remaining provisions from the Katrannik family, and the summer of 1933, when, supervised by guards, skeleton-like peasants collect the harvest from fields which are covered with the bodies of the deceased. Little Andriyko Katrannik loses his parents, his grandmother, his brother and his sister; the boy is the only member of the family who lives to see and tell of what he had to witness.

The film opens with a series of subtitles narrating the course of Ukrainian history after 1917:

> After the collapse of the Russian Empire in 1917, the enslaved nations struggled for independence. The Ukrainian People's Republic was suppressed and forced to join the Soviet Union. When Stalin had acquired full power at the end of the 1920s, the communist party sought to establish control over all walks of life through systematic terror. The Ukrainian peasantry became the first victim of Stalin's renewed enserfment. Stalin singled out independent peasants as 'enemies of the people' and 'kulaks'. Soon the entire Ukrainian nation became an 'enemy of the people'. Decrees were issued in 1932 which led to the death of millions. During the winter and spring of 1933, terror was applied through the coercive confiscation of food and livestock. The larger part of the confiscated grain was exported, and the returns were used to finance the industrialisation of the Union.

Effectively, the opening of the film uses a take on the general historical context to shape the emotional perspective of the audience. From the very beginning, the film presents the Famine as a consequence of the stand-off between two ideologies, communism and nationalism and as a result of the struggle between the forces of 'darkness' and the 'light'. Already the first sequence in the film, the service in the church, is climactic and circumscribes the entire conflict. 'God loves us', preaches the priest in this episode, 'all that is left to us is love, too. Forget about who owes someone something; purify your souls from all evil'. The moral of an all-embracing redemption as exposed in this sequence of *Golod-33* is clearly connoted with 'being Ukrainian'.

The Ukrainian character is challenged by the morality (or rather, in the language of the film, the amorality) of the party officials and agents of industrialisation. As the henchmen of the OGPU, the political police shatters into the church, bewildered Ukrainian peasants, wearing emblematic white blouses, rally to safeguard icons and other cult objects. The sequence culminates in a symbolic act: the communists topple the bell from the bell tower; it bursts when hitting the ground. Simultaneously, the screen collapses and the emerging black and white picture visually highlights the ascetic atmosphere of the film. Similar emotive episodes, like the horrors of life threatened by starvation, piles of dead bodies or scenes of humiliating requisition of provisions, are continuously interspersed throughout the narrative axis of the film, juxtaposing Ukrainian spirituality with the communist lack thereof.

One could mention, besides the humiliation of the older believers, the destruction of the churches and the ransacking of the peasant huts for the last remaining bits of grain as examples of what the followers of the party are capable of. The communist moral void culminates in a scene in which unarmed peasants are mowed down in their attempt to reach the mill where the sequestered grain is stored (see below), or another sequence depicting how the bodies of the deceased are simply thrown from a train.

Victimisation and Selective Commemoration

Tellingly, only Ukrainians suffer in Yanchuk's film, in full accordance with the key phrase of the introduction: 'The whole Ukrainian nation became an enemy of the people.' Thus suffering occurs as a marker of nationality. *Golod-33* is saturated with motifs of suffering and martyrdom; one might even say that the whole film is built on the rhetoric of victimisation[6]. Ukrainian identity is defined by its readiness for sacrifice and martyrdom and, consequently, by an ethic of Christian love. If one of the characters in the film runs the risk of compromising his or her Ukrainian identity, national affiliation is passed over in silence. Hence the 'problem of the local executors of the terror; those not in the leading positions in the party, but the hundreds and thousands of local activists that participated in the requisition of grain and decided the fate of their fellow Ukrainians'[7] is passed over in silence.

The film does not conceal, however, that there have been Ukrainian Communists who tried to resist central authorities. One of the earlier sequences of the film, for example, is devoted to the chairman of the *kolkhoz* 'Daybreak of Socialism', who, upon receiving the order to deliver 90 per cent of the grain to the state, shoots himself, as he is aware of the fact that this order amounted to 'a death warrant to the peasantry'. Yet the film does not suggest that the chairman should be regarded as a victim as well: his end is depicted as being no more than the death of a typical Stalinist official killing himself in front of a portrait of Lenin. Apparently, death is the only logical option left to solve the conflict of identities, as the identity of being Ukrainian and victim should not be conflated with the identity of being communist and perpetrator. By sustaining this distinction, the film retrospectively helps to preserve an untainted image of the national community.

Hence the criteria defining whether one element is worthy of decent commemoration or of oblivion is tied to the role the given element plays in the contemporary processes of national consolidation. Theories of collective memory concur that any commemoration of the past is highly selective. What is remembered depends directly on what we choose to remember, in accordance with the requirements of the present. If memories of an event in the past threaten to challenge or subvert our present identity, they are highly prone to be forgotten.[8] It goes without saying that it is very difficult to achieve a consensus on such a problematic period of Ukrainian history like the Famine; and its coverage in an all-encompassing way is by no means an easy task. Hence we should not be concerned with the question about 'how it all has really happened', but rather examine the strategies of representation with the help of which the 1932–33 Famine is transformed into an exemplary traumatic past. How did the authors of *Golod-33* solve the task of the reconstruction and adaptation of a collective trauma?

Processes of forgetting, of selection and of reconstruction are prerequisites for a collective accommodation of individual memory of traumatic events within the framework of dominant values and beliefs in a society, and thus with cultural conventions more generally.[9] If a certain aspect of the remembered past contradicts a contingent concept of identity, it will be consigned to oblivion in the long run. Memories erode gradually: initially critical aspects will be removed from the foreground and consequently forgotten. Thus a more acceptable image of the past is constructed step by step.

Strategies of Representation

Yanchuk likewise suggests his own scenarios in which certain aspects of everyday life acquire cultural meanings which they did not carry intrinsically and are consequently transposed to the level of a symbolic existence removed

Figure 10.1. Oles Yanchuk, Death of the mother, still from *Golod-33* (1991)

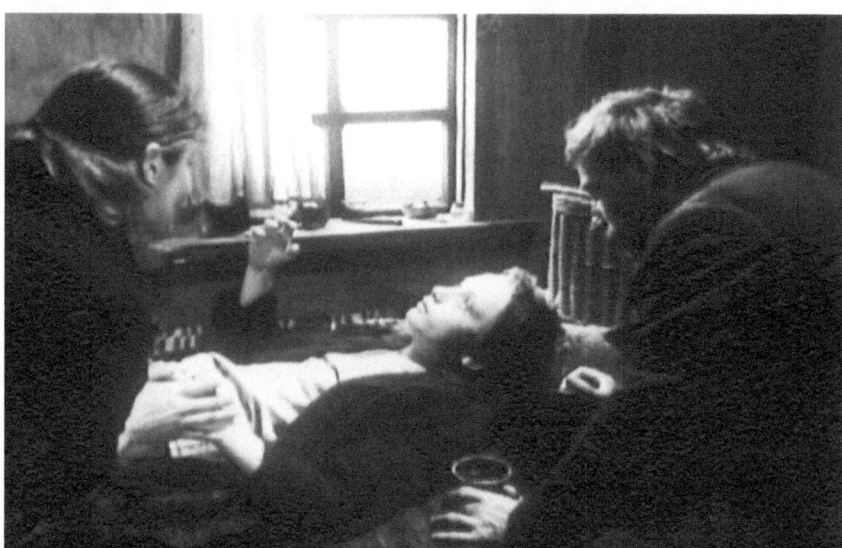

from their initial mundane context. One characteristic episode of the film may serve as an example:

> Just finishing their customary thin soup, the Katrannik hear a knock on the door. It turns out to be one of the communist among their fellow villagers. 'Show me, where's your grain?' – 'They have taken it all, come on!' – 'Taken it all? Instead of giving your excess to the state, like any conscientious citizen, you say they've taken it all!' This dialog develops into a sequence which shows the expropriation of all remaining provisions; as a result the Katrinnik family is left to starve. The grandmother starts to lament and begs the executioners not to take the last remnants away. She is brutally knocked over and falls to the floor. In this sequence it is more than obvious that the authors of the film *Golod-33* suggest a matriarchal interpretation of traditional Ukrainian society. It is the senior female member of the family who confronts the intruders and who bravely retorts that all the grain has been taken away already. And it is precisely the same grandmother who tries to restrain them when they attempt to sequester the last remaining provisions. This evokes a chain of associations: woman – (grand-)mother – protectress. It is not difficult to guess what the last link in this chain of associations is supposed to be: the blow from a rude communist does not just bring an old woman or the mother down, but forces Ukraine down to her knees.

Throughout the film, similar recognisable symbols of humiliation accrue, one after the other, heightening the suspense. Finally the omnipresence of unburied corpses carries the conflict beyond the limits of political opposition and points to the transgression of intercultural norms in the treatment of the bodies of the deceased.[10] The climax of suffering is demonstrated in a grotesque sequence showing huge and sinister red soldiers who encircle a dilapidated and inoffensive Ukrainian cottage which is just barely illuminated by a single ray of light. The peasant hut, the incarnation of the unspoiled character of the Ukrainian peasantry, the embodiment of the national spirit for nineteenth-century writers, is trampled to the ground by the oversized, muddy boots worn by Bolshevik soldiers. The collective trauma is thus translated into a cinematographic image or into a symbol. Images and symbols substitute something in essence incomprehensible by conventional and comprehensive representations of humiliation.

To some extent, the close up perspective selected by Yanchuk for his approach to the Famine offers likewise a sounding board for the creation of distinctive symbols as well as for omissions. Indeed, the focus on individual representations of collective suffering is one of the customary strategies of conventional narratives. As an American reviewer once remarked with reference to representations of the Holocaust, 'the death of 6 million is beyond human comprehension; hence empathy, the death of six is not'.[11] The agony of one tangible family is comprehensible for everybody due to the fact that each spectator automatically projects this family's suffering onto his own life experience. The focus on an individual tragedy allows passing over all aspects threatening the national identity and adopting a substitute image of the collective trauma: 'In the case of unpopular events, which may divide the collectivity, the memory of the group members who took part in the event is put forward and their individual tragedy is accepted. The sociopolitical cause of the trauma is forgotten'.[12]

Even if events displayed in *Golod-33* are connected to the Katrannik family's life, the relationship of the five family members comes across as very dry and schematic. Each of them is drearily carrying his or her individual cross. Family relations are reduced to uninspired exchanges of questions and answers and to the fulfilment of abstract roles and tasks. Before us we do not see Miron Katrannik with his wife and children, but abstract 'fathers', 'mothers', 'children', if not 'victims' and 'martyrs' according to their structural function.

The terms 'sacrifice/victim' (*zhertvo*) and 'martyr' are clearly interrelated, yet they bear a semantic difference. Theological interpretations of the sacrifice, as quoted in the classical studies by Marcel Mauss and Henri Hubert[13], see the 'sacrifice' as a gift that people present to God in the hope of establishing some forms of communication. In the primary meaning 'sacrifice' occurs exclusively as an object, whereas later the idea of a conscious self-sacrifice found its prototype with the crucifixion of Christ. The term 'martyr' is certainly closer to this secondary interpretation of a 'sacrifice'; it carries the idea of a conscious sacrifice to its logical consequence. The subject and the object of the sacrifice are amalgamated inseparably in one.

In *Golod-33* the chalice in which, during church services, the wine is symbolically transformed into the blood of Jesus Christ, becomes highly important. One might even call it one of the central 'characters' of the film. We have already mentioned the sequence in which church property is looted and in which the peasants rally to defend icons and the church's treasury. Even among other items within church treasury, the chalice clearly stands out. After having been handed it, a woman clutching the chalice looks into the camera as if to emphasise this particular significance. Further in the film the fate of the Katrinnik family and the history of the Famine more generally evolve around the chalice: at the request of his fellow villagers, Miron hides the chalice from the communists.

Conspicuously, in the sequence involving the chalice the rhetoric of victimisation corresponds closely to the rhetoric of martyrdom. This is particularly obvious in the sequence in which Miron Katrannik is tortured. Heroically suffering threats and intimidations, he refuses to reveal his secret. It is finally his wife who, in the face of her own death, promises to render the chalice to the henchmen in return for her husband and daughter (the latter already deceased by that time). Yet as she suddenly dies, the enemies are left with empty hands. Her death is certainly not accidental: if realism or the mother's survival instincts would have required her to take the grain, she has to die in the film's narrative to preserve the unrestrained positive image of the Ukrainians.

Between Soviet Cinematography and Early-Christian Rhetoric

It is also interesting to analyse the final sequences of the film in this light. Emaciated by starvation, the men in the village, Miron Katrannik among them, decide on a desperate undertaking: they gather to go to the mill where confiscated grain is stored. The mill is guarded by Red Army soldiers who open fire upon the 'aggressors' without any hesitation. The film takes an interesting turn here: When the Red Army soldiers open fire the peasants do not discontinue their advance. Why would the peasants advance in the face of their sure death?

On the one hand, the iconography of the episode refers to the representation of Bolshevik heroism in early Soviet films, for example the storming of the Winter Palace in Eisenstein's *October* (1927) and Michail

Figure 10.2. Oles Yanchuk, Peasants approaching the mill where the sequestered grain is stored, still from *Golod-33* (1991)

Romm's *Lenin in October* (1937). In at least two respects *Golod-33* inverts the logic of these iconic representations. Firstly, we see how the victorious revolutionary workers fire on their (former) allies, the peasants. And secondly, in contrast to the storming of the Winter Palace, the assault on the mill is a failure. From hindsight, by the way of contrast with the correct national interpretation of events, this inversion unmasks the deceptive character of the Soviet images.

In this context it is worthwhile to consider potential allusions to the Soviet Ukrainian cinematographic tradition as well; and in particular to its towering figure, Aleksandr Dovzhenko. Interestingly, such allusions are almost absent; at least as far as *Zemlia* (Earth), Dovzhenko's seminal film on collectivisation, is concerned. As a matter of fact, Dovzhenko's representation of the transformation in the Ukrainian village, filmed already in 1929, served as the main point of reference for what had become known as the Ukrainian poetic cinema during the 1960s and 1970s. Consciously or unconsciously, Yanchuk avoided reference to the classical cinematographic representation of Ukrainian collectivisation. Dovzhenko's *Zemlia*, still a silent movie, may well be characterised by the term monumentality,[14] as it depicts the peasants' way of life as monumental, and it shows monumental characters living in harmony with nature. Yanchuk's film, on the contrary, puts the emphasis on the individual, by focusing on the Katrannik family.

Even in mass scenes, like the one confronting the peasants and the soldiers, there is no monumentality. Exactly for that reason the scene recalls early Soviet cinematography, when emphasis was still put on the masses as one actor and not the individual within the crowd. In this respect, *Golod 33* reminds us not only of *October* or *Lenin in October*, but also, to a degree, of Dovzhenko's 1939 film *Shchors*, narrating the life and death of an ethnic Ukrainian equivalent of Chapaev, a famous red commander of the Civil War and 1930s film hero. This film was made already by a completely different Dovzhenko, a Dovzhenko who had gone through vitriolic criticism for *Zemlia* and one who had witnessed his film being withdrawn from the movie theatres. In the 1939 film about Shchors, Dovzhenko used widescreen technology and many long shots, for example in one scene when red soldiers approach an invisible enemy across a snow covered plain. Here we see indeed some iconographic proximity with *Golod 33*. Beyond that, there is a sense of tragedy common to both scenes.[15]

Beyond the cinematographic allusions, the episode with the mill all too obviously lacks realism. Soberness and the instinct of self-preservation would have required the peasants to stop and reconsider their tactics, instead of advancing to face a certain death. In the end of the day they had embarked on their endeavour to preserve their own lives and those of their relatives. The length of the sequence and some of its obtrusiveness, resulting from the different angles from which we see the surviving peasants advance past their already killed neighbours, suggests again that the film adheres to principles other than those of realism. This sequence, loose in the sense of a documentary logic, becomes much more intelligible if we read it in the context of the early-Christian rhetoric of martyrdom.

According to common representations, early Christians willingly met their end under the sword of the executioner or in the arena of the circus in anticipation of the posthumous salvation of their souls. Beyond that, the church fathers actively supported this conviction. Tertullian, for example, captured the spirit of his time when he wrote in his affirmative appeal to the martyrs:

> Let the spirit hold converse with the flesh about the common salvation, thinking no longer of the troubles of the prison, but of the wrestle and conflict for which they are the preparation [...] let the spirit set clearly before both itself and the flesh, how these things, though exceeding painful, have yet been calmly endured by many [...] and have even been eagerly desired for the sake of fame and glory; and this not only in the case of men, but of women too, that you, O holy women, maybe be worthy of your sex.[16]

Incidentally, the Christian teaching on martyrdom comprises one additional aspect absent in the film *Golod-33*: the link between martyrdom and the idea that sins are absolved. As the Ukrainian nation is depicted throughout the film as being essentially without sins, the film nonetheless presents the readiness of the Ukrainian peasants to die in the hail of Bolshevik bullets as a voluntary and fully conscious sacrifice; as an act of Christian martyrdom for the *future* salvation of Ukraine.

In the film *Golod-33*, the Ukrainian past is generally represented through narratives of suffering and martyrdom. This reflects developments of the recent past as traditional forms of narratives built around heroes lost much of their appeal during the second half of the twentieth century. Histories focussing exclusively on perpetrators, it seems, have no great future either as they misrepresent the belief of the individual in his or her own capacities.[17] Obviously histories of victims and sacrifices are more compatible with the current mood.

Staring in captivation at the chalice, little Andryiko Katrannik in a close-up mutters 'It sparkles like a star from the sky'. The boy's expression explains the symbolic charge of the golden chalice. As the Ukrainian nation was a chosen people, destined to martyrdom; the nation had to suffer in order to finally fulfil its mission. In the film, the mission to rescue the chalice, the quintessential spiritual treasure and symbol of moral dignity, falls upon a single Ukrainian family, the Katranniks.

Any interpretation of the situation must take into account the extraordinary importance of the mechanism of psychological plausibility. In the words of Stephen Bertman, '[t]he nation transforms the events of the past in order to create a psychologically more acceptable image of the past. Events that do not fit in are excluded; people and political regimes alike prefer sweet oblivion to painful memories'.[18] The film represents the Famine as a well thought-out and rationalised act of suffering for ideas and convictions, bypassing those episodes that might create symbols potentially subverting the intended message.

As a matter of fact, the tragedy of the Katrannik family is presented as a spiritual torment. The loss of the family members has nothing in common with the physical death of bodies emaciated by starvation. Rather their passing away is rendered as the moment when the soul leaves the surface of the earth. Already in the first sequences of the film Miron, having a vision, mutters: 'Like crusaders they have come to destroy us. Their flags only look as if they were red. They are dark. We will perish, as we cannot live like demons'. This comment explains the unprecedented level of the conflict: This is not about conflict between people, but the perpetual confrontation of two absolute powers, of good and evil.

'Have you heard that the Antichrist is back? There are many Antichrists these days. One came from our midst, but he is not one of us', the narrator apocalyptically states at the end of the film. The escalation of the conflict at the end of the film brings the conflict between good and evil to a distinct conclusion: this film is not about the confrontation between class or group morals; this film is not merely about the killing of one part of the population by another, it is in essence accounting for the return of the Antichrist.

In other words, the film juxtaposes two chains of identity. On the one hand there is Ukraine, linked to the positive national norms and values and Christendom, on the other there is the internationalist Soviet Union, linked to evil and the Antichrist. In 1991, these associations must have read for a Ukrainian audience like just another argument for the secession from the USSR with the aim of independent state-building. Against this backdrop the launching of the film on the eve of the 1991 referendum was extremely timely.

One-of-a-Kind

That said, this adequateness in the historical setting of 1991 has in the long run proven to be one of the film's main deficiencies. Frank Ankersmit stressed that a 'narrative scope only comes into being when one compares narrative interpretations with rival interpretations. If we have only one narrative interpretation of some historical topic, we have not got any'.[19] The same might hold true for visual iconography. If we have only *one* visual representation of a historical event, for example the Famine, we can hardly talk about having any at all. However a comparison with the cinematographic representation of the Holocaust, the exemplary collective trauma par excellence, is telling. In the case of the Holocaust, at least two different models of visual representations have developed. The first is embodied by Stephen Spielberg's *Schindler's List*, the second by Claude Lanzmann's *Shoah*. The only fictional film on the Famine, by contrast, has been glorified to such a degree that it has become difficult to mount any critique in public.

Why is the kind of representation of the historical trauma chosen by the authors of *Golod-33* problematic? We have already noticed that the main feature of the film is its construction of a Ukrainian identity that rests exclusively on the status of sacrifice, victimhood and martyrdom. It makes no difference in this context whether we deal with sacrifices in their 'objectified' form, or with martyrdom which reconciles subject and object. In any case, the positive characters in the film work exclusively in the mode of sacrifice and martyrdom. The overall hallmark of both processes is narrativisation, in that every individual act is inscribed into a teleological scheme. The ideological demands of the period in which the film was created grafted their teleology upon the history of the Famine. Distinctively, according to the prevalent interpretation, the sacrifice serves as a prerequisite for communication with the sacral sphere while martyrdom confirms the conviction of those who suffer it. The film *Golod-33* consciously inserts such a teleology (and therefore also sensibility and meaning) into the process of annihilation of Ukrainians, basing its interpretation on a rhetoric of victimisation and martyrdom. To be sure, such a teleology would neither have been intrinsic to the Ukrainian Famine nor to any other form of mass murder in the course of the twentieth century. Implanting a spiritual dimension into the conflict between Ukrainian peasants and Stalinists, the film *post factum* predetermines the events of the 1930s. The suffering of the Ukrainian nation is represented not as a tragic episode of the past, but rather as an important impulse for the creation of independent Ukrainian statehood in the future. In that sense, collectivisation and hunger acquire an inevitable quality. The victims among the peasantry become martyrs for the just cause, sacrificing their lives for the future wellbeing of Ukraine as without the tragic past of the nation no stable national identity could have been constructed. Unwittingly, the film thus contributes to a rehabilitation of the atrocities it was intended to condemn.

Translated from Russian by Christian Noack

Notes and References

1 See the chapters by Kulchytskyi and Marples in this volume.
2 Georgii Kasianov, 'Razrytaia mogila: golod 1932–1933 godov v ukrainiskoi istoriografii, politike i massovym soznanii', *Ab Imperio* 3 (2004): 237–69 (45). See also Kasianov's contribution to this volume.
3 Vasil' Barka, *Zhovtyi kniaz'* (reprint, Kiev: Dnipro, 1991). It deserves mentioning that the *Yellow Prince* was Barka's only work to be included in school curricula in independent Ukraine. In 2011, however, it was taken out of the programme as a compulsory reading and recommended for individual study.
4 Georgii Kasianov, 'Boi za istoriiu', *Novoe Literatunoe Obozrenie* 83 (2007), at http://magazines.russ.ru/nlo/2007/83/ka8.html (accessed 10 November 2011).
5 Larysa Brukhovets'ka, *Prikhovani fil'mi* (Kiev: ArtEk, 2003), 73.
6 In Ukrainian and Russian, the term *zhertva* denotes both *victim* and *sacrifice* [translator's note].
7 Kas'ianov, 'Razrytaia mogila', 265.
8 Cf. Kharal'd Vel'tser [Harald Welzer], 'Istoriia, pamiat' i sovremennost' proshlogo', *Neprikosnovennyi zapas* 40–41 (2005), at http://magazines.russ.ru/nz/2005/2/vel3.html (accessed 26 October 2011).
9 Juanjo Igartua, Dario Paez, 'Art and Remembering Traumatic Collective Events: The Case of the Spanish Civil War', in James W. Pennebaker, Bernard Rim, and Dario Paez (eds), *Collective Memory of Political Events: Social Psychological Perspectives* (Mahwah, NJ: Lawrence Earlbaum Associates, 1997), 79–102 (80).
10 One of the most horrible episodes of the film represents a variation of the motif of 'disrespect for the human body': After the mass shootings, bolsheviks dump the bodies

of the killed and wounded into a ditch, with trunks of wood interspersed, and burn them. The scenes showing cannibalism can also be linked to this motif.

11 Quoted from Annette Insdorf, *Indelible Shadows: Film and the Holocaust* (Cambridge: Cambridge University Press, 2003), 6.
12 Igartua, Paez, 'Art and Remembering Traumatic Collective Events', 83.
13 Cf. Henri Hubert, Marcel Mauss, *The Sacrifice: Its Nature and Function* (Chicago: University of Chicago Press, 1981); See also Rene Girard, *Violence and the Sacred* (Baltimore: Johns Hopkins University Press, 1977).
14 On *Zemlia* see Jerzy Toeplitz, *Geschichte des Films 1895–1933* (Munich: Rogner and Bernd, 1987), 345–6 and the richly illustrated iconographic essay 'Philosophy, Iconology, Collectivization: "Earth" (1930)', by Raymond John Uzwyshyn, available at http://rayuzwyshyn.net/dovzhenko/Earth.htm (accessed 1 June 2012).
15 Cf. Toeplitz, *Geschichte des Films*, 975–6.
16 Tertullian, *To the Martyrs*, excerpts from chapter four, available at the *Sophia Project*, http://www.molloy.edu/sophia/tertullian/tertullian_martyres_txt.htm (accessed 2 May 2011).
17 Vel'tser, 'Istoriia, pamiat' i sovremennost' proshlogo' (see note 9).
18 Stephen Bertman, *Cultural Amnesia: America's Future and the Crisis of Memory* (Westport: Praeger, 2000), 63.
19 Frank R. Ankersmit, 'Six Theses on Narrativist Philosophy of History', in Frank R. Ankersmit, *History and Tropology: The Rise and Fall of Metaphor* (Berkeley: University of California Press, 1994), 33–43 (41).

Part IV

NEW SOURCES AND NEW APPROACHES TO THE IRISH AND UKRAINIAN FAMINES

Chapter 11

IN SEARCH OF NEW SOURCES: POLISH DIPLOMATIC AND INTELLIGENCE REPORTS ON THE HOLODOMOR

Jan Jacek Bruski
Jagiellonian University, Krakow

In recent years we have witnessed a crucial breakthrough in research into the Holodomor. Although many questions are still hotly debated, historians differ with regard to interpretations of the events rather than to the basic facts. A consensus on the list of the most important research areas is beginning to emerge.[1] Undoubtedly, the opening of Soviet archives and the fast processing of new archival sources played a key role. Among them are recently declassified materials, for example documents issued by the Stalinist leadership, state and party administration or the secret services. Beyond that, accounts given by witnesses who went through the hell of the Holodomor have added significantly to the picture.[2]

Documents of foreign provenance which include mainly reports produced by the diplomatic, consular and intelligence services of those states which had missions in the territory of the Soviet Union during the 1930s have likewise contributed to our knowledge. Sources of that type appear to be of interest for at least two reasons. On the one hand, they disclose many previously unknown facts concerning the course of events in Ukraine in 1932–33 and supplement the picture created by the Soviet materials. On the other hand they offer the key to an understanding of the wider, international context of the Ukrainian tragedy. The analysis of these documents brings us closer to answering many important questions: how was the Famine on the Dnieper perceived by foreign diplomats and what was the public opinion abroad concerning them? Were other countries aware of the scale of the human disaster in Ukraine, and to what extent? And, finally, what was the reaction of foreign governments to the news coming in from the USSR?

It is necessary to point out that prior to the opening of Soviet archives foreign sources had been consulted in the first place. It was as early as the mid-1980s that a special US Congress Commission made thorough use of them in its investigation of the circumstances surrounding the Great Famine.[3] Shortly afterwards special editions of documents on the Holodomor which had been found in the archives of the United Kingdom, Germany and Italy were published. Two of the publications deserve special attention: a selection of Italian documents edited by Andrea Graziosi and a model edition of British documents prepared by a team of Ukrainian researchers from Canada.[4]

Regrettably, Polish archives did not attract any attention for a long time. Today we know that the services of the Second Polish Republic – the neighbouring state with a large Ukrainian minority of its own most keenly interested in the developments on the Dnieper – were probably best informed about the details of the Ukrainian tragedy. These Polish sources are well worth taking into account if only for the role of the 'Polish factor' in Soviet Ukraine, notably the longstanding Soviet fear of Poland's interference and the support it could offer to Ukrainian aspirations for secession. This fear has clearly influenced a number of key decisions made by Stalin in 1932–33, in other words, it may have significantly contributed to a drastic aggravation of the Kremlin's policy towards the Ukrainians.[5]

It is only in the last two or three years that several studies and editions of documents including Polish sources have been printed. Two publications are especially worth mentioning. One of them is a comprehensive volume on the Famine in Ukraine, published in the series *Poland and Ukraine in the 1930s and 1940s: Unknown Documents from Secret Service Archives*, containing, inter alia, several dozen reports prepared by the Polish branches in the USSR.[6] The other was edited by the author of this chapter. It includes exclusively diplomatic and intelligence documents, and was published by the Polish Institute of International Affairs.[7] Both volumes were published four years ago to mark the 75th anniversary of the Great Famine.

The previous lack of interest in Polish archive materials is all the more striking when one realises that they, despite their fate during and after World War II, have been preserved in a relatively good condition. As a result, we have an almost complete set of documents on the Holodomor produced by Polish diplomatic and intelligence missions, which comprises several hundred detailed reports, analyses and studies from 1931–34. The actual dispersal of these documents, however, constitutes a serious obstacle for researchers. The most important ones are currently kept in three archives. Probably the most valuable materials can be found in the Central Military Archives (*Centralne Archiwum Wojskowe*; CAW) in Warsaw, though many important sources are housed in another institution located in the Polish capital as well, namely the Archives of Modern Records (*Archiwum Akt Nowych*; AAN). Additionally, unique materials are held in Moscow. They consist of the extensive archive of Polish interwar intelligence, *Oddział II Sztabu Głównego Wojska Polskiego* (the Second Bureau of the Main Staff of the Polish Army), confiscated in 1945 by the Red Army and now kept in the Russian State Military Archives (*Rossiiskii Gosudarstvennyi Voennyi Arkhiv*; RGVA) among other so-called 'trophy files' (*trofeinye fondy*).[8]

On which sources did Polish information on the Holodomor rely? The current situation in Ukraine was monitored by the officials of the diplomatic legation in Moscow – mainly the Polish military attaché and the commercial councillor. However, the most convenient vantage points were two missions in Ukraine itself: the Polish consulate general in Khar'kiv, the capital of the Ukrainian SSR at the time, and the consulate in Kiev.[9] These missions carried out typical consulate functions but they also acted as undercover agencies for the Polish intelligence services.[10] Their employees gathered invaluable information during their numerous journeys across Ukraine, which were made available by all means of transport[11] and through their contacts with clients who visited the Polish offices. The exchange of information with foreign diplomats, especially those representing Italy and Germany, added to the picture.[12] Also of no small importance was the analysis of official publications and the Soviet press. The number of local newspapers regularly subscribed to by the Polish missions illustrates the significance attached to sources of this kind. In the autumn of 1933, the consulate in Kiev, for example, held as many as 115 titles.[13]

Information collected through various channels reached the Polish authorities in the form of reports. The distribution lists included the Polish General Staff, various departments of the Ministry of Foreign Affairs, and, at times, the Ministry of Industry and Trade, the Ministry of Agriculture, the National Institute of Export and the *voivodship* offices in Lwów (L'viv) and Łuck (Lutsk). Particularly important documents were published in a confidential newsletter titled *Przegląd Informacyjny 'Polska a Zagranica'* (*Informational Survey 'Poland and Abroad'*), which appeared in several dozens of numbered copies. The Polish elites' perception of the events in the USSR was also affected by *Biuletyn Wschodni Ministerstwa Spraw Zagranicznych* (*The Eastern Bulletin of the Ministry of Foreign Affairs*), which was a bit more widely distributed. Unfortunately, it ceased to appear in the second half of 1932.

What picture emerges from the Polish documents? It is not surprising that Polish observers keenly followed the developments of the so-called Stalinist revolution, and above all the campaign against the Soviet peasants. Reports from the USSR and especially Ukraine contain a lot of information about the dispossession of peasant land and forced collectivisation. They also include news of repressions, like deportations of alleged *kulaks*. These deportations, conducted under inhumane conditions, were in fact a form of extermination, or 'the mass execution of undesirable elements for the Soviet leadership', as the commercial councillor of the legation in Moscow put it.[14] All instances of peasant opposition against the new agricultural policy were scrupulously reported – from passive resistance and the sabotaging of official decrees, through acts of individual terror aimed at village 'activists' to the forming of regular insurgent units undertaking skirmishes with the units of GPU and the army. As early as the turn of 1930 Polish diplomats were fully aware of the fact that on the European territory of the USSR the centres of fiercest opposition were located in Ukraine and in the Northern Caucasus, areas populated in large numbers by ethnic Ukrainians.[15]

Although the Polish reports were often formulated on the spot, they make many accurate predictions. They repeatedly gave a negative assessment of the future consequences of collectivisation. As early as autumn 1930 it was pointed out that mass repressions of peasants and the removing of economic incentives which could stimulate agricultural production were certain to lead to a severe food crisis in the near future.[16] Therefore the outbreak of famine in Ukraine, where the Bolsheviks' new policy assumed particularly drastic forms, came as no surprise for the authors of the Polish reports. They had systematically been providing information about the oncoming disaster. The tragedy had its roots in the formulation of exaggerated targets for grain procurement (Russian *khlebozagotovki, khlebosdacha*) which Ukraine was supposed to implement by the end of 1931. To achieve these declared aims, the authorities took draconian coercive measures. 'Nowhere else, apart from the Northern Caucasus, was grain procurement pursued with such ruthlessness as to actually amount to the confiscation of almost the whole agricultural production of the peasants', affirmed the head of the Polish consulate general in Khar'kiv, Jan Karszo-Siedlewski.[17]

These methods did not facilitate the execution of the unrealistic plan. However even its partial implementation resulted in, as the Polish commercial councillor in Moscow wrote, 'excessive amounts of grain being pumped out of the Ukrainian village'.[18] The first symptoms of the crisis were mentioned in the Polish reports dated February 1932.[19] Three months later Polish observers no longer harboured doubts as to the correct assessment of the situation. In May, Henryk Jankowski, the consul in Kiev, reported:

> In towns like Vinnytsia and Uman there are cases of people who have collapsed from weakness and emaciation and have to be removed from the streets every day. The situation in the country is even worse, where [...] starvation, banditry and murders happen on a daily basis.

Jankowski reported that lack of food afflicted not only individual peasants, 'who had long been feeding themselves on potato peelings, acorns and the like', but also collective farms.[20] The reports were confirmed by the councillor Adam Stebłowski from Khar'kiv, who wrote about the raging famine and places where 'everything has been eaten, even cats and dogs'.[21]

The Famine of the spring of 1932 turned out to be only a prelude to the real tragedy. The effect of the Bolsheviks' policy on the peasants was that they became more and more apathetic and ceased to display any interest in cultivating the land. The authorities decided to break this passive resistance with force. Again they imposed an exorbitant plan of production and grain deliveries on Ukraine which was supposed to be executed at all costs and by all available means. In the summer and autumn of 1932 the Polish observers reported on new measures in the campaign aimed against Ukrainian peasants. As a result, Polish reports analysed repressive directives, such as 'On the Safekeeping of Socialist Property', that permitted the death penalty for petty theft of food, or the introduction of the so-called 'black boards' (*chernye doski*) onto which whole Ukrainian *raions* (middle-level administrative units) were entered for failing to supply their quotas of grain. As a consequence they were deprived of all supplies and cut off from the rest of the country by police and army blockades.[22] A number of preserved documents report on the course of important party conferences in July and September 1932 which were supposed to break the Ukrainian communists' resistance against the agrarian policy enforced by Moscow. It is worthwhile to note that Polish diplomats immediately directed their attention to the ominous role of the two emissaries, Viacheslav Molotov and Lazar Kaganovich, sent by Stalin, in the crushing of local opposition and the acceleration of the repressive campaign against the Ukrainian peasantry.[23]

Although in the autumn of 1932 Soviet authorities did not manage to collect the planned amount of grain, the Ukrainian countryside had nevertheless been cleaned out of all reserves and again faced the spectre of famine. Yet the worst was still to come. Stanislav Kulchytskyi convincingly argues that at the turn of 1932 and 1933 Stalin consciously decided to escalate the Famine in Ukraine and to use it as a repressive instrument against the peasantry.[24] One of the elements of this 'terror-famine' was the actual blockade of villages. The Soviet security services undertook a ruthless battle against peasants wandering across towns or cities in search of something to eat. A secret directive closed the borders between starving Ukraine and Soviet Russia for fugitives. It must be emphasised that those symptomatic developments did not escape the attention of the Polish observers and were scrupulously listed in their reports sent to Warsaw.[25]

At the beginning of 1933, the villages, beset by successive disciplinary requisitions, began to run out of their last food reserves. In February the head of the Polish consulate in Kiev alarmingly stated that '[a] vast percentage of the population in villages is suffering from malnutrition. The death rate is enormous'. He also reported on a widespread sense of indifference and resignation among peasants and an 'almost complete deadening of life' in the countryside.[26] We could adduce further, still more shocking, quotations from the reports. The Polish documents undoubtedly give a very vivid picture of the worsening – week by week, month by month – of the famine disaster in Ukraine. Polish observers realised that a food crisis, triggered by the abortive agrarian policy, was something present in many regions of the USSR, and not only in Ukraine did it take the form of actual famine. Information about it was passed on through both diplomatic channels and intelligence agencies. However, reports made it clear that it was only in the Ukrainian SSR and the Northern Caucasus that the Famine reached the catastrophic proportions which could result in the biological annihilation of whole social groups.

The disaster reached its peak in 1933, in the period preceding the new harvest. Several dramatic intelligence reports from that time stress that villages were desolate and in a state of ruin. The mission in Khar'kiv reported that

> Villages that used to be inhabited by five or six thousand people – now (15 June) have 20–30 families […] Due to the lack of people who bury dead bodies, in some villages corpses were initially thrown into the cellars of deserted houses, and when there were no people to do the job of throwing corpses into cellars, corpses lay unburied at home for a long time […] As a result, in some almost empty villages, there is an unbearable stench in the air.[27]

An agent from Kiev also reported on deserted village houses and dozens of unburied corpses lying on roads and in fields.

> There is no sight of cats or dogs, all of them have been eaten. In forests there are many half-wild people who feed on mushrooms, moss and roots. On the roads one can often see peasant families fleeing from the countryside on horse wagons – in no specific direction.[28]

In June 1933 the head of the consulate general in Khar'kiv reported that

> some villages have become completely deserted […] Generally, the Ukrainian countryside now has no more than 60 per cent of the

population, the rest have died or run away to cities. Cases of cannibalism are increasingly heard of.[29]

The theme of cannibalism recurs in the Polish reports of this period. We can read in one of them:

> Quite a reliable informant of Berdychiv says that in the evenings on the outskirts of the town a real hunt for children is taking place. No mother puts a child on the street after nightfall. Despite this, there are cases of children being stolen from their homes. The remains of dead horses are dug up and there are also cases of the eating of the deceased by their families – after several days of waiting for a coffin and the permission for burial. The hunger is most severe in the countryside. In a number of *raions*, such as Tsvetkovs'kyi, Zvenyhorods'kyi, Umans'kyi, Buts'kyi, Tarashchans'kyi and partly Berdychivs'kyi, cannibalism became a kind of addiction.[30]

Other equally shocking aspects repeatedly mentioned in the reports by the Polish diplomats and intelligence agents include police manhunts for abandoned children and fugitives from villages as well as the killing of emaciated persons with special injections.[31]

In the months of May and June 1933, people slowly dying from hunger became commonplace in the cities. A Polish agent reported from Kiev:

> The cases of death from starvation in the streets and in the courtyards are counted now not in tens, but in hundreds daily. Every night, trucks and horse-drawn wagons circling the streets collect the dead in the streets and markets, gardens and courtyards. Once in the morning I witnessed four trucks that carried the dead and people dying of hunger away from the main railway station. I was told that this happened every day. What confirms the number of such deaths is the fact that administrators of individual houses often have to wait three to four days, after alerting the municipal authorities to collect the corpses of *besprizornye* [orphans not looked after] or peasants, who while searching for food scraps and a place to sleep died from starvation in the courtyard or on the stairs. During two nights – on 3–4 and 4–5 June – at the Catholic cemetery 'Baikova Gora' about two thousand dead bodies were buried in forty pits. I saw the final stage of the burial, since the graves are located near the Polish military cemetery. Two huge vats of lime were put in place and every layer of corpses was covered with lime and a very shallow layer of soil. However it should

be explained that only part of the corpses is buried in cemeteries – and that there is a certain order: for two nights corpses are transported to one cemetery, for the next two – to another, etc. (Kiev has five open cemeteries). The majority of the dead are buried in suburban fields, gardens, etc. Unfortunately, determining the exact number of corpses collected each night is impossible. I know from a completely reliable source that every night this number ranges around 700 corpses.[32]

Reports being sent from Ukraine were so terrifying that Polish authorities often did not want to believe all of their details. In particular, the head of the consulate in Kiev, Stanisław Sośnicki, received a reprimand from his superiors. In January 1934, he was rebuked by the legation in Moscow, which accused him of 'generalising too much [...] the information about famine, misery, persecution of the population, the fight against Ukrainianess etc.' The Polish *chargé d'affaires*, councillor Henryk Sokolnicki, wrote that Sośnicki had seemed to be 'too mesmerised by the applicants coming [to the consulate] to ask for help'. These people –Sokolnicki added – 'can often give a number of interesting details', but could not be a reliable source of data about the general situation – especially since they had a personal interest in exaggerating their stories.

The Polish representative in Kiev responded immediately. In a letter of 31 January Sośnicki confirmed his assessment of the events on the Dnieper and emphasised that the main source of his information – indeed identical to the information provided by other foreign diplomats – were not petitioners, but personal observations he had made during his trips across Ukraine. The consulate's data 'on misery, persecutions, the fight against Ukrainianess' – he stated categorically – 'are being thoroughly analysed, verified and only then communicated in reports'.[33]

Diplomatic reports also give an estimated number for casualties of the Holodomor. Polish observers almost unanimously talked about at least 5 million, though it is difficult to establish the grounds for those estimates.[34] The desolate villages and whole regions they passed through during their journeys across the country constituted a tangible proof of the enormous losses which Ukraine must have suffered. On numerous occasions these reports also mentioned that tens of thousands of new settlers – mainly Byelorussians, Russians, and Jews – were brought in by official policy to colonise deserted areas.[35]

It is interesting to note that Polish diplomats differed in their opinions concerning the reasons for the catastrophe. Stanisław Sośnicki, the consul in Kiev, writing about the 'mistakes' of the Soviet authorities and an unsuccessful 'experiment', seemed to blame doctrinarian agrarian policy and the blindness of the Bolsheviks, who let the situation slip out of control.[36] Other conclusions can be drawn from the observations of Karszo-Siedlewski, the head of the Polish mission in Khar'kiv. He noted that the disastrous Famine affected an area of clearly defined boundaries, and this could only be explained by the authorities acting deliberately:

> The famine does not refer to the south of Russia as such but to Ukraine itself, because when you cross the northern boundary of the Ukrainian SSR, the picture radically changes. In the Central Chernozem Oblast [the Black Earth region in the RSFSR], which does not differ much from Ukraine as far as the climatic and economic situation is concerned, the condition of the peasants is incomparably better. This means that the policy of the central government towards Ukraine was much more ruthless and predatory than towards neighbouring provinces of the RSFSR, with the exception of the Northern Caucasus.[37]

Karszo-Siedlewski formulated this thesis on the basis of his observations made during a journey by car from Khar'kiv to Moscow.

> What intrigued me most during the whole journey was the difference between what villages and fields looked like in Ukraine and the neighbouring TsChO [Central Black Earth Oblast], and even infertile areas around Moscow. Ukrainian villages are in decay, they are empty, deserted and miserable, cottages half-demolished, with roofs blown down; no new houses in sight, children and old people are more like skeletons, no sight of livestock. [...] When I found myself in TsChO soon afterwards [...] I had the impression of crossing the border from the state of the Soviets to Western Europe.[38]

It should be pointed out that a substantial group of Polish documents concerns not only the Soviet authorities' crackdown on Ukrainian peasants, but also a campaign started in 1933 against the Ukrainian intelligentsia. We have at our disposal dozens of reports on the collapse of the so-called policy of Ukrainisation, successive purges in the Ukrainian Communist Party, the rout of Ukrainian scientific and educational institutions, deportations and arrests of the intelligentsia, and finally – the ongoing Russification of public life in Ukraine.[39] It should be emphasised that the Polish observers – unaware of the inside stories of decisions made in the Kremlin – were deeply convinced about the link between the two phenomena: a blow dealt to the Ukrainian countryside and an attack on the nationally conscious elements in cities. They attributed it to a change in Soviet nationality policy. According to Polish diplomats, changes in Ukraine could be closely linked with the new stage

Stalin's Soviet Union had just entered into; the stage of building a new empire based primarily on the Great Russian ethnic component. The head of the consulate general in Khar'kiv rightly noticed at the end of 1933:

> Mass persecutions and arrests cannot be explained or justified by peril on the part of the Ukrainian national movement. [...] The real cause of the action lies in the planned, far-sighted long-term policy of the Moscow leaders, who are more and more becoming imperialists, strengthening the political system and borders of the state.[40]

The impact that the spectre of a 'Polish threat' has exerted on the Kremlin's Ukrainian policy has already been pointed at earlier. It would seem fair to note that these Soviet fears could be deemed justifiable to a degree, if the course of events accompanying forced collectivisation in the early 1930s is taken into account. In particular, it hardly seems coincidental that Soviet authorities met with the most stubborn resistance against collectivisation precisely in those regions of Ukraine bordering with Poland. Presumably against the backdrop of the experiences during the Civil war a decade earlier, the local peasantry expected the imminent outbreak of war and was probably increasingly welcoming the prospect of a Polish military intervention which would have ended Bolshevik rule. Signs of such sentiments of the population were carefully observed and frequently reported by the Polish consular missions in Ukraine.[41]

Stalin, of course, was fully aware of this situation. It should be added that he did not trust the Ukrainian communists any further than the Ukrainian peasantry. He regarded the former as nationalists in disguise and thought them to be only too susceptible for Polish influence. Most certainly this was one of the constant and most nagging 'headaches' for the general secretary. An excerpt from his letter to Lazar Kaganovich clearly illustrates the way Stalin perceived Ukrainian matters including possible Polish interference. Under the impression of latest news about the deteriorating situation in Ukraine and the Ukrainian communists' dissatisfaction with the party's agrarian policy, Stalin wrote to his close collaborator on 11 August 1932:

> The chief thing now is Ukraine. Things in Ukraine are terrible. It's terrible in the party [...]. It's terrible in the GPU. If we don't make an effort now to improve the situation in Ukraine, we may lose Ukraine. Keep in mind that Pilsudski is not daydreaming, and his agents in Ukraine are many times stronger than *Redens* [the head of the Ukrainian GPU] or *Kosior* [the secretary general of the Ukrainian party] think. Keep in mind that the Ukrainian Communist party (500,000 members,

ha-ha) includes not a few (yes, not a few!) rotten elements, conscious and non-conscious *Petliurites* [followers of the Ukrainian emigré leader Symon Petliura, assassinated in 1926; in the Soviet propaganda jargon an equivalent to the term 'Ukrainian nationalists'] as well as direct agents of Pilsudski. As soon as things get worse, these elements will not be slow in opening a front within (and outside) the Party. [...] We must set the goal of transforming Ukraine as quickly as possible into a real fortress of the USSR, into a genuinely exemplary republic. [...] Without these and similar measures (ideological and political work in Ukraine, in the first place in her border districts and so forth), I repeat – we may lose Ukraine [...][42]

In fact such fears were somewhat exaggerated, to put it mildly. We know now certainly that against the backdrop of the situation in 1932–33 Poland was not eager to get involved in internal Soviet matters or to start a risky game over Ukraine. Actually the complex developments in the international arena almost inevitably prompted Warsaw rather to seek agreement with Moscow. Indeed, Stalin himself was aware of the delicate position that the USSR's western neighbour was in at the time. Correctly recognising the essential dilemmas of the Polish foreign policy, he did not hesitate to use the moment and gave the signal for a rapprochement with Warsaw. The point of departure for a significant, if short-lived Polish-Soviet détente was the conclusion of a non-aggression pact in July 1932. It brought tangible benefits to the Polish side, but at the same time severely restricted its freedom of political manoeuvre. Presumably the shift in the relations between Moscow and Warsaw seriously affected, inter alia, the situation in Ukraine. It is very likely that Stalin perceived this as a perfect opportunity which would not present itself soon again. Realising this and using Poland's current passivity on Ukrainian matters, the Soviet leader decided to finally crush all the signs of the emancipatory tendencies on the Dnieper.

Indeed, some of the Polish diplomats openly suggested this connection in their reports.[43] They also pointed out that obvious signs of a Polish-Soviet rapprochement had changed the attitude of the Ukrainian peasants towards Poland. Ascertaining this in December 1933, consul Kurnicki wrote: 'they [the peasants] stop perceiving us as their possible "saviours" and rather transfer their hopes to the Germans'.[44] Two years later the same diplomat stated:

[The Ukrainian villagers] saw in Poland their last resort and very seriously calculated upon the possibility of an armed conflict [...] However the Pact ended the expectation of foreign help. Thus in the mind of the broad masses the Soviet power became an ultimate ruler of their life and death.[45]

Given the limitations of a chapter, it is impossible to fully discuss all the aspects reflected in Polish documents and their relevance for research on the Holodomor.

Therefore, approaching the conclusion, I would only like to point out some of the important issues highlighted in these sources, but not mentioned earlier. Among them are such questions as: the lobbying efforts of the Ukrainian diaspora seeking the public recognition of the famine disaster in an international forum, the situation of the Polish national minority in Ukraine during the famine years, and the influence which the events on Ukrainian soil exerted on Polish-Soviet relations. All these questions are highly important and interconnected with many other under-researched areas in Ukrainian and international history of the 1930s. Perhaps the use of previously unknown Polish documents will not fundamentally change our view of the period. Undoubtedly, recently declassified Soviet archival materials are more important in this respect. Nevertheless, I am convinced that Polish sources may contribute significantly to a better understanding of the events of 1932–33 and help to answer numerous detailed questions that still have to be answered in relation to the Holomodor.

Translated by Alicja Waligóra-Zblewska and Christian Noack

Notes and References

1 The main controversies focus on the question whether the Holodomor was intentionally provoked by the Stalinist leadership or not. A positive response would imply classification of the Ukrainian Famine as an act of genocide. Such a view presents the position of, inter alia, the seminal study of Robert Conquest, *The Harvest of Sorrow: Soviet Collectivization and the Terror-Famine* (Edmonton: University of Alberta Press, 1986). A new, well-founded variant of this interpretation is provided by Stanislav Kul'chyts'kyi – *Holodomor 1932–1933 rr. iak henotsyd: Trudnoshchi usvidomlennia* (Kiev: Nash chas, 2008). See also Kulchytskyi's and Marples' contributions to this volume. For different conclusions compare: Robert W. Davies, Stephen G. Wheatcroft, *The Industrialisation of Soviet Russia*, vol. 5: *The Years of Hunger: Soviet Agriculture, 1931–1933* (Basingstoke: Palgrave Macmillan, 2004); Viktor Kondrashin, *Golod 1932–1933 godov: Tragediia rossiiskoi derevni* (Moskva: ROSSPEN, Fond Pervogo Prezidenta Rossii B. N. El'cina, 2008).

2 Valerii Vasyl'iev and Iurii Shapoval (eds), *Komandyry velykoho holodu: poizdky V. Molotova i L. Kahanovycha v Ukrainu ta na Pivnychnyi Kavkaz 1932–1933 rr.* (Kiev: Heneza, 2001); Oleg V. Khlevniuk, Robert U. Devis (Robert W. Davies), L. P. Kosheleva, E. A. Ris, L. A. Rogovaia (eds), *Stalin i Kaganovich: Perepiska 1931–1936 gg.* (Moskva: ROSSPEN, 2001); Valentyna Borysenko, Vasyl' Danylenko, Serhii Kokin, Oleksandra Stasiuk, Iurii Shapoval (eds), *Rozsekrechena pam'iat': Holodomor 1932–1933 rokiv v Ukraini v dokumentakh HPU-NKVD* (Kiev: Stylos, 2007); Ruslan Pyrih, *Holodomor 1932–1933 rokiv v Ukraini: Dokumenty i materialy* (Kiev: Instytut Istorii Ukrainy NAN Ukrainy, Vyd. Dim

Kyievo-Mohylians'ka akademiia, 2007); *Ukrains'kyi holokost: Svidchennia tykh, khto vyzhyv*, vols 1–6, edited by Iurii Mytsyk and Liudmyla Ivannikova (vols 1–4) and Iurii Mytsyk (vols 5–6) (Kiev: Vyd. Dim Kyievo-Mohylians'ka akademiia, 2003–2008).

3 Proceedings of this commission were summarised in *Investigation of the Ukrainian Famine. Report to Congress Commission on the Ukraine Famine. Adopted by the Commission April 19, 1988, Submitted to Congress April 22, 1988* (Washington, DC: United States Government Printing Office, 1988). This edition also contains a valuable documentary appendix. See also Kulchytskyi's contribution in this volume.

4 Andrea Graziosi, '"Lettres de Kharkov". La famine en Ukraine et dans le Caucase du Nord à travers les rapports des diplomates italiens, 1932–1934', *Cahiers du Monde Russe et Soviétique*, vols 1–2 (1989): 5–106; idem, *Lettere da Kharkov. La carestia in Ucraina e nel Caucaso del Nord nei rapporti dei diplomatici italiani, 1932–33* (Torino: Giulio Einaudi, 1991); Marco Carynnyk, Lubomyr Y. Luciuk, Bohdan S. Kordan (eds), *The Foreign Office and the Famine. British Documents on Ukraine and the Great Famine of 1932–1933* (Kingston: Limestone Press, 1988). Another precious edition is that of German diplomatic documents: Dmytro Zlepko (ed.), *Der ukrainische Hunger-Holocaust. Stalins verschwiegener Völkermord 1932/33 an 7 Millionen ukrainischen Bauern im Spiegel geheimgehaltener Akten des deutschen Auswärtigen Amtes. Eine Dokumentation aus den Beständen des Politischen Archivs im Auswärtigen Amt, Bonn* (Sonnenbühl: Verlag Helmut Wild, 1988). See also some documentary studies, based on this kind of sources: M. Wayne Morris, *Stalin's Famine and Roosevelt's Recognition of Russia* (Lanham: University Press of America, 1994); Wsevolod W. Isajiw (ed.), *Famine-Genocide in Ukraine, 1932–1933. Western Archives, Testimonies and New Research* (Toronto: Ukrainian Canadian Research and Documentation Centre, 2003); Étienne Thévenin, *France, Allemagne et Autriche face à la famine de 1932–1933 en Ukraine*; available at http://colley.co.uk/garethjones/james_mace.htm (accessed 18 May 2010).

5 On the impact of the 'Polish factor' on the events of 1932–3 in Ukraine see: Terry Martin, *The Affirmative Action Empire: Nations and Nationalism in the Soviet Union, 1923–1939* (Ithaca: Cornell University Press, 2001), 273–308; Timothy Snyder, *Sketches from a Secret War: A Polish Artist's Mission to Liberate Soviet Ukraine* (New Haven: Yale University Press, 2005), 99–114.

6 The bilingual, Polish – Ukrainian, edition: *Pol'shcha ta Ukraina u trydciatykh-sorokovykh rokakh XX stolittia*, t. 7: *Holodomor v Ukraini 1932–1933* = *Polska i Ukraina w latach trzydziestych-czterdziestych XX wieku*, t. 7: *Wielki Głód na Ukrainie 1932–1933*, edited by Jerzy Bednarek and others (Warszawa-Kijów: Instytut Pamięci Narodowej – Komisja Ścigania zbrodni przeciwko Narodowi Polskiemu, Ministerstwo Spraw Wewnętrznych i Administracji RP, Wydzielone Archiwum Państwowe Służby Bezpieczeństwa Ukrainy, Instytut Badań Politycznych i Narodowościowych Narodowej Akademii Nauk Ukrainy, 2008). English language version: *Poland and Ukraine in the 1930's–1940's. Unknown Documents from the Archives of the Secret Services. Holodomor: The Great Famine in Ukraine 1932–1933*, edited by Jerzy Bednarek and others (Warsaw-Kiev: The Institute of National Rememberance – Commission for the Prosecution of Crimes against the Polish Nation, Ministry of Interior and Administration Republic of Poland, The Security Service of Ukraine Branch Sate Archives, Institute of Political and Ethno-National Studies at the National Academy of Sciences of Ukraine, 2009).

7 Jan Jacek Bruski (ed.), *Hołodomor 1932–1933: Wielki Głód na Ukrainie w dokumentach polskiej dyplomacji i wywiadu* (Warszawa: Polski Instytut Spraw Międzynarodowych, 2008). Some documents from this edition were translated into Russian: Ian Iacek Bruski, 'Bol'shoi golod na Ukraine v svete dokumentov pol'skoi diplomatii i razvedky', *Evropa. Zhurnal*

Pol'skogo Instituta Mezhdunarodnykh Del 6, no. 4 (2006): 97–152; available at http://www.pism.pl/zalaczniki/Europa21Bruski.pdf (accessed 18 May 2010). Some additional Polish materials can be found in Robert Kuśnierz (ed.), *Pomór w 'raju bolszewickim'. Głód na Ukrainie w latach 1932–1933 w świetle polskich dokumentów dyplomatycznych i dokumentów wywiadu* (Toruń: Wydawnictwo Adam Marszałek, 2008).

8   For more information on the *Holodomor* files in the archives in question see: 'Wstęp', in Bruski, *Hołodomor 1932–1933*, LXII–LXV; Jan Jacek Bruski, 'Nieznane polskie dokumenty na temat Hołodomoru. Efekty rekonesansu archiwalnego w Moskwie', *Nowa Ukraina*, nos. 1–2 (2008): 64–70; available at http://www.nowaukraina.org/nu1_2-2008/09_Bruski.pdf (accessed 18 May 2010).

9   The consulate general in Khar'kiv, established in 1924, was continuing the mission of the Polish diplomatic legation, active in Ukraine in 1921–23, before all the prerogatives in the field of Soviet foreign policy were transferred from the republican governments to the all-Union *Narkomat Inostrannykh Del*. The second Polish consulate – in Kiev – was founded only in 1926. After moving the capital of Soviet Ukraine to Kiev, in mid-1934, the Polish outposts changed their roles – the consulate in the new capital gained the rank of a consulate general, while the mission in Khar'kiv was downgraded. The latter was closed in 1937, the former ceased to exist in September 1939 only.

10   During the Holodomor practically all prominent officials of the Polish consular missions in Ukraine were closely collaborating with military intelligence. A list of them includes among others the two subsequent heads of the Polish consulate general in Khar'kiv – Adam Stebłowski and Jan Karszo-Siedlewski, consuls – Tadeusz Pawłowski (Khar'kiv), Henryk Jankowski and Stanisław Sośnicki (both Kiev), and a vice-consul Piotr Kurnicki and his wife Zofia in Kiev.

11   They traveled mainly by car and by train, but occasionally also by plane. The latter way of traveling enabled Polish diplomats to observe larger areas and to assess the state of fields, harvest progress, etc.

12   Both countries had their offices in Ukraine: Germany – the consulate general in Khar'kiv and consulates in Kiev and Odessa; Italy – the vice-consulate in Khar'kiv. There was also an Italian consular mission in Novorossiisk (on the territory of the Russian Soviet republic), which reported inter alia on the situation of the Kuban Ukrainians. For examples of a two-way exchange of information between Polish and foreign diplomats see: Adam Stebłowski to the Ministry of Foreign Affairs, Khar'kiv, 21 May 1932, and Lt. Colonel Jan Kowalewski to the Chief of the Second Bureau of the Main Staff, Moscow, 24 January 1933, in Bruski, *Hołodomor 1932–1933*, doc. 24, p. 64; doc. 58, p. 185; reports by Bernardo Attolico from 7 April 1933 and by Sergio Gradenigo from 6 January and 16 August 1933, in Andrea Graziosi, *Lettere da Kharkov*, doc. 25, p. 137; doc. 30, p. 154; doc. 43, p. 202; William Strang to John Simon, Moscow, 26 September 1933, in Carynnyk, Luciuk, Kordan, *The Foreign Office and the Famine*, doc. 50, pp. 312–13.

13   Piotr Kurnicki to Lt. Jerzy Niezbrzycki, Kiev, 22 October 1933, in Bruski, *Hołodomor 1932–1933*, doc. 144, p. 425.

14   Antoni Żmigrodzki to the Trade Department of the Ministry of Industry and Trade, Moscow, 18 March 1930, AAN, Collection: Ambasada RP w Moskwie, Box 48, p. 394.

15   Numerous Polish reports on this subject could be found in: AAN, Collection: Ministerstwo Spraw Zagranicznych RP, 1918–1939, Boxes 10000, 10040, 10041; CAW, Collection: Oddział II Sztabu Generalnego/Głównego WP, I.303.4.2995. Precious analyses were also regularly appearing in *Biuletyn Wschodni Ministerstwa Spraw Zagranicznych*, available for example in Biblioteka Narodowa (National Library) in Warsaw.

16 Cf. for instance: an economic report by Lt. Colonel Jan Kowalewski, (not dated, not before the end of October 1930), AAN, Collection: Attaché wojskowy przy Ambasadzie RP w Moskwie, Box 92, p. 411.
17 Jan Karszo-Siedlewski, 'Kwestja narodowościowa na Ukrainie Sowieckiej według stanu na 1.V.1933 r.' ('The Nationality Question in Soviet Ukraine on 1 May 1933'), 8 May 1933 (an elaboration prepared for the Polish consular meeting in Moscow), in Bruski, *Hołodomor 1932–1933*, 264.
18 Antoni Żmigrodzki to the Trade Department of the Ministry of Industry and Trade, Moscow, 7 May 1932, in Bruski, *Hołodomor 1932–1933*, doc. 20, p. 48.
19 Adam Stebłowski to the Eastern Division of the Ministry of Foreign Affairs, Khar'kiv, 1 February 1932, in Bruski, *Hołodomor 1932–1933*, doc. 11, pp. 31–2.
20 Henryk Jankowski to the Polish envoy in Moscow Stanisław Patek, Kiev, 11 May 1932, in Bruski, *Hołodomor 1932–1933*, doc. 22, p. 59.
21 Adam Stebłowski to the Eastern Division of the Ministry of Foreign Affairs, Khar'kiv, 21 May 1932, in Bruski, *Hołodomor 1932–1933*, doc. 24, p. 63.
22 'Sytuacja materjalna ludności na Ukrainie' ('The material situation of the population in Ukraine') (a report by the Polish consulate general in Khar'kiv), 16 October 1932; Henryk Sokolnicki to the Polish legation in Moscow, Khar'kiv, 30 November 1932; Jan Karszo-Siedlewski's report, Khar'kiv, 4 February 1933; in Bruski, *Hołodomor 1932–1933*, doc. 46, 50, 61, pp. 142–6, 159–66, 191–4.
23 A press report by the Polish consulate general in Khar'kiv no. 9/32 (for the period 1–15 July 1932), 22 November 1932, CAW, Collection: Oddział II Sztabu Generalnego/Głównego WP, I.303.4.3043, p. 274–283; Zdzisław Miłoszewski, 'Zbiory zbóż na Ukrainie w 1932 r. i perspektywy na "chlebozagotowski"' ('The Grain Harvest in Ukraine in 1932 and the perspectives of *khlebozagotovki*'), Khar'kiv, 26 September 1932; and Adam Stebłowski to the Eastern Division of the Ministry of Foreign Affairs, Khar'kiv, 17 October 1932, in Bruski, *Hołodomor 1932–1933*, doc. 39, 47, pp. 116–25, 147–51.
24 Kul'chyts'kyi, *Holodomor 1932–1933 rr. iak henotsyd*, 228–361.
25 A report by Jan Karszo-Siedlewski, Khar'kiv, 4 February 1933; Henryk Sokolnicki to the Eastern Division of the Ministry of Foreign Affairs, Moscow, 27 February 1933; Henryk Jankowski to Stanisław Patek, the Polish envoy in Moscow, Kiev, February (before 9) 1933; in Bruski, *Hołodomor 1932–1933*, doc. 61, 67, X, pp. 191–4, 201–8, 669–71.
26 Jankowski to Patek, Kiev, February (before 9) 1933, in Bruski, *Hołodomor 1932–1933*, doc. X, pp. 669–71.
27 A memo by the official of the Polish consulate general in Khar'kiv, 19 July 1933, in Bruski, *Hołodomor 1932–1933*, doc. 114, p. 341.
28 An anonymous report from Kiev, 6 June 1933, in Bruski, *Hołodomor 1932–1933*, doc. 100, p. 303.
29 Jan Karszo-Siedlewski to Józef Beck, the Polish minister of foreign affairs, Khar'kiv, 12 June 1933, in Bruski, *Hołodomor 1932–1933*, doc. XV, pp. 678–80.
30 An anonymous report from Kiev, 6 June 1933, in Bruski, *Hołodomor 1932–1933*, doc. 100, p. 302.
31 Jan Karszo-Siedlewski to the Polish legation in Moscow, Khar'kiv, 17 March 1933; Józefina Pisarczykówna (alias 'Ola Osmólska', 'X.22') to Lt. Jerzy Niezbrzycki, Khar'kiv, 13 June 1933; a report by Piotr Kurnicki, Kiev, July (between 12 and 23) 1933; in Bruski, *Hołodomor 1932–1933*, doc. 77, 102, 115, pp. 233, 305–6, 346.

32 An anonymous report from Kiev, 6 June 1933, in Bruski, *Hołodomor 1932–1933*, doc. 100, p. 302.
33 Henryk Sokolnicki to the Polish consulate in Kiev, Moscow, 24 January 1934; Stanisław Sośnicki to Sokolnicki, Kiev, 31 January 1934, in Bruski, *Hołodomor 1932–1933*, doc. 178, XIX, pp. 533–4, 685–7.
34 'Sytuacja na Ukrainie' ('Situation in Ukraine'), *Przegląd Informacyjny 'Polska a Zagranica'*, no. 40, 10 October 1933 (an article based on a report by Jan Karszo-Siedlewski); an annual report by the Polish military attaché Lt. Colonel Jan Kowalewski, Moscow, 21 February 1934, in Bruski, *Hołodomor 1932–1933*, doc. 138, 186, pp. 396, 559.
35 Two reports by Stanisław Sośnicki, Kiev, September (between 3 and 5) and November (after 11) 1933; Piotr Kurnicki (alias 'Napoleon Nalewajko', 'Ku') to Lt. Jerzy Niezbrzycki, Kiev, 29 November 1933; a report by Jan Łagoda, the assistant of the Polish commercial counselor in Moscow, 11 April 1934; in Bruski, *Hołodomor 1932–1933*, doc. 128, 147, 152, 192, pp. 368, 431, 446, 583.
36 Stanisław Sośnicki to the Polish legation in Moscow, Kiev, September (between 3 and 5) 1933, in Bruski, *Hołodomor 1932–1933*, doc. 128, p. 372.
37 Jan Karszo-Siedlewski, 'Kwestja narodowościowa na Ukrainie Sowieckiej według stanu na 1.V.1933 r.' ('The Nationality Question in Soviet Ukraine on 1 May 1933'), 8 May 1933, in Bruski, *Hołodomor 1932–1933*, doc. 91, p. 264.
38 Jan Karszo-Siedlewski to Stanisław Patek, the Polish envoy in Moscow, Khar'kiv, 31 May 1933, in Bruski, *Hołodomor 1932–1933*, doc. 96, p. 295.
39 Extensively on this subject: 'Wstęp', in Bruski, *Hołodomor 1932–1933*, XLII-L. See also: Jan Jacek Bruski, 'Między ukrainizacją a rusyfikacją. Sowiecka polityka narodowościowa na Ukrainie w ocenach dyplomacji i wywiadu II RP', in Jan Machnik, Irena Stawowy-Kawka (eds), *Prace Komisji Środkowoeuropejskiej PAU*, vol. 17, (Kraków: Polska Akademia Umiejętności, 2009): 7–27.
40 A memorandum by Jan Karszo-Siedlewski, Khar'kiv, 6 January 1934, in Bruski, *Hołodomor 1932–1933*, doc. 96, p. 295.
41 'Wstęp', in Bruski, *Hołodomor 1932–1933*, XXIII.
42 Quote from Martin, *The Affirmative Action Empire*, 297–8. See also Kulchytskyi's chapter in this volume.
43 For example: a report by the Polish deputy commercial counselor in Moscow, Jan Łagoda, Moscow, 11 April 1934, in Bruski, *Hołodomor 1932–1933*, doc. 192, p. 576.
44 Piotr Kurnicki's letter to Jerzy Niezbrzycki, Kiev, 2 December 1933, in Bruski, *Hołodomor 1932–1933*, doc. 153, p. 449.
45 A report by Piotr Kurnicki, Kiev, 1 March 1935, CAW, Collection: Oddział II Sztabu Generalnego/Głównego WP, I.303.4.1993, subfolder: Ku 1934–1935–1936.

Chapter 12

ORAL HISTORY, ORAL TRADITION AND THE GREAT FAMINE

Maura Cronin
Mary Immaculate College, Limerick

A chapter attempting a discussion of oral history and tradition as a source for the study of the Irish Famine must surely start with a story. This story was told to me by my mother about her own maternal grandmother, Mary Skehan, the wife of a comfortable farmer in the upland region of north Waterford. In a tradition passed down to her daughter and her granddaughters, Mary was presented as a woman of great generosity. During the Famine, so my mother told me, Mary Skehan was never known to turn a poor person away from her door and yet, despite her constant giving, her meal-bin was never empty.[1] She died when my mother was a child – almost a century ago – yet the story lives on, transmitted by me to my children and to anyone else who cares to listen. So here we have an authentic piece of oral history about the Great Famine. Or do we? Is this story oral history? And is it about the Famine?

Oral History and Oral Tradition

This piece of family lore, its theme of generosity rewarded familiar in all folklores, illustrates many of the complexities of the oral as a source for historical research. In the first place, it raises questions regarding the distinction between oral history – the first-hand evidence of individuals – and oral tradition – tales passed on from one generation to the next.[2] But oral tradition may begin as oral history, mutating gradually from first hand narration to stories that open with 'people used to say that [...]', shaped by the personal and collective mediation that, over time, remove the told tale from the lived experience.[3] Mary Skehan's story probably originated in the late 1800s in the personal testimony of a neighbour, cousin or passing 'knight of the road', then metamorphosed into a semi-miraculous tale in family folklore, transmitted onward from the Skehans' upland locality to the home of Mary's daughter and grandchildren, eight miles to the south, to spread subsequently through space and time to admiring, mildly amused or even bored audiences.

The story has a second significance in the context of the present volume. It suggests how the oral does not remain oral forever: through its present committal to print, Mary Skehan's story moves from orality to text, ensured survival but shorn of the vibrancy of the spoken word and of its 'layers of meaning and directions of interpretation'.[4] In this it resembles other famine stories, originally orally transmitted but now buried in nineteenth-century memoirs and politically inspired newspaper articles, or included in the Irish Folklore Commission collections of the 1930s onwards.[5] This archive, which includes responses to a questionnaire circulated on the occasion of the famine centenary in 1945, represents the formalisation of private collection efforts carried on sporadically over the previous decades.[6] The idea of a state-backed collection of folklore was spurred by both the requirements of nation-building in the immediate post-independence period and the need to preserve memories in danger of obliteration by ongoing social, economic and linguistic change.

Such a realisation was not new: 60 years previously Canon John O'Rourke decided that 'the leading facts' of the Irish Famine should be compiled and published without delay, since 'that testimony of the most valuable kind, namely contemporary testimony, was silently but rapidly passing away with the generation that had witnessed the scourge'.[7] Although a number of fictional works based on the famine period had been published from the 1860s onwards, there was no attempt at a detailed account of the disaster until O'Rourke's book appeared.[8] His work was a model of painstaking research in the documentary record of the 1840s but was also informed by his own (sketchily outlined) memories and by other personal testimonies of the famine. O'Rourke, in fact, seems to have been the first to give serious consideration in a largely non-polemical context, to the still living memory of the calamity, much as Brother Luke Cullen had done 40 years previously in relation to memories of the 1798 rebellion in Wicklow.[9]

Historians and Oral History

For over a century after the publication of O'Rourke's work, however, Irish historians proved wary of the oral as a historical source, so much so that Beiner, during his several years in the Irish Folklore archive at University College Dublin researching the 1798 Connaught rebellion, met no other historians similarly engaged.[10] Nor is there much reference to popular memory in the many recent academic works on the Famine, which largely rely (as, indeed, did

O'Rourke) on the 'firmly constructed, reliable and permanent' documentary sources from the famine period itself.[11] In her 1997 analysis of historical research on the famine, Mary Daly rightly cast doubt on the capacity of oral tradition to greatly improve our understanding of the events of the 1840s, echoing the objection noted by Portelli that 'memory and subjectivity tend to "distort" the facts'.[12] However, recent work by Cormac Ó Gráda, Niall Ó Cíosáin, Cathal Poirtéir and Guy Beiner give a more nuanced view of the role of oral tradition in historical research, and the present chapter is to a great extent a synthesis of their work, shot through with some reflection on the insights offered by family tradition.[13]

While the contemporary record – private and public correspondence, local newspapers and the records of the poor law – allow us to witness the events of the Famine unfolding, the evidence available in the oral tradition is marred by the time lag between event and narration. As Ó Gráda suggests, songs may be the exception to this rule of dilution by time, their wording largely unchanged from one generation to the next and their themes resonant of a time now gone – 'fossilized like contemporary written documents, without subsequent filtering'.[14] But the narrated memories are more problematic. Though those recounted by O'Rourke in 1874 and Rossa in 1898, along with the random references appearing in the late nineteenth-century press, were certainly first-hand accounts of the events of the 1840s, their recording 40 years after the Famine may well have dulled their detail and accuracy. The time lag is even more serious in the case of the stories (like that of Mary Skehan) in popular currency in the 1920s and collected by the Irish Folklore Commission from 1935 onwards, separated as they were from their origins by several decades and up to four generations. Most of the respondents to the famine questionnaire of 1945 were born a quarter century after the Famine, and this time gap is reflected time and again in the narratives: 'Old people here say they heard from their fathers', 'Long years ago I heard an old man say [...]'; 'In my young days I used to hear old people discuss [...]'[15]

This distance between event and narration has inevitably led to the obliteration of memories, a phenomenon not unique to the Irish experience – in Ethiopia memories of poems composed during the famine of the mid-1980s had faded only a decade after the event.[16] But such 'porosity of memory' may be due as much to people's *unwillingness* to remember as to their inability. Had Mary Skehan's family – farmers of forty-acre holdings of good land in the early 1850s – done well out of post-famine consolidation, and does this explain why no other famine-related narratives surfaced in the family lore?[17] On the other side of the Comeragh mountains, my father's maternal aunts and uncles parried any questions about the events of the 1840s through which their parents had lived – though whether this was due 'self-protectiveness' in relation to their own experiences, or to an understandable reluctance to call up distressing memories in the presence of young people, is not now clear.[18] The Irish Folklore collection narratives display a similar circumspection regarding famine-related topics, 'distancing [...] the informant's source, usually an immediate ancestor, from the starving people'.[19] This 'othering' of the famine experience took a number of forms. Firstly, as Poirtéir and Ó Cíosáin have shown, the worst effects of the famine were almost always described as having been felt in other areas, and this despite the census evidence of sharp population decline in the home districts of the narrators. Neither, despite the considerable attention given in the narratives to workhouses and soup kitchens, was there any reference to informants' family members having recourse to these sources of relief or, indeed, of stealing food to evade starvation.[20]

Another type of distance, too, colours the oral evidence, i.e. the social distance between the narrator and those who form the subjects of the narrative. Purportedly coming 'from below', oral tradition is in some ways as much a view 'from above' as is contemporary elite testimony from coroners, clergymen, landlords, philanthropists and officials. This is true of the first-hand narratives of the late nineteenth century: when O'Donovan Rossa wrote his memoirs he was prominent in advanced nationalist circles in Irish-America; O'Rourke was parish priest of Maynooth, while most of those whose testimony he recorded were also priests or doctors.[21] The same perspective from 'above', 'outside' and post hoc, applies in different ways to the family and local oral traditions collected since the later nineteenth century. Ó Cíosáin estimated that the Irish Folklore Commission's informants were largely drawn from the ranks of the small farmers – those whose forebearers had survived the Famine – their narratives reflecting the value system of their class.[22] That 'remembering and retelling are indeed influenced by the social frameworks of memory', as Portelli expressed it, is also clear in the story of Mary Skehan, recounted as it was in a family of solid farmers.[23] Their retelling of her story, while no doubt accurately celebrating her charity (replicated in two subsequent generations of strong-minded and open-handed women), also firmly confirmed her and their position in the ranks of the 'respectable' farming class – givers of charity and with a longstanding stake in the area. It is no accident, surely, that the story took shape in the hey-day of what Hoppen termed *agricola victor* – i.e. when farmers, on the cusp of changing from tenants to proprietors, came to be looked on as the backbone of Irish society.[24] Or was the story an example of 'screen memory', that term borrowed from psychoanalysis and describing the recall of one memory to repress recollection of another – perhaps in this case the erasure of family 'survivor guilt' by the emphasis on individual charity?[25]

On the other hand, it would be misleading to over-emphasise these different types of distance between narrator on the one hand and subject and event on the other. O'Rourke recorded not only the memories of priests and doctors but also of more humble individuals like the old man who, in the mid-1850s, described the virtual disappearance of the village of Bridgetown outside Skibbereen in the famine years. Moreover, the doctor and priests he spoke to were not merely detached *observers* of the Famine: their activities in the later 1840s put them in immediate danger of contracting famine fever, while some experienced at first hand the pangs of hunger.[26] As for Rossa, his own family had felt the effects of the crop failure of the 1840s and the ensuing hunger – though not to the point of starvation – and those memories were very clear in his mind 50 years later. Nor, indeed, does he appear to have exaggerated his own personal experience of the disaster:

> Some years ago, in Troy, New York, I was a guest at the hotel of Tom Curley of Ballinasloe. Talking of 'the bad times' in Ireland, he told me of his own recollection of them in Galway, and asked me if I ever felt the hunger. I told him I did not, but that I felt something that was worse than the hunger [...] the degradation into which want and hunger will reduce human nature.[27]

Though Rossa's guilt concerned no more than how he had eaten a penny bun without sharing with his siblings, it does link issues central to oral testimony and tradition – i.e. the parallel existence of three different and sometimes competing narratives identified by Ó Ciosáin as the 'global', the 'popular' and the 'local'.[28] The global he defines as largely national in scope (what might be termed the 'grand narrative') and frequently derived or influenced by written sources. The local, at the far end of the scale, concerns fragmentary memories of events, places and individuals. The third level, the popular, focuses largely on a 'stylised repertoire' of motifs and narratives that seek to illustrate or attach meaning to the unexplainable. Rossa's anecdote reflects all three levels: its focus is local and personal; the theme of abandonment of kin (even in the small matter of failing to share a bun) serves as a motif of how disaster upsets normal human relationships; and the chapter in which the anecdote appears, 'How England Starved Ireland', belongs to the grand narrative of anglophobic Irish nationalism.

The Grand Narrative

The backdrop of a grand narrative reminds us, as researchers, that what appears to be purely oral tradition is also shaped by the documentary record.[29] As the twentieth century dawned, memoirs, school histories, poems and popular fiction became ever more accessible to an increasingly literate population.[30] Some of these injected an anti-English element into famine narratives, particularly in the 1880s and 1890s when near-famine conditions prevailed in the west and the nationalist press deliberately called up phantoms of the 1840s, warning that 'the demon of English famine again broods over enslaved, impoverished and unhappy Ireland' while the inclusion of famine memories in Rossa's 1898 *Recollections* had an equally polemical purpose.[31] But even more powerful in popularising an Anglophobic interpretation of the Famine was John Mitchel's *Jail Journal*, in print since 1854.[32] The powerful, elegant and lucid writing style ensured that this work, with its underlying political message, was in the 1920s passed on to bright pupils by their teachers as an example of 'good English'.[33] Mary Skehan's granddaughter, a conduit of the generosity story, was given the *Jail Journal* in her local convent school by one of the teaching sisters (herself a contributor to the Irish Folklore Commission collection) whose cultural and religious influence remained with her for decades.[34]

Thus, by the 1920s when Mary Skehan's story was passed on to her granddaughter's generation, still more so by the time the Irish Folklore Commission began its work in the 1930s, there was already a well-established and widely disseminated corpus of written work on the Famine, at least some of which combined with and coloured local and family memories of the event. This cross-fertilisation of oral tradition by written sources is clearly evident in some contributions to the folklore collection. While still centring on the local, such famine narratives cite detailed and specific information in relation to the Famine, information directly echoing the published record:

> The enormous amount of work in relieving the distress that ensued proved altogether beyond the scope of the Board of Guardians. Relief works were started and charitable organisations came to relief of the dying people but finally the Government had to give the Guardians authority to assist people outside the workhouses and outdoor relief was given in 1848 for the first time.[35]

Consider how different this last contribution is to the following which, while consistent with the grand narrative (emphasising the damage done by half-cooked food), departs from the common terminology (e.g. 'soup kitchen' becomes 'soup house') in a way that suggests the surviving memory of a local reality:

> The soup house was where Mrs [David] Fitzgerald is now. They had a big boiler and they used to put about a sack of meal into it, and two strong old men stirring that with two sticks. Sometimes that [porridge] wouldn't be half boiled, and it would give them colics and kill them. They used to take it away in wooden cans on their heads, very thin. Those that were in charge of it would take home whatever remained.[36]

To some extent, this 'contamination' of the 'local' by the 'global', of oral tradition by the grand narrative, resulted from the way the Irish Folklore Commission's questions had been framed. This was not necessarily a matter of imposing a Mitchel-type interpretation on famine memories (and, incidentally, the Mary Skehan story was devoid of Anglophobia), a temptation that was admirably resisted by the Commission – no mean feat in the 1930s when the requirements of nation-building could have swamped those of academic enquiry. Indeed, the questionnaire used by the Folklore Commission collectors was devised by historians so as to counteract nationalist presuppositions about the Famine.[37] But this in itself subjected the narrated memories to a different type of prior mediation, the questions reflecting the priorities of academic historians accustomed to documentary evidence rather than opening the doors to what was really 'remembered' at local level.[38] In the case of the famine memory collection, therefore, there was a tendency, if not to pre-shape the informants' answers, then to shape the way in which they searched their memories. Moreover, one has to consider the influence that 'school history' of a nationalist type exercised on the narratives of the Folklore Commission's informants. If extracts from A. M. Sullivan's *Story of Ireland* were being recited at Gaelic League *feiseanna* in west Clare in the first decade of the twentieth century and Mitchel's *Jail Journal* was being read 20 years later by senior pupils in some convent schools in Waterford, then the tailoring of the local to fit the global narrative may have come as much from below as from above.[39]

Memory and Motif

When informants to the Folklore Commission deviated from the precise themes of the questions posed, however, the most formulaic narratives could be shot through with arresting images – the memories of people's mouths stained green from eating weeds, living children on their dead mothers' breasts, snow-sprinkled bodies lying in ditches, dogs eating the unburied dead.[40] Such images can be interpreted on two levels. Firstly, as Ó Cíosáin shows, they serve as motifs to represent the reversal of the natural order in a period of chaos, just as Rossa's memory of and remorse for secretly eating the penny bun stuck in his mind for half a century.[41] But their role as motifs should not detract from their essentially accurate representation of physical realities, all of which appear in the contemporary record, and are replicated time and again in accounts of more recent famines and, in a somewhat different context, of war atrocities.[42] Moreover, bringing together the local and popular levels of narration described by Ó Cíosáin, they were remembered not only because they represented in a universally understood way the enormity of the calamity, but because they were burned into people's minds by their highly emotional impact and by their frequent association with the local and familiar. One Kerry contribution to the Irish Folklore collection, understated rather than otherwise, illustrates this fusion of the visual, the emotional, the real and the symbolic:

> [...] There were seven or eight of them there. A neat little family, white heads. My uncle Mick used to cry when he used be telling the story [...] Five of them died [...] Years after, my father was ditching near the ruin [of their house] and he found the bones. An old man and a child, the arm of the old man was wound around the child.[43]

The perpetuation of memory and the mapping of events through a combination of the local and popular levels of narrative is also clear in the way that places and events are closely linked. Rossa, for example, remembered into his old age the spot on the road where he and his family parted in 1848 as they left for America and he returned to Skibbereen.[44] Many of the accounts collected by the Folklore Commission, too, pinpointed clearly the location of a soup distribution centre, or of townlands emptied of their population by the Famine. Sometimes a physical relic remained to confirm past events in local memory – the shards of a soup boiler, the ruins of a deserted *clachan*, or the clear traces of roads leading from nowhere to nowhere, the remnants of a road-building relief work.[45] The memories of Famine – just like those of the 1798 rebellion examined by Beiner – were then further preserved in place names, sometimes euphemistic like 'the Green Road', sometimes self-explanatory like *Bóithrín na Déirce* (the alms road), 'Famine Road' or *Reilg a' tSlé* (the Famine Graveyard).[46] But there was also a more conscious interlinking of local memory and commemoration when religious devotionalism literally reshaped the physical form of objects directly connected with the famine experience. Such was the case of 'TW', one of O'Rourke's informants who, in his Bantry boyhood, had seen the hinge-bottomed coffin repeatedly used for carrying the famine dead to the grave – a memory frequent in the Irish Folklore collection of 50 years later. 'TW' procured such a hinged coffin and had it made into three large crosses, one of which he gave to O'Rourke, so as to link death with the Christian hope of resurrection and to preserve the memory of those who had died.[47]

Telescoping and Blaming

As Glassie stressed, oral tradition 'is unsteady about dates and loose in its handling of causative sequence'.[48] Personal testimony and oral history are notoriously careless with orthodox chronology. Their ensuing telescoping of time – memories or narratives of one period being merged with those of another – is typical of oral testimonies regarding the Famine.⁴⁹ Such telescoping characterises the story of Mary Skehan, reminding us that precision and looseness can co-exist in the same orally transmitted narrative. At one level, she was a real person, identifiable in the census of 1901 and 1911, a formidable little woman dimly remembered by her older grandchildren as well as in the folklore of her own family.⁵⁰ At another level, she was a casualty of the oral tradition's telescoping of time: born in 1843, she was only a small child during the Famine, so her career of generous giving belongs not in the 1840s but in the later decades of the nineteenth century. Or, perhaps the stories had inadvertently leap-frogged a generation, originally relating to Mary's mother who did live through the famine of the 1840s. Or was the story's reference to the famine simply a hook upon which to hang a moral lesson about charity, a lesson reflecting the home and school influences that shaped the outlook of those passing on the story?

How does oral tradition throw light on the issues of 'responsibility, culpability and blame' which obsessed nationalist polemicists like Mitchel and Rossa, and had come to colour the popular view of history by the early twentieth century?⁵¹ Many narratives collected by the Irish Folklore Commission apportioned blame ('Our local landlord always turned those seeking aid or food from his door [...]') – frequently to the detriment of historical accuracy, as in the case of the Offaly landlord, Richard Gamble, whose efforts to alleviate suffering during the Famine were given scant credit in the retrospective popular version of events.⁵² Not all those blamed were landlords, nor was the allotting of blame confined to the rural context. When, in the early twentieth century, a young lad in Cork city asked about the Honan family commemorated in the local Catholic church they had funded, his rural-born mother lost no time in denouncing them as having made their money exporting corn during the Famine.⁵³ Whether this country woman, born three decades after the Famine and far from Cork city, was adopting the city's folklore or transposing rural oral tradition into an urban setting is impossible to say, largely because the Irish Folklore Commission did not collect material in the cities. The anecdote does, however, echo the combined resentment and begrudgery (sometimes open, sometime oblique) that characterised many folklore references to 'grabbing' farmers, shopkeepers and those who benefitted from the famine-related misfortunes of others.⁵⁴

Yet even where the oral tradition pointed an accusing finger at individuals, especially landlords, it was more in their role as local villains rather than as representatives of a class. Even Rossa, who denounced landlords collectively as 'the English in Ireland', proved more benign when recalling the local reality:

The landlord of Renascreena in my day was Thomas Hungerford, or Cahirmore [...] a quiet kind of a man [...] God be good to him; he was not, that I know of, one of those evicting landlords that took pleasure in the extermination of the people.[55]

Almost half a century later, one highly articulate Mayo informant highlighted for the Irish Folklore Commission this gap between the negative popular view of landlords on the one hand and what remained in the local oral tradition on the other:

> It seems somewhat unorthodox to record written encomiums on Irish landlords as a rule, yet it has been conceded on all sides that Samuel Bournes was a generous and a charitable man. Whatever his motives, he was indeed a philanthropist.[56]

Thus, the oral tradition proved remarkably immune to polemical contamination and generally avoided blaming any one agency for the tragedy of the 1840s. Instead, the popular narrative (Ó Cíosáin's third narrative level) sought supernatural or moral explanations for the disaster – a 'visitation of God', a just punishment for the people's wastefulness or laziness in the past.[57] As one west Cork narrative put it: 'Old people said it was God's will to have the famine come, for people abused fine food when they had it plenty. I heard it for a fact that spuds were so plentiful that they were put on the fields for manure'.[58] How long such narratives continued to circulate in the wider community is unclear, but they certainly impinged on my own childhood in the 1950s when my mother, Mary Skehan's granddaughter (who included no anti-English or anti-landlord strand in her narrative) greeted wastage of food with the warning that it was such waste that 'caused the famine'.[59]

Conclusion

So what light is cast on the Great Famine by oral history and tradition? The limitations of the oral as a historical source are clear: it can be 'contaminated' by documentary sources and by popular misconceptions of the past; it tends to telescope events from different periods and to read the past through the eyes of the present; and it can 'forget' as much as it 'remembers'. This brings us back to where we started, to Mary Skehan's story. Is the story oral history? Not really: it may have begun as such, but well over a century after its first narration it has entered the realms of oral tradition – not the clear-cut account of 'what happened' but a complex mixture of fact, image, allegory, wishful thinking and a family's self-projection. And does it relate to the Great Famine? Hardly, since its central figure lived after that event and her generosity – probably the only *real* part of the story – was exercised in the later part of the nineteenth century.

But like the oral record generally, the story should not be dismissed. Even if it smacks of home-grown hagiography, of an idealisation of family and past, it is in Vansina's words 'the representation of the past in the present [...] reflecting both past and present in a single breath'.[60] The story may tell us relatively little about the Famine of the 1840s, but it does tell us something both about how individuals and communities *wish* to remember and how values in the present can shape and be shaped by the past. It also raises questions as to how social status, gendered authority roles and significant individuals (mothers, fathers, grandparents, teachers) determine the selection and transmission of memory.

Notes and References

1. Mary Murphy, née Hickey, regarding her grandmother, Mary Skehan of Kilbrack, Rathgormac, County Waterford. This story was told on many occasions between the mid-1950s and 2000.
2. For a comprehensive and sympathetic discussion of this folk theme, see Cormac Ó Gráda, *Black '47 and Beyond: The Great Irish Famine in History, Economy, and Memory* (Princeton: Princeton University Press, 1999), 213–15.
3. Patrick Hagopian, 'Secondary revision and the memory of the Vietnam war', *History Workshop* 32 (Autumn 1991): 142–3.
4. Alessandro Portelli, 'A dialogical relationship. An approach to oral history' at http://www.swaraj.org/shikshantar/expressions_portelli.pdf (accessed 26 August 2010).
5. Diarmuid O'Donovan Rossa, *Rossa's Recollections 1838–1898* (Shannon: Irish University Press, 1972 [first edition: New York, 1898]); *Irish World and American Industrial Liberator* (New York), 16 April, 28 May 1898; *Nation*, 26 September 1872.
6. The Irish Folklore Commission was established in 1935 and was succeeded in 1972 by the Department of Irish Folklore at UCD, where the archive is currently located. See http://www.ucd.ie/folklore/en/ (accessed 11 June 2012).
7. Canon John O'Rourke, *The Great Irish Famine* (Dublin: Veritas, 1989) (originally Dublin: James Duffy, 1875), xv.
8. William Carlton, *The Black Prophet: A Tale of Irish Famine* (Belfast and London: Simms and McIntyre, 1847); *The Farmer of Inniscreen: A Tale of the Irish Famine in Verse*, (London, publisher anon., 1863); Elizabeth H. Walshe, *Golden hills: A Tale of the Irish Famine* (London: Religious Tract Society, 1865); 'Ireland', *Forlorn, but not Forsaken: A Story of the 'Bad Times' in Ireland (ie the Famine of 1848)* (Dublin: publisher anon., 1871).
9. Myles Ronan (ed.), *'98 in Wicklow: The Story as Written by Rev. Bro. Luke Cullen ODC (1793–1859)* (Wexford: *People* Newspaper Office, 1938).
10. Guy Beiner, *Remembering the Year of the French: Irish Folk History and Social Memory* (Madison: University of Wisconsin Press, 2007), xi.
11. Patrick Hickey, 'Famine, Mortality and Emigration: a Profile of Six Parishes in the Poor Law Union of Skibbereen, 1846–47', in Patrick O'Flanagan and Cornelius Buttimer (eds), *Cork: History and Society* (Dublin: Geography Publications, 1993), 873–918; Christine Kinealy, 'The Response of the Poor Law to the Great Famine', in Gerard Moran, Raymond Gillespie and William Nolan (eds), *Galway: History and Society* (Dublin: Geography Publications, 1996), 375–93; Paul Thompson, 'Believe it or not: Rethinking the Historical Interpretation of Memory', http://epa-web.soe.ucy.ac.cy/courses/EPA731/Believe, 2 (accessed 6 November 2009).

12 Mary E. Daly, 'Historians and the Famine: a Beleaguered Species?', *Irish Historical Studies* 120 (Nov. 1997): 591–601; Portelli, 'A dialogical relationship', 4.
13 Ó Gráda, *Black '47 and beyond*; Niall Ó Cíosáin, 'Approaching a Folklore Archive: the Irish Folklore Commission and the Memory of the Great Famine', Folklore.FindArticles. com, http://findarticles.com/p/articles/mi_2115/ai_n8693730/ (accessed 5 November 2009); Cathal Poirtéir, *Famine Echoes* (Dublin: Gill and Macmillan, 1995).
14 Ó Gráda, *Black '47*, 217.
15 Ó Gráda, *Black '47*, 199; Irish Folklore Commission, 1072: 185–230. William O'Dowd, born 1863, County Leitrim; Poirtéir, *Famine Echoes*, 49, 217, citing Sean Rowley, Rossport, Co. Mayo and Ned Buckley, Knocknagree, Co. Cork.
16 Cormac Ó Gráda, *Famine: A Short History* (Princeton: Princeton University Press, 2009), 39.
17 *Griffith's Valuation*, Co. Waterford, Parish of Mothel, townlands of Kilbrack and Graigavalla.
18 In conversation c. 1975 with Thomas Murphy (born 1896). His grandmother, Mary Cooney, was born in 1826, so must have had quite clear memories of the Famine. Her sons and daughters were born between 1858 and 1877. Census of Ireland 1901, Co. Waterford, Townland of Toureen East, District Electoral Division of Knockaunbrandaun; Thompson, Believe it or not', 7.
19 Carmel Quinlan, '"A Punishment from God": the Famine in the Centenary Folklore Questionnaire', *Irish Review* 19 (1996): 68–80; Ó Gráda, *Black '47*, 212–13.
20 Ó Gráda, *Black '47*, 206–8; Ó Cíosáin, 'Approaching a folklore archive'.
21 R. V. Comerford, 'Canon John O'Rourke, Historian of the Great Famine' in T. Kabedebo (ed.), *Beyond the Library Walls: John Paul II Annual Lectures* (Maynooth: St Patrick's College, 1995), 8–22.
22 Ó Cíosáin, 'Approaching a folklore archive'; Ó Gráda, *Black '47*, 212.
23 Portelli, 'Dialogical relationship', 5.
24 K. T. Hoppen, *Ireland since 1800: Conflict and Conformity* (London: Longman, 1998), 89. The family's position as comfortable farmers can be traced back to the early 1850s when both maternal and paternal forebears held farms ranging from 40 to 50 acres (ranging from £36 to £43 valuation) as tenants of Walter Mansfield and the Marquis of Waterford. *Griffith's Valuation*, Co. Waterford, Parish of Mothel, townlands of Kilbrack and Graigavalla.
25 Patrick Hutton, 'Scholarship on Memory and History', *The History Teacher* 33, no. 4 (Aug. 2000): 539.
26 O'Rourke, *Great Irish Famine*, 157, 211; Donal Kerr, *A Nation of Beggars? Priests, People and Politics in Famine Ireland, 1846–1852* (Oxford: Clarendon Press, 1994), 43, 171.
27 O'Donovan Rossa, *Recollections*, 122.
28 Ó Cíosáin, 'Approaching a Famine Archive'.
29 Mary Daly, 'Historians and the Famine', 599.
30 From the 1880s onwards Famine-related works (fictional and historical) included Charles E. Trevelyan, *The Irish Crisis: Being a Narrative of the Measures for the Relief of the Distress Caused by the Great Irish Famine of 1846–7*, (London: Macmillan, 1880); William Patrick O'Brien, *The Great Famine in Ireland and a Retrospect of the Fifty Years 1845–95, with a Sketch of the Present Condition and Future Prospects* (London: Downey, 1896); Edward Newenham Hoare, *Mike: A Tale of the Great Irish Famine*, (London: Christian Knowledge Society, 1898); Vaughan Nash, *The Great Famine and its Cause* (London: Longman, 1900).
31 *Irish World and Industrial Liberator* (New York, 28 May 1898); *Nation*, 22 July 1887, 6 Mar. 1897.
32 John Mitchel, *Jail Journal: Or Five Years in British Prisons*, (New York: Citizen Office, 1854).

33 Memory of Mary Murphy (b. 1912) regarding the Mercy Convent School in Portlaw, Co. Waterford.
34 In conversation with Mary Murphy c. 1980.
35 Poirtéir, *Famine Echoes*, 139, quoting Tomás Aichir, born 1859, of Kilmaley, Ennis, Co. Clare.
36 Poirtéir, *Famine Echoes*, 143, quoting Pádraig Mhichíl Uí Shúilleabháin, b. 1867, Meall and Róistigh, Sneem, Co. Kerry.
37 Ó Cíosáin, 'Approaching a folklore archive'; Canon O'Rourke also circulated a questionnaire to his respondents, but there is no evidence as to what questions it included, O'Rourke, *Great Irish Famine*, xv.
38 Carmel Quinlan, 'Punishment from God', 85. The Commission's questions identified the main Famine-related issues as the first appearance of blight, the spread of cholera, the establishment of fever hospitals, the running of the workhouses and relief schemes, emigration, evictions, the attitude of 'well-to-do families and priests', the experience of proselytism.
39 *Clare Journal*, 20 July 1908; *Clare Champion*, 23 Feb. 1907. I am indebted to Caroline Maguire, PhD researcher in the History Department, Mary Immaculate College, Limerick, for this reference. *Feiseanna* (*feis* singular) were competitions run by the Gaelic League to foster an appreciation of Irish language and culture from the 1890s onwards.
40 Roger J. McHugh, 'The Famine in Irish Oral Tradition', in R. Dudley Edwards and T. Desmond Williams (eds), *The Great Famine: Studies in Irish History, 1845–52* (Dublin: Browne and Nolan, 1956), 419–22; Poirtéir, *Famine Echoes*, 85–115.
41 Ó Cíosáin, 'Approaching a folklore archive'.
42 Karol Ssemogerere, 'Famine in Uganda: Lessons from Uganda's Oral History', *Monitor Uganda*, 23 September 2009, http://www.reliefweb.int/rw/rwb.nsf/db900SID/MUMA-7U84TXZ (no longer accessible, 31 May 2012); Myra MacPherson, *Long Time Passing: Vietnam and the Haunted Generation* (New York: Signet, 1984), 587.
43 Poirtéir, *Famine Echoes*, 93, citing Eibhlín Bean Phádraig Uí Shúilleabháin, Sneem Co. Kerry.
44 O'Donovan Rossa, *Recollections*, 142.
45 The *clachan* was a settlement comprised of a number of houses clustered together, the land held by their occupants being organised on a communal basis. See Kevin Whelan, 'The Modern Landscape: from Plantation to Present', in F.H.A. Aalen, Kevin Whelan and Matthew Stout (eds), *Atlas of the Irish Rural Landscape* (Cork: Cork University Press, 1997), 79–80.
46 Beiner, *Remembering the year of the French*, 214; Patrick Hickey, 'Famine, Mortality and Emigration: a Profile of Six Parishes in the Poor Law Union of Skibbereen 1846–7', in Patrick O'Flanagan and Cornelius Buttimer (eds), *Cork: History and Society* (Dublin: Geography Publications, 1993), 888; Poirtéir, *Famine Echoes*, 132–65.
47 O'Rourke, *Great Irish Famine*, 213, 289 (footnote 28); Poirtéir, *Famine Echoes*, 182–96.
48 Henry Glassie, 'Folklore and History', address to the 1986 Minnesota Historical Society annual conference. http://collections.mnhs.org/MNHistoryMagazine/articles/50/v50 i05p188=192.pdf (accessed 6 November 2009).
49 Ó Gráda, *Black '47*, 195–6.
50 Census of Ireland, 1901 and 1911, Co. Waterford, District Electoral Division of Rathgormac, townland of Kilbrack.
51 Christine Kenealy, *A Death-Dealing Famine: The Great Hunger in Ireland* (London: Pluto Press, 1997), 6. By the 1930s, the term 'Black 47' had become something of a short-hand term

for the Famine in the Irish local press: *Leitrim Observer*, 1 Apr. 1934, *Munster Express*, 9 Feb. 1940, 19 June 1946.

52 T. P. O'Neill, 'The Famine and Offaly', in William Nolan and T. P. O'Neill (eds), *Offaly: History and Society* (Dublin: Geography Publications, 1998), 691; Poirtéir, *Famine Echoes*, 200, citing Séamus Reardon, Boulteen, Eniskeane, Co. Cork.

53 In conversation with Thomas Murphy, born 1896, c. 1965; Robert Honan was listed as a merchant at Patrick's Quay, Cork, in *Slater's Directory for Ireland* (Manchester: Slater, 1846).

54 Roger McHugh, 'The Famine in Irish Oral Tradition', 429–30.

55 O'Donovan Rossa, *Recollections*, 15–16.

56 Poirtéir, *Famine Echoes*, 206–7, quoting Michael Corduff, Rossport, Ballina, Co. Mayo.

57 Niall Ó Cíosáin, 'Approaching a folklore archive'.

58 Poirtéir, *Famine Echoes*, 40, quoting Bill Powell, Enniskeane, Co. Cork.

59 Memory of the author in relation to her mother, Mary Murphy (née Hickey) c. 1960.

60 Jan Vansina, *Oral Tradition as History* (Madison: University of Wisconsin Press, 1985), xii.

Chapter 13

MAPPING POPULATION CHANGE IN IRELAND 1841–1851: QUANTITATIVE ANALYSIS USING HISTORICAL GIS

Mary Kelly
National University of Ireland, Maynooth

A. Stewart Fotheringham
University of St Andrews

Martin Charlton
National Centre for Geocomputation, Maynooth

The spatially uneven nature of the impacts of the Irish Famine have been recognised by both historians and geographers[1] and research that has examined the Famine at various spatial scales has shed much light on its uneven impact on the human landscape of mid-1840s Ireland.[2] However, the regionally varied nature of the event makes it difficult to understand its impacts at the national scale. This is because of the difficulty of assessing the extent to which local processes that may have contributed to the worsening of conditions for people in different areas operated at the national scale. The emphasis on local areas that characterises much of the literature on the Irish Famine in part contributes to this difficulty. We have much detailed research for particular villages, parishes, poor law unions and counties, but little comparative or national analysis.[3] Recent research has attempted to bridge the gap between local and national perspectives on the Famine by constructing a geographical information systems (GIS) database of local attributes at electoral division (ED) level for the entire island.[4] Electoral divisions are administrative units first introduced to Ireland in the mid-1840s for the purposes of rate collection and were also used as the unit for census data collection. There were 3,439 such divisions in Ireland at this time.[5] Having a database of information at this scale, for this particular period in Irish history, means that we can begin to examine the attributes that characterised areas experiencing very different levels of population change and to explain why some areas suffered more than others.

In this chapter we discuss the GIS database that has been constructed and the manner in which it can be used to further Irish Famine research. The first part of the chapter deals with the uses of GIS in historical research and outlines the rationale for constructing a GIS database of local attributes for the Irish Famine period. In the second part of the paper we discuss the ways in which this database can be used to bridge the gap between local and national analysis by enabling us to measure statistically the relationship between particular local attributes and population change. Here we discuss regression analysis to measure the relationships between different ED attributes and population decline at the national level, and geographically weighted regression (GWR), a form of regression analysis that allows us to examine the extent to which these relationships varied locally. In doing so we suggest how GIS has much to contribute to Irish Famine research and to historical research more broadly.

GIS as a tool for collating, managing and analysing spatial data originated in the 1960s and is now widely used across a range of disciplines.[6] However, while GIS has not traditionally been associated with the humanities and social sciences outside geography, the spatial turn in the humanities and social sciences coupled with the increasing digitalization of humanities research has led to the emergence of humanities GIS and historical GIS as distinct fields in their own right.[7] Essentially GIS involves the integration of a database of spatial information, for example a set of census records, with a digitised map, for example a set of ED boundaries, and a set of tools that facilitate mapping, measuring and analysing the data. Thus, using the records, the map and the tools, various aspects of local information can be mapped facilitating the visualization of spatial patterns. For example, we can map population or aspects of population, for each ED through time and look for spatial patterns and trends. We can then look for possible explanations for patterns or trends through linkage to other attributes. This is not novel, but GIS makes the process much easier and facilitates the detailed examination of large datasets not previously possible. For example here we report on an historical database of over 100 variables that we have constructed and mapped for 3,439 EDs for the decade 1845–51.

The Rationale for Constructing an Historical GIS

The reasons for constructing a GIS database through which we can re-visit the Irish Famine period and re-examine its effects on the human landscape are two-fold. Firstly, we know that the impacts of the Famine, measured in terms of population decline, were not felt evenly across the country. This has been borne out by those that have mapped population change at various scales but also by the wealth of local studies which demonstrate the significance of local contexts and local responses.[8] What we do not know and would like to know is what the extent of these variations across the county was and what might have caused such variation. Secondly, the vast literature on the Irish Famine contains a number of possible explanations for why the Famine had such an enormous effect on the population in certain areas, both in terms of death and emigration.[9] Overpopulation on the eve of the famine, over-dependency on a single crop, the uneven distribution of resources; land clearances; agricultural rationalization and improvement; the expansion of commercial farming; a growing underclass of landless or land-poor, an inadequate welfare system and the laissez faire ideology of the day have all been put forward as possible explanations.[10] While arguments can be made for each of these, it is more likely that population decline in different regions resulted from a combination of these factors and that combinations varied over space. Freeman's mapping of population density, for example, has shown that pressure on land was not an island-wide phenomenon but had a distinct geography and that while there was significant population decline in areas where there was pressure on land (notably in the west), there were also areas of high population density which were less affected by the Famine.[11] The overpopulation thesis therefore only tells part of the story. Constructing a GIS database that includes information about levels of population decline in local areas as well as information on the existence or extent of a range of possible explanatory variables which we can use to map, measure and analyse variables and their relationship to population decline, can help us to complete the story.

Constructing the Database

Local variables were collected at the level of electoral division for the entire island using the population census and the agricultural census data of 1851. Electoral divisions, of which there were 3,439 in 1851, were first introduced into Ireland as an administrative unit in 1838 through which the Irish poor law system was to be administered and census data collected.[12] As divisions took time to be established, the 1841 census enumerators collected the census of that year at the then traditional townland and parish level. The 1851 census enumerators, however, recalculated the 1841 returns at electoral division level so as to facilitate comparison between pre- and post-famine Ireland. In doing so, the census enumerators have left us with a valuable lens through which spatial comparisons can be examined but which has not yet been used in Irish famine research. Data presented in the census returns include total population per ED in 1841 and 1851, male/female ratio 1841 and 1851, the number of inhabited houses, uninhabited houses and houses under construction in both 1841 and 1851 as well as the poor law valuation for 1851. From this additional data can be calculated, including population density and people per building so as to provide us with a measure of population pressure or overcrowding while valuation per acre provides us with a measure of land value. Also extracted from the census of population was the number of people living in urban settlements for both 1841 and 1851 which provides us with a measure of the extent to which EDs were urbanised. Here we defined urban as a place that had over two hundred people living in a settlement of over twenty houses.

The agricultural census was first established in 1847. This census collected crop data at electoral division level and livestock numbers at barony level. However, comparative use of the agricultural census before 1851 is problematic due to the fact that the electoral divisions were still evolving and not compatible with those of 1851. However, the 1851 agricultural census provides detailed information on the numbers of cropped acres on different classifications of farms sizes as well as on the amount of land in each electoral division under grass, woods and plantations, fallow and uncroppable and waste. Evidently this agricultural census provides us with a perspective on the immediate post-famine landscape which in many respects does not reflect that of pre-famine Ireland, particularly in terms of potato cover which in 1851 was only 40 per cent of what it had been in 1841. The number and sizes of farm holdings also underwent a dramatic transformation during this period. However, as outlined by Bourke, there were approximately 14 million arable acres in Ireland in 1841, a number similar to that in 1831 and 1851.[13] Thus while we know that the 1851 census situation was dramatically different to that of 1841, in the absence of an alternative source on agriculture for this period we used the 1851 census as an indication of the geographical distribution of different kinds of agricultural patterns in different areas – if not the extent. On the basis of this, the extent of land in each ED under particular crops was calculated as well as the proportion of cropped land in each ED devoted to particular crops. Crops examined included grain (wheat, oats, barley, bere and rye), meadow, and potatoes.[14] Also calculated from the agricultural census was the population density per acre of cropped land using both the 1841 population figures and the 1851 figures to give a measure of the uneven pressure on cropped land both before and after the Famine and the manner in which this pressure lightened over the course of the period.

Finally, additional geographical variables were calculated using tools incorporated within the GIS. Distances from the coast and from the nearest port as well as proximity to the workhouse and to towns were calculated for each ED. This information was included as the coast may have provided people with an alternative food supply, ports were points of departure and attracted large numbers of people, while towns, and in particular workhouse towns, were places towards which people gravitated in search of relief. Finally, mean elevation, a measure of agricultural marginality, was calculated for each electoral division and included as a variable in the database. Smyth's work on Burncourt in Co. Tipperary has shown that in the decades preceding the famine tenant farmers were increasingly forced onto more marginal upland areas to accommodate the expansion of commercial farming in the more fertile lowlands.[15] Similarly, Jones-Hughes's work on east Leinster shows that while this area in general suffered less population decline relative to the rest of the country, it was the remoter hills of north Meath and the upland areas of Wicklow that suffered greatest losses.[16]

Using the Database

Having constructed a database of local variables at ED level for the entire island, these were inputted into a historical GIS based on a digitised set of 1851 ED boundaries and mapped at this spatial scale. Visualising these variables at ED level provides us with a very detailed perspective on spatial patterns of population change in Ireland during this period, as well as on the variables that might have affected this change. Figures 13.1–13.4 show 4 of these maps, starting with per cent population decline (Figure 13.1), the variable that we would like to explain. As can be seen from this map, population decline during the famine decade was spatially uneven. While it is well known that the west generally suffered greater population losses than the rest of the country, this map shows that the geography of population decline was more complex than previous regional analyses suggest. While there were areas of high population decline in the west, interspersed with areas of more moderate population loss as well as population gain, notably in towns. Also evident is that while Ulster and Leinster fared better than Munster and Connaught, some areas within these provinces suffered similar levels of decline to those in the west and south. EDs in north Meath and west Wicklow for example suffered over 40 per cent population loss as did places in Co. Tyrone.

Figure 13.2 shows the percentage of land in each ED under crops. Here we see that electoral divisions in the east contained significantly more proportions of cropped land than in the west where land was less fertile. Parts of Galway and Mayo had less than 10 per cent of the ED area under crop cultivation. This stands out in marked contrast to places in the east were over 90 per cent of the ED area was under crop cultivation. However, also evident are clusters of intense crop cultivation around Cork, Limerick, and Donegal. Land valuation (Figure 13.3) showing valuation per acre as recorded in the 1851 census confirms the east/west divide. Most of the counties on the western seaboard were valued at less than 50 pence an acre (with some parts being valued at less

Figure 13.1. GIS map per cent population change

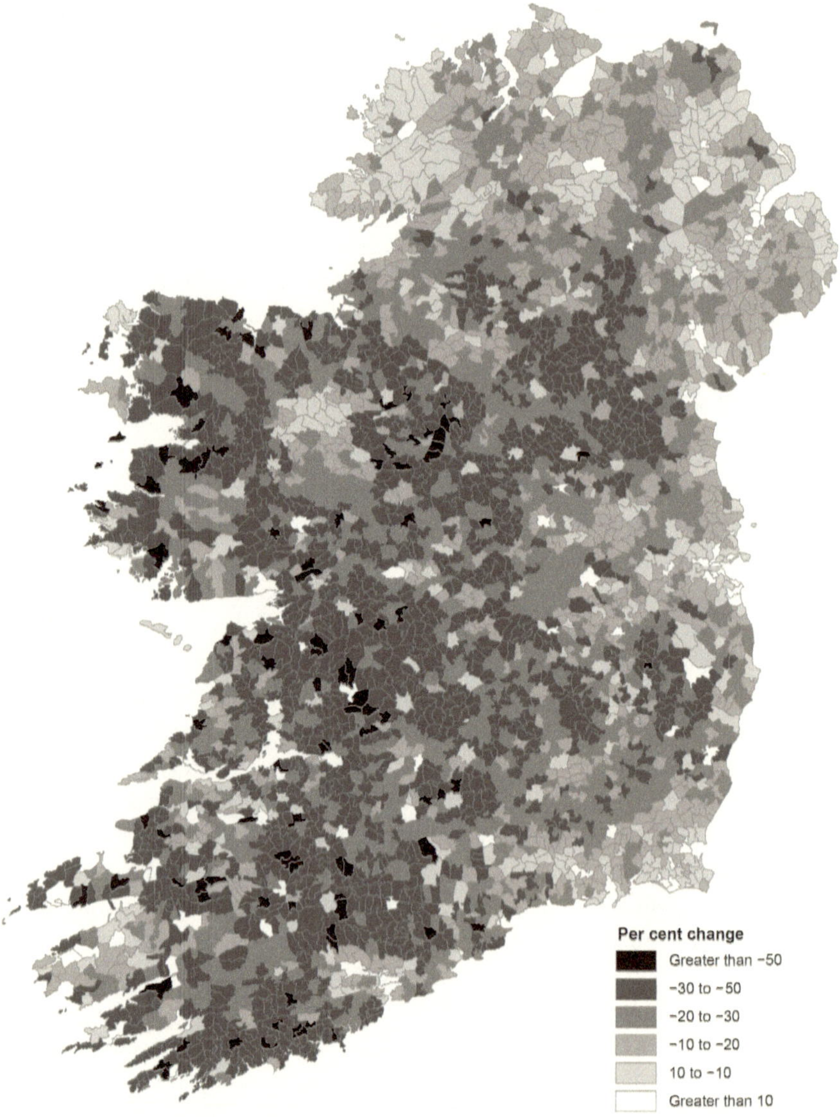

than half a penny an acre) while those in the east tended to be valued at up to and over one pound. However, parts of Wicklow, Wexford and Antrim had land values as low as in the west. Figure 13.4 shows population density per acre of cropped land using the 1841 population data on the 1851 crop data, as a measure of pre-famine pressure on land. Pressure on the land was greatest in the west where land was less fertile and less valuable, and particularly so on

Figure 13.2. GIS map per cent of cropped land in each ED 1851

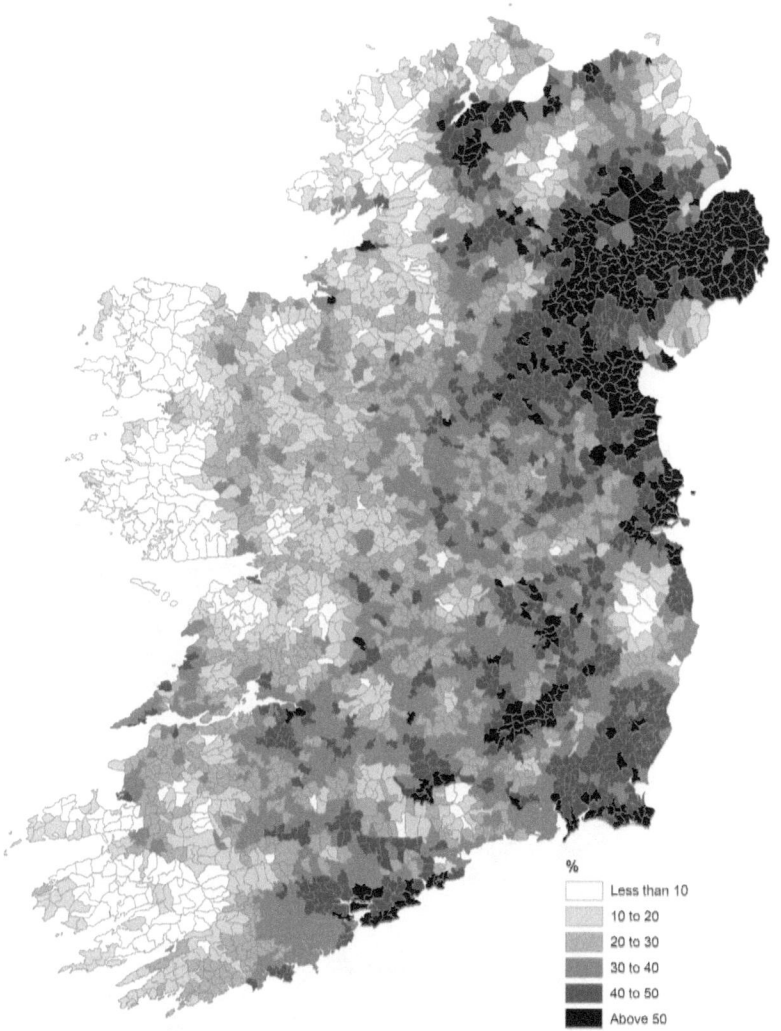

the western seaboards of Galway, Mayo, North Clare, West Donegal as well as in parts of Fermanagh and Leitrim.

Other variables in the database include the spatial distribution of different kinds of crops. Figures 13.5–13.8, for example, show the percentage of land under wheat, oats, potatoes and meadow, respectively, in 1851. Wheat was primarily a commercial crop and, while in decline in 1851, represents larger farmer

Figure 13.3. GIS map valuation per acre

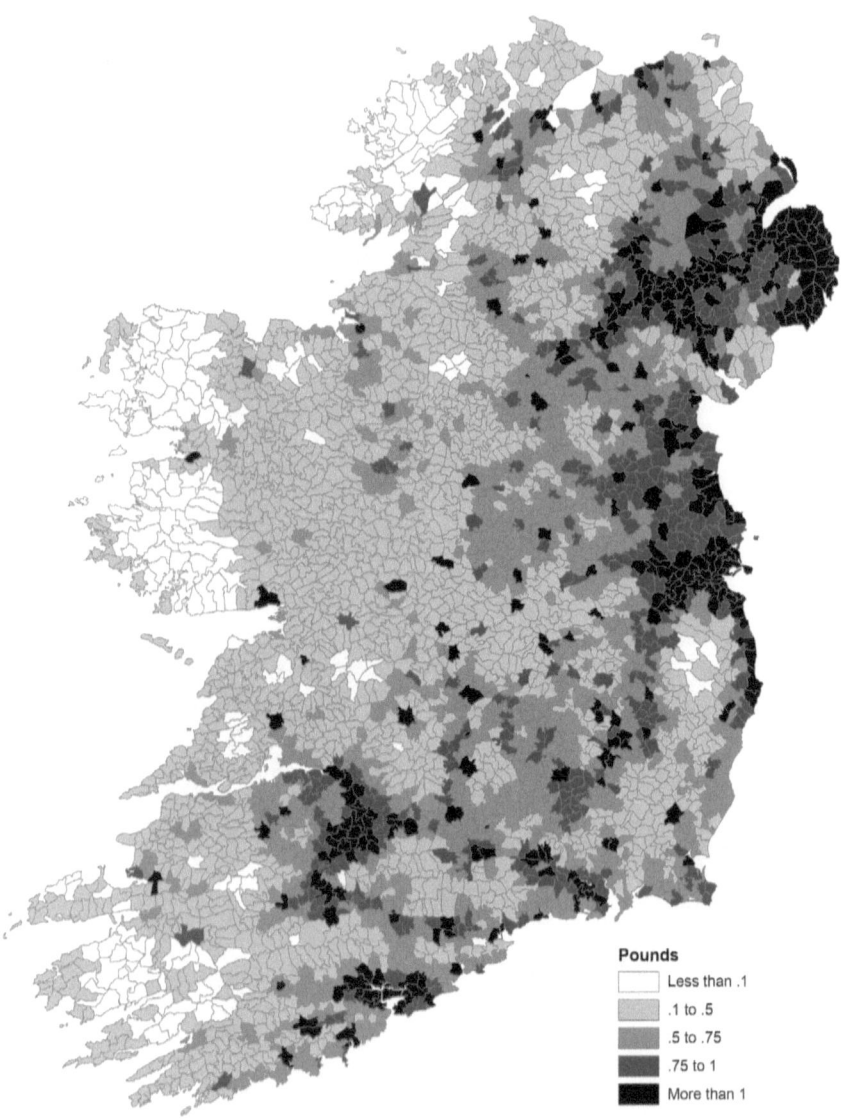

interests (Figure 13.5). Oat crops were the most geographically widespread in 1851 (38 per cent of all crop acres were under oats) probably because of the fact that it was used both for sale and for on-farm consumption and was used as an alternative to potatoes during the famine crisis.[17] Additionally, 15 per cent of crop acres in Ireland in 1851 were under potatoes. Potato cultivation was,

Figure 13.4. GIS map population density on cropped land 1841

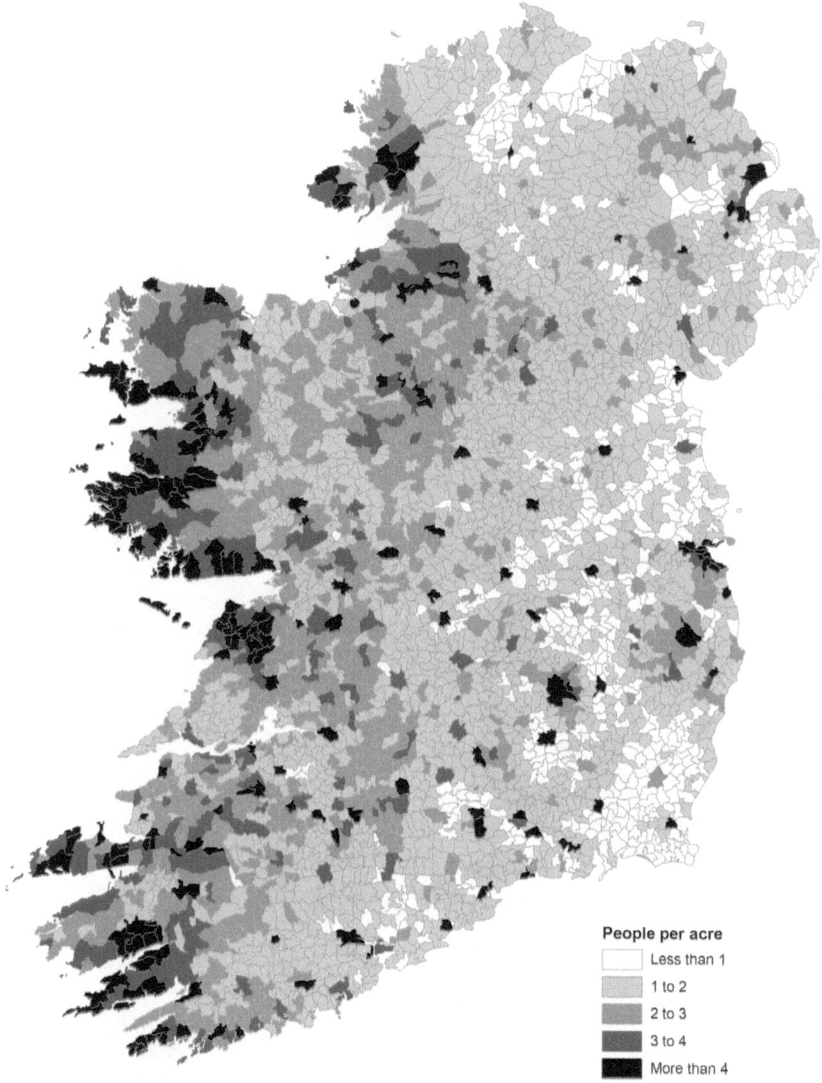

however, heavily concentrated in the west and south. Some EDs in Galway, Mayo and west Cork had over 50 per cent of their crop area under potatoes. Finally, meadow, a fodder crop, constituted 21 per cent of crop acres, which was found on all farm sizes but constituted the main crop on larger farms (above a hundred acres). These larger meadow-orientated farms were located on more up-land regions. In parts of the Kerry and Wicklow mountains, for example,

Figure 13.5. GIS map percentage of crop land under wheat

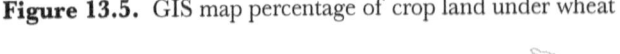

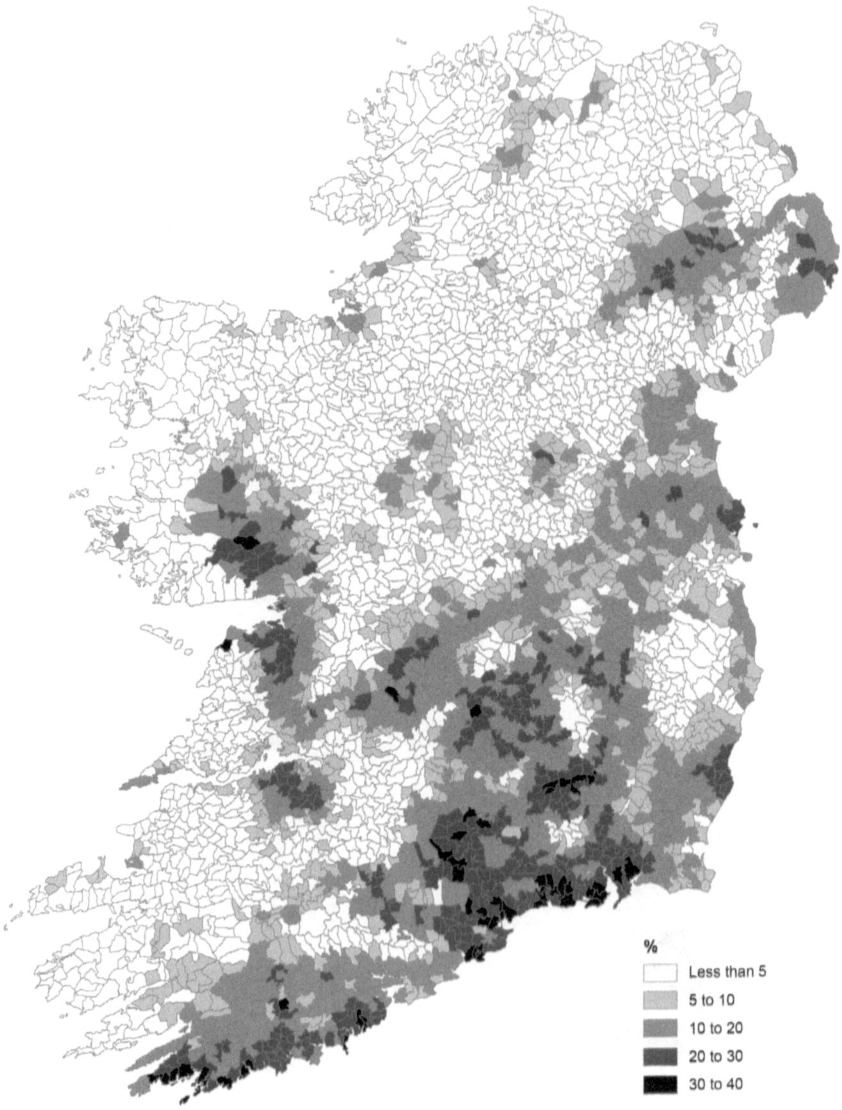

meadow covered over 50 per cent of crop area. Some, although not all, of these EDs were places which suffered heavy losses during the Famine.

Locational variables such as distance to the coast, distance to the nearest port and accessibility to towns and workhouses are also included in the database. Distance to the coast (Figure 13.9) was measured using the distance from the centroid of each ED to the coastline. Jones-Hughes's work on east Leinster

Figure 13.6. GIS map percentage of crop land under oats

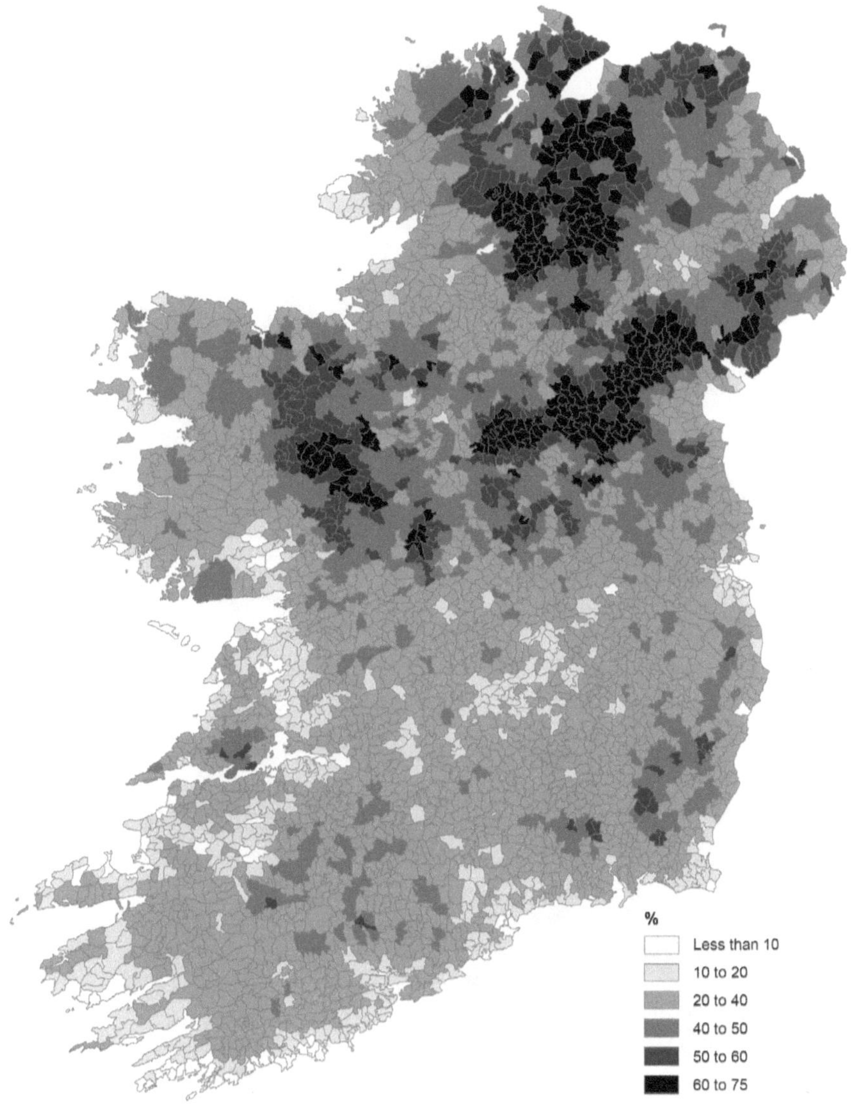

shows that large numbers of people sought refuge in coastal areas during the Famine resulting on the settlement of strands and dunes, while within the 21 parishes that stretch along the coastline from the Malahide Estuary to Dundalk Harbour population decline was less than half the national average.[18] Distance to the nearest port was measured from Freeman's pre-Famine Ireland port map.[19] Ireland was well served by port towns in the 1840s which acted as points

Figure 13.7. GIS map percentage of crop land under potatoes

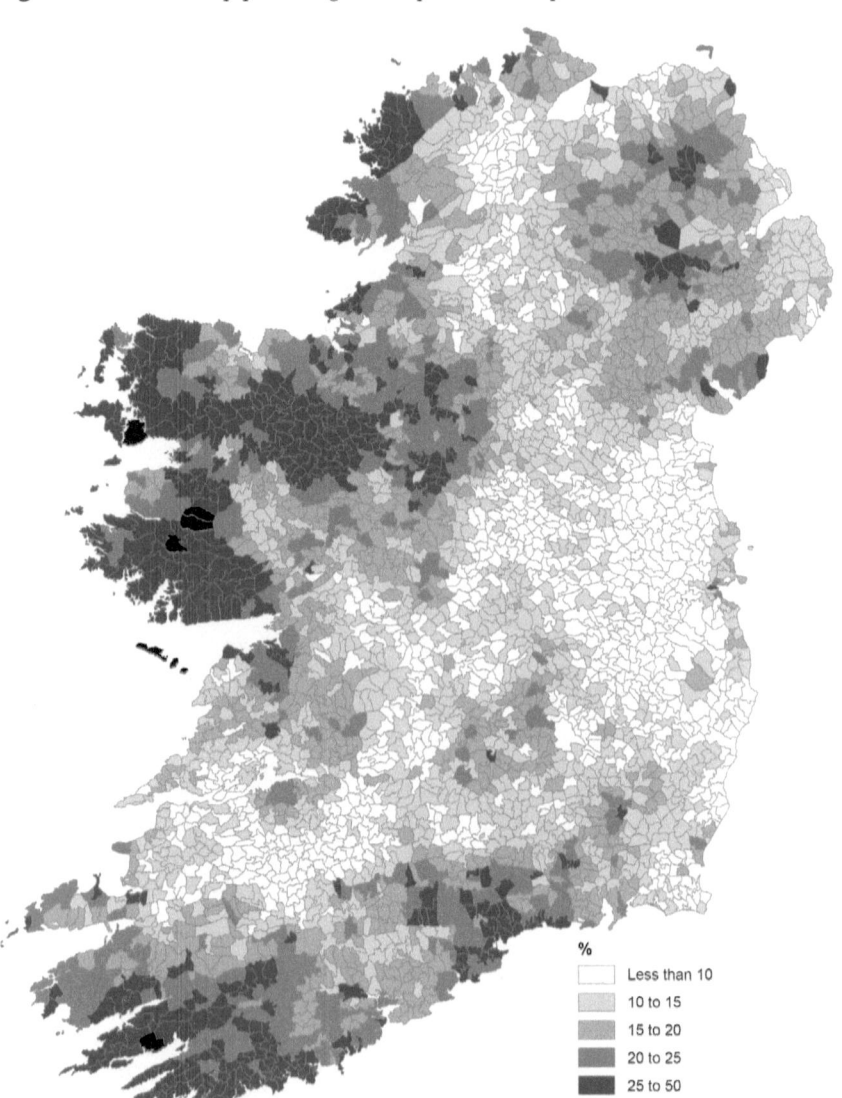

of departure as well as points through which relief supplies were shipped. Notable exceptions include Donegal and Clare, counties which did not have established ports. Port towns may therefore have been places towards which people gravitated with the intention of emigrating or in the hope of availing of relief then being shipped in. The population of Queenstown for example increased by 7,000 people between 1841 and 1851, while Kingstown increased by 4,000.

Figure 13.8. GIS map percentage of crop land under meadow

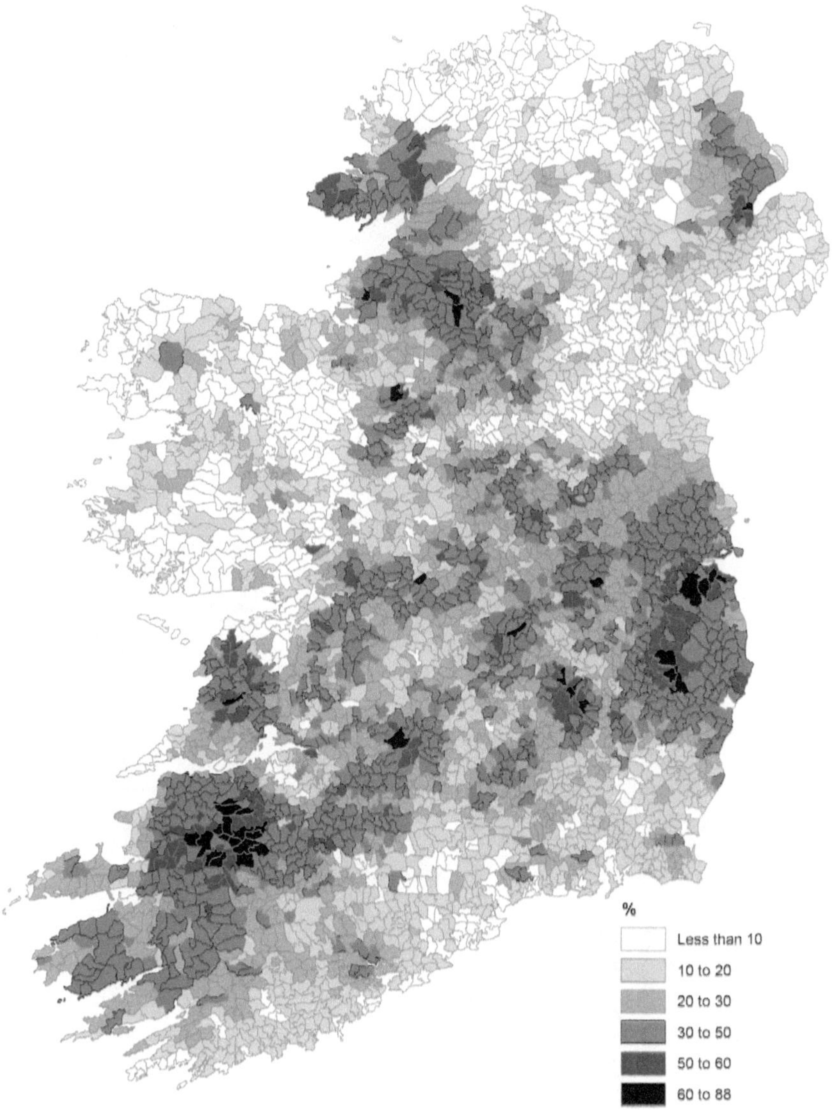

Accessibility to the workhouse (Figure 13.10) was calculated on summed inverse distances to workhouses. The 1851 census records show that 167 EDs contained a workhouse, an auxiliary workhouse or both. Some of these institutions housed large numbers of people. Those in Killarney, Kilrush and Cork City had populations of over 4,000 people in 1851, while Listowel had over 4,000 people in its workhouse in the town and a further 1,000 people in

Figure 13.9. GIS map distance to the coast

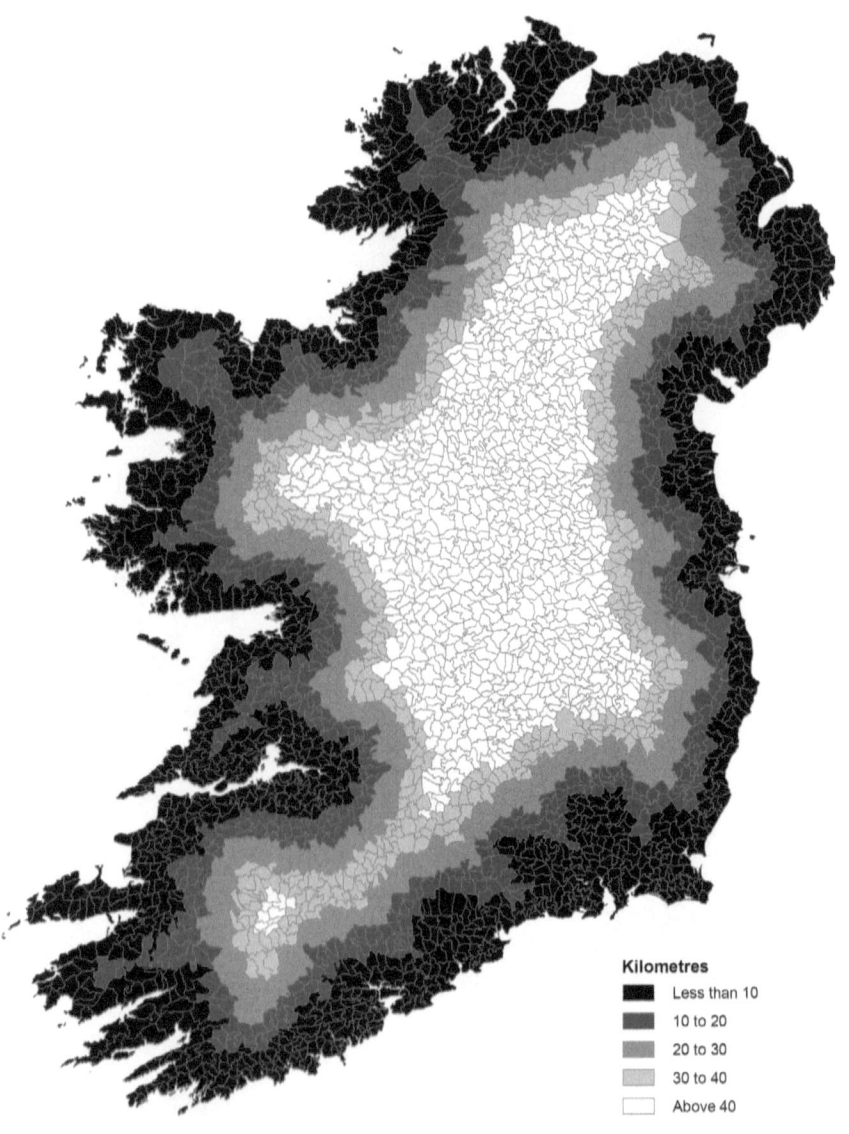

an auxiliary workhouse outside the town. These figures may have been much higher during the famine period when workhouses, which had initially been avoided by the Irish poor, quickly reached full capacity. In many instances nearby buildings were also used by workhouse administrators to house the destitute. Contemporary reports provide vivid descriptions of people with emaciated appearances clamouring at workhouse doors, Indian corn depots

Figure 13.10. GIS map workhouse accessibility

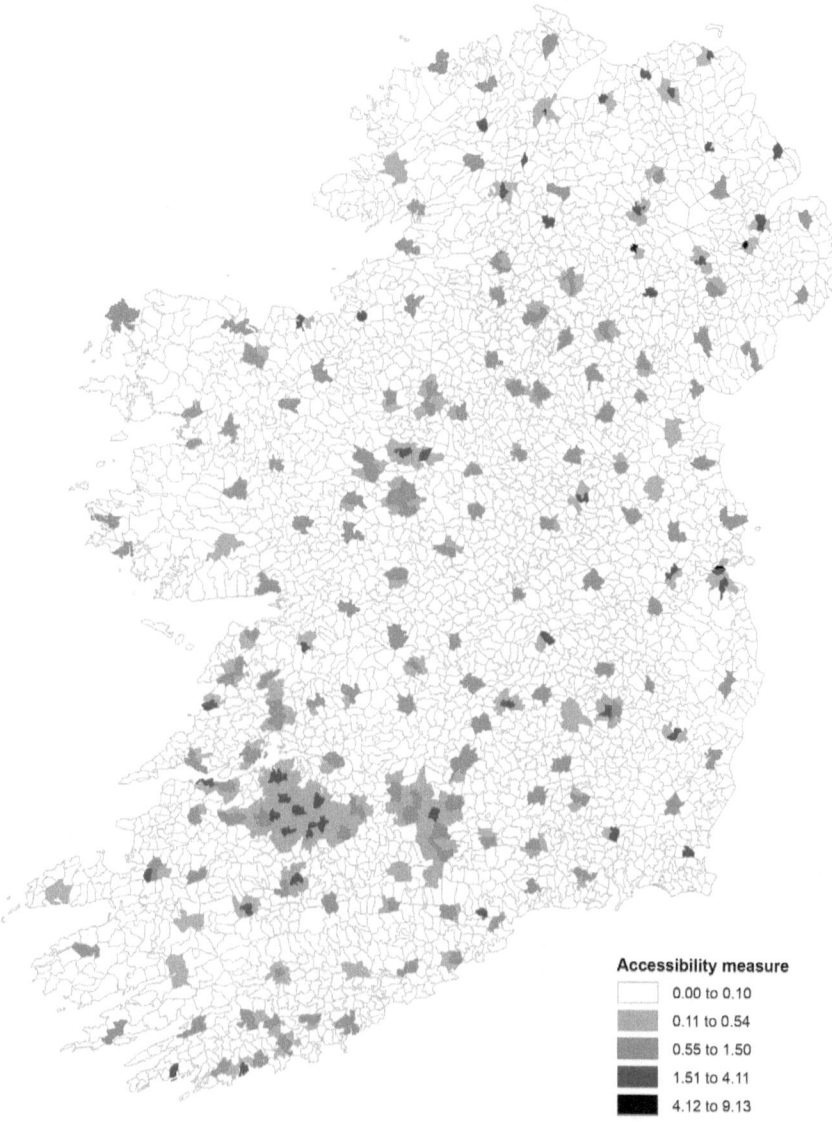

or soup kitchens located nearby, in search of relief.[20] The existence of a workhouse either as a place which housed large numbers of paupers or as a place towards which people gravitated in search of outdoor relief had a bearing on the changing population levels, both of workhouse towns and of nearby EDs. In 1841, 18 per cent of the population were living in urban settlements, 15 per cent of which were in towns of over 1,000 people. By 1851,

25 per cent of the population were living in urban settlements and 3.5 per cent of were living in institutions.[21] Given this urban and institutional growth, at a time when the death rate in towns was high (William Wilde reported that over 260,000 people died in urban workhouses alone), the influx of people towards workhouse towns must have been great.

However, while GIS allows us to visualise the spatial distribution of the variables that may have impacted on population change, having the data available in an historical GIS at a consistent set of territorial units means that we can use statistical analysis to examine the relationship between these variables and population decline. Using a set of six variables from the database,[22] we carried out a regression analysis to examine the relationship between them and population decline. Those selected were population density on cropped land, percentage of ED under grain cultivation, percentage of ED under potato cultivation, proximity to a workhouse, accessibility to urban areas, percentage of population living in urban settlements, distance to the coast and mean elevation.

The results of this analysis are summarised in order of importance in the table below. The parameter estimates are a measure of the relationship between each variable and population decline. Negative estimates indicate that as the variable increases, population decline was more severe, while positive estimates indicate that as the variable increases, population decline was less severe. The parameter estimate for population density on cropped land is −14.9. This means that on average across the country, if population density on cropped land within an ED rose from five people per acre of crop land to six people per acre, the population decline over the decade for that ED would have increased by around 15 per cent. As the unit of measurement for each variable varies (person per square kilometre, percentage of land under grain, average holding size) we use t-values (parameter estimates divided by their standard error) to provide us with a standardised measure of the relationship. This allows us to eliminate insignificant relationships (values between 2 and −2) and to order variables in terms of the strength of their relationship.

The variable with the strongest relationship with population decline is population density on cropped land, a measure of rural population pressure. As outlined above, as population density on cropped land increased, i.e. as resource scarcity increased, population decline was more severe. Similarly as both the percentage of cropped land under grain (an indicator of commercial farming) and average holding size increased, population decline also increased. Also found is that as the percentage of an ED living in towns increased population decline was less severe. Thus the impacts of the Famine were more severe in more rural areas. As both the proximity to towns and to workhouses increased, population losses were greater, presumably as people migrated into both towns and workhouses, in search of relief. Interestingly, the effects of the Famine were less severe in EDs more heavily dependent on potatoes in 1851. It may be that in 1851, EDs in which potatoes were again being intensively grown were those that suffered less in population terms than others, so producing this positive relationship. Finally, as distance to the coast increased population decline increased (indicating that the effects of the famine were more severe inland) and as mean elevation decreased population decline increased. The relationship between population decline and distance to the coast can be explained by the fact that coastal regions may have offered an alternative food supply while ports may have experienced population increases as people gravitated towards them with the hope of emigrating or of receiving food from incoming relief supplies. The result for mean elevation showing that population decline was less severe in more upland regions can be explained by the fact that population numbers in these areas were in general low and population decline less than in more densely populated areas.

Effect	Parameter estimates	T value	Population decline was more severe when:
Population density on cropped land	−14.919852	−27.79	Higher population density on cropped land*
Grain cultivation	−0.335679	−15.64	Greater proportion of cultivated land under grain in 1851
Average holding size	−6.730804	−15.16	Areas had larger holding sizes
Per cent population urban	0.183011	9.11	EDs had a lower percentage of population living in urban areas in 1841
Workhouse accessibility	−4.008397	−8.08	Nearer to workhouses
Urban accessibility	−4.872450	−5.91	Nearer to towns
Potato cultivation	1.682499	3.62	Less cultivated land under potatoes in 1851
Distance to the coast	−0.625783	−3.44	Farther away from the coast
Mean elevation	0.007511	2.47	On less upland regions

*Variable calculated using 1841 population data and 1851 crop data

However, while these regression results make sense and in many respects support explanations put forward in the literature they do not take into account the possibility that relationships being examined might have varied across Ireland. One of the problems with standard or 'whole map' regression analysis is that the parameter estimates are global averages that could mask any local variation. Jones-Hughes and Smyth, for example, have both shown that population decline was greater in some of the more upland regions in Tipperary and Wicklow.[23] Similarly, the relationship between other variables outlined above and population decline might well have varied from place to place. In order to examine such a possibility we use GWR to calibrate the model instead of traditional global regression. GWR is a statistical procedure for measuring spatially varying relationships that produces a locally disaggregated set of parameter estimates for each relationship.[24] These local estimates and associated local t-values can then be mapped to examine any spatial variation in the relationships being examined.

Figures 13.11 and 13.12 show the parameter estimate maps for two variables used in the model, percentage of cropped land under grain and mean elevation. The global result for grain on cropped land was −16.64 indicating that EDs with a higher percentage of land under grain suffered more severely during the Famine in terms of population decline. This might be explained by the fact that the expansion of commercial farming in the decades preceding the 1840s may have forced rural populations into more marginal land therefore leading to increased vulnerability prior to the Famine or to the fact that grain production may have expanded in the wake of the rural depopulation that began to occur after 1845. However, the parameter estimate maps for this variable show that this was not the case on the island as a whole. In this analysis the relationship between grain cultivation and population decline was found to be negative only in certain parts of the county, Sligo and Roscommon in Connaught as well as Tipperary, Cork and North Kerry in Munster (areas indicated in black and diagonal stripes). Over much of Ulster as well as parts of south and east Leinster, Connaught and south Munster the relationship between percentage of land under grain crops and population decline was positive. In these areas (indicated in grey and horizontal stripes) population decline was less severe in EDs with a higher proportion of crop land devoted to grain cultivation.

With regard to mean elevation, the global result was 2.7 indicating that, in general, upland areas did not suffer as much as lowland areas. This, as outlined above many have been due to the fact that, averaged over the island as a whole, population densities on higher areas were lower than in lowland regions and population decline, therefore, was more prevalent in EDs with lower elevations. GWR results for this variable show that this was the case only

Figure 13.11. GWR local parameter estimates for mean elevation

Figure 13.12. GWR local parameter estimates for percentage grain on cropped land

in parts of the county, in the Kerry mountains for example, as well as in parts of Monaghan. However, in parts of east Galway and Kildare the relationship between mean elevation and population decline was negative. In these areas EDs with higher mean elevations suffered greater losses.

Conclusion

As outlined by Gregory and Ell, the uses of GIS include the facilities for storing and managing large quantities of spatial data, for visualising spatial patterns and measuring various spatial attributes, relationships and differences.[25] In this paper we have demonstrated how GIS can be used in Irish Famine research both in terms of storing and managing historical and spatial data and in terms of their visualisation and analysis. Here we have mapped and measured the spatially uneven nature of population decline during this period in Irish history, built up a database of possible explanatory variables that might help us to explain why some areas suffered more severe population decline than others, and measured both the relationship between these variables and population change at a global level and the extent to which these relationships varied across space. The significance of this research lies in the fact that it enables us to bridge the gap between national trends and local contexts, by providing a framework through which the characteristics of local areas, both in terms of their location on the island and the social and physical conditions that prevailed within them, are included in the overall analysis. Also of importance is the extent to which this database can be extended as additional data become available. Information on assisted migration programmes or relief schemes for example could be incorporated within this GIS to help us better understand the role of local responses and extend the analysis.[26] Historical GIS therefore enable researchers to build up more complete datasets on events in history that allow us to explore the manner in which processes vary over space and through time, and to examine this variation at different scales of analysis. While this chapter has focused on a particular event in Irish history, GIS and the kind of analyses that they allow can be applied to other historical contexts and consequently have much to offer historians and historical geographers elsewhere.

Notes and References

1 Cormac Ó Gráda, *Ireland's Great Famine: Interdisciplinary Perspectives* (Dublin: UCD Press, 2006); Liam Kennedy, Paul Ell, Margaret Crawford and Leslie Clarkson, *Mapping the Great Irish Famine: a Survey of the Famine Decades* (Dublin: Four Courts Press, 1999).

2 P. J. Duffy, 'The Famine in County Monaghan', in Christine Kinealy and Trevor Parkhill (eds), *The Famine in Ulster* (Belfast: Belfast Ulster Historical Foundation, 1997), 169–96; James Grant, 'The Great Famine in County Down', in Lindsay Proudfoot (ed.), *Down: History and Society* (Dublin: Geography Publications, 1994), 327–52; R. A. Harris, 'Ballykilcline and Beyond', *Irish Studies Review* 15 (1996): 39–42; Patrick Hickey, *Famine in West Cork: the Mizen Peninsula Land and People 1800–1852* (Cork: Mercier Press, 2002); Ignatius Murphy, *A People Starved: Life and Death in West Clare* (Dublin: Irish Academic Press, 1996); Patrick Hickey, 'Famine Mortality and Emigration: a Profile of Six Parishes in the Poor Law Union of Skibbereen', in Patrick O'Flanagan and Cornelius Buttimer (eds), *Cork: History and Society* (Dublin: Geography Publications, 1995), 873–918; Tom Yager, 'Mass eviction in the Mullet peninsula during and after the Great Famine', *Irish Economic and Social History* 23 (1996): 24–44.

3 Ó Gráda, *Ireland's Great Famine*.

4 A. Stewart Fotheringham, Mary Kelly, and Martin Charlton, 'The Demographic Impacts of the Irish Famine: Towards a Greater Geographical Understanding', *Transactions of the Institute of British Geographers* (forthcoming) Citation: 2012 doi: 10.1111/j.1475-5661.2012.00517.x.

5 E. M. Crawford, *Counting the People; a Survey of the Irish Censuses, 1813–1911* (Dublin: Four Courts Press, 2003), 39.

6 J. T. Coppock, and D. W. Rhind, 'The History of GIS', in David J. Maguire, Michael F. Goodchild and David W. Rhind (eds), *Geographical Information Systems: Principles and Applications. Volume 1: Principles* (London: Longman Scientific and Technical, 1991), 21–43; Tor Bernhardsen, *Geographic Information Systems: an Introduction* (New York: Wiley, 2002).

7 Ian Gregory, and Paul Ell, *Historical GIS: Technologies, Methodologies, and Scholarship* (Cambridge: Cambridge University Press, 2007); Ian Gregory and R. G. Healey, 'Historical GIS: Structuring, Mapping and Analysing Geographies of the Past', *Progress in Human Geography* 31, no. 5 (2007): 638–53, Anne Kelly Knowles, *Past Time, Past Place: GIS for History* (Redlands: ESRI Press, 2002); Anne Kelly Knowles, *Placing History: How Maps, Spatial Data, and GIS Are Changing Historical Scholarship* (Redlands: ESRI Press, 2008); Atsuyuki Okabe, *GIS-based Studies in the Humanities and Social Sciences* (Boca Raton: CRC/Taylor and Francis, 2006), David J. Bodenhamer, John Corrigan, and Trevor M. Harris *The Spatial Humanities: GIS and the Future of Humanities Scholarship*, (Indiana: Indiana University Press, 2010).

8 Kennedy et al., *Mapping the Great Irish Famine* W. J. Smyth, 'Map-making and Ireland: Presences and Absences', in Crawford Art Gallery, *(C)artography: Map-making as Artform* (Cork: Crawford Art Gallery, 2007), 4–14. For local studies at various scales see note 2 above.

9 Joel Mokyr, *Why Ireland Starved: A Quantitative and Analytical History of the Irish Economy, 1800–1850* (Boston: Allen and Unwin, 1983).

10 For discussion on overpopulation see T. W. Freeman, *Pre-famine Ireland: A Study in Historical Geography* (Manchester: Manchester University Press, 1957); Kenneth Connell, *The Population of Ireland 1700–1845* (Oxford: Oxford University Press, 1975); D. B. Grigg, *Population Growth and Agrarian Change: an Historical Perspective* (Cambridge: Cambridge University Press, 1980); for a discussion on overdependence on the potato see Kevin Whelan, 'Pre- and Post-famine Landscape Change', in Cathal Póirtéir, (ed.), *The Great Irish Famine* (Cork: Mercier Press, 1995), 19–33; for a discussion on the uneven distribution of resources see Christine Kinealy, *A Death-dealing Famine: The*

Great Hunger in Ireland (Dublin: Pluto Press, 1997); Ó Gráda, *Ireland's Great Famine*; W. J. Smyth, 'Landholding Changes, Kinship Networks and Class Transformation in Rural Ireland: a Case Study from County Tipperary', *Irish Geography* 16, no. 1 (1983): 16–35. For a discussion on the laissez-faire ideology of the day see Peter Gray, *Famine Land and Politics: British Government and Irish Society 1843–1850* (Dublin: Irish Academic Press, 1999); David Lloyd, 'The Political Economy of the Potato', *Nineteenth Century Contexts* 29, nos. 2–3 (2007): 311–35.
11 Freeman, *Pre-Famine Ireland*.
12 Gerard O'Brien, 'The Establishment of Poor Law Unions in Ireland 1838–1943', *Irish Historical Studies* 33: (1982–3): 97–120.
13 P. M. A. Bourke, 'The Use of the Potato Crop in Ireland in Pre-Famine Ireland', *Journal of the Statistical and Social Inquiry Society of Ireland* (1967–8): 72–96; P. M. A. Bourke, 'The Extent of the Potato Crop in Ireland at the Time of the Famine', *Journal of the Statistical and Social Inquiry Society of Ireland* (1959): 1–35.
14 In an attempt to get a sense of the extent to which the geography of potato cultivation changed over the period we examined the county totals in Bourke's analysis of the 1844 potato survey (ibid) against that of the totals for 1851. Here we found that while there was a significant decrease in acres under potatoes between 1844 and 1851, in terms of the proportion of overall potato acres per county, the picture is relatively stable.
15 Smyth, 'Landholding Changes'.
16 Tom Jones-Hughes, 'East Leinster in the Mid-Nineteenth Century', *Irish Geography* 3, no. 5 (1958): 227–41.
17 Bourke, 'The Extent of the Potato'.
18 Jones-Hughes, 'East Leinster', 239.
19 Freeman, *Pre-Famine Ireland*.
20 John Killen, *The Famine Decade: Contemporary Accounts, 1841–1851* (Dublin: Blackstaff Press, 1996); John O'Connor, *The Workhouses of Ireland: the Fate of Ireland's Poor* (Dublin: Anvil Books, 1995).
21 In 1851 18.2 per cent of the population were living in towns with over one thousand inhabitants, 3.7 per cent in towns with between two hundred and one thousand inhabitants and 3.5 per cent in institutions (*Census of Ireland for the year 1851*).
22 Procedure for model selection outlined in Fotheringham et al.
23 Jones-Hughes 'East Leinster'; Smyth 'Landholding Changes'.
24 A. Stewart Fotheringham, Chris Brunsdon and Martin Charlton, *Geographically Weighted Regression: the Analysis of Spatially Varying Relationships* (Chichester: Wiley, 2002); A. Stewart Fotheringham, Martin Charlton and Chris Brunsdon, 'The Geography of Parameter Space: an Investigation into Spatial Non-Stationarity' in *International Journal of GIS* 10, (1996): 605–27.
25 Ian Gregory and Paul Ell, *Historical GIS: Technologies, Methodologies, and Scholarship* (Cambridge: Cambridge University Press, 2007).
26 P. J. Duffy, 'Disencumbering our Crowded Spaces: Theory and Practice of Estate Migration in Mid-Nineteenth Century Ireland', in P. J. Duffy (ed.), *To and from Ireland: Planned Migration Schemes c. 1600–2000* (Dublin: Geography Publications, 2004), 79–104; Mary Daly, 'The Operations of Famine Relief, 1845–57', in Cathal Póirtéir (ed.), *The Great Irish Famine* (Cork: Mercier Press, 1995), 123–34.

INDEX

Aalen, F. H. A. 243n
Ambroziak, A. 144n
Anderson, E. A. 102n
Andrews, H. 72n
Ankersmit, F. R. 209, 211n
Antrim, Co. 193, 250
Antze, P. 15n
Archdeacon, T. J. 112n
Ardess, 163n
Arel, D. 186n
Arendt, H. 109–10, 113n
Assmann, A. 3, 13, 14n, 15n, 16n
Assmann, J. 14n, 140n
Attolico, B. 228n
Augusteijn, J. 71n

Baidaus, E. 46n
Balitskii, V. 27
Bammer, A. 15n
Bandera, S. 48n
Barka, V. 198, 200, 210n
Bednarek, J. 227n
Beiner, G. 163n, 232–33, 238, 241n, 243n
Beiner, R. 100n
Berdychiv, 221
Berdychivs'kyi, 221
Berghahn, V. R. 99n
Bernhardsen, T. 266n
Bertman, S. 208, 211n
Bew, P. 71n
Bilen'kyi, S. 186n
Bilonozhko, S. 102n
Blair, T. 107, 189
Bodenhamer, D. J. 266n
Borysenko, V. 226n
Boston, 118

Bourget, I. 116–17, 122–24, 126, 129–33, 136, 142n
Bourke, P. M. A. 61–62, 72n, 248, 267n
Bowen, D. 196n
Brockie, G. 83, 91, 101n
Broderick, J. 84
Brooklyn, 106, 111
Brown, A. D. 15n
Brown, T. N. 73n
Browne, H. 110, 113n
Brownson, O. 140n
Brukhovets'ka, L. 210n
Brunsdon, C. 267n
Bruski, J. J. 10, 13, 33n, 48n, 227n, 228n, 229n, 230n
Buckley, M. B. 137–38, 141n, 143n
Buckley, N. 242n
Bunting, E. 192, 196n
Burke, T. 163n
Buts'kyi, 221
Buttimer, C. 241n, 243n, 266n
Byron, R. 155, 164n

Cahalane, P. 58, 71n
Callan, 164n
Callery, J. and A. 67
Carlow, 163n
Carlton, W. 241n
Carras, C. 99n
Carty, J. 82, 85–86, 101n
Caruth, C. 14n
Carynnyk, M. 227n, 228n
Casserley, D. 82, 86, 101n
Cavan, Co. 163n
Central Black Earth (region), 31, 223
Central Chernozem Oblast: *see* Central Black Earth (region)

Charbonneau, A. 140n
Charlton, M. 10, 14, 266n, 267n
Cherniavs'kyi, V. I. 43, 49n
Clare, Co. 120, 237, 243n, 256
Clarkson, L. A. 72n, 265n
Cleveland, 164n
Coghlan, V. 195n
Collins, M. E. 83, 90
Comerford, R. V. 8, 242n
Conlon-McKenna, M. 194
Connaught, 232, 249, 262
Connell, K. H. 61, 72n, 266n
Connolly, J. 5, 57, 58, 71n
Conquest, R. 6, 21–22, 24, 32n, 36–41, 47n, 48n, 170, 226n
Cook, T. 126
Coolahan, J. M. 101n
Cooney, M. 242n
Coppock, J. T. 266n
Cork (city), 56, 137, 150, 157, 239–240, 257
Cork, Co. 63, 67, 249, 253, 262
Corporaal, M. 15n, 71n
Corrigan, J. 266n
Coulby, D. 99n
Cousens, S. H. 61, 72n
Crawford, E. M. 72n, 265n, 266n
Crimea, 23, 172
Cronin, M. 10, 13
Crotty, R. 61, 72n
Crowley, J. 103
Cullen, L. 232
Curran, J. J. 138, 143n
Cusack, C. 15n, 71n

Dalrymple, D. 48n
Daly, M. E. 162n, 195n, 233, 242n, 267n
D'Anieri, P. 102n
Danilevs'ka, O. 84, 95, 102n
Danilov, V. 20, 25, 32n, 33n
Danylenko, V. 226n
D'Arcy McGee, T. 117, 128, 130, 133, 136
D'Arcy Ryan, M. 141n
D'iachenko, S. 197
Davies, R. W. 22, 32n, 38–41, 47n, 48n, 226n
de Keghel, I. 101n
de Valera, E. 56, 59, 71n, 146

De Vere, A. 120, 141n
Delargy, J. H. 59
Demchenko, M. N. 43, 49n
Derry, Co. 163n
Des Rochers, J. 142n
Devis, R. U.: *see* Davies, R. W.
Dietsch, J. 16n, 47n
Dnipropetrovs'k, 49n, 95
Doherty, G. 101n
Dombrain, J. 108
Dompierre, R. M. 140n, 142n
Donegal, Co. 249, 251, 256
Donnelly, Jr, J. S. 62–63, 71n, 72n, 128, 142n
Dooley, T. 72n
Doolough, 164n
Dovzhenko, A. 206–07
Dowd, P. 117, 130–33, 136–37, 139, 143n, 144n
Doyle Driedger, S. 122, 142n
Drach, I. 184n, 184n
Dublin, 11, 52, 54–55, 57–58, 69, 90, 99n, 111, 148, 150, 163n
Dubord, G. 139, 144n
Duffy, J. 69
Duffy, P. J. 265n, 267n
Dunbar, R. 195n
Dundalk, 255
Duranty, W. 40, 48n
Dziuba, I. 184n

Edwards, R. D. 59–60, 71n, 72n, 73n, 162n, 243n
Eisenstein, 205
Ell, P. S. 72n, 265, 265n, 266n, 267n
Ellman, M. 39, 47n, 48n, 49n
Enniskillen, 163n
Erikson, K. 1, 14n
Erll, A. 4, 15n
Eustace, N. 144n

Fanning, C. 119, 141n
Farren, S. 101n
Fegan, M. 122, 142n
Fermanagh, Co. 163n, 251
Figes, O. 48n
Fitzgerald, M. 141n
Fitzpatrick, C. 138

INDEX

Fitzpatrick, M. 194, 196n
Fitzsimon, E. 71n
Fludernik, M. 15n
Fokin, V. 169
Foster, R. F. 73n, 85, 101n, 101n, 154, 164n
Fotheringham, A. S. 10, 14, 266n, 267n
Frankel, D. 163n
Frawley, O. 15n
Freeman, T. W. 247, 255, 266n, 267n

Galway, Co. 150, 163n, 235, 249, 251, 253, 265
Garvey, A. 103
Gillespie, R. 148, 163n, 241n
Girard, R. 211n
Gkotzaridis, E. 72n
Glassie, H. 238, 243n
Gleeson, D. T. 73n
Göbner, R. 16n
Gonne, M. 57
Goodchild, M. F. 266n
Gorbachev, 40, 91
Grabovich, G. 185n
Gradenigo, S. 228n
Grant, J. 265n
Gray, P. 53, 71n, 73n, 162n, 163n, 267n
Graziosi, A. 216, 227n, 228n
Green, A. 99n
Green, R. 101n
Greene, S. A. 184n
Greenfeld, L. 100n
Gregory, I. 265, 266n, 267n
Grigg, D. B. 266n
Grosse Île: *see* Grosse Isle
Grosse Isle, 115, 121, 126, 129, 135–36, 138–39, 143n, 147
Gundara, J. 99n
Gutman, Y. 15n
Gwynn, S. 82, 86, 101n

Hagopian, P. 241n
Haines, R. 71n
Halbwachs, M. 3
Hamel, T. 124, 125 fig. 6.1., 126, 130, 136
Harper, J. 126–27
Harris, R. A. 266n
Harris, T. M. 266n

Haverty, M. 69, 73n
Hayden, M. 82, 86, 101n
Hayden, R. M. 187n
Hayden, T. 164n
Healey, R.G. 266n
Healy, G. 58
Heaney, S. 108
Heretz, L. 47n
Hetherington, R. 195n
Hickey, P. 241n, 243n, 266n
Hill, J. 72n
Hincks, F. 124
Hirsch, M. 15n, 140n
Hitler, A. 44
Hoppen, K. T. 234, 242n
Hosking, G. A. 37, 47n
Hubert, H. 204, 211n
Hutchinson, J. 100n
Hutton, P. 242n
Huyssen, A. 147

Igartua, J. 210n, 211n
Ignatieff, M. 99n, 100n
Il'enko, Y. 170
Insdorf, A. 211n
Irvinestown, 163n
Isajiw, W. W. 227n
Ivannikova, L. 227n

Jankowski, H. 218–19, 228n, 229n
Janmaat, J. G. 8, 102n
Janssen, L. 15n, 71n
Javorskii, V. 184n
Jilge, W. 15n
Jones, C. 99n
Jones-Hughes, T. 249, 254, 262, 267n
Jordan, J. A. 138, 143n, 144n

Kaganovich, L. 23, 27, 29, 33n, 36, 42, 44, 47n, 48n, 219, 224
Kamenka, E. 100n
Karszo-Siedlewski, J. 218, 223, 228n, 229n, 230n
Kasianov, H. 9, 13, 47n, 66, 184n, 197, 210n
Kasyanov, G.: *see* Kasianov
Katzer, N. 16n
Kaufmann, E. 80, 100n

Kazakevych, H. 1, 14n
Keansburg, 164n
Kearney, R. 163n
Keenan, C. 9, 10, 12
Kelleher, M. 51, 71n, 112, 118, 122, 140n, 142n, 195n
Kelly, M. 10, 14, 266n
Kelly, N. A. 163n
Kennedy, L. 62, 71n, 72n, 265n, 266n
Kenny, S. 164n
Kerr, D. A. 71n, 73n, 242n
Kerr, J. 112n
Kerry, Co. 253, 262
Khar'kiv 10, 30, 42, 44, 185n, 217–20, 223–224, 228n, 229n, 230n
Khlevniuk, O. V. 47n, 226n
Kickham, C. J. 55, 56
Kiev, 6–11, 41, 44–45, 173, 188n, 198–99, 217–18, 220–222, 228n, 230n
Kildare, Co. 163n, 265
Kilkee, 120
Kilkenny, Co. 150, 164n
Killarney, 258
Killen, J. 267n
Kilrush, 258
Kindler, R. 16n
Kinealy, C. 73n, 144n, 193, 196n, 196n, 241n, 244n, 265n, 266n
King, J. 9, 140n, 142n, 143n, 144n
King-Mahon, 67
Kingston, 119
Kingstown, 257
Kirkpatrick, R. 83, 90, 101n
Kissane, B. 100n
Kissane, C. 97, 102n
Khlevniuk, O. V. 47n, 226n
Khrushchev, N. S. 19
Knowles, A. K. 266n
Kohn, H. 79, 80, 100n
Kokin, S. 226n
Komarov, Y. 102n
Kondrashin, V. 226n
Kordan, B. S. 227n, 228n
Kosheleva, L. P. 47n, 266n
Kosior, S. V. 42, 46, 48n, 224
Kots, M. 185n
Koulouri, C. 99n
Koval', M. V. 83, 84, 102n

Kowalewski, J. 228n, 229n, 230n
Kravchuk, L. 91, 95, 167–72, 184n
Krawchenko, B. 32n, 37, 47n, 100n
Kremen, V. 95
Kremenchuk (district), 49n
Krylach, E. 101n, 102n
Kuban (region), 21–23, 29, 30–31, 45, 93–94, 228n
Kucheruk, O. 83, 95, 102n
Kuchma, L. 11, 95, 168, 172–74, 185n
Kul'chitskii: *see* Kulchytskyi
Kul'chyts'kyi: *see* Kulchytskyi
Kulchytskyi, S. 7–8, 13, 32n, 35, 46n, 47n, 83–84, 93–94, 96–97, 101n, 102n, 184n, 185n, 188n, 210n, 219, 226n, 227n, 229n, 230n
Kulchytsky: *see* Kulchytskyi
Kurnicki, P. 225, 228n, 229n, 230n
Kurnosov, Y. 83, 102n
Kuromiya, H. 38–39, 41, 47n, 48n
Kuśnierz, R. 228n
Kuzio, T. 80, 96, 100n, 102n
Kwasniewski, A. 185n
Kymlicka, W. 100n

Łagoda, J. 230n
Lally, S. 191, 193
Lambek, M. 15n
Landsberg, A. 15n
Lanzmann, C. 209
Lartigue, J. J. Bishop. 133
Lawson Lucas, A. 10, 195n
Leavitt, S. 144n
Lebedeva, Y. H. 84, 102n
Lee, J. J. 68, 73n, 162n
Leinster, 249, 255, 262
Leitrim, Co. 163n, 251
Lemkin, R. 106
Lenin, 25, 27, 40, 202
Leningrad, 42
Levy, D. 15n
Lieven, D. 14n
Limerick, 120–121, 150, 152, 164n
Limerick, Co. 120, 152, 163n, 249
Listowel, 258
Lloyd, D. 267n
Longford, Co. 150
Luciuk, L. Y. 227n, 228n

INDEX 273

Luk'ianenko, L. 170
Lusiak-Rudnits'kyi: *see* Lusiak-Rudnitskyi
Lusiak-Rudnitskyi, I. 23, 32n
Lutzeier, E. 192, 196n
Lytvyn, V. 184n

MacCurtain, M. 83, 89–90, 101n
MacDonagh, O. 59, 72n
Mace, J. 21–22, 32n, 47n, 170
Machnik, J. 230n
Macken, W. 190
MacNeill, E. 84
MacPherson, M. 243n
Magee, J. 88, 101n
Maguire, C. 243n
Maguire, D. J. 266n
Maguire, J. F. 9, 115–19, 126, 128–40, 140n, 141n, 142n, 143n, 144n
Maguire, M. 195n
Maguire, W. A. 62, 72n
Maier, R. 98, 101n, 102n
Maksudov, S. 49n
Malahide Estuary, 255
Mark-FitzGerald, E. 9, 69, 163n, 164n
Marochko, V. 35, 46n
Marples, D. 8, 14, 15n, 33n, 48n, 210n, 226n
Marsden, W. E. 77, 99n
Martin, F. X. 83, 101n
Martin, T. 48n, 49n, 227n, 230n
Massachusetts, 111
Mashchenko, M. 170
Maume, P. 71n, 73n
Mauss, M. 204, 211n
Mayo, Co. 120, 148, 153–54, 163n, 164n, 249, 251, 253
McAleese, M. 111
McBride, I. 15n, 73n
McCarthy, J. 56, 71n
McCormack, C. 190
McCormick, M. 110
McDonald, J. 83, 91, 101n
McGowan, M. 128, 142n
McHugh, R. 64, 73n, 243n, 244n
McKeown, A. 190, 193, 196n
McLaughlin, E. 151
McMahon, C. 143n
McMahon, R. 144n

Meagher, T. J. 73n
Meath, Co. 249
Medvedovskaia, 23
Melentyeva, M. 46n
Merridale, C. 49n
Middell, M. 16n
Miletta, M. 103
Miller, K. A. 68, 73n, 147, 163n
Miller, P. M. 163n
Mills, J. E. 123
Misan, V. 84, 95, 102n
Mitchel, J. 55, 57–58, 64–66, 69–70, 71n, 73n, 128, 236–37, 239, 243n
Mokyr, J. 62, 72n, 163n, 266n
Molotov, V. 29, 36, 42, 219
Monaghan, Co. 265
Montreal, 115, 117–19, 121–24, 126–30, 133–34, 136–137, 139–40, 141n
Moody, T. W. 83, 101n
Moonan, G. A. 82, 86, 101n
Moran, G. 241n
Morash, C. 51, 56, 64, 71n, 73n, 148, 163n
Moroz, O. 180
Morpurgo, M. 190–92, 196n
Morris, M. W. 227n
Moscow, 6, 20, 28, 31, 36, 40, 42–44, 46, 91, 95, 167, 173, 183, 217–19, 222–25, 229n, 230n
Movchan, P. 175, 184n
Mulcahy, B. 82, 100n, 101n
Mullan, D. 163n
Mullen, M. 190
Mullin, J. V. 104, 112n
Munster, 249, 262
Murphy, I. 266n
Murphy, J. H. 69, 71n, 72n, 73n
Murphy, M. 241n, 243n, 244n
Murphy, M. O. 8, 69, 103, 110–112, 141n
Murphy, P. D. 140n
Murphy, T. 242n, 244n
Murray, D. 54
Mysan, V.: *see* Misan, V.
Mytsyk, I. 227n

Nash, V. 242n
Nassau County, 111
Neal, F. 196n
Neill, K. 83, 90, 101n

Newenham Hoare, E. 242n
New Jersey, 111, 112n
New York (city), 55, 108, 111, 118–19,
    127, 141, 147–48, 155, 235
New York (state), 8–9, 103–04, 106, 108,
    110, 112, 156–61
Nicholson, A. 119, 141n
Niezbrzycki, J. 228n, 229n, 230n
Noack, C. 210, 226
Nolan, W. 241n, 244n
Nora, P. 3, 14n, 15n, 147
North Caucasus, 24, 26, 30, 36–37, 39,
    44–45, 94, 218, 220, 223
North Clare, 251
North Kazakhstan (region), 94
Nove, A. 24, 32n, 38, 47n
Novorossiisk, 228n
Nowlan, K. B. 60

O'Brien, George. 57–58, 71n
O'Brien, Gerard. 267n
O'Brien, K. 143n
O'Brien, W. P. 53, 71n, 242n
O'Callaghan, M. 162n
Ó Cíosáin, N. 73n, 233–35, 237, 240,
    242n, 243n, 244n
O'Connell, D. 85
O'Connor, J. 267n
O'Doherty, E. 160, 163n
O'Donoghue, T. A. 100n, 101n
O'Donovan Rossa, D. 57, 233–39, 241n,
    242n, 243n, 244n
O'Dowd, W. 242n
O'Flaherty, L. 58
O'Flanagan, P. 241n, 243n, 266n
O'Gallagher, M. 121, 122, 140n,
    142n, 143n
Ó Gráda, C. 14n, 62, 64, 71n, 72n, 73n,
    112, 141n, 162n, 233, 241n, 242n,
    243n, 265n, 266n
O'Herlihy, T. 58, 59, 72n
O'Leary, J. 143n
O'Mahony, M. 141n
O'Neill, T. P. 59, 72n, 244n
O'Reilly, B. 126–28, 136, 138, 142n, 144n
O'Rourke, J. 52–53, 59, 65, 71n, 73n,
    232–35, 238, 241n, 242n, 243n
O'Sullivan, P. 140n

Oak Forest, 164n
Odessa, 228n
Okabe, A. 266n
Oliver, K. 73n, 162n, 163n
Osborne, S. G. 120–21, 141n
Osmolovs'kyi, A. 102n
Osyka, L. 170

Paez, D. 210n, 211n
Panchenko, P. 35, 47n
Papash, O. 10, 13, 185n
Parkhill, T. 197n, 265n
Pataki, G. 111, 112n
Patek, S. 229n, 230n
Pavl'chko, D. 184n
Pawłowski, T. 228n
Pearse, P. 57
Peel, R. 54, 88
Pennebaker, J. W. 210n
Petliura, S. 30, 33n, 48n, 225
Petrovs'kyi: see Petrovskyi, H. I
Petrovskyi, H. I. 43, 49n
Piattoeva, N. 102n
Pilling, A. 194, 196n
Pilsudski, 48n, 224–25
Pizzuti, M. 152, 164n
Plamenatz, J. 100n
Pohrebins'kyi, M. B. 48n
Póirtéir, C. 73n, 146, 196n,
    233–34, 242n, 243n, 244n,
    266n, 267n
Poltava (district), 169
Ponochovnyi, M. 49n
Popson, N. 102n
Portelli, A. 233–34, 241n, 242n
Postyshev, P. 31, 49n
Pothier, L. 142n
Proudfoot, L. 265n
Providence, 164n
Pyrih, R. 33n, 226n

Quebec, 9, 115–18, 122, 126, 128,
    131, 133–40, 144
Queen Elizabeth II, 113n
Queen Victoria, 57, 61, 68
Queens, 111
Queenstown, 256
Quinlan, C. 242n, 243n

INDEX 275

Raymond, C. 141n
Redens, 48n, 224
Rees, D. 190
Rees, E. A. 47n
Rhind, D. W. 266n
Riabchuk, M. 185n, 186n
Richards, Fr. 129–30, 133
Richman-Kenneally, R. 143n
Ricœur, P. 15n
Rigney, A. 4, 15n
Rim, B. 210n
Ris, E. A. 226n
Robinson, M. 116, 139, 140n, 154
Roddan, J. T. 118
Rogovaia, L. A.: see Rogovaya, L. A.
Rogovaya, L. A. 47n, 226n
Romm, M. 206
Ronan, M. 241n
Roscommon, Co. 151, 163n, 262
Rostov, 23
Rothberg, M. 4, 15n
Rowley, S. 242n
Rubach, M. 49n
Rudin, R. 144n
Russell, J. 65, 69–70, 86
Russell, L. 111

Sadlier, M. A. 118–19, 141n
Šapoval, J.: see Shapoval, Y.
Schissler, H. 99n, 102n
Schöpflin, G. 80, 100n
Seidman, K. 144n
Serbyn, R. 32n, 37, 47n
Sevastopol, 172
Sevigny, A. 140n
Shabad, S. 47n
Shapoval, I.: see Shapoval, Y.
Shapoval, Y. 15n, 35, 46n, 84, 102n, 226n
Shostak, P. 49n
Shulman, S. 100n
Simon, J. 228n
Simonenko, P. 175
Simpson, P. 142n
Singer, A. 103, 110, 112
Skehan, M. 231–34, 236–37, 239–40, 241n
Skibbereen, 52–53, 61, 63, 150, 235, 238
Skrypnyk, M. 44, 49n

Sligo, Co. 163n, 262
Smith, A. D. 80, 100n
Smith, M. 190
Smyth, W. J. 249, 262, 266n, 267n
Snyder, J. 99n
Snyder, T. 227n
Sobolewski, P. 83, 91, 101n
Sodaro, A. 15n
Sokolnicki, H. 222, 229n, 230n
Sośnicki, S. 222, 228n, 230n
Soysal, Y. N. 102n
Spielberg, S. 209
Ssemogerere, K. 243n
Stalin, J. 3, 6–7, 10, 12–13, 19, 20–27,
    29–32, 33n, 36–40, 42, 44–46, 48n,
    49n, 81, 92–95, 167, 200, 202, 216,
    219, 224–25
Stasiuk, O. 226n
Staudter, T. 164n
Stawowy-Kawka, I. 230n
Stebłowski, A. 219, 228n, 229n
Stepanenko, V. 80, 100n
St John, P. 64
St John (New Brunswick), 119
Stout, M. 243n
Strang, W. 228n
Sub-Saharan Africa, 109, 112
Subtelny, O. 100n
Sullivan, A. M. 237
Suny, R. G. 48n
Swinford, 153–54, 164n
Symonenko, S. 49n

Tabachnyk, D. 174
Taniuk, L. 197
Tarashchans'kyi, 221
Tauger, M. B. 37, 41, 47n
Taylor, S. J. 48n
Terekhov, R. 42–43
Tertullian, 207, 211n
Thévenin, E. 227n
Thompson, P. 241n, 242n
Three Rivers: see Trois Rivières
Tierney, M. 83, 89–90, 101n
Tipperary, Co. 54, 147, 249, 262
Toeplitz, J. 212n
Tolle, B. 147–48, 163n
Tottle, D. 47n

Tracevskis, R. M. 185n
Trevelyan, C. E. 65, 242n
Trigger, R. 140n
Trois Rivières, 126–27
Tsvetkovs'kyi, 221
Turchenko, F. H. 84, 93–95, 97, 102n
Tyrone, Co. 249

Ulster, 193, 249, 262
Uman, 218
Uman District: *see* Umans'kyi
Umans'kyi, 42, 221
Uzwyshyn, R. J. 211n

Valone, D. 144n, 163n, 164n
Vansina, J. 241, 244n
Vard, C. 195n
Vasyl'iev, V. 226n
Vaughan, W. E. 62–63, 71n, 72n
Vel'tser, K. (Harald Welzer) 210n, 211n
Velychenko, S. 100n
Vlasov, V. 84, 95, 102n
Volga (region), 26, 31, 93–94
Volhynia (region), 174
Voronezh (region), 98

Waligóra-Zblewska, A. 226
Walsh, R. 83, 91, 101n
Walshe, E.H. 241n
Warsaw, 216, 219, 225
Wemheuer, F. 16n

Westport, 52, 108
Wexford, Co. 106, 111, 163n, 250
Wheatcroft, S. 22, 32n, 38–41, 47n, 226n
Whelan, K. 243n, 266n
Whitney, C. 37, 47n
Wicklow, Co. 52, 232, 249, 250, 253, 262
Wilde, W. 260
Wiles, P. 37, 47n
Williams, T. D. 60, 72n, 73n, 162n, 243n
Wilson, A. 100n, 102n
Wilson, L. 147, 163n
Wood, C. 65
Woodham-Smith, C. 60, 65, 72n, 73n, 108, 195n

Yager, T. 266n
Yanchuk, O. 185n, 197–204, 206
Yanukovich, V. 178
Yushchenko, V. 6, 9, 36, 46, 47n, 167–68, 174, 176–82, 186n, 188n, 198

Zaitsev, O. 102n
Zatons'kyi, V. P. 43, 49n
Zelenin, I. 20, 32n
Zgurovskyi, M. 95
Zhulinskii, M. 170, 184n
Zisels, J. 23
Zlepko, D. 227n
Žmigrodzki, A. 228n, 229n
Zvenyhorods'kyi, 221

www.ingramcontent.com/pod-product-compliance
Lightning Source LLC
Chambersburg PA
CBHW021821300426
44114CB00009BA/264